The London Boys

For Mum and Dad who gave me my name and started all this.

The London Boys

David Bowie, Marc Bolan and the 60s Teenage Dream

Marc Burrows

PEN & SWORD HISTORY

First published in Great Britain in 2022 by
Pen & Sword History
An imprint of
Pen & Sword Books Ltd
Yorkshire – Philadelphia

ISBN 978 1 39900 843 3

Typeset by Mac Style
Printed in the UK by CPI Group (UK) Ltd, Croydon, CR0 4YY.

Pen & Sword Books Limited incorporates the imprints of Atlas,
Archaeology, Aviation, Discovery, Family History, Fiction, History,
Maritime, Military, Military Classics, Politics, Select, Transport,
True Crime, Air World, Frontline Publishing, Leo Cooper, Remember
When, Seaforth Publishing, The Praetorian Press, Wharncliffe
Local History, Wharncliffe Transport, Wharncliffe True Crime
and White Owl.

For a complete list of Pen & Sword titles please contact

PEN & SWORD BOOKS LIMITED
47 Church Street, Barnsley, South Yorkshire, S70 2AS, England
E-mail: enquiries@pen-and-sword.co.uk
Website: www.pen-and-sword.co.uk

Or

PEN AND SWORD BOOKS
1950 Lawrence Rd, Havertown, PA 19083, USA
E-mail: Uspen-and-sword@casematepublishers.com
Website: www.penandswordbooks.com

Contents

Acknowledgements

This book began at birth. You name a kid after Marc Bolan, and you've basically set them up to be fascinated with the romance of rock 'n' roll for the rest of their life. You see David Bowie's 'Ashes To Ashes' video at the right stage of childhood and you're either terrified or fascinated. In my case, it was both. I've dedicated this book to my parents, but I want to expand on that here because that simple decision: to choose the cooler spelling in tribute to a pop legend, less than four years gone at that point, is a pretty profound one. It's probably not the most important thing my parents ever did for me, but it's something I've always loved them for, just as I've always loved Marc's music. To Russ Burrows and Julie Williams, for this and for so much more, thank you.

I'd like to show my appreciation to everyone at Pen & Sword for taking a chance on this idea and believing that just because someone can write a biography of a fantasy author, they can also tackle the social history of pop. I assume you've realised that that's what this is, right? I'd especially like to thank Jonathan Wright, Charlotte Mitchell, Lori Jones and Laura Hirst for their help and patience.

The cover of this book, I'm sure you'll agree, is BEAUTIFUL – that's the work of Andrea C. White, who has an incredible knack for injecting real magic into an image. If I get my way she will be doing my covers forever. Please investigate her stuff.

I'm extremely appreciative of Stephanie Kays, Allen Warren (with whom I go back further than I thought), Mark Laff and Tony Visconti for sharing their memories with me (admittedly in Visconti's case it was while I was interviewing him for *The Guardian*), and of Kevin Cann and Clifford McLenehan for the invaluable work they did preparing the way with the excellent timelines they've written of Marc & David's lives.

This book was edited by Melanie Clegg, an incredible author and historian in her own right and the woman who introduced me to the hobby of 'palacing'. She is one of the maddest and most brilliant people I know, and her advice, encouragement, warmth and careful eye have made this book so much better than it would ever have been without her. If you're looking for a definition of posh, they once shot an episode of *Lovejoy* in her house.

I'd also like to take this opportunity to thank Andrew O'Neill for their constant encouragement, support and friendship. Similarly, I will always appreciate the presence in my life of Biff & Kim, Rich Jennings, Pete Gardner, Christa

Bloom-Burrows, Andy Heintz, Jez Miller, Thea Heintz, Cat Lee, Laurie Black, Katy Brent, Amanda Angus, Cara Ballingall, Katie Singer, the entire island of Orkney, Rob Wilkins, Gurinder Chadha, Francine Carol, Joanna Hagan, Catherine Anne Davis, Ana Cecilia Escobar, Mary Kate Jordan, Clara Paniago, Declan Cashin, Jen Wilson, Nicola Keaney, Princess Wylde and Rachel Tyson, all of whom – sometimes without knowing it – have offered crucial support during the difficult gestation of this project. It takes a village to raise a child. It takes a small city to write a book.

Finally, to Nicoletta, thank you for *everything*.

Introduction

This is not a story about two pop stars. It's a story about time. And context. And music – above all, it's a story about music. It's about how two boys, born in the same city; a blasted and knocked down city, a wrecked city in a shattered country, at opposite ends of the same year, were shaped by their culture so that they could, in turn, shape that culture right back. It's a story that begins in scratchy monochrome and rises through faded sepia tones into the brightest of bright technicolour. It's *The Wizard of Oz*, but with guitars and drums and great haircuts. It's about clothes and sex and time and place and men and women. It's the story of a very specific version of London at a very specific time. And it's the story of those boys.

Looking back from the 21st Century we have the benefit of seeing the whole picture, something only the most farsighted citizens of Britain recovering from the war could do. We know what's on the horizon. We know about rock 'n' roll, about The Beatles, about teenagers and televisions, about swinging London and Bobby Charlton and *Carry On* movies and 'Space Oddity' and the miner's strike and the three day week and 'Ride A White Swan'. We know what's coming. Oppression and poverty will give way to modernity and excitement to create a flashpoint in youth culture. A unique node. The children born in 1947 were moulded in the spirit of that transition, becoming part of the fabric of that modern world as it took shape. 1947 not only saw the birth of our heroes, Marc Bolan and David Bowie, but also Elton John, David Essex, Queen's Brian May, Steve Marriot of The Small Faces and Humble Pie, Dave Davies of The Kinks, Ronnie Wood of The Faces and The Rolling Stones, Mick Fleetwood of Fleetwood Mac, Brian Johnson of AC/DC and Greg Lake of Emerson, Lake and Palmer. It was a slightly older musical generation that kick-started the rock revolutions of the fifties and sixties, but the class of '47 shaped and defined so much of the popular culture that followed. They would, between them, own the 1970s. And it all began in an England that was broken, cold and miserable.

This is a story about two boys. Not stars. Not yet. Sometimes they were friends, sometimes rivals, but mostly they were just acquaintances. The nature of their relationship is far less important than you'd think. This is a story about how they became what they became. It'll take about twenty three years, and I promise it's worth the journey.

This is the story of the London boys.

Prologue: 'Oh, That's Really Polaroid'

The last day of the London boys was always going to descend into drama, farce and high camp. It has been fifteen years of friendship, rock 'n' roll rivalry and temper tantrums; why change now? For Marc Bolan, weeks away from his thirtieth birthday but just days away from the car accident that will kill him, opportunity is once again knocking and he is grasping it with both hands.

This is 7 September 1977, ATV Studios, Manchester; the last day of filming on Bolan's kid-friendly music show, *Marc*. It's a new sort of gig for the once-bopping elf, in which he does cheeky links to camera between mimed versions of T.Rex hits and new tunes. He also gets to further his self-bestowed reputation as the 'Godfather of Punk' by hosting the punchiest names in New Wave. Guests on the show have included such upstarts as The Jam and The Boomtown Rats, and today's recording will feature punks-proper Generation X and power-pop pub rockers Eddie and The Hot Rods. It will also include the British TV premiere of '"Heroes"', the new single from the other London boy, David Bowie.

History will be kind to the *Marc* show, seeing it as a passing of the torch from one rock generation to another, with a cleaned-up and slimmed down Bolan shimmying once more for the masses. In 2002 biographer Mark Paytress wrote in *The Guardian* about how Marc was 'feted by the new wave of punk iconoclasts'. However, if history is being kind then it has probably not watched the show lately. There's token punk-era snot in every episode and Marc himself is clearly having a ball, but *Marc* is padded with unspeakable naffness that no amount of campy Bolan high-jinx can quite sell. There's Paul Weller's strut and Billy Idol's snarl, sure, but there's also Showaddywaddy, the Bay City Rollers and Mud; plastic glammies that had usurped T.Rex's teenybopper crown and were now themselves on the downward slide. We get Thin Lizzy and Hawkwind, but also Robin Askwith, the soft-porn star of the cheeky *Confessions of a Window Cleaner* movies. Every episode features a dance troupe, Hearts Throb, performing cringey routines to a minor hit of the day. By comparison, *Top of The Pops'* Legs & Co look cooler than Kraftwerk.

If it wasn't for a decade of London boy friendship, Bowie's appearance in such company would be more than strange. David isn't like the young punks; an up-and-comer needing exposure to a more mainstream audience. Nor is he on the slide and in need of a leg-up like the 'Rollers or Mud (or – it has to be said – Marc himself). He's an elder statesman now, a respected name celebrated for pushing the envelope sonically on his recent album *Low* and the forthcoming *"Heroes"*, while still wielding commercial clout. His single 'Sound and Vision' had reached number three back in February. The previous year he had played a six-night stand at the Wembley Empire Pool, the enormodome arena where T.Rextasy had reached its screaming, knicker-wetting zenith when Bolan headlined two shows there in 1972. That was Marc's commercial peak. David hasn't even hit his yet. The London boys are no longer rivals. David has won. He's here to do his mate a favour.

Marc and David have cemented their friendship again as the glam wars of the early seventies recede into the past. For a few years the pair had eyed each other's success with jealousy; lobbing an astonishing run of classic pop singles at one another and playing tug-o-war with producer Tony Visconti, like two stray dogs with a particularly interesting bit of rope. These days an easy and comfortable relationship has been reinstated. Marc and his partner, Gloria Jones, were guests at two Bowie shows in Finland during 1976's *Isolar* tour; David had just received a print of his new film, *The Man Who Fell To Earth*, and had excitedly screened it for them. Back in March, Bowie had stayed for four nights at Marc's home in London during his stint playing keys on Iggy Pop's famously debauched solo run. The two old friends had worked on music together, an all too rare occurrence despite their long association. One track, 'Madman', of which a few rough-sounding recordings survive, held a lot of potential; a spiky, glammy stomp of the sort Bowie's fans thought he had abandoned with his Ziggy Stardust catsuits. In Marc Bolan's hands it could well have been a proper, snarling monster of a hit. Marc would play the tape to anyone who would listen, saying he intended to build his next album around the track. He also talked of plans for them to make a film together, though given Bolan's tendency to talk-up a movie career that never ended up happening, that seems less likely.

Both have been through the wringer as the glam years gave way to the coke-fuelled excesses of the mid-seventies; David's star rising, Marc's falling, David a grinning skeleton, surviving on milk and peppers, Marc bloated from brandy and a bad diet, both existing at the bottom of a bag of white powder as they dealt with the respective pressures of success and comparative failure. They seem to have survived the worst of it. Both men are, if not quite clean, then certainly looking healthier than they have in a while and in good spirits. Marc is tiny and delicate, skinnier than he's been in years, preening in leopard-print catsuits or tight jeans. As for David, as Tim Lott wrote in *Record Mirror*, 'Bowie looked more Adonis in blue jeans than a Belsen boy. Lean though not gangly, easy moving, oiled. The complexion is *Cosmopolitan*-fresh. He looks no older than 20'.

That David was appearing at all was testimony to the affection he felt for his old friend. Bolan might have once been a sparring partner, but Bowie would hardly be thrilled at the association with those other, lesser survivors of the glam years. When TV host Russell Harty had asked him if he'd 'heard of the Bay City Rollers' back in 1975, he had barely been able to keep the amused contempt from his face. Even Thin Lizzy, a comparatively 'cool' rock band were, in Bowie's eyes, beneath him. He'd been baffled when he'd heard Visconti had been working with them, and also slightly affronted that such straightforward rockers were keeping his long-term producer from obeying his summons. And while, yes, okay, in a country with just three TV stations any telly exposure, even a teatime show with a badly animated cartoon audience and a dance troupe, is not to be sniffed at – even so, everyone is aware that Bowie doesn't really need this. He's throwing a bone to Bolan and his co-manager, Jeff Dexter, another one-time mod and London boy who'd been part of the sixties underground scene in which the two would-be stars had learned their craft. Marc, for his part, is thrilled. For David, it's a favour for an old friend; for Bolan, it's an opportunity and it's all about the optics. Unbeknownst to Bowie and his team, publicist Keith Altham and EMI's promotions manager Eric Hall have dragged every sympathetic journalist they can find up the M6 to Manchester, keen to sell the pair as rock elders and co-conspirators; the London boys, together at last. Marc Bolan and David Bowie, sharing the spotlight as equals.

Things go swimmingly all morning. David arrives accompanied only by his personal security, Tony Mascia, the Italian-American bruiser who rarely leaves his side. Marc is all puppyish excitement, presenting his superstar friend with a sunburst Stratocaster to use on the show and instructing his guitar tech, Cliff Wright, to look after the erstwhile Thin White Duke's every need. There's a slight moment of tension when it turns out that the current line up of T.Rex includes former Bowie side-men Herbie Flowers and Tony Newman, the rhythm section that had nearly staged a walk-out over a pay dispute during David's *Diamond Dogs* tour. Hatchets are soon buried though, and everyone descends into the comfortable groove of old friends reacquainted; Herbie, after all, had been the bass player on 'Space Oddity'. Everyone goes way back. The plan is for Bowie to sing live over a backing track, recorded that morning with the T.Rex line up. This causes two moments of potential awkwardness. The first comes when he asks Flowers what key '"Heroes"' is in. Herbie mistakenly says 'E', though the song is actually in the slightly lower and more comfortable key of 'D'. Still, if David notices he doesn't say anything, and the song is performed a whole tone higher than the original version.[1] Bowie is a great singer, easily coping with the change, so it's not a big deal. A bigger problem comes when Marc realises that, despite his expectations, he is not going to be playing guitar

---

1. Flowers discussed this in an interview conducted by Bolan superfan John Bramley for his book *Beautiful Dreamer*. Flowers says he hoped his old boss didn't think he did it on purpose. Bowie was, admittedly, an instinctive rather than technical musician, but it does seem strange that he didn't know what key his song was in.

on David's song. This is gutting as the more time he spends on stage with David, the more the two will be presented as equals; something he dearly wants. Taking the stage to play with his friend on '"Heroes"', one of the most sublime things Bowie will ever write, should have been a crowning moment. However, just as Marc's instinctive careerism means he knows how well this moment could play for him, David's equally careerist instincts know that, as a guitarist, Marc simply isn't right for the track. He's a rock 'n' roll player, and '"Heroes"' is a far more precise and delicate beast. It's ego against ego. David is the bigger star, but it is, after all, Marc's show. Bowie is adamant and ultimately wins: Marc is not going to be part of his number. The band nails the track with David covering guitar duties using the gifted Strat – which Marc insists he keeps – and a hastily set-up amp to recreate Robert Fripp's distinctive, feedback-driven part. It's around this point that Bolan starts drinking.

Marc is becoming increasingly anxious, but tries to put it aside, and the morning passes with something of a party atmosphere. Bodyguard Mascia isn't letting anyone near Bowie, but Marc has no such entourage. The various press and label execs brought in for the occasion flit in and out of his dressing room, where Marc is a gracious host; hugging and kissing old acquaintances and sharing his drinks. Eddie and The Hotrods are there too, waiting with their gear to record their hit song, 'Do Anything You Wanna' and making the occasional barbed comments at Bolan's camped-up antics. They arrived in town yesterday and have been hanging around the studio all morning. They may have to wait for some time. Marc and David are working on a collaboration, 'Standing Next To You'[2], a rough jam that will close the show, and are enjoying themselves. No-one is in a hurry. Generation X, stuck on the motorway somewhere, haven't even arrived yet. Eventually rehearsals are completed without Billy Idol's missing men – the crew will just have to manage without a dry run. Things are already over-running, but not disastrously so. At one point the floor manager complains that Marc is too controlling. Bolan points out whose name is in lights above the stage.

Somewhere around lunchtime the David Bowie entourage arrives, including more security; David's PA, the famously protective Corinne 'Coco' Schwab; and RCA America's fearsome press agent, Barbara DeWitt who is not impressed at the amount of journalists casually swigging the free wine kept flowing by Altham and Hall. Team Bowie starts turfing out anyone they suspect is unnecessary to the show, including the aforementioned floor manager, who happens to be Granada TV's union representative. This will prove to be a mistake. Various London music hacks play a game of cat and mouse with Bowie's bodyguards as they attempt to stay on the studio floor. Producer Muriel Young, who has known both London boys since they were upstart teens hanging around the set

---

2. Called on some bootlegs 'Sleeping Next To You'.

of her proto-pop programme *The Five O'Clock Club*, is becoming increasingly irate as various bands, studio managers, record executives and stars find assorted reasons to complain. Generation X finally arrive, three hours late, having broken down somewhere on the M1 and without any of their gear. They hastily borrow a bass from a reluctant Paul Grey of the Hot Rods, and are told they can use the studio's in-house drum kit and amps. A cherry red Les Paul guitar is handed over for use by a still-cheerful Bolan, who impresses the young punks with his charisma and warmth. 'Let's do it!' he tells them. 'It's going to be great'. The band's singer, Billy Idol, a lifelong fan, and his teenage bandmates look at each other. No-one can believe how short Marc Bolan is in real life. They discuss smashing the guitar during their spot, just for the look of the thing, but cooler heads prevail.

At some point Jeff Dexter returns from a trip to pick up Marc's other manager, Tony Howard, from the airport, only to find the door to the studio barred by a large and unenthusiastic Bowie staffer, who informs them that the set is closed. A row breaks out as various parties demand to see various other parties. Marc and David, preoccupied with their number, don't even register what's happening at first. It's all sorted out, eventually, more or less, but it's taken up a lot of time. Jeff will later describe this as one of the worst nights of his life. David is suitably ashamed on behalf of his entourage, claiming no knowledge of their behaviour or instructions. He might even be telling the truth. Marc, feeling that events are slipping out of his control, retreats embarrassed to his dressing room with tears in his eyes and two bottles of wine he's half-inched from David's rider.

Recording of the show proper gets underway, and the clock ticks ever on. An unrehearsed Generation X, playing live rather than miming as the other bands are, are forced through take after take on their borrowed gear as the crew struggle to get things covered. At one point they're asked to cut their song down by fifty percent to try and get the schedule back on track. Their manager threatens to pull them and do *Top of the Pops* instead. 'This is a new group called, er, Generation X', says Marc for the fifth time. 'They have a lead singer called Billy Idol, who's supposed to be as pretty as me. We'll see'. He sniffs daintily on a pink carnation, resplendent in an even pinker satin shirt, tied just above his navel, with his name written across the front. There's some homophobic sniggering from the Hot Rods' Barrie Masters, still waiting to perform. If anything it pushes Marc to be even more gloriously camp.

Despite the numerous delays and retakes, Generation X, doing 'Your Generation', are great. The Jam and Boomtown Rats are all very well, but Gen X are proper punks and their storming energy elevates the whole programme. This is only their second ever TV performance, and their first time playing live in front of the cameras; they never lose the energy and excitement they're getting from the opportunity. Idol isn't quite as pretty as Marc, but it's clear that a star has been born.

Next up, Marc, now in a one-piece leopard-print catsuit, a smokey eye and kitten heels, attempts to mime to a new, rocked-up version of his classic 'Debora'. It's an oldie, pulled from the Tyrannosaurus Rex catalogue. It had been a minor hit when he cut it with Visconti back in '68, and had left David green with envy at his friend's success. Possibly, its inclusion today is a reminder of the time Marc had first pulled ahead. But possibly not. This is a slinkier, full band arrangement, which would give new life to the song if Bolan could just manage to lip sync it properly. Alas he never does. Matters are not helped by issues with the playback, the wrong verses emerging in the wrong order. More time is taken up, and Marc never quite nails a convincing mime, though his pouting performance looks great all the same.

It's time for David to record '"Heroes"', and all but essential personnel are evacuated. It's a song most in the room have never heard before, and a performance which those watching in the studio, including a few crafty hacks hiding behind curtains to avoid the heavies, are unlikely to ever forget. *Record Mirror*'s Tim Lott is absolutely entranced: 'You can't help but be transfixed by the man, transported', he will later write. 'Nothing exists during "Heroes" except that astonishing rhythm line'. Ten feet from the stage, Generation X's drummer Mark Laff stands open-mouthed. '"Heroes"' instantly becomes his second favourite song of all time (second, he says, because no-one can have a true favourite song). *Melody Maker*'s Chris Welch has also managed to hang on to his spot and is awestruck by the performance. If Marc was hoping that he could make a point by wheeling out 'Debora', David has absolutely trumped him. Welch will later speculate that Bowie had been waiting all day to sing a song in which he literally declares himself king, with his old rival relegated to his queen. It's a mesmerising performance, even transposed up a key, stretching David's voice to its upper limit when the octave jumps in the second verse. Much of the song is delivered straight down the barrel of the camera. He learned that trick on *Top of the Pops*, all those years ago. He's singing to us, in our living rooms. *Nothing* will tear *us* apart. David, wearing nothing fancier than a denim shirt, blue jeans and his sincerity, is captivating. Everyone has goosebumps.

David's performance has clearly been the stand out moment of the show, if not the whole series, but the recording isn't over yet. It's time for the London boys to do their big number. Marc, now wearing jeans, Cuban heels and a vest, and David, having found a pair of aviator shades, are set up in front of Flowers, Newman and T.Rex keyboard player Dino Dines. Marc addresses the viewers. 'Thank you' he says, breathless, slightly slurring, 'for all the boys in the band, David, everybody, all the cats … you know who they are. This is a new song!' David counts in with '1-2-3 …' before the 'four' is replaced by one of those blood-thirsty Bolan howls of 'YEAH!' and the song, a stomping twelve bar blues, kicks in. Bowie's people have graciously let everyone back into the studio to witness the moment. 'It's MONSTER' says EMI's Eric Hall, but he says that about everything. Billy Idol praises the discoish beat, which then stutters to a stop. The microphone has given Marc an electric shock and he's halted the song. A brief rejig and we roll again, David playing it cool, Marc – now quite drunk – bouncing like an excited puppy and grinning like an idiot, finally sharing the stage with his friend. It's a moment of real, obvious joy. Even David cracks a smile. As the pair turn to the microphones Marc stumbles and falls off the lip of the low stage, causing his comrade to burst out laughing. 'Can someone fetch a wooden box for Marc to stand on?' he says[3]. Everyone prepares for a third take, but the clock is ticking and the end of the working day is getting closer and closer. The crew are only supposed to be filming until 7pm. The floor manager asks for the Hot Rods who, twenty-four hours after arriving in town, are finally getting their chance. Marc and David are having none of it, and launch into a jam with Flowers, Newman and Dines. The clock strikes seven. The lights go out, the amps suddenly go quiet. The cameras are off. The union rules are strict – the day ends at 7pm. The power has been cut. No overtime.

No-one can quite believe it. 'Come on man,' begs Marc, 'this is me and David, it's a one-off, it might never happen again'. But no-one is budging. The floor manager is also the union rep, remember, and having been overruled by Bolan all day and then unceremoniously thrown out of his own studio by Bowie's security, he is not in the mood to grant favours. 'Just give it a bit longer – the song's only going to last another couple of minutes', pleads Gen X's Mark Laff, to no avail. The crew are packing up their gear. Eddie and the Hot Rods stand at the side of the stage. They've still not recorded their number and will have to come back another day. They are furious. Everyone is. Marc is devastated, crying openly. The lads from Generation X, taking advantage of the confusion, load the studio's drum kit out the door and have off with it. Punk, after all, has a reputation to uphold.[4] Later, in the control room, everyone watches the footage, desperately hoping it can be salvaged. Even Marc sees the funny side as he takes his tumble from the stage in the last seconds of his last TV performance. 'Oh, that's really polaroid', laughs David. 'You've got to keep that in'. That night, the two reconvene in London and make up over dinner, revisiting their old King's Road haunts where, according to Bolan biographer Paul Roland, they get sozzled on wine and baffle tourists by shouting 'I'm Marc Bolan!' and 'I'm David Bowie!' at passers by.[5] It is the last night they will spend in one another's company. By the time their only performance together airs, on 28 September, Marc Bolan will be dead.

---

3. The 'to stand on' is often omitted in reports of this incident, creating a ghoulish joke in light of Marc's death the following week. Chris Welch's piece in *Melody Maker* is quite clear on the full line, though.
4. They were subsequently banned from Granada TV for ten years.
5. Roland is unclear on who shouts what, so we can't know how confused people actually were.

Barely a week later, in the early hours of 16 September, Marc's car, a mini, driven by Gloria Jones with Marc in the passenger seat, loses control as it takes a hump-back bridge, and swerves off the road near Barnes in North London. The mini hits a steel-reinforced concrete post and the front portion of the tiny car crumples. Gloria breaks her jaw. Marc is killed instantly. His funeral is held just days later in Golders Green, near to his old North London stomping ground. David flies in from Switzerland to attend. Also present are Rod Stewart, Dana Gillespie, Steve Harley, Tony Visconti and a host of others, London boys, honorary and actual, all of them.

As Bowie's limo pulls up outside the crematorium, winding its way through the assembled fans, he hears a familiar voice calling 'David! David!' June, Marc's estranged wife, has not been invited to the funeral but has come anyway, only to be turned away at the gate. David invites her into his car and causes a minor scandal by sneaking her into the service. He sits next to Visconti and weeps openly. Singer Dana Gillespie, who has known both David and Marc for as long as they have known each other, will later say that this is the only time she has ever seen him have such a sincere emotional reaction to anything. According to Bowie biographer and *Mail on Sunday* critic Lesley-Anne Jones, writing in her book *Hero*, that night David and June, who had shared endless evenings with Marc in the sixties when none of them were anyone in particular, playing music in parks or jamming in Visconti's tiny Earl's Court flat, seek comfort from their grief in one another.

The following day, feeling reflective, David drives to Beckenham, to Haddon Hall, the location of so much scheming, planning, dreaming. The base from which he had planned his ascent. The shabby, once-grand building is still there. Just as he had left it. And because even in those moments you can never truly escape your history; his former landlord spots him from a window, comes out to greet him and hands over a bill for unpaid rent.

For David, Marc's death represents a final severance from the earliest days of his career. Though their paths had taken very different courses from the mid-seventies onwards, their bond was like none other in his life – friends that for years had mirrored each other's progress. They had a perspective on one another that was unique to their relationship, a product of so much shared history. That is gone now. David, against some fairly hefty odds, has survived the seventies. Marc hasn't. In a very new, very real sense, he is alone.

Chapter One

Bombsite Boys

The Second World War had left London ravaged; pockmarked with bombsites, its population displaced. Across the city rows of terrace houses sported jagged spaces, like the gaps in an old man's teeth. Two million of Britain's homes had been destroyed in the Blitz. 80% of those were in the capital. Born just two years after the final attacks on London, both David and Marc had childhoods shaped literally by the aftermath of war. It was impossible to live in the city and not be close to the evidence of the German assaults, but Bowie and Bolan had it particularly bad. Marc hailed from East London, Stoke Newington, close enough to the Luftwaffe's prime target of the Docklands to receive a vicious hammering during the Blitz, and terrifyingly close to some of the most devastating rocket attacks of the war. To this day the nearby Walthamstow Marshes has a spot marked 'Bomb Crater Pond' on maps, after a V2 rocket blast gouged a sizeable hole in the ground which was left to gradually fill with water. The young Marc Bolan, like every child in the city, played in the wreckage of war.

Many of the bomb sites surrounding David Bowie's childhood home in Brixton were the result of a particularly dubious bit of misdirection. In 1944, the Nazis had unveiled the V1 rocket; the 'flying bomb' nicknamed the 'doodlebug' by Londoners who were left terrified as they listened for its distinctive engine to cut out, signalling that the pilotless plane was about to fall to earth and explode. Fearing the damage the new weapon could inflict on the city, officials hatched a plot to protect London's most important zones. British double agents, operating behind enemy lines, fed misleading reports that the V1s were overshooting their targets. The Germans responded by shortening the range of the weapons, meaning valuable central London was spared the worst of the bombardment. The downside, of course, is that the doodlebugs invariably hit the mostly working class southern parts of the city. It's estimated that perhaps 2,000 lives were saved by the tactics, though that would be small comfort to the residents of those Lambeth streets disproportionately devastated by the attacks. The misinformation campaign was eventually discontinued due to the ethical concerns it raised, though not before significant damage had been done in Lewisham, Lambeth, Clapham, Camberwell, Battersea, Bermondsey and Brixton.

The war may have ended by the time the boys were born, but its shadow was long, especially in London where a population of eight million people were trying to reconstruct their lives and adapt to an annoyingly transitional 'new normal'. Still, there was plenty happening in which a city still traumatised by the shattering fear of the Blitz could find renewed hope: the Labour government's new welfare policies were gradually taking shape, free health care for all had been established by the National Health Service Act the previous year and would be up and running by 1948 and child benefit had been introduced in 1946, providing families with a minimum guaranteed income. Free, compulsory education had been extended to the age of fifteen, and whatever they may eat and drink at home, all children were entitled to free milk at school. The national mood was buoyed by the engagement and, later that year, marriage of Princess Elizabeth to Philip Mountbatten. Restrictions on foreign travel imposed during the war were finally lifted and, above all, nobody was dropping bombs on anyone else's house.

As the post-war period recedes into ancient history, it's difficult to fully appreciate the sense of comfort, security and relief that all of this would have brought to the boys' parents. They knew they were bringing their babies into a world in which the whole family would probably survive the week. The absence of nightly raids, still fresh in the memory for so many, meant that even the shabbiest of houses would likely still have a roof tomorrow. They could plan a trip to the pictures to see *Black Narcissus*, *Miracle on 34th Street* or the first Ealing Comedy, *Hue and Cry*, safe in the knowledge that the local Odeon would still be standing when Saturday night rolled around. They could go to work, or send their children to school and be relatively confident that they'd find more than a crater full of twisted metal and chunks of brick when they arrived. None of this could be guaranteed during the first half of the decade. David and Marc were born into relative security, if not actual prosperity. The end of the war gave them, at the very least, a life of mostly peace (though not quiet), as well as providing them with some very interesting and absurdly dangerous places to play as boys.

The war years felt like the pivot-point of the century: things couldn't – and shouldn't – be the same. The world had been reshaped, metaphorically, politically and – in London, certainly – literally. Change was in the air. That atmosphere couldn't last.

By 1947 the United Kingdom was in poor shape and spirits were low. As it turned out, things hadn't changed all that much. Money was scarce and restrictions were still necessary. David and Marc's earliest memories were of scarcity. Rationing would remain in place until 1954; each adult family member was entitled to a weekly allowance of thirteen ounces of meat, one-and-a-half of cheese, six ounces of butter, one ounce of lard, eight ounces of sugar, just two pints of milk and a single egg. Needless to say, few cakes were baked in those early years. One of the harshest winters on record meant that those staples that had helped families through the worst of the wartime restrictions – root vegetables, powdered egg – were now as scarce as milk and butter had been. For most of their childhood, our London boys were required to make just seven ounces of sweets last seven long days. The brutal winter led to a fuel crisis, with mandatory power blackouts brought back for the first time since the war and many businesses, particularly factories, forced to close. Several never re-opened, adding increased unemployment and strikes to the country's woes. Office workers were asked to complete their work by candlelight. Charles Dickens' image from *A Christmas Carol* of 'the clerk in the tank', shivering under a comforter, deprived of coal for the fire, was as applicable to David Bowie's father working in the London of 1947 as it had been to poor Bob Cratchit in 1843. Television broadcasts were once again paused, and even radio output was limited.

The end of hostilities in Europe brought immediate peace, but also came with the clang of the falling iron curtain and the first signs of a Cold War that would dominate geopolitics until the 1990s. Hitler was gone, but Stalin was probably far more powerful than he had ever been. The horrible new atomic weapons that had brought about Japanese surrender were ominous and terrifying. The relief of VE and VJ Day gave way to uncertainty and fear. The unity of purpose the push for victory had created was gone. Britain was still living under wartime conditions but without a war to justify them. In his book *Never Had It So Good* the historian Dominic Sandbrook quotes one despairing housewife at the time: 'We won the war,' she says. 'Why is it so much worse?'.

David Robert Jones was born into this freezing, dark and blasted city at 9am on 8 January 1947, during the coldest month Britain would see in the entire twentieth century. By a neat coincidence, of the sort that Bowie would have had to invent if it didn't happen to be true, his birth took place twelve years to the day after that of fellow pioneering rock 'n' roll iconoclast, Elvis Presley. Possibly the date is sprinkled with stardust – Shirley Bassey, the actors Ron Moody and Roy Kinnear and the American comedian Soupy Sales, whose sons would be Bowie collaborators many years down the line, were all born on 8 January – but, then again, probably not. Millions of 8 January babies have failed to achieve international icon status. Still, if we're buying into the myths and mysticism of the Bowie story there's plenty to be going on with: a midwife present at the birth declared that David had 'been here before'. When pushed to explain the comment, she simply said that 'it's his eyes. They're so knowing.' It's the kind of thing that, to this day, the more traditional sort of midwife says to new mothers, and there's probably not a great deal to read into the comment except to say that the mythical aspects of David's story began on day one. [1]

---

1. Tracking down the origin of this quote proves tricky – it's repeated in almost every book about Bowie published since the eighties, but doesn't surface earlier than the account written by his former manager, Kenneth Pitt, in 1983, suggesting this was a story recounted by David himself, or one of his parents, who knew Pitt well. It's certainly not a claim Bowie seems to have publicly repeated himself.

Though he would grow up essentially lower-middle class, David's earliest years still fit the poor-lads-done-good mythos of the London boys, in which, as Tony Visconti, a long-term collaborator of both Bowie and Bolan, says, they were 'poor, working class lads who had a Beethoven symphony in their heads'. David was born at home, which was very typical at the time, in a modest three-floored terrace at 40 Stansfield Road, a stone's-throw from Brixton tube station. The house was home to two other families for most of the time that the Joneses lived there. Bowie biographer Lesley-Ann Jones (no relation), in her colourful telling of his life, makes a lot of the walls of peeling paint, the floor of curling lino and the windows still sporting the criss-cross of tape used to minimise the damage of bomb blasts during the Blitz. While we can't *quite* account for the accuracy of this description, it's true that the area was far from affluent. In one of David's first major press interviews, with Penny Valentine for *Disc* in 1969, he would recall the children who would come to school with their shoes falling apart and the 'people deprived' that surrounded him.

On the surface, the start of Marc Bolan's life was very much the same. He was born later that year, on 30 September, eight miles and some 45 minutes, by bus and tube, to the north of David's house, just before another notably vicious winter ripped through the country. Born Mark Feld, the future Marc Bolan opened his eyes for the first time in Hackney General Hospital; the transition from home to hospital births as the norm was underway by now, and young Marc's entry into the world was, as a result, a little more modern than David's. Alas, we do not know the midwife's verdict on the spiritual history of the tiny soul born that day, which is a shame, nor do we know if – as Marc himself claimed in his song 'Cosmic Dancer', he 'danced himself right out the womb'. Whether the same stardust was sprinkled on the date of 30 September as 8 January we can only speculate; however it would probably please Marc to know that one of the earliest recorded figures to share his birthday was Rumi, the thirteenth century Persian mystic whose poetry would, via a lineage of influence, resonate with Marc's own.

Not far from the hospital was Marc's first home, at 25 Stoke Newington Common, another three-storey Victorian terrace. Both the Feld and Jones households were old and draughty, neither had central heating or hot water, and both boys would grow up sharing a room with their older brother, relying on piles of blankets, hot water bottles and the cuddles of their parents to keep them warm through the long winters that brought the country to a halt during the grim late forties and early fifties. There was, however, a very telling difference between the two households: the Felds rented their home, paying 15 shillings a week for four rooms split over two floors. David's family owned theirs outright.

Throughout his life, Marc would spin yarns about his backstory; claiming to be, amongst other fancies, descended from French aristocracy, a dabbler in the occult, and a member of a violent street gang. One important and much-repeated claim, however, was absolutely true: his background was solidly working class London. His mother, Phyllis, hailed from across the city in Fulham. Her own mother was a cleaner, and her father an apparently quite unsuccessful green grocer. She met Simeon 'Sid' Feld, a short, talkative sailor, seven years her senior, from a devout Jewish family, in 1944 while both worked in a munitions factory near Earls Court. Sid was the son of a Whitechapel meatpacker with a sideline in bare-knuckle boxing, descended from Russian, Spanish and Polish Jews that had fled antisemitic regimes in Europe at the turn of the century. The pair were married in January 1945, with Phyllis already pregnant with their first son, Harry (which may account for their fairly short courtship) and moved to Stoke Newington, where Sid found work as a lorry driver.

Though Phyllis came from a traditional Church of England background, Sid's family very much leaned into their Jewish heritage and, while not especially religious, the couple raised their two sons more-or-less in that tradition. East London in general, and Stoke Newington and neighbouring Stamford Hill in particular, had (and still has) a significant Jewish population that very much influenced the character of the neighbourhood. The Felds were a large family – Sid was one of six siblings – and Marc grew up surrounded by cousins, aunts, uncles, second-cousins and close family friends, all part of a tightly knit, inclusive and largely Jewish community. Marc would walk his younger cousins home from school, babysit for members of the extended family, and, when he was older, help with running his mother's fruit and veg stall on Soho's Berwick Street, or assist his father in his second job; assembling market stalls in the East End early on weekend mornings. That's not to say that Marc was an especially generous or giving child, though one of his cousins, Stephanie Kays, does describe him as having 'a very sweet nature'; such acts were simply the norm in such close, family-focused communities as the one the Felds inhabited. Marc's parents doted on their sons and indulged Marc in particular, but the whole neighbourhood was one that looked out for one-another. Clothes were mended and swapped between families as children out-grew them, kids played street games together, watched over by whichever local adult was closest. The Jewish aspect of the area played into this. Antisemitism was rife, especially in East London, where the Blackshirts of Oswald Mosley's British Union of Fascists had focused many of their protests, so it was natural that the community would look after its own. Even outside of the Jewish households though, neighbourhoods in the East End have always been tightly knit.[2]

Mark Feld grew up in a tight community as part of a large, close family that watched over him, included him and frequently indulged him. Everyone knew the Felds, and though Sid and Phyllis' mixed Jewish/Christian marriage would have raised a few eyebrows, their inclusion in the community smoothed over

---

2. There is an entire soap opera dedicated to this.

any old scandals. Over in Brixton, however, it was a different story. The family of David Jones were keeping themselves to themselves. It's not a huge surprise – Sid and Phyllis' mixed faith marriage may have been a little unconventional, but it wasn't really that uncommon; David's Brixton home housed a far more scandalous story.

Heywood Stenton 'John' Jones, the father of the future David Bowie, met Margaret 'Peggy' Burns in 1945 shortly after returning from the war. It's worth pausing here to note that neither of David's parents, nor Marc's father, went through life using their given name. Heywood, Margaret and Simeon became John, Peggy and Sid, just as Mark Feld and David Jones would become, amongst other names, Marc Bolan and David Bowie. Both boys grew up knowing instinctively that identities were not set in stone; that names and social conventions were not hard and fast rules that must be followed. They would go on to try out – and then discard – personas and names as if they were masks or costumes. Bowie, in particular, would make a career out of it.

John and Peggy fell for each other quickly, and moved to London together before the year was out. They purchased the house on Stansfield Road in 1946, and by the end of the year Peggy was heavily pregnant with the couple's first and only child together. Which all sounds pretty conventional, if rather hurried by modern standards – although in the post-war years, when marriages and births spiked, such a quick turn-around wasn't especially unusual. What was rather less common was the fact that the couple weren't living alone. With them was John Jones' first wife, Hilda, and a young daughter, Annette, the product of an extramarital affair in which John had become involved before the war.

Robert Jones, David's paternal grandfather, had been a partner in a successful footwear business – The Public Benefit Boot Company – in his native Yorkshire, and had died during the First World War, with his wife following soon afterwards. At eighteen their son, Heywood, inherited the not-inconsiderable sum of £3,000 from his parents' estate[3] and headed south to London, to soak in the jazz and the nightlife and make his mark on the world. There he met and, in 1933 married, Hilda Sullivan; a nightclub singer and the daughter of a music hall performer, whose family had fled Austria as the Nazis began to extend their influence there. Announcing that he would make her a star, John plunged two thirds of his inheritance into a touring revue to showcase the abilities of his new wife, now known as 'Chérie – The Viennese Nightingale'. Sadly, the venture never really took off, and instead the couple opened a Soho nightclub, the 'Boop-A-Doop' piano bar, which according to David, ended up catering to boxers, gangsters, sex workers and the other colourful characters that comprised the underbelly of thirties London. The club, like the revue, turned out to be a money pit and eventually John would leave showbusiness for a job in public

---

3. To put that figure into context, the house he would later buy in Brixton cost just £500.

relations with Dr Barnardo's Homes, a long-established and respected children's charity, joining the company in 1935. He would stay with them for the rest of his life, becoming head of PR in 1956.

The pair's marriage was tempestuous, and never really recovered from the early disappointments of the club and Hilda's failed singing career, for which she always blamed her husband. By the time John took the job at Barnardo's the couple had already separated and reconciled at least once, so it's perhaps not totally surprising that, during an extended business trip to Birmingham, he became involved with another woman; apparently a nurse, though no other details of her life are known. What possibly *was* surprising is that when that affair resulted in a pregnancy, Jones confessed everything to his wife and the pair agreed to bring up the baby together. The arrangement, alas, couldn't last and their marriage crumbled shortly thereafter. This was 1938. A year later, war broke out and John, already a member of the Territorial Army, enlisted as a rifleman in the Royal Fusiliers, leaving Hilda to bring up another woman's child alone.

Peggy Burns' journey to Stansfield Road contained its own share of twists and turns. Coming from a much less affluent background than her future husband, Peggy grew up in Tunbridge Wells, a commuter town in the south of England. According to Ken Pitt's *Bowie: The Pitt Report*, young Peggy was a local beauty with a striking fashion sense and David would later tell his wife, Angela, that his mother had been the first woman in her town to wear trousers. She was, apparently, likeable and warm, but also naive and impressionable; to the point of becoming a supporter of Oswald Mosley's British Union of Fascists because she thought the characteristic black shirts were 'rather becoming'. It's fairly safe to assume that there was no genuine antisemitism in Peggy's nature, however – shortly after the Blackshirts incident she became involved with a young Jewish man, Jack Rosenberg, a kitchen porter in the hotel where she worked as a nanny. It's perhaps testimony to her naivety that the twenty four year old Peggy soon found she was pregnant. Rosenberg promised to marry her, but vanished before the ceremony could be arranged. Their son, Terence Guy Adair, born in 1937, was given his mother's surname. Six years later, while working in a munitions factory during the war, Peggy fell pregnant again; this time due to an affair with a married man. She gave birth to a daughter, Myra Ann, but gave her up for adoption before she was a year old. David would grow up with his half-brother Terry, but never got the chance to know his two half-sisters, Annette and Myra Ann. He would later speculate – in some distress – to his school friend, George Underwood, that his mother had been a 'prostitute' during this time, having discovered letters hidden at home that seemed to suggest it.

Demobbed at the end of the war, having fought in France, North Africa and Italy, John Jones resumed his employment with Dr. Barnardo's. It was while visiting one of the charity's children's homes in Tunbridge Wells that he met

Peggy, now working as a server in the Ritz cinema. The pair were apparently instantly smitten with each other. John moved his new love to London later that year and when Peggy found that she was pregnant, the obvious move was to buy a house in which to raise their child. There was, of course, a snag – John Jones was still technically married, and Hilda Jones was entitled to half of the couple's savings. They hit upon an arrangement; John and Hilda would buy a property together and, likely for propriety's sake, both live there – alongside Peggy – with Hilda moving out once a divorce had been arranged, taking with her John's daughter, Annette, whom she had raised alone while he had been fighting abroad. When John ultimately sold the house half of the proceeds would be given to his daughter.[4] Thus it was, on that freezing January night, that David Jones' very conventional home-birth took place in a rather unconventional home. John and Hilda's divorce, granted on the grounds of his infidelity, was finalised eight months later, on 11 August 1947 and wasting little time, he and Margaret Jones were married on 12 September. Much later, in 1960, the couple would legally re-register David's birth and have his birth certificate amended, making their son (who had been born out of wedlock) the legitimate product of their marriage. Peggy's first child, ten-year-old Terry, moved to Stansfield Road from Tunbridge Wells, where he had been living with his grandparents, in 1948. Peggy had put up with a lot to establish her family and had insisted that, now matters were settled, her elder son should join the household too. John agreed, apparently reluctantly, and Terry's surname was changed from Burns to Jones. He and David would share a bedroom for many years.

These experiences mattered. A baby's brain develops more in its first three years than at any other stage in its life. Studies by the Bezos Family Foundation, the children's charity set up by Amazon founder Jeff Bezos, found that children as young as three months old can be affected by the moods and emotions of the people around them; their sense of the world and how to interact with those that they encounter within it is formed by watching their parents. How they are treated, who they are exposed to, the atmosphere in the home; all of these contribute in a very fundamental way to the development of personality and social skills, and a significant portion of a brain's architecture is impacted by these very early experiences. It's not an exaggeration to say that these parts of Marc and David's lives helped shape the very different, and yet very similar men they became. Had they not been born in the austere post-war years, had they not had *these* families at *this* time, they could never have become *those* artists.

Life in the Jones household was uncomfortable and frosty, and that left its mark. In 1997, on the occasion of his fiftieth birthday, David would tell *Interview* magazine that there was 'an awful lot of emotional and spiritual mutilation

---

4. John actually reneged on this when he sold the house in 1953, using the money to buy his family's new home in Bromley instead.

[that] goes on in my family ... I think to a certain extent it's touched me in various ways over the years'. David would grow up hero-worshipping his older brother Terry, and yet had to watch him be constantly treated as an outsider by the family. When the rest of the Jones household moved to Bromley in 1953, Terry, now fourteen, would stay behind in Brixton. In another interview, this time for a US documentary called *David Bowie: Sound & Vision*, Bowie talked about how the 'dark secrets in the cupboard of his family meant he grew up feeling alienated and apart from his peers.

John was a supportive and friendly father, though physically very hands-off, while Peggy – apparently a natural with children when she was younger – had become frostier as she grew older. Hugs were rare in the Jones household, and compliments rarer. As David's school friend, George Underwood, once said, 'even David didn't like his Mum'. Angela, David's future wife, writing in her memoir *Backstage Passes*, would peg many of the adult Bowie's worst traits – emotional coldness, restlessness, a need for control – on the environment in which he was raised. It wasn't all he learned, however. Young David Jones learned public relations at his father's knee; seeing first hand the importance of creative presentation and reputation, and learning the art of manipulation.

While David's early years contributed to an emotional distance, Marc's stoked what would eventually become a fairly titanic ego, hidden behind an easy and disarming manner. Marc's parents doted on him, adored him. Phyllis, in particular, treated her youngest child as if the sun shone from his very behind. Marc responded well to the attention; to being told he was talented or handsome or clever, to knowing that he was loved. He was always small for his age and, as small children often do, expanded his personality to make up the difference. Young Marc was a dreamer, and his parents encouraged him in this, they also instilled in him the importance of looking smart and put together. All of this would pay off.

To grow up in the late 1940s and early 1950s, as we have seen, was to bear witness to massive social change from the very front lines. Both London boys were in a good position to watch. The tail end of the forties saw a ramping up of immigration to Britain.[5] The most iconic representation of which was the arrival of the *SS Empire Windrush* at Tilbury Dock, downriver in Essex, on 22 June 1948; a passenger liner that carried 492 people, mostly young men, each seeking a new life, from Kingston in Jamaica. The *Windrush* was not the last such vessel, and over the coming months and years 15,000 people would arrive from Jamaica alone, with another 13,000 coming from India. All in, 57,000 immigrants came to the UK from Commonwealth countries in those post war years in search of a new life, creating what would later be referred to as 'The

---

5. Though not to the extent that the right wing press of the time made out. In fact, Britain was a net *exporter* of people until the end of the twentieth century.

Windrush Generation'. By 1971, 650,000 people in Britain traced their origins to the West Indies, Bangladesh, India and Pakistan.

London, as it always had, would feel the biggest impact of immigration to the UK. While it's important to remember that the city, as a major port and the hub of a vast trading empire, had been a cultural melting pot for most of its history and had always welcomed newcomers, the arrival of the *Windrush* Generation inevitably left its mark; fundamentally changing the areas of the city where immigrants settled, influencing music, culture, food and language. Two such areas were East London, the home of the Feld family, and Brixton, where the Jones household resided. Both boys, in different ways, grew up affected by their mixed cultural communities.

Despite many claims in later life that his South London origins meant he'd been raised soaked in Caribbean culture ('I grew up in an 'ouse full of Blacks', he fibbed to one interviewer in the 70s) Bowie's family actually moved away before the new arrivals had started to properly settle in Brixton[6], which became one of the UK's best-known hubs of Black life. However, that doesn't mean the multicultural nature of the area didn't have an impact. His brother Terry stayed on, immersing himself in music and culture. David hero-worshipped his brother, and absorbed many of those influences. He would go back to the area regularly as a teenager: 'It left great, strong images in my mind,' he told *Time Out* in 1983, when he became involved in a campaign to save a local youth centre. 'All the ska and bluebeat clubs were in Brixton, so one gravitated back there. Also it was one of the few places that played James Brown records.'

Even in those very early years the area would have an ambience that the young Bowie would definitely have picked up on. Many of the local houses were owned by the legendary Trinidadian pianist Winifrid Atwell, who would rent them to performers, variety artists and show business types, and there's some speculation that it was this 'showbizzy' element that drew John Jones, the former nightclub impresario, to the area. David Arden, the younger brother of legendary music manager Don Arden and the uncle of Sharon Osbourne, was raised in Brixton around the same time and told Bowie biographer Dylan Jones about the reggae and jazz records available on market stalls. A neighbour of the Joneses, Annie Briggs, remembers the 'technicolour clothing' and 'lilting speech' of the market, soundtracked by buskers and street performers, cockney and Caribbean culture rubbing shoulders, creating a melting pot that no child could fail to be impacted by.

Marc, already part of a marginalised Jewish community, also felt a kinship with the latest arrivals. His own great grandparents had been immigrants themselves, coming to London for a better life. 'It was fairly multi-cultural even

---

6. Or, as his future manager Ken Pitt once rather unpleasantly put it, 'before the tidal wave of black immigration destroyed the character of an English community'.

then, we had children from all over the world,' says Stephanie Kays, Marc's cousin. 'It was very multiracial. We loved that. It made us more accepting. I was in awe of them, these families that come thousands and miles to make a life on our little island. We embraced it.' Marc and his brother and cousins were raised in an atmosphere of activism and anti-fascism, which they all soaked in. 'He couldn't handle injustice or conflict', says Stephanie. 'He'd break up fights and get people to sing a song'.

London, as a hub of immigration, was inevitably also a hub of racism. For many, the newcomers were alien. The historian David Kynaston, in his book *Family Britain, 1951-1957*, relays reports of Londoners shocked that a 'coloured person' might know English and understand 'proper' money ('they would grab your hand and then shout to all of the bus that your hands were warm' remembers one new arrival), one Christian man from the West Indies, settling in Camden and attending a local church, was told politely by the vicar that the congregation was 'not comfortable around Black people'. By the sixties, those uncomfortable feelings had turned into outright resentment, leading to riots and violence. Racism was not just found on the streets, either. In 1955, Harold Macmillan, then Foreign Secretary, noted in his diary that even the prime minister, Anthony Eden, thought 'Keep Britain White' to be a 'good slogan'.

Though the Feld family was not universally open minded – one of Marc's cousins actually fled the country because his wife 'wasn't comfortable with the *Windrush* Generation' – they were, by and large, actively resistant to the racism they too suffered from. Ridley Road in Dalston, a short hop and skip from Stoke Newington, was the the focal point for the fascist rallies of Oswald Mosley's Blackshirts and his new Union Movement party, goaded beyond antisemitism by the increase in Commonwealth immigrants. The '43 Group', formed by Jewish ex-servicemen in East London, was formed to combat and campaign against Mosely's fascists, as was the '62 Group', another Jewish-led anti-fascist venture formed a few years later. Marc's neighbourhood was abuzz with this sort of activism. As Stephanie Kays says, hatred of injustice was 'a very family thing':

> 'Our grandmothers, they used to fight blackshirts on Ridley Road market in the 1930s. They worked on Tobacco Docks in Limehouse, they were quite attractive girls, they'd get free cigarettes and would hang around Ridley Road puffing away. They'd go two at a time and stand each side of a blackshirt, puff on the cigarettes, look at each other, wearing loads of lippy and mascara and the bright blue eye shadow, they'd look as glamorous possible, wink at each other, then wink at the Nazi, who thought his luck was in, and as they were smiling they'd plunge their cigarettes into his eyes and then run as fast as they could. That was our family.'

Arguably the immigration of the 1940s and 1950s shaped and changed the culture of the city as much as the war had done, though with obviously far more positive results. For the London boys multiculturalism was second nature, a way of life. Racism was an anathema to both. They would grow up obsessed with Black music and Black idols, both would be heavily influenced by Black artists in their own music and, perhaps most tellingly, both would eventually settle down with Black women and father biracial children. It's another example of how this era of London's history was uniquely impactful on the boys and how they would see and understand the world.

By the mid 50s we have our two London boys, growing up on either side of the city, divided by the river and by an even wider gulf of social class, but connected by the sociological and historical context of those lean, post-war years of cold austerity and want. One nourished by a loving community, one isolated by family scandal, both soaking-in the city around them. But it was not geography or sociology that would unite the London boys in common purpose, it was music. Their love affair with culture, both Black and otherwise, was only just beginning.

Chapter Two

Awopbopaloobop Alopbamboom!

The prize for surviving the grim austerity of the post war years was pop music. For those young enough to swerve national service (compulsory for all 18-21 year olds between 1949 and 1960), entering the blush of youth as rationing was lifted (1954) and able to earn money of their own just as the market was flooded with desirable commodities like clothes, records, magazines, cars and concerts; a gift was given that has been taken for granted by every generation since. It's a gift denied to those whose teenage years were blighted by wars, or rationing, or want: *youth*. A late childhood. A teenagerdom. An extended adolescence. Indulging in teenage fancy had previously been something enjoyed only by the privileged few, even when there *hadn't* been a war to fight. In the 1930s the concept of 'the teenager' – an autonomous consumer group that were neither children nor adults – was only just starting to take hold when it was interrupted by the air-raid sirens. It was still normal for working class kids to go straight from the school to the factory, growing quickly from short trousers to settled workers with a two-up-and-two-down terrace house and a couple of kids of their own on the horizon. That shifted in the 1950s, a decade in which every young person began to realise their god-given right to augment their hormonally-charged growth spurt with experimentation, a cold Coca-Cola and a poster of a pop star on their wall. The playfulness of childhood was allowed to gradually fade into adult responsibility, rather than being shunted painfully off the board as the grown-up world took hold. Pop music wasn't the only manifestation of this, but it was the most potent, the most thrilling. For Marc and David it became a way of life.

It's important to note that, first and foremost, the music that blew the minds of our London boys – the music that changed the world, really – was American. Geoff MacCormack, a life-long friend of David's who first met him in 1954 at Burnt Ash Junior School in Bromley, sees Americana as absolutely key to unleashing the pent-up energy of Britain's youth. 'The Britain we grew up in was really quite grubby', he told Bowie biographer Dylan Jones, 'the music was bad, there was no decent food and everything was grey, so when American music came along it fundamentally changed everything.'[1] David was in a good

---

1. Peter Prickett, also a pupil at Burnt Ash, agrees. 'Everything seemed grey', he told another biographer, Paul Trynka for his book *Starman*. 'We wore short grey flannel trousers, grey socks, grey shirts. The roads were grey, the prefabs were grey, the bombsites … made of grey rubble'. I'm writing this book in 2022 and the roads are *still* grey, so we probably have a ways to go yet.

position to hear this stuff. Despite settling into a job in the charity sector, John Jones – David's father – never lost the showbiz bug he'd picked up as a tour promoter and nightclub impresario. He would help organise fundraiser concerts and events for his job at Dr Barnardo's, schmoozing talent and industry types. One night in 1955, a few years after the family had moved from Brixton to the more comfortable South London suburb of Bromley, a contact gifted John a box of 45 RPM singles imported from the US, which he happily took home for his son. David, all of eight years old, went through the whole box, playing both sides of each, fascinated. He found Fats Domino, the likeable boogie-woogie pianist most famous for 'Blueberry Hill' and 'Ain't That a Shame'; he found Chuck Berry, who used his guitar to play thrilling blues rock like a man with a pickaxe plays a quarry wall. There was Frankie Lymon and the Teenagers, the teenage doo-wop sensations whose cheeky, 13-year-old singer had a sweet soul belt. Most importantly, he found Little Richard's 'Tutti Frutti'. Right then, as the needle hit the groove of the vinyl, as a raw, utterly sexual voice with a little rip in its top end, yelled 'A-WOP-BOP-A-LOO-BOP-A-LOP-BOM-BOM!' and cued an irresistible twelve-bar swing, whooping and screaming like nothing he had ever heard before, as a sax solo ripped across an instrumental break, the eight-year-old David Jones' world changed forever. In that two minutes and twenty-four seconds, somewhere inside that little boy, David Bowie stirred for the first time.[2]

We should pause here for just a second to discuss Little Richard, because his influence on the young Bowie is fairly profound. Before he was the self-styled 'innovator, the originator and the architect of rock 'n' roll', he was plain old Richard Wayne Penniman … except there was never *anything* plain about the kid nicknamed 'Lil Richard' by his family. In his teens he sang in church but was banned from the congregation for 'screaming and hollering'. After that he would sing for the preachers, snake oil slingers and travelling shows that came through his hometown of Macon, Georgia until he eventually became (or so it's claimed – Richard was as prone to self-mythologising as Marc and David) the disciple of a local religious leader called 'Doctor Nubilio'; a flamboyant and terrifying figure who wore colourful turbans and capes, carried a black stick and, apparently, the actual blackened, shrivelled corpse of a baby with clawed feet and horns, which he called 'the devil child'. Richard became his herald, singing on the street to pull passers-by in to see the Doctor preach, all the time watching and learning, taking from Nubilio the importance of flamboyance, performance

2. One version of this story recounted by David himself claims that the family gramophone played only 78 rpm discs, and that he had to manually speed up the platter to get his new treasures to play correctly. This feels a little like Bowie mythmaking. For starters it's unlikely anyone could have any kind of transformative experience with a record played like that, it would sound horrible. Secondly, 78s – as the name suggests – spin *faster* than 45s, so actually he would need to have slowed the turntable down, not speed it up.

and the enduring power of being deeply weird.[3] Later, as one of the first true rock stars, Richard would perform in brightly coloured baggy suits that hung off of his skinny frame, draping down to huge, 26 inch hems at the ankle, a thin pencil moustache across his upper lip, looking like it had been drawn on with a magic marker. He wore orangey pan-stick make-up so thick you could write your name on his face with your fingernail without touching his skin, augmented with smokey eye shadow and mascara. His hair was backcombed, cascading and bubbling into his fringe as he slammed the heel of his court shoe into his piano keyboard and screamed bloody murder. When he spoke he was *outrageously* camp, but somehow also managed the brim and vigour and passion of a southern preacher. Between songs, he would fake heart attacks onstage. There was nothing, absolutely nothing, in the monochrome world of post-war Britain even remotely like Little Richard. David was taking notes.[4] He would see Richard perform several times, begging his mother to take him to a recording of the TV show *Jukebox Jamboree*, where the star would be appearing for the first time. After seeing the 1956 rock 'n' roll flick *The Girl Can't Help It*, which featured a Little Richard live performance, he resolved to learn the saxophone and become one of the four horn players in his band. That same film, a full-colour rock 'n' roll extravaganza starring Jayne Mansfield ('It's got the HEAT! And the BEAT! For your happiest time!' screamed the poster) was played across the country, dazzling a generation. On the other side of the city, Mark Feld was awed, and 200 miles north in Liverpool four teenage skiffle players suddenly saw their future. David, meanwhile, would say that his first play of 'Tutti Frutti' was the moment he 'saw God'.

It didn't end, or even begin, with Little Richard. The new music coming from America supercharged British youth culture. It wasn't its American-ness *per se* that made rock 'n' roll stand out; American music had been part of British culture for decades, from Cole Porter and George Gershwin, to Bing Crosbie and Frank Sinatra to the more recent imports of jazz and swing music. Rock 'n' roll was different, though. It was unflinching, almost brutally primitive, an evolution of Black blues and hard R&B, with a dash of white country and swing to sweeten the pot. Above all it was incredibly sexy; based around throbbing basslines, chugging guitars, hammered keys, vocal yelps and howls and a rock solid beat, loud in the mix. To a nation of kids raised on Vera Lynn and Al Martino, Max Bygraves, George Formby and Doris Day, it was like heavy metal, gangsta rap, punk rock and acid house all rolled into one inflammatory whirl. Even its name was sexual: 'rock 'n' roll' was first used to describe the new sound

---

3. As the rock historian and comedian Andrew O'Neill says in their excellent *A History of Heavy Metal*, 'and this why you'll never be as cool as Little Richard'.
4. Bowie would later claim to keep a framed picture of Little Richard getting out of a red Cadillac at every recording session he did, telling Nile Rogers, the co-writer and producer on 1983's *Let's Dance*, that the picture embodied the feel of the album he wanted to make.

by the American DJ Alan Freed in an effort to blur racial divides in the music he played, previously thought of as Black rhythm and blues or white pop. Before that, 'rock 'n' roll' had been Harlem slang for sex.

Oddly, though, despite the heady, multi-racial musical orgy gradually spreading across the US, it took a chubby, white, thirty-something country singer-cum-rockabilly-band-leader to kick the door open for the UK's own rock revolution, and it was this affable everyman – rather than the freakazoid extravagance of Little Richard – that first grabbed the attention of most of the nation's youth, alongside that of an eight year old Mark Feld.

There's an argument that Bill Haley's 'Rock Around The Clock' is the most influential record ever made, and it deserves some attention here because it truly did inform the musical landscape that both Bolan and Bowie emerged, blinking, into. It's certainly one of the best selling records ever, having shifted somewhere in the region of 25 million copies in the last 65 or so years. It doesn't rock as hard, or as raunchily as songs by Little Richard, Chuck Berry or Jerry Lee Lewis, but it does have a kind of primal power. That opening, 'one-two-three-o'clock-four-o'clock ROCK!', is probably the most recognisable five seconds of music ever recorded, yet its journey from a New York recording studio to mainstream British success and, ultimately, the ears of the future Marc Bolan is based almost entirely on happenstance.

Haley himself, when compared to the other early rockers, hardly looks like teen-idol material. He was thirty at the time (old in rocker terms), tubby and broad and dressed like Colonel Sanders, in a tan suit and a bootlace tie, or a tartan jacket and tank top with a dicky bow. He curled his fringe into a greased quaver on his forehead, and possessed a face that was big and round and friendly, like Thomas The Tank Engine. As Nik Cohn says in his pioneering history of pop, *Awopbopaloobop Alopbamboom!*, 'when he sang, he grinned hugely and endlessly, but his eyes didn't focus on anything'. Much of his music had more in common with the big-band era than the teenage lust of rock 'n' roll (check out the sax solo on 'Rock Around The Clock', it's pure Glenn Miller); he would stand out in front, bopping from side to side with his guitar while his backing band, The Comets, stood in a line behind him in matching suits: guitar, upright bass, accordion[5], drums, saxophone, piano. The band would bop side to side too, stepping forward one at a time for their solo. Occasionally the bassist would climb his bull fiddle and rock back and forth, or splay himself across it, laid horizontally on the floor, practically humping the instrument as he hammered the strings, while the sax player walked around on his knees or flipped onto his back. This was pure rockabilly. It wasn't as thrilling as Little Richard, but it was entertaining. It was a show. Musically, Haley's previous hits, 'Shake, Rattle and Roll' and 'Crazy, Man, Crazy' were

---

5. Surely the coolest use of an accordion in music history?

boogies rather than rockers, a whitened take on the heavier, bluesier end of show-band swing.

He'd cut 'Rock Around The Clock' in 1954 as the b-side to another tune, 'Thirteen Women (and only one man in town)', a minor hit (reaching 23 on the US Billboard) that came and went, thus a song now considered a watershed moment in pop came close to vanishing into obscurity, potentially delaying the graduation of rock 'n' roll as the dominant force in youth culture by years. Fortunately, one of the people that bought 'Thirteen Women' was nine-year-old Peter Ford, an R&B obsessive living in California, who happened to flip the 78 RPM shellac disc to the b-side at just the right time. His father was a Hollywood A-lister, Glen Ford; a respected actor who had just been cast as the lead in an upcoming movie for MGM called *Blackboard Jungle*. The movie's producer, Pandro S. Berman visited the Ford residence in the run-up to filming, and heard young Peter spinning records in the family's music room. Impressed with the youthful energy and clattering beat on show, which he felt chimed with his movie's themes of teenage rebellion, Berman took a few discs away with him and played them to his own children to gauge opinion. 'Rock Around the Clock' fit the tone of the movie so perfectly one of his daughters assumed it had been written for the film. Thus when *Blackboard Jungle*, a tale of juvenile delinquency in high schools, opened in March 1955 the first thing its audiences heard, booming through the huge movie theatre speakers, was 'ONE TWO THREE O'CLOCK FOUR O'CLOCK ROCK!'. People promptly went nuts. Hearing a tune on a jukebox or the radio was one thing, but a cinema sound system, even in the fifties, was another entirely. This was an overwhelming, life-changing experience. Kids would get up and spontaneously jive in the aisles, cheering and stomping, heading back time after time just to hear the soundtrack.[6] America's teenagers had finally found a sound that spoke to them. By July it had become the first rock 'n' roll record to top the Billboard pop charts, and it only took that long because – at first – no-one could find a copy: record stores hadn't even heard of it; at least until Decca got wise and sorted out a reissue. This time, 'Thirteen Women (and only one man in town)' was banished to the b-side. It stayed at the top for eight weeks, and you can see why: 'Rock Around The Clock' may not have had the pure adrenalin or sex of some of the other early rock, lacking the thunder of Jerry Lee Lewis or the slinkiness of Elvis, who was just beginning his rise at the same time, but it's hard to deny that it's a corker of a dance record. That iconic intro promises a party that is simply never going to stop. Haley's delivery isn't anything to get the heart pumping but the breathless lyrics absolutely are, and that's before you get to the guitar solo, a properly cool ten seconds or so of

---

6. *Blackboard Jungle*, by the way, is also a very good film; far better than a later movie, *Rock Around The Clock*, rushed out the following year to capitalise on the song's success.

electrifying shredding.[7] As an added bonus it popularised 'rock' as a musical buzzword.

The hype around 'Rock Around The Clock' crossed the Atlantic to Britain before *Blackboard Jungle* itself did, propelled on a wave of newspaper outrage about the deviant sounds emerging from the US. The BBC was still very much basing its content on old standards and light-entertainment, so kids on the hunt for the riotous new sounds from across the pond sought out American Forces radio if they were lucky enough to live near a base, and the pirate Radio Luxembourg if they weren't. Haley had already had a British hit the previous December with the slightly safer sounding 'Shake, Rattle and Roll', and 'Rock Around The Clock', released on a German label, had actually made the top 20 in January 1955 before dropping out of sight – months before *Blackboard Jungle* had even hit in America. The following November, after months of fevered excitement, Decca's re-release made number one. It became the first record to sell over a million copies in the UK, and would go on to be the top selling song of the whole decade.

Rock 'n' Roll had arrived in Britain, which was handy, because Britain had been waiting for it: teenage culture in the UK had started to swell throughout the early fifties but it felt rootless and toothless compared to the candy-striped, leather jacketed American version. 'Rock Around The Clock' changed that. It was a focus, a pressure valve. Haley himself became, briefly, the symbol of teenage rebellion. The song was adopted as an anthem by the Teddy Boys, one of Britain's first true working class youth subcultures, all Edwardian suits, brothel creeper shoes and duck-ass haircuts. Its appearances in cinemas, first in *Blackboard Jungle* and later in the cash-in *Rock Around The Clock*, which featured nine Bill Haley tunes, inspired genuine riots; slashed seats and thrown cushions and jiving in the aisles. Such was the hysteria, police were dispatched to screenings, marching any kids that got too boisterous out of the theatre. The press had a field day. Writing in the *Daily Herald* film critic Anthony Carthew claimed that rock 'n' roll made him 'physically sick', concluding that 'many American teenagers are either mentally deficient or brutal thugs'. 'It is deplorable,' warned a characteristically frothing *Daily Mail* editorial in September 1956, 'It is tribal. And it is from America. It follows ragtime, blues, dixie, jazz, hot cha-cha and the boogie-woogie, which surely originated in the jungle.' A kicker line reveals the real issue at the heart of the establishment outrage: 'We sometimes wonder whether this is the Negro's revenge.' By now the Windrush generation was weaving itself into British life, and elements in

---

7. The solo to 'Rock Around The Clock' was performed by seasoned session player Danny Cedrone, and far from unique to the song. It was actually something of a signature move of his – he played exactly the same solo on at least two other records, including Haley's own 'Rock This Joint', a sort of dry-run for 'Rock Around The Clock' in 1952. Cedrone sadly died after a nasty fall just before *Blackboard Jungle* made his signature solo into one of the most iconic guitar licks ever recorded.

the press felt that traditional ideas of what Britain should be were slipping from their grasp. The moral outrage at rock 'n' roll played into this. Bill Haley's first trip to the UK was met with scenes of mass hysteria.[8] Many years later he appeared on a TV show which, in a spectacular display of variety booking, also featured the nationalist Tory MP Enoch Powell, fresh from authoring his notorious and bluntly racist 'Rivers of Blood' speech. Backstage, Powell made a bee-line for Haley and shook his hand. When asked why a member of the cabinet was so keen to meet this mere peddler of low-brow jump music, Powell replied that Haley was 'the most influential figure of our age'.

The song became a rallying cry in Britain, not necessarily for revolution, racial harmony or a new world, but for the existence of *youth*. It was the first real sound of genuine teenage excitement, and though Powell was entirely wrong about Haley, who was merely John the Baptist to Elvis Presley's Messiah, he was right in recognising 'Rock Around the Clock' as emblematic of a sea change in British youth culture.

Up in Stoke Newington, Mark Feld, all of eight years old, was largely oblivious to this outrage, and was obsessing over an entirely different American import: Davy Crockett. Marc and his brother Harry, keen Saturday afternoon movie goers, were fans of Disney's *Davy Crockett: King of the Wild Frontier*, the tale of the legendary coonskin-hatted American frontiersman. The film had spawned a hit single, performed by the actor Bill Hayes: the likeably jaunty 'Ballad of Davy Crockett,'[9] a treasured 7" single of which was given to the boys and played on repeat in their small bedroom. Sid Feld, their father, seeing how delighted his sons were, took himself off to a record store to buy another Bill Hayes single for them. Alas, Sid – not the most culturally switched on of the Feld family – picked up a disc by someone with *very nearly*, but not quite, the right name. Thus that evening, when Sid returned to the house on Stoke Newington Common, it was with a copy of Bill *Haley*'s 'Rock Around The Clock'. Life for his younger son would never be the same. 'I was so disappointed,' Marc told *Melody Maker* in 1970, 'until I heard the record. Then I threw Bill Hayes out the window and rocked. I've been rocking ever since'.

To summarise: a movie producer overheard a nine-year-old boy in California playing an obscure b-side by an artist who happened to have nearly the same name as a British eight-year-old's new favourite singer … and that's why we have glam rock.

David and Marc were boys in the right place at the right time. Bill Haley had broken down the door, and the rest of America's big-name rockers soon barrelled through after him, notably – and definitively – the instantly iconic Elvis Presley, the preposterously charismatic teenage good ol' boy from Tupelo,

---

8. And eventual disappointment when people actually got a look at him.
9. Hayes, remarkably, is still acting at the time of writing, aged 96.

Mississippi who would soon define the modern pop star in a way that has never really changed. Both boys were huge Presley fans. Marc would parade down the streets of Stoke Newington singing 'Teddy Bear' and 'Blue Suede Shoes', obsessed by Elvis's grace and power, practicing his hip-swivels in the mirror. When David discovered that he and the 'king of rock 'n' roll' shared a birthday he was 'mesmerised', as he would tell *The Telegraph* in 1996. 'I couldn't believe it. He was a major hero of mine[10], and I was probably stupid enough to believe that it actually meant something'. American rock 'n' roll pushed both boys into music; they soaked it up from their opposite corners of London, making it part of their identity and swearing it would be part of their futures. Fortunately, one parent per London boy was happy to encourage the preposterous idea of rock 'n' roll stardom in their respective darling son. Peggy Jones had little interest in David's musical ambition, but her husband was keen to enable it, and would take him to the many charity concerts and events he helped organise for Dr Barnardo's. David's cousin, Kristina, remembers a trip to the Royal Variety Performance, as she told Dylan Jones for his book *David Bowie: a Life* –

> I remember one afternoon in the late 50s when David was introduced to Dave King, Alma Cogan, and Tommy Steele. 'My son is going to be an entertainer too,' [his father] said. 'Aren't you, David?' 'Yes, Daddy.'[11][12]

The solidly working class Sid Feld, by contrast, had little time for Marc's daydreams of rock stardom. He regarded rock 'n' roll as a passing fad, something that would never put dinner on the table, however much Marc would promise that he'd one day buy his parents a Cadillac and a big house of their own, as Elvis had for his. Phyllis, however, who adored her youngest son, could rarely refuse him anything. Her own mother, Elsie, had told her that Marc would rise to the top when she'd first seen him as a baby. Phyllis believed it.

It was the younger of the two that started first. The happy accident with Bill Haley in 1956 lit a white hot flame in young Mark Feld. Sid and Phyllis, doting parents that they were, allowed him to spend the money he was earning helping his dad assemble market stalls at the weekend on singles. He had Eddie Cochran

---

10. One of many ways in which David Bowie and Public Enemy's Chuck D differ.
11. It's likely that she was misremembering this slightly as the three artists mentioned never played the same Royal Variety performance – King performed in 1955, Steele in 57 and Cogan in 58, though it's also possible that David was taken to all three. Still, we do know that David and Kristina saw early British rocker Tommy Steele at the Rainbow in Finsbury Park in 1956 and were introduced to Steele backstage.
12. There's a bit in Tony Zanetta and Henry Edward's book, *Stardust: The Life and Times of David Bowie* which claims that young David once stood in front of his head master and, asked what he wanted to be when he grew up, proclaimed 'I want to be a pop idol'. The story is probably apocryphal, since few other books or articles on Bowie have ever backed it up, but it was compelling enough to be included in Todd Haynes' 1998 film *Velvet Goldmine*, a thinly veiled, fictionalised account of the life of a 70s glam rock star, which was intended as a real biopic focussing on the Ziggy Stardust years … until Bowie kiboshed the use of his songs.

and Elvis, Buddy Holly and Gene Vincent, Chuck Berry and Carl Perkins. The real deal. He would blast the songs at maximum volume on the cheap radiogram in the small bedroom he shared with his brother, prompting the downstairs neighbours to hammer on the ceiling with a broom. Marc's listening became absolutely obsessive; he would press his ear against the speakers straining to hear the clicks and intakes of breath and the sound of the pick hitting strings on 'Blue Suede Shoes.' By 1957 bopping to tunes in his bedroom was no longer enough; he needed to be making this glorious noise himself. The previous year, Sid had made him a makeshift drum kit out of wooden fruit boxes salvaged from the market, held together with elastic bands and augmented by an old snare drum. It never felt enough – it just didn't scream rock 'n' roll. Really, only one instrument could. One day, leafing through his mother's *Sunday Pictorial* newspaper on the bus to his grandparents' house, Marc caught sight of a line drawing of an acoustic guitar and knew that it was all he had ever wanted. Elvis played an acoustic guitar. Billy Haley and Eddie Cochran played hollow-body guitars that basically looked like acoustic guitars. Guitars *were* rock 'n' roll. They were its essence,[13] as a 1958 piece in *ABC Film Review* said, 'the guitar has become a kind of status symbol for a type of music that, although it may only have a short life is certainly having a merry one'[14]. The instrument cost either £9 or £14 (reports vary), but either way it was more than the family bought home in a week; that was okay, though – as with almost any luxury item at the time it was available on the 'never never' – via hire-purchase – and the doting Phyllis Feld was happy to keep up the monthly repayments. Thus on 30 September that year, Stoke Newington's latest rocker unwrapped the birthday present that would change his life.

Learning to play this new treasure was initially irrelevant: the important thing was to *own* it. Marc would spend hours in his room, perfecting his wiggles and struts as he emulated Elvis in the mirror, chopping out a hopeless noise on the out-of-tune strings. The first song he attempted was 'Hound Dog', in the charts at the time and probably Presley's raunchiest, rawest record. Things like chords and tuning were unimportant– he just mashed the strings and rocked. It was a prop; a channel for his inner rock 'n' roller to come out. Marc would carry his guitar, caseless, around the neighbourhood just to be seen with it. By now he'd learned to style his hair like Elvis and duck walk like Chuck Berry. Rock 'n' roll was everything. The next stage was to form a band.

Fortunately Marc wasn't the only proto-rocker in Hackney. He and a school friend, Stephen Gould, would jangle and clang on their guitars together, making up songs and perfecting their Elvis sneers. Other local kids drifted in as well, united by their love of the new sounds, among them siblings Susan and Glenn

---

13. Jerry Lee and Little Richard might disagree, but that was David's territory.
14. They were very wrong about one of these three claims.

Singer, their cousin Helen Shapiro, who had an extraordinary singing voice, and a school friend of Gould's, Melvyn Fields. The six children with rudimentary chord skills, two guitars, a ukulele, a snare drum and a bass made from a tea chest, a broom handle and a bit of washing line, rehearsed a short set of chart hits including Elvis's 'Hound Dog', 'Teddy Bear', 'Don't Be Cruel' and 'Got a Lot O' Livin' To Do', the Everly Brothers' 'Bye Bye Love' and Buddy Holly's 'That'll Be The Day', practicing in the Goulds' living room. They even managed a handful of low-key gigs, performing for cups of tea and the odd shilling in a local cafe or entertaining the kids who had to trudge back to school for lunch during the holidays while their parents were at work. Marc would later mythologise his first group, retrospectively naming them 'Susie and the Hula Hoops' (a name neither Gould nor Shapiro remembers), and claiming a history of gigs in London that simply didn't happen. There's a solid reason why Bolan would later play up this brief chapter of his career, of course: Helen Shapiro would beat him to pop stardom by almost a decade, having a string of top ten hits between 1960 and 1962, and at fourteen became the youngest female solo act ever to have a UK number one – a record she still holds. Highlighting his early link to Shapiro deepened Marc's backstory, and plumping up the significance of 'the Hula Hoops' enhanced his credentials as a born popstar. In fairness to Marc, he did stand out amongst his peers: he was the youngest in the group, a whole school year below his friends, chubby, short and a little bolshy with a magnificent Elvis quiff – the only kid anyone knew that had managed to get the hair right. He carried his guitar everywhere and was, even then, obsessed with clothes and fooling around with girls. The 'Hula Hoops' were just children playing at rock stars really, but their later pedigree makes their existence a genuinely interesting pop footnote.[15]

The summer of 1957 also saw the young David Jones try his hand at singing in public, though it would be another year before he drew level with Marc and gained his junior rock 'n' roller merit badge. David joined the local church choir, as his beloved Little Richard had done; though it's unlikely that rattling off 'All Things Bright And Beautiful' and 'My Lord Is My Shepherd' at St Mary's in Bromley would have provided quite the same rush Richard got from singing gospel in the American south. This particular gig was rather short lived ('not long enough to dirty a surplice,' writes former manager Ken Pitt) but it did give him an opportunity to sing for his supper for the first time.[16] The boys would get paid five shillings to sing at events like weddings, and a bonus day off school if the service took place midweek. It also gave him two lifelong friends in fellow choristers George Underwood and Geoffrey MacCormack – both of whom

---

15. And not just for Shapiro and Bolan. Stephen Gould also had a smattering of minor hits in the 70s under the name Steven Johnson, while Susan and Glenn Singer and Melvyn Fields all had careers in music in one form or another.

16. Or at least for his communion wafers, and tea and biscuits after the service if he was lucky.

joined him in the local Cub Scout troop. Both would play roles in his musical development, as well as being among the very few friends he took through his entire life.

As the year progressed, the boys' taste in music deepened, though guided in different ways. Marc's musical education came from the radio, the movies and – most excitingly – seeing recordings of the live TV pop shows *Oh Boy!*, *Boy Meets Girl* and *Wham!* at the Hackney Empire on Saturdays, where he became the first amongst his friends to discover British rockers Billy Fury, Marty Wilde and, best of all, Cliff Richard, whose classic 'Move It' was another pivotal moment. More thrilling still was the day Eddie Cochran performed – Marc was allowed to carry the great man's guitar into the venue after hanging around the stage door on the off-chance he could blag his way backstage. Of all the American rockers Cochran was perhaps the most perfectly formed: beautiful, ridiculously cool, innovative and a genuine teenager, meaning that when he sang 'C'mon Everybody', 'Summertime Blues' and 'Twenty Flight Rock' he imbued them with relatable frustration, fury, boredom and lust in a way few other artists of his era did. Cochran was killed in a car crash in 1960, aged just 21, forever freezing him in his youth. Marc was obsessed. All of this, plus a habit of hanging around Soho's coffee bars when he should have been helping his mum on her Berwick Street fruit and veg stall, meant he had the jump on most of his friends in terms of music. When he bought a copy of Carl Perkins' 'Blue Suede Shoes' (the shop had sold out of the Elvis version) and discovered that Perkins had not only recorded the song first, *but had actually written it*, he felt like he was unlocking rock's secrets.

David's education was different. Marc had to flounder around, finding what he could, learning what he could, absorbing it all piecemeal. David had a guide. Not only did his father move in a fairly impressive showbusiness circle, but his half-brother Terry returned from his national service toward the end of 1957 and the pair once again shared a room. Terry's time living in Brixton as the Windrushers settled in, not to mention his travelling with the military, meant he was soaked in music that was far from the beaten path of suburban Bromley. David was already a pop fan, to this Terry added jazz, especially John Coltrane, Eric Drolphy and both Charlies, Parker and Mingus, on top of blues, soul, Caribbean bluebeat and the big band crooners – Tony Bennett, Frank Sinatra, Dean Martin. David not only had rock 'n' roll, he now had the building blocks that comprised it. It was the teenage thrill of pop that gave him the biggest buzz, but David lapped up these tangentially related genres too, and in his head began to assemble the musical jigsaw that linked them all together, seeing the joins and the edges.

John Jones, as always, was happy to indulge his son's musical passions, though drew the line at getting his little boy any serious gear at first. Instead he helped him put together a kind of pop starter kit, buying him a cheap tin guitar and a ukulele and helping him build a classic tea-chest bass, in which a bit of washing lined provides the note, a broom handle gives the tension and a wooden box becomes a resonator. Such cheap and home-made instruments, alongside washboard percussion and kazoos stuck in watering cans, were the building blocks of skiffle – the DIY British rockabilly which ran alongside and intermingled with the rock 'n' roll boom, blurring the line. In 1957, British teens were as likely to be listening to Lonnie Donegan's 'Rock Island Line' as they were Bill Haley or Little Richard. Skiffle had originally been jug-band music, an off-shoot of New Orleans jazz knocked out on homemade instruments, a 'skiffle' being a name for the tiny gigs thrown in front rooms to fund a musician's rent. It was imported to the UK when British jazz obsessives started to get into the raw blues of Leadbelly and Muddy Waters[17]. Jazz heads like Ken Coyler, who would go on to play with Donegan, took trips to New Orleans, saw the jug bands and came back inspired; they wanted to nod to the sophistication of jazz, the power of blues and the inventive flair of the DIY Louisiana crowd. The pure racket and bare-bones simplicity of the resulting sounds stuck out like a sore thumb amid the British radio landscape of Vera Lynn and Glenn Miller. Skiffle – before Haley and the slicker American singers changed the game – became the sound of British rock.

Despite the presence of a tea chest bass in Susie and the Hula Hoops [sic], Marc never really vibed with skiffle – it wasn't sexy or slick enough – and only had eyes for the pure rock 'n' rollers. Bowie, on the other hand, loved the genre. Perhaps it was due to his interest in jazz and blues, both of which had a more obvious influence on skiffle than they had on straight rock 'n' roll, or perhaps it was simply because a skinny white lad in English suburbia could never really pass himself off as the next Little Richard, but had a good shot at being the new Lonnie Donegan. David and his new friends were inspired by the excitement of music they could actually create themselves; that didn't need the finesse required to play piano like Jerry Lee or guitar like Chuck Berry. Punk would inspire people in a similar way twenty years later, as would hip-hop in early 80s New York. Skiffle gave David the tools to finally make a proper racket of his own.

George Underwood, one of his two closest friends, was as inspired by the sounds as David was, and the two bonded over their love for skiffle. Underwood had managed to acquire a guitar of his own, a Höfner acoustic, and was already playing as a duo with a family friend, so quite naturally the two boys took to making music together. In the summer of 1958, the boys were taken on a camping trip to the Isle of Wight with their Cubs troop and insisted on bringing their skiffle starter kit with them – David's uke and tea chest bass – which they used to entertain the boys around the campfire during a (presumably

---

17. Lonnie Donegan discovered a treasure trove of blues 78s in the library of the US embassy in London, and would spend hours absorbing the sounds; often leaving with some of the best cuts hidden under his jumper.

welcome) interval in all the Ging-Gang-Goolie-ing. Oddly enough, one of the songs performed that night was 'The Ballad of Davy Crockett', the very tune that indirectly led Marc Bolan to rock 'n' roll. As George Underwood would tell Paul Trynka in his book *Starman*: 'neither of us had a claim to virtuosity, but we wanted to sing'.

Both London boys had now found their early rock 'n' roll groove. As we can see from their various friends, from Stephen Gould and Helen Shapiro to George Underwood and Geoffrey MacCormac, they were hardly unique amongst 1950s school children. They weren't the first generation to graduate into rock 'n' roll: that honour fell to the older kids, the teens who were in a position to take their new passions seriously; the generation that produced the Beatles, the Rolling Stones and the Who. David and Marc (and Elton and Rod and Freddie and all the rest) were their younger brothers, watching fascinated in the wings as pop music was forged before their eyes but still too young to do anything more than play make believe rock 'n' rollers.

Still, even amid these nascent sparks we can start to trace the difference between the two boys. Mark Feld was all flash and fizz, trying to run before he could walk, playing gigs before he could even play chords. He didn't just want to *play* music, he wanted to be a *star*. David Jones, on the other hand, with his worldly father and cool older brother, was already taking being *musical* more seriously. That doesn't necessarily make David the more authentic of the two children – they were both so undeveloped that there's little to read into the comparison. It's more that David, middle class and suburban, had the opportunity to explore the details of his new obsession, to be studious about it and learn. He had mentors. Phyllis Feld indulged and doted on her little boy, sure, but John Jones actually had an inkling of the world he was encouraging his son into. His support was more constructive, which meant that David's earliest musical experiences were more focused and finessed. Marc, working class, raised in the inner-city and with no real mentors to learn from, didn't have the same roadmap. He was making it up as he went along.

It's obviously reductive to apply these very early musical adventures to either of the boy's later careers. They were children; too young to be doing anything but making as glorious a noise as they could as they channelled the exciting new sounds they were discovering. It *is* tempting, though. Tempting to see those early flashes reflected in the shape of the rock stars they became: the excitable bopper and the serious artiste. It wasn't as simple as that, not in 1957, 1967 or 1977, but if you squint you can just about make out those shapes as they formed. The London boys both had a long way to go, and many, many costumes to try on and discard before anyone paid any real attention, but as the fifties, a decade that had seen post-war want give way to carefree consumerism, drew to a close Marc and David had already seen glimpses of the future they wanted. The bright light of the sixties hurtled toward them, and both boys turned to face it head on.

Chapter Three

Mod n' Art

For both London Boys the swinging sixties began with Soho, and Soho began with the 2 I's,[1] the most famous of the 'expresso' bars scattered across the city, in which young people who were unable to gain entry to pubs and clubs could get jacked on tiny coffees, hit the jukebox and watch live music until the early hours of the morning. It was hardly the most salubrious of locations for a youth culture revolution, and yet one happened all the same. The 2 I's, located at 59 Old Compton Street on the site of what is now an upmarket fish and chip restaurant, was shabby. Upstairs was a small bar, wallpapered like your nan's spare bedroom with a counter that only had space for a coffee machine and some bottles of pop, while one side of the room was dominated by a jukebox filled with mostly-American 45s. The few stools would be occupied by shifty-looking regulars with names like 'Tom Football Head', 'Iron Foot Jack' and 'Jerry the Bat'. Other frequent punters included – genuinely – a pair of out-of-work ex-cons, always looking to be hired as someone's rhythm section. Once or twice the Kray twins popped in. Lurking behind the bar might be Paul 'Dr Death' Lincoln or 'Rebel' Ray Hunter, the Australian wrestlers that leased the place from the Irani brothers, the original managers that had given the cafe its name. The street-level bar was largely irrelevant though. The good stuff happened downstairs, in a tiny basement, scarcely the size of the average terrace house living room. Filling one side of the room was the stage; just boards on milk crates on which bands would cram themselves, with their singers forcing their voices through the ancient PA system. An electric fan hung on the wall, puttering uselessly. The walls themselves had been painted black by a helpful local songwriter and 2 I's regular called Lionel Bart, who would go on to pen any number of tunes for first wave British rockers before branching out into musical theatre and hitting pay dirt with *Oliver!*. Alas, Bart hadn't put much oom-pah-pah into his painting and decorating: the badly mixed paint rubbed off against anyone who leaned against it, which was inconvenient since the place was usually packed with kids, sweating, smoking and filling the air with their coffee-and-nicotine breath, which condensed and ran down the already streaky walls. It was fetid. Revolting. And yet, somehow, as the fifties ticked toward the sixties, it was also the most exciting place in the city. The 2 I's was where the skiffle boom and British rock 'n' roll were born. It's where Tommy

---

1. Pronounced 'Two Eyes'.

Steele, Adam Faith and Cliff Richard were discovered, where Vince Taylor and the Playboys and Johnny Kidd and the Pirates swapped band members like trading cards; where managers, agents and pop hopefuls would hang out, eyeing each other suggestively, working out how one could use the other. It was in the 2 I's where Allan Williams, the Beatles' first manager, became reacquainted with the talent-scouting proprietor of the Kaiserkeller Club in Hamburg, leading to the deal that sent the future-fab-four to Germany for an essential crash course in stagecraft and amphetamine abuse. On the door would be the volatile, charismatic hard-nut bouncer, Peter Grant – who would later put those exact skills to use as the manager of Led Zeppelin. Acts were mostly paid in coffee and Coca-Cola. By the time Marc discovered the place in 1958, its reputation as somewhere to be seen was well established. Its notoriety had not led to a noticeable improvement in the facilities and decor, but it *had* inspired a new sign above the door proclaiming it to be the 'home of the stars'; a claim it was still making years later, long after the stars had moved on to clubs like the Marquee and the Flamingo; venues that had proper stages and didn't require punters to nip back to the nearest tube station to use the loo.[2, 3]

Young Mark Feld, all of eleven years old, was a lunchtime regular in the 2 I's. By 1958 his mother, Phyllis, was following in her father's footsteps working on a fruit and veg stall on Berwick Street market, and would drag her son along to help. Marc, of course, couldn't be relied upon to do anything as sensible as working on a market stall and so doting Phyllis would slip him a few coppers and let him loose to explore Soho.

The 2 I's was an obvious first target for Marc, who knew its reputation. With characteristic tale-spinning he would later tell journalists of seeing a pre-fame Cliff Richard being thrown from the venue, and attending one of Tommy Steele's first performances; both of which were probably untrue – it's far more likely that he discovered those artists at the Hackney Empire when they performed on the *Oh Boy!* TV show. Marc was mostly attracted by the jukebox, which gave him access to the American rock 'n' roll records he loved so much, and which were played all too infrequently on British radio. It further deepened his understanding of music, and gave him a taste for the more authentically Black sounds coming over from the US: Bill Doggett, Ray Charles, the Drifters, the Coasters and more. Sometimes this chubby little boy with the Elvis hair helped serve coffees when he should have been helping his mother on the stall, just so he could hear the music. What became clear to Marc was that the 2 I's

---

2. Even during the beat group boom of 1963 the reputation of the 2 I's had some power. The Beatles, on their early trips to the capital, would always visit. It was just what you did.

3. The 2 I's eventually closed in 1970. A shadow of its former self it may have been, but the old place had done well; keeping its doors open through Britain's first full generation of rock and pop, and only closing them as the wind changed and the era that had begun with Lonnie Donegan and Cliff Richard finally ended with the breakup of the Beatles.

was somewhere people got *discovered*. He knew that svengalis like Larry Parnes, the manager of Billy Fury, Tommy Steele, Johnny Gentle and a host more, hung around the bar on the hunt for talent. Even as an eleven-year-old novice he had sufficient charisma to batter the staff into letting him perform, though his mother believed they only did so to shut him up. At some point in autumn 1958, Marc and his fellow Hula-Hoop Stephen Gould played a short lunchtime gig at the 2 I's under the name 'Rick and Ellis' (Marc was 'Ellis', naming himself after a local eccentric who lived on a canal boat – the first occasion that we know of where Marc developed a separate identity under which to perform.) The two had worked up a short set as they searched endlessly for a fourth chord to learn, and among the songs played that day were Eddie Cochran's 'Summertime Blues' (sung by Marc) and Elvis' '(You're So Square) Baby I don't Care' (sung by Stephen). Alas, no-one in the 2 I's that day seemed to see the potential in a bequiffed eleven-year-old attempting Eddie Cochran's smoulder. Stephen was just thrilled to have played the gig, but Marc was devastated that it hadn't led to anything. That evening he shut himself in his room, livid that his dreams had been foiled. It's our first glimpse at both the bullish self-confidence and slightly-deluded entitlement that would come to define his career. He had genuinely thought the show was his ticket to rock fame.

While Marc was getting an education in the coffee bars of Soho, his future friend David was gathering knowledge in a more dependably middle class and suburban way, having passed the Eleven Plus and advanced into secondary education. The Eleven Plus was a fairly pivotal bit of education policy in the post war period: children were assessed at eleven years old and, in theory, based on the results, would then proceed to an educational establishment that matched their needs; thus the super bright kids wouldn't be neglected by teachers trying to help those lagging behind, and those that struggled would not have to keep up with a curriculum more suited to quicker readers and the academically inclined. In theory, everyone benefited. In practice, of course, the well-schooled middle class families always fared better and got to go to grammar and technical schools that groomed them for the professional world; meaning they could *continue* to be well-schooled and middle class and raise well-schooled, middle class children of their own. Meanwhile, working class kids in rougher areas, with parents who were less well educated, limboed under the bar, went to poorly provisioned secondary modern schools and left to get jobs, raise families and become the next generation of poorly educated working class parents. By the late sixties, most experts had accepted that this was a problematic system that (via the perpetual motion of the British class system, rather than by design) kept everyone in their place. Mark Feld would take his exam the following year and, predictably enough, head off for a short-lived career at the local comprehensive. David Jones, however, passed the Eleven Plus with flying colours and, along with his closest friend, opted for the all-boys Bromley Tech over the local grammar.

There's a much-repeated idea that Bowie was a product of 'art school', as John Lennon, Brian Eno, Pete Townshend and the whole of Pink Floyd were, and that a period studying high-falutin' conceptual thinking elevated him above the less enlightened rockers of his era (you could count Bolan in that). It's not entirely the case, though it's beyond doubt that the schools themselves were key to the development of the wider era. 'If you want to try to find somewhere from which you could say the whole sixties culture comes from, it was the art schools,' the designer Pearce Marchbank told Jonathan Green for his book *Days In The Life*. 'You were bombarded with a lot more than just a set syllabus. ... The fact that we were technically being trained to design ceramic pots or books or theatre sets was irrelevant.' The era of the art-school pop star was indeed beginning at the same time that David was finding his way into music, but the art schools themselves didn't have a monopoly on progressive education. Accessible mainstream schooling was, for the first time, being viewed at least by some, as having a *creative* role, in which young people could develop their critical and artistic thinking rather than merely gain the necessary knowledge to operate in the job market. It ties back to the relatively new idea of extended youth, and young people as a distinct social group, rather than merely older children or proto-adults. For the first time, teenagers below the wealthy classes were encouraged to develop who they *were* ... not just what they could do for a living. Education was being redesigned, with mixed results admittedly, to allow the post-post-war children to find their niche rather than fall into the established grooves of their parents. Art schools were part of that. For the first time, pretty much ever, normal British kids were told that creative pursuits could be more than admirable hobbies.

David's school, Bromley Tech, was a good example of this. It wasn't an art college, but it did have a far more committed approach to what we now refer to as 'the liberal arts' than many of the grammar schools of the day. It was a natural next step from Burnt Ash, the primary school David had attended after the family moved to Bromley, which had a progressive-for-the-time emphasis on music, art, creative writing and movement classes[4]. Modern schools for their darling boy were part of the reason the family had quit bombed-out Brixton for the suburbs – it's unlikely the inner city establishments of Lambeth would have provided him with as many opportunities to find his path. Still, opting for a tech college was a slightly unexpected choice for a boy as bright as David, who did well enough in his exam to comfortably qualify for a grammar school place, and it took a little convincing as John and Peggy were initially reluctant. Grammar schools, after all, primed you for a *career* (rather than the mere 'job' a secondary modern pupil could hope for), while Technical Schools were a weird half-way house where you emerged with either a very specific trade; like graphic design

---

4. Though not so liberal that one friend of David's could avoid a pretty thorough telling off for bringing in 'Rock Around the Clock' during a 'Christmas listening party'.

or electrical engineering, or else were let loose into the world with the vaguest of portfolios and even vaguer prospects. David was determined to go to the more creative establishment, however, which despite having a fairly traditional set-up (singing old hymns, special assemblies that banned Jewish and Catholic pupils, Hogwarts-style houses) was also art-school adjacent (literally – Bromley College of Art was next door) with a respected and creative art department that existed within the stuffier structure of the main school.

Why was the arty aspect so important to David? One obvious reason was his friend George Underwood, who by now had decided that commercial art was a career path he could explore. Going to Bromley Tech kept David close to his best friend and musical foil while he tried to work out what his own future could hold. The more liberal feel of the school meant that the pair could play music together, taking their guitars into art lessons and practicing their harmonies in the quadrants and under stairwells at break time and between classes. George's presence would have given David an immediate impetus to try his hand at the tech. However, there was another arguably more important figure that helped form the young Bowie's creative instincts, shaping an outlook that would have been suffocated by the idea of a grammar school – his older brother, Terry.

A lot has been written over the years about Terry Jones/Burns, the son born after Peggy Jones' teenage fling with a Jewish scullery boy. Most of it focuses on his mental health problems, and those issues shouldn't be downplayed: Terry was a troubled young man, who would eventually be diagnosed with schizophrenia and hospitalised. His later illness, treatment and tragic death by suicide in 1985 would have a dramatic and much-analysed effect on David, who was afraid of his own potential for mental instability. [5] He would tell his first wife, Angela, that when he lost control through drink or drugs he could 'feel the madness within' him. He was referencing a pattern of mental illness in his mother's family, which included instances of schizophrenia and other psychological issues experienced by his grandmother and three of his aunts. It's worth noting that some of David's relatives, including his cousin Kristina, have said such claims have been overstated, not least by David himself, and blamed the diagnoses on the attitudes of the time as much as on genuine trauma.

It's unfortunate that Terry's memory should be so caught up in the mythology of madness that has grown up around Bowie's background[6] when his biggest

---

5. The fear was genuine, though he could be guilty of playing up to it in interviews. In 1976 he told *Rolling Stone*'s teenage wunderkind (and future Hollywood director) Cameron Crowe that 'insanity runs in my family', echoing a comment he'd make in *Playboy* a few years later ('It's a nice thing to throw out at parties, don't you think? Everybody finds empathy in a nutty family. Everybody says, "Oh, yes, my family is quite mad." Mine really is. No fucking about, boy.'). He'd made similar statements throughout his early career.

6. The 2021 movie *Stardust*, a fictionalised account of Bowie's 1971 US promo tour, makes David's fear of following his brother into psychiatric care the spine of its plot. The Bowie estate gave the movie pretty short shrift, denying permission to use any original music.

contribution to his younger brother's development was far more important than any subsequent tragedy: it was Terry that gifted David *art*. Not so much in the sense of visual arts, of drawing and painting – though those did follow – but in his interest in pure, fluid, unrestrained creativity. Terry introduced David to jazz, ensuring that his tastes in music went further and were altogether more sophisticated than the chart hits of Lonnie Donegan and Elvis. Terry lived and breathed thoroughly *cool* art. He was a fan of the beat writers, giving David a copy of Jack Kerouac's *On The Road* and enthusing about Allen Ginsberg, Lawrence Ferlinghetti and other pioneers of new American culture. During his national service he had been stationed with the Royal Airforce in Aden, a British imperial outpost located in contemporary Yemen, where he'd seen combat during local uprisings, about which he had stories aplenty. He was well read, well travelled, opinionated, charming, good looking and enthusiastic. You can see why he made such an impression on the young Bowie. Terry worked for Amalgamated Press, a Fleet Street publisher of books, comics and newspapers, meaning he was not only knowledgeable and well informed about worldly matters, but also well placed to explore London's musical nightlife. David hero-worshipped his brother, and would ingest everything Terry threw at him, hanging on his tales of trips into the West End to rummage in record stores and watch live jazz and cabaret, listening rapt as he held forth about his favourite music, literature and art. The impressionable eleven-year-old would absorb this stream of ideas and opinions to store and replicate later. With all of this swimming around his head, alongside the fizzing power of rock 'n' roll, it's not a huge surprise that David couldn't stomach the idea of a school life defined by algebra, Latin and grammar.

David started at Bromley Tech in September 1960 and began the next phase of his education with a significant stroke of luck. The form that he and George were assigned to was overseen by a master that was also new to the school, Owen Frampton, a former commercial artist and designer who had been brought in to run the art department. It was Frampton – whose son, Peter, went on to considerable fame as a musician himself – that nurtured the seeds of creativity in David that Terry had first sown. Frampton was allowed to develop the school's art programme in a way that was beyond the norm for a suburban tech, allowing the first years, who were just eleven and twelve, to study the subject properly. Bromley Tech was one of the first schools in the country to take art seriously at every level, establishing a route into the art college next door for creatively inclined students. According to David, three quarters of his art class went on to study the subject at a higher level. Frampton, known by the students as 'Ozzy', was in some ways a typical form tutor of the age; strict when he needed to be, donning a mortar board for special occasions and not hesitant in applying the slipper to an unruly backside, never quite shaking off the military discipline he'd learned as an artilleryman during the war. He was well versed in the classical and technical traditions of his subject, but was also keen on modern art. His pupils learned about *concepts* as well as techniques. It was Frampton that introduced David to Egon Schiele, the Austrian impressionist whose work was a huge influence on his later aesthetic, notably the cover art for his albums *"Heroes"* and *Lodger*. Crucially, Frampton was also a guitarist and encouraged his students to play music. Between them, Terry Burns and Owen Frampton broadened David's world beyond the standard pop 'n' roll fare of many of his peers. Through them, he came to understand creativity as an abstract as well as direct form of communication. Frampton claimed that David was 'completely misunderstood' by the majority of the teaching staff, but in art class and under his form tutor he thrived, learning that everything – including himself – was a canvas on which to project, in one form or another, his creativity.

One way in which David began to express himself more and more was through his appearance, starting off with modifying his school uniform. Again, it was Owen Frampton who partly inspired an interest in clothes – the teacher would push at the edges of school-masterly attire, coming in wearing cavalry twill trousers and suede shoes. Fashion was introduced in lessons in the form of design and techniques, and David and his friends tied that to the idea of self-expression and conceptualisation that lay at the core of Frampton's approach. As future Bowie manager Ken Pitt writes in his biography, *Bowie – The Pitt Report*, 'it gave them a taste for fashion and they dreamed of wearing such daring things as elastic-sided boots, string ties and twelve-inch bottoms'. David would come to school in tapered trousers and fashionable Denson's 'Hi-Poynter' shoes, which both showed off his cutting-edge sense of style and betrayed the affluence to which he was becoming accustomed. Though by no means wealthy, John Jones' rise at Dr. Barnardos meant that David was better off than many of his friends ('The comfortable circumstances of his life contrasted sharply with me and many of the other boys,' one school friend, Len Routledge, reported to Paul Trynka for his book *Starman*). Eventually, as David experimented with dying his hair temporarily with food colouring and plucking his eyebrows, even the liberal Mr Frampton was forced to remind him that the school did still have *some* sartorial standards. Still, in Frampton, David had found a teacher that understood him. 'I accepted his actions as a means of projecting his personality,' Frampton told biographer Dylan Jones, 'and of that he had plenty!'

It was the influence of America that prompted many of the cultural shifts of the era, and David's little suburban bubble was no exception to this. The young Bowie, like many of his contemporaries, saw America as a mystical land of accelerated pop culture, movie stars, rock 'n' roll and excellent, excellent clothes. It wasn't just the likes of Elvis that made an impact on David's growing sense of style, either – he idolised US president John F Kennedy, styling his hair after him and attempting to copy his look, combing Bromley's better class of shops for 'Italian trousers', and borrowing money from his dad to buy a dark green tweed suit with a 'bum-freezer' jacket from Burton. That specific mix of styles – Americana via European designers (specifically French and Italian), sharp cuts and silhouettes and an abiding interest in modern jazz and beat poetry meant that Bowie was already chiming with a youth subculture which would eventually be given a label distilled from the 'modernist' jazz enthusiasts of the last 50s. Without really meaning to, David had joined the first wave of Mods and his interests in fashion, music and art led him inexorably to Soho's coffee bar culture and clothes shops. To the north of the city, Mark Feld was in lockstep.

Like David, Marc's life would come to be dominated by clothes. The flip from Bill Hayes to Bill Haley had brought about his first big sea-change – from childhood to adolescence in a few minutes of bopping. The next paradigm shift would be just as fast. Marc recounted the story to *Rolling Stone*'s Michael Thomas in 1972, during the magazine's first big T.Rex feature.[7] The way Marc tells it, at some point in 1960, some time before his Eleven Plus, he was sitting outside his house on Stoke Newington Common dressed in all his rock 'n' roll finery. He had on his drainpipes, his shirt – modelled on one he'd seen the Everly Brothers and Ricky Nelson wearing – his immaculate Cliff Richard hair, his 'black and white rock 'n' roll shoes, very rare in England'. Just being seen. Just being Marc. At that moment, a Teddy Boy walked past; a proper one. The Teds were distilled rock 'n' roll back then, the first true, widespread working class youth culture. They represented the essence of the British yankophile rocker; bastardising expensive Edwardian suits into an approximation of the gear donned by the US rock 'n' rollers. The Teds were reviled by the more polite corners of society, they were seen as – and to be honest, often genuinely were – no-hopers; disillusioned kids searching for meaning in the wrecked England of the 50s, resenting school, expecting little from work, losing themselves in an identity constructed from bits and pieces which they floated on second-hand American rocker culture; a mish-mash of Edwardian Britain's discarded threads, America's bang-up-to-date sounds and some dances – the Creep and the Stroll – all of their own. Nik Cohn, writing in the late 60s in his book *Awopbopaloobop Alopbamboom*, likens the Teds to the gangs in a post-apocalyptic dystopia; packs of young men roaming, 'brawling and smashing at random … All they did was break things, windows, and locks and bones. There was nothing else to do.' Dick Hebdige, meanwhile, sums up their ethos rather poetically in his sociology classic *Subculture, The Meaning of Style* – they were 'on the outside in fantasy'.

Of course, when you're eleven what the Teds *actually* were, was *cool*. They were older boys in artful uniforms, reeking of menace and Brylcreem and doing whatever the hell they wanted. Plus they could grow proper Elvis sideburns,

---

7. Which, naturally, means we have to apply the usual possibly-too-good-to-be-true filter, kept handy for any story told by Marc Bolan to the press during his pomp.

which even the most perfectly kitted out pre-teen rocker couldn't manage without the aid of an eyeliner pencil or a stick of charcoal. So it was with a mixture of approval and envy that young Marc noted the picture-book Ted as he strolled by on his rockin' way, presumably to break something or punch a toff. And then, just as Marc was looking wistfully at this perfect, rock 'n' roll blend of the past and the present ... the future walked by.

It was wearing orangey-brown baggy tweed trousers, dark green winklepicker shoes with buckles on the side, a dark green shirt with a high collar and a fine dark blazer jacket 'with drop shoulders, one-button cutaway' that stopped short at the base of the spine. Its hair was worn longer and clean, combed neatly and parted in the centre. It was, in almost every respect, the exact opposite of a Teddy Boy. Twin heart-shapes bloomed in Marc's eyes and the greasy rocker he'd admired a few minutes before was suddenly just a thuggish dinosaur. 'The *impact* of having just seen what one thought was really a trendy looking Teddy Boy, and then seeing this cat,' Marc told *Rolling Stone*. 'Just the image of him! To this day I still can't trace how he *got* like that. But I knew something was going on'. The future's name was Martin Kauffman and he was a 'face' – what was occasionally thought of as a 'Modernist' and, later, just a 'Mod'. Martin Kauffman isn't going to come up in our story again – we only know his name from that one interview Marc gave, fourteen years later. His is just a walk-on part. It just happens to be a walk-on that would change Marc's world. According to his interview, Marc spent the next hour or so following his new style icon around the area, trying to figure the magic out – where was this stuff from? How did it work? Within a few days he was putting his new look together. Mark The Mod was about to enter the scene.

Like David, Marc talked his most compliant parent into getting him a Burton suit (although it's worth noting that while John Jones advanced his son the cash to buy a suit outright, Phyllis Feld got Marc's on hire-purchase), and soon found the nooks and crannies of the city, accessible by bus, where a smart lad could get himself set up with the right gear. He got his neighbour, Mrs Perrone, who worked as a cobbler, to make him a bespoke leather waistcoat (a treasured possession since they were so rarely made in his size) and made-to-measure shoes, several pairs in fact, in lizard and snake skin, or so he claimed, though she finally drew the line when he demanded a new pair 'every other day'. He soon found alternative footwear options – black 'mock-croc' winklepickers from Stan Bartholomew in Battersea, the originator of the style; boots from Anello & Davide in Covent Garden, the store that would later kit out The Beatles; suits made at Alfred Bilgorri near Liverpool Street. He'd get cardboard-stiff child-sized Levi 505's from Connick's, a tailors on Kingsland High Street in Dalston, as the adult ones his friends were nicking from a shop on Leman Street in Whitechapel were way too big, no matter how much he tried to shrink them in the bath. He never went anywhere without a tightly rolled, smart umbrella.

Over the next few years it was clothes, more than music, that would dominate Marc's life as he gravitated to like minded (and similarly dressed) 'faces' in his local hangouts; the Fairsport amusement arcade in Stamford Hill (aka the *'Schtip'* – a Yiddish word meaning 'to take, to take', so named because that was what it did to your money), the local cinema, the new bowling alley. Later he would brag that he'd 'always been a star ... even if it was just of three streets in Hackney'. It was more or less true – not everyone *liked* Marc, he rubbed a lot of people up the wrong way and didn't have the people pleasing knack that made David the centre of his own mini-cult down in Bromley. A lot of people found him arrogant, bolshy, a little full of himself. As a result he had to learn to handle himself in a fight, becoming a master of grabbing an opponent by the lapels and nutting them viciously in the mouth – hence a reputation, according to one contemporary who spoke to the *Hackney Gazette* in 2020, as a 'hard nut'. Although some people found him annoying, others were completely charmed, and he had plenty of friends – of which he tended to be regarded as the ringleader, despite being the youngest and the shortest. One thing everyone could agree on, though – he looked *great*. The biggest mystery, of course, was how a poor-as-a-church-mouse East End twelve-year-old managed to afford hand-made shirts, new suits and apparently innumerable pairs of shoes. Many of his classmates assumed there was a certain amount of light pilfering involved, either of items themselves or of the money to pay for them, and by Marc's own admission there was always a bit of that going on. There was also, however, an innate ingenuity in Mark Feld, and a degree of sheer hustle and chutzpah. He could glad-hand and talk his way into anywhere. He was also canny, realising he was small enough to buy the cheaper children's sizes and modify them. He even learned to make his own gear.

Not for the first or last time, Marc and David were present for a changing of the guard in British culture. David watched the flourishing of suburbia as it was infected with art school conceptualism and began to see a future for himself that wouldn't involve getting the train into London with a bowler hat and umbrella, to a job in the civil service or a bank or somewhere else similarly mundane. In Stoke Newington, Marc – who occasionally actually did augment his smartly rolled umbrella with an equally smart bowler hat, despite going nowhere near anything resembling a real job – was present for the last gasp of one distinctly British working class subculture – the Teds – and the rise of the next one. East London was one of the first outposts of the Mods, way before they evolved into the anoraked-and-scootered *Quadrophenia* culture of the 60s and 70s.[8] In Marc's day, the scene was much less focused and codified than

8. It was a subculture very much demonised by the press and unpopular with the public, not least with their arch-enemies, the 'rockers'; the biker gangs that had evolved from the Teds and who would happily start a ruck with a Mod on sight. Many a well dressed young man found themselves wearing a target on their back.

it would become. Most Mods didn't even think of themselves as such, and Marc and his fellow 'ace faces' would be appalled at any association with the cardigan-wearing, middle class trad-jazz beatniks that lent the 'modernists' and thus the Mods their name. The stinky sweaters and scrappy beards of the trad crowd, though equally at odds with both the mainstream and the Teds, were the very antithesis of the sharp-dressed boys in Stamford Hill, who were more likely to use the word 'face' than 'Mod' to describe a contemporary. Despite a certain vagueness in their parameters and naming conventions, the Mods of the early 60s – who were retrospectively given that title – were every bit a cohesive youth culture … just one based around the width of a tie and the cut of a shirt rather than any shared political or social agenda. They weren't a part of working life, and most of the faces that had jobs worked in low-skilled office roles and spent their meagre wages on brogues and tweed. They weren't usually grammar school pupils either, often coming from the most intensely working class areas of the city. What they *did* manage to do was adopt a style that would simultaneously fit in everywhere – work, school, out on the town – and yet be distinct from everyone else in those environments. The signals they sent to the world were simple: 'we are not one of you, we reject you', while the signals they sent to each other were small but very specific. The East London faces would jealously watch their contemporaries, weighing up a thousand minute details to decide who looked the best. One of the reasons Mark Feld divided opinion among his contemporaries is that half of his friends were in awe of his style and the other half resented him for always, somehow, having the edge on them.

In 1962, when he was just fourteen, Marc and two of his fellow local faces, Peter Sugar and Michael Simmonds, both twenty, were interviewed for a lifestyle magazine called *Town*, for an issue subtitled 'The Young Take the Wheel'; an attempt to snapshot Britain's youth culture of the time. In an article headlined 'Faces Without Shadows' (which incidentally never uses the word 'Mod') Marc outlines his manifesto to reporter Peter Barnesly, emphasising the need to exist in the moment. 'You've got to be different from the other kids,' says Marc. 'You've got to be two steps ahead.' He went on to wax lyrical about the 'haddocks' in his class showing off the sort of suits he was wearing 'three years ago'. Since three years earlier he'd been perfecting Cliff Richard's sneer in a chubby face sandwiched between a greased pompadour and an Everly Brothers shirt, the comment seems a bit rich. Still, the article is a fascinating read in which young Marc spins the myth of these 'individualists' well. He certainly has *Town*'s Peter Barnsely convinced of his seriousness, if not his ability to carry that spirit into any kind of future. 'Where is the goal toward which he is running as fast as his impeccably shod feet can carry him?' he writes of Marc. 'It is nowhere. He is running to stay in the same place'. Marc enjoyed the notoriety the piece brought him, but never forgave *Town* for its one irredeemable sin –

the issue took a few months to come out, by which time the outfit he sported in the pictures was, in Mark Feld's world, hopelessly out of date.

In one respect, *Town* had it very wrong indeed. Later that year, Marc and fellow face Jeff Dexter found themselves, as they occasionally did, at the all-dayer Sunday Sessions at the Lyceum club, just off the Strand. At one point Marc turned to his friend, gesturing in annoyance at the rammed dance floor. The problem? 'Too many Mods.' Despite what *Town* might claim, the London boys were doing anything but running on the spot.

Chapter Four

Count Me In

When you're an impressionable teenager *every* year is a banner year, in which something happens to define your future – especially if you happen to be living in a time of accelerated and unprecedented social change. That said, 1962 and 1963 contained more genuine watershed moments for David and Marc that would echo into their careers and set them up as the artists they became, than perhaps any others in their lives. A lot of things started in those years. It was in 1962, for example, that George Underwood punched David Jones in the face in a fight over a girl, landing his friend in hospital after what was previously thought to be merely a black eye 'just exploded' (David's words) leading doctors, at one point, to worry he was going to lose his vision or even the eye itself. In the end the only real damage was to a muscle that controlled the contraction and dilation of his pupil, leaving his right pupil permanently dilated and making his eyes appear to be different colours. It made him visually unique, and he learned to lean into it; either to subvert his natural prettiness or enhance his conceptual oddity. [1]

1962 is the year that the Felds upped sticks and left Stoke Newington, rehomed by the council in a prefab[2], way across town in Wimbledon. It ripped the 'king of three streets in Hackney' away from his little kingdom, and when he returned some months later to visit his friends in Stamford Hill, he found himself to be yesterday's news. He'd thought that the *Town* article would mean he'd depart the area as something of a local legend ... actually it just made him a pariah, a delusional show-off in last season's suit. If he was to establish a reputation in Wimbledon he would have to start from scratch – his solution was simply not to bother. South West London might be where he put his head down, where he sought solitude, reading books and writing songs while he had the place to himself in the daytime, and ate his Friday night dinner with his mum and dad, but his social life was now focused mostly in Soho. The move across town also, finally, ended his mutually ambivalent relationship with education. He survived a few weeks at a local comprehensive

---

1. Much as sharing a birthday with Elvis delighted David, he also felt his eye condition brought him closer to Little Richard, who always said he was born with 'a big eye and a little eye'.
2. A prefabricated house – the cheap-to-build 'temporary' houses used by the British government as a band aid for the post-war housing crisis. You will be unsurprised to learn that many people ended up living in them for decades. Marc's family certainly felt they were better off there than in their old Stoke Newington flat.

school – Hillcroft – but couldn't muster the enthusiasm to stay, especially with no social circle; an issue not helped by his appearance in *Town* which, to some of his new classmates, made him look, to put it mildly, a bit of a prat. Eventually he just stopped turning up until the school made it official and expelled him ('I only had about six months to go anyway. I just didn't go anymore. No-one seemed to mind.'[3]) after which Marc bounced through a few menial jobs, flipping burgers in a Wimpy, working in a clothes store, but his heart was never in it. He'd been told for years that he was worth more than the standard working class life-cycle of school-job-family-repeat and had managed to carve out a childhood and adolescence that he felt confirmed that belief – he'd been in a magazine! He'd played the 2 I's! He had owned the finest leather waistcoat in East London! And now, what? Scrubbing ketchup off plates in Wimpy? Mark Feld knew he was better than that. He was going to be a *star*. He knew it as well as he knew anything. He knew exactly *which* star, as well: despite the changing music and fashion scenes, and the incredible American 45s he was exposed to while hanging out in the 2 I's, or hearing them pumped onto the dancefloor of the Lyceum, Marc's favourite artist in the world was still Cliff Richard. *Summer Holiday*, Cliff's milquetoast classic musical, was a particular eye-opener. He came out of the theatre determined that his career would follow a similar path: Soho, the stage, the studio, the silver screen.[4] 'But you can't sing,' his friend Jeff Dexter told him. 'I'll learn,' came the reply.

When Marc later recounted the story of his life to journalists, this was the point when he'd insert a lengthy and mostly fictional stay in Paris, where he apparently lived in a '40-room mansion' with a 'very powerful wizard' for six months. Occasionally he would say he worked as a chauffeur, which is a bit of a tough sell – Marc Bolan never learned to drive. A trip to Paris did happen – we'll get to that later – but it wasn't in 62 or 63, and it wasn't for six months. Marc inserted this point of his backstory like someone trying to explain a gap in their resume. Without it there'd be an awkward blank space.

In a way it's not surprising that Marc, despite considering himself the coolest of cats, was still into Cliff: there wasn't much else happening. By the early sixties there was a general sense that rock music had run its course, with the biggest American names all out of action, one way or another. Elvis had been tamed by conscription into the army and would come back a balladeer, Little Richard had found God again and turned his back on pure rock, Chuck Berry was in prison after transporting a 14-year-old girl over state lines and seducing her, Jerry Lee Lewis had become *persona non grata* after marrying his thirteen-year-old

---

3. Quoted in *Marc Bolan – A Tribute*, an official(ish) biography/tribute published in 1978 – I've not been able to source the origin of this quote, though it's apparently from 1972.

4. It's possible he took the film's theme of 'no more working for a week or two' to heart. Marc barely lifted a finger for the next three years.

cousin[5], and Buddy Holly and Eddie Cochran were dead. Pop music continued, but without its pioneers it became anodised. The music industry swelled to the point that the 'industry' part was growing more important than the 'music' part, losing some of rock's danger and the sex in the process.

In Britain the biggest names; Cliff, Tommy Steele, Billy Fury, Adam Faith, even Lonnie Donegan soon stopped trying to give the impression that they were any kind of authentic rocker, each becoming, in his own way, a light entertainer; appearing in cheap variety shows and 'quota quickie' movies[6]. The Music Hall tradition had never been far from the British entertainment industry, and as much as the early English rockers aped their American counterparts, they all knew deep down that they were just another turn on the variety bill. An engagement at the Palladium and a chance to shake hands with Princess Margaret beckoned at the top end of success, though they were more likely to be shaking hands with Buttons or Captain Hook in a Christmas run at the Wigan Hippodrome.

There were many, particularly in the media and music business, that assumed rock 'n' roll was a fad that had run its course. And, in a way, they were right – after all, the three chords and twelve bars of the average rock hit could only be replicated so many times. Chuck Berry's imprisonment alone meant that the public, at the very least, had a few years respite from hearing the same song over and over with different words. There's real, visceral thrills in how Berry articulates the teenage experience and chops at his guitar, but there's not much in the way of tonal variety. The music in the charts, the odd gem aside, was largely uninspiring: Bobby Vee, Pat Boone, Frank Ifield. The idea of rock as nothing but a fad wasn't helped by short-lived crazes like the Twist or the Cha-cha, and novelty records like Mike Sarne and Wendy Richard's 'Come Outside'. Pundits and industry types weren't looking for the next evolution of rock, they were looking for the fad that would replace it.

On New Year's Day 1962, a Scouse four-piece called The Beatles, who had gained quite the following in the North of England, auditioned for Decca Records' A&R Dick Rowe. He turned them down, reportedly saying that 'groups are out; four-piece groups with guitars particularly are finished' (a quote he subsequently denied.[7]) That decision has entered music industry legend, becoming a shared terror that had A&R men jerking awake in the middle of

---

5. There is an uncomfortable trope around southern rockers and young teenage girls – Elvis met his future wife, Priscilla, in 1959 when he was 24 and she was just 14.

6. These were British-made films knocked out cheaply to satisfy a government mandate that cinemas must show a certain amount of home-grown releases in any given year. Many an actor, director and screenwriter owed their start to the quota-quickies.

7. Though the decision to turn down the Beatles is usually attributed to Rowe, it's possible it was actually another executive. The whole affair wasn't quite as open and shut as reports suggest, the label produced acetates of several songs that were considered for possible singles before deciding against signing the band, and Rowe believed in them enough to offer to get a record pressed anyway if they could pay for it themselves. That is, of course, another story for another time.

the night, drenched in a cold sweat. Nobody wanted to miss the next Beatles. The perception of Rowe as a visionless dimwit, however, is actually very unfair. Leaving aside that a hungover producer (the session took place at 9am on New Year's Day, don't forget) oversaw a nervous and exhausted Beatles as they delivered a lacklustre audition that didn't really stand out from any of the other guitar bands Rowe saw that week; rock music really *had* started to feel stagnant – rock 'n' roll wasn't really registering for the new generation of kids, while the first wave of rock fans were graduating to sensible lives and safer tastes. Here were four working lads from Liverpool, fresh from entertaining the hookers, dockers and sailors of Hamburg, knocking out an hour or so of American R&B – the sound of the last decade. Most A&Rs would have done exactly what Rowe did.

The teen crowd had moved on to lighter pop, while the hipsters' choice of the time was a revival of pre-war English folk music, a movement obsessed with authenticity and detail. Even more widespread and even more serious was trad jazz, often known simply as 'trad', favoured by discerning, po-faced, badly dressed young men interested in progressive politics and poetry. At the start of the decade a lot of tastemakers felt that trad, genuinely, could be the next musical paradigm. 'The top men of trad are entertainers,' BBC radio presenter Brian Matthew wrote in his 1962 book *Trad Mad*, referring to the likes of Acker Bilk and Kenny Ball, 'and they are really going to set their seal on this decade.'

Though any number of screaming girls in Liverpool's Cavern Club could have predicted exactly what might happen next, most people – especially not the grown-up professionals of Tin Pan Alley – never saw The Beatles coming, or could have foreseen how they would change everything for everyone. The band auditioned for EMI a few months later, this time in the relaxed presence of the genial producer George Martin; who fell for their charm and wit as much as their abilities. They allowed him to mould them sonically into something more palatable – which included an enforced change of drummer. Their success across the next few years[8] would be the backdrop against which David and Marc would make their first serious stabs at pop fame. What the music biz types hadn't accounted for was that the teenagers who'd bought guitars in '56 and '57, after hearing Elvis and Bill Haley, had started to get *good*. Rock 'n' roll, as they had known it, was indeed dead and buried, but it had sown the seeds of the revolution to come ... and with David and Marc and their peers, the one after that as well.

All of this is why it was probably jazz, rather than rock, that was on David's mind at the end of 1961 when he begged his father for the money for a saxophone. It's telling that he didn't ask for a guitar, the ultimate symbol of

---

8. Something of an understatement.

rock 'n' roll – David wouldn't own a decent guitar until 1965. Instead he opted for a more technical, more challenging option. He'd coveted the instrument since that first electrifying listen to Little Richard's 'Tutti Frutti' years before. His big-brother's crash course in jazz alongside the vivid descriptions of live music in Kerouac's *On The Road* had only sharpened his interest. David was also showing the canniness that would mark much of his later career: the school was full of guitarists and singers, but no-one else was offering to form the horn section. It's an undoubtedly *cool* instrument, enabling the player to throw shapes and pose. It's also relatively easy to get a tune out of, at least compared to other members of the brass family, while making a sound most people listening will be impressed by. Plus, since a sax part rarely runs through the whole song, there's plenty of scope for singing too. The sax was David's way in.

Never knowingly under-indulged, by spring David had obtained not one but two saxophones. The first was his 1961 Christmas present, a beautiful cream-coloured Grafton alto sax with brass keys. He was delighted, and set about learning his favourite Little Richard solos. The Grafton has some notoriety in sax circles – the design was conceived as an affordable alternative (at around £55, it cost half of what most saxophones would fetch), which made it a tempting beginner's option. The saving was made by constructing it from injected acrylic plastic rather than the traditional metal, unfortunately this made the instrument much less robust than a standard sax and tonally a little odd, producing by turns a harsh, honking sound and a dull, raspy wheeze. In the hands of a master it could be used to great effect – jazz legend Ornette Coleman leaned heavily into its limitations to create a unique, almost a-tonal sound – but the fourteen year old David Jones was no master horn player [9] and it soon became clear that he'd need a more versatile instrument if he was to advance. Of course, what David wanted, David got. Within a few weeks, somewhere around David's fifteenth birthday, John Jones was escorting his son up to Tottenham Court Road to find a new saxophone. This time he chose a 1930s Conn New Wonder Series II tenor, a model nicknamed the 'Chu Berry', after the horn played by the great jazz sideman Leon Brown 'Chu' Berry. It was a more reliable, versatile and expensive instrument, paid for on hire-purchase. The Conn sax became Bowie's horn of choice – he was still using it on his records twenty years later. Unfortunately, George Underwood's tasty punch delayed David's advancement on the instrument, and it wasn't until the spring of 1962 that he finally got his act together and applied himself seriously. The first step was to find someone to give him lessons – but who? The answer, obviously, was 'the very best'.

By the age of fifteen the young Bowie was used to getting his own way. He was cherished by his parents, who balanced their lack of familial warmth with indulgences: not many kids in Bowie's day could wheedle their way out

---

9. To be honest, he never would be.

of grammar school, or get taken backstage to meet the stars at concerts or, indeed, be bought two saxophones within a few weeks of each other. The previous year he had written to the US Embassy in London and politely asked if they had any magazines that might explain the rules of American Football, having discovered the sport via US Forces Radio, which broadcast games for troops stationed abroad. It had become – briefly – a new obsession[10], further fuelling his fascination with all things American. The Embassy were delighted to accommodate a British kid enthralled by their national sport, and invited David to watch some pre-taped games and chat with the captain of the US Navy's local team. They also surprised him with a gift of a helmet and shoulder pads. He and George Underwood, who had tagged along, were photographed for the *Bromley and Kentish Times*, resplendent in their immaculate shirts and winklepickers.[11] Life for young David Jones had a habit of working out in just the way he wanted it. So when he and his brother brainstormed saxophone teachers and realised one of the country's best jazz saxophonists lived locally, David knew immediately what he needed to do.

Ronnie Ross is occasionally described as 'David Bowie's saxophone tutor', which is both literally true and also a misleading way to characterise his career. In truth, Ross wasn't a saxophone teacher at all – David was apparently one of the few people he ever schooled on the instrument. What he was, at least according to a 1958 issue of *Jazz Today*, was 'a titan of British Jazz'. Ross had played at the famous Newport Jazz Festival in Rhode Island as part of the International Youth Band – the only Brit in the line-up – and toured the US, where he'd received the 1959 'New Star' Award in the jazz bible *DownBeat* magazine. He would go on to play with The Beatles on the *White Album*. What he *wasn't* known as at the time, was a sax teacher – especially not for fifteen-year-old herberts with little to no experience on the instrument. David, of course, didn't know this and simply looked him up in the phone book and asked nicely – and persistently – for lessons. Ross was initially resistant but eventually gave in to this charming and compelling youth, inviting him to his home in Orpington the following Saturday. The skinny 'conservative and shy' (Ross' words) schoolboy with the newly mismatched eyes, and the experienced jazz pro with a cracked Keith-Richards growl in his voice rather hit it off – Ross was impressed enough with the boy's enthusiasm and knowledge of the genre,

---

10. He would also get very into baseball later in the year, even joining a local team. Naturally, John bought him a proper catcher's mitt.

11. This, apparently, wasn't David's first press appearance. In the mid-50s the family had spent some time living in Harrogate, Yorkshire while John worked out of the Dr. Barnardo's office there. During their stay, the Queen herself paid a visit to the area; David, somehow, ended up right in front of her, and a snap of the moment – according to Bowie – made it onto the cover of a local paper. This story is difficult to corroborate: there *was* a royal tour of Yorkshire in 1954, but none of the local coverage appears to show the young Bowie. Still, if it's true it's yet another example (and perhaps the first such) of David finding himself in the right place, at the right time, and doing exactly what was needed to find the limelight.

specifically the work of Charlie Parker, to agree to give him fortnightly lessons at £2 a go, despite his initial assessment being that he was 'bloody awful'. David, as he'd tell *Rolling Stone* a few years later, simply thought 'he was *so cool*'. He had eight lessons with Ross in total, across sixteen weeks. In that time he learned how to blow and breathe and place his fingers, and a little music theory. Perhaps more importantly he learned a lesson that reinforced the conceptual thinking Owen Frampton had been impressing on him at school: 'I told him that sax playing was all about the sound you had in your mind,' he told Ken Pitt in *The Pitt Report*, 'not just reproducing the notes on the paper'.[12]

Eight lessons was apparently all David felt he needed, and by the summer of 1962 he was champing at the bit to put his new skills to use with a real band. There may have been a paucity of electrifying material in the British charts, but the country was by now stuffed with an underground scene of young beat groups – formed, as we've seen, by those kids who'd fallen under the spell of rock 'n' roll in the 50s. The older ones, the generation that would comprise the first wave of the British beat boom, were already sniffing around the edges of the London scene, and the music industry was snuffling curiously back at them. The Beatles would record their first session at EMI's Abbey Road studios on 6 July. A week later, a group of preposterously young, middle-class blues enthusiasts would play their first show at The Marquee on Charing Cross Road using their new name; 'The Rolling Stones'. That summer a band called The Detours, who attended Acton County Grammar School in another London suburb, would move their lead guitarist, Roger Daltrey, to vocals after their original singer quit, cementing a line up of Daltrey, guitarist Pete Townshend and bass player John Entwistle. By 1964 they'd be called The Who. Up in Muswell Hill, to the North of the city, two brothers – Ray and Dave Davies – formed the Ray Davies Quartet and played their first gigs. It would take two years before they'd finally settle on a name: 'The Kinks'. In schoolyards across the country the beat boom was starting to bubble – once the Beatles released 'Love Me Do' in October it would be ready to boil off the stove.

Though David wasn't aware of the coming revolution, he was being pulled by the same tides. Live rock 'n' roll had found its way to Bromley Tech while he'd been nursing his injured eye – George Underwood (very much adding insult to injury) had been invited to form a band to play at a school fundraiser, assembling an outfit called George and the Dragons and performing a raucous set in the middle of the event. He would later say that had David and he been on good terms (the incident at the start of the year rather hung over their friendship at the time) and had David not been off sick, he would almost certainly have been involved too. The show was enough fun to give Underwood

12. Years later, Bowie would book Ronnie Ross to play sax on 'Walk on the Wild Side', the single he was producing for Lou Reed. He claimed that Ross hadn't made the connection between the boy he'd taught in 1962 and the super-star he was meeting now – although that seems rather unlikely.

the performing bug, and he would join a couple of local bands – The Spitfires and The Hillsiders – in the coming months, before bagging a gig singing for a Bromley act called The Konrads, already gigging regularly at youth club dances and parties. His main qualification for the job was that he owned his own amplifier, though it helped that he also possessed a very masculine, Presley-esque swagger: He *looked* like a star. Once George was in a proper band, David, who had finally forgiven him, begged to be let in too. Underwood agreed, even saying that David could sing a few numbers; Joe Brown's 'A Picture of You' ('He looked a bit like Joe Brown in those days', Underwood told Kevin Cann for his book *Any Day Now*) and Bruce Channel's 'Hey! Baby', while George took care of the rest of the set, which included Billy Fury's 'It's Only Make Believe' and Curtis Lee's 'A Night At Daddy Gee's'. The new lineup, featuring Mssrs Underwood and Jones, made its live debut at Bromley Tech's PTA fete, performing on the steps to the school's main entrance, where they augmented their set with instrumentals by The Shadows. An impressed Peter Frampton, who accompanied his parents to the event, also remembers David taking lead vocals on an Elvis number. This first proper show, which took place a week or so after David's final sax lesson, substantially over-ran with the band only leaving the stage once exasperated music teacher Brian Lane had the power turned off. The powers that be might have been able to end that particular gig, but David Jones was a lost cause – he was in a real band now, he was playing real shows, and he wasn't going to stop for anyone. The electricity had been cut, but a fuse had been lit. 'I could tell he was determined,' Underwood would tell Dylan Jones, years later. 'I think he almost dreamed it before he did it. It was a dream that came true.' Though Underwood would eventually fall away from the group amid some inter-band politics – 'Even though they still had my amplifier,' he grumbled – the slightly-renamed Kon-Rads (David insisted on inserting the dash) would become Bowie's primary focus for the next year or so, over and above his schooling, his Saturday job in a local record store or the full time job at an ad agency that Owen Frampton helped him secure after he graduated from Bromley Tech the following summer. The band gigged solidly throughout 1962 and 1963, playing dancehalls, youth clubs, birthday parties, working men's clubs and coffee bars, mostly in the Bromley area but occasionally venturing into London proper. Toward the end of 1962 they hooked up with a new drummer, Dave Hadfield, an older boy who had played with Cliff Richard when the two were still at school. His credentials and apparent professionalism were enough for the band to somewhat cynically give their original drummer (and founding member) Dave Crook[13] the boot. The line up of the Kon-Rads fluctuated from five to eight members, sometimes on a per-gig basis, and it's fair to say that the rest of the group didn't quite have

---

13. The Kon-Rads were a very Dave-heavy band.

Bowie's sense of ambition. Even the more seasoned David Hadfield struggled to keep up. 'He had thousands of ideas, a new one every day,' he told biographer Peter Doggett in his 2011 book *The Man Who Sold The World*. 'That we should change the spelling of our name, our image, our clothes, all the songs in our repertoire [and] sketches of potential logos'. For a band that were mostly in it for the fun, the drinks, the girls and to make a few bob here and there, it was sometimes a trying experience. 'I could always remember David as being difficult,' Stella Patton, one of the group's occasional backing singers, told Dylan Jones. 'The band all wore the same clothes, but he didn't like that[14]. He always had an exercise book with him and he would always be scribbling, writing down lyrics.' David, though never technically the group's lead singer, was undoubtedly their driving force – to him this was more than just an excuse to get onstage and impress girls[15]. This was *music*. It was *serious*. It's in the Kon-Rads that we first start seeing Bowie playing with the ideas of conceptualisation that he'd picked up from art and jazz. At the end of 1962, he created a Christmas card featuring the band in silver waistcoats (Hadfield is listed as their manager) which he then printed cheaply, got his bandmates to sign and sent out to local venues to drum up business. The Christmas card is interesting for one very notable reason – Bowie signs his name not as David Jones, but as 'Dave Jay' – the first example we know of him assuming a stage name.

The Kon-Rads are only a tiny part in the London boys' story – they never made it to the charts, they barely made it out of Bromley, but they were David's first true musical playground. Sure, they mostly knocked out tracks by Elvis, the Shadows and (later) The Beatles, with the odd self-penned number thrown in – some of David's first original songs – but the young Bowie was always pushing them to be something more. At one point he suggested that they change their name to 'Ghost Riders' and adopt a cowboy image, announcing he was changing his name as well. In keeping with his new wild west theme – which the rest of the band rejected anyway – he decided to christen himself after a real-life figure featured in the John Wayne movie *The Alamo*, and for a few months he went by the name of 'Jim Bowie', before reverting back to another variation of 'David J'.

He could be ruthless, a characteristic that both he and Bolan shared across the next two decades. He may not have been the lead singer, but it was always 'Dave Jay' that audiences remembered – David put his band in matching green blazers, mohair trousers, white shirts and striped yellow ties. The neat uniform benefited one member in particular: four of the boys looked physically very similar, with non-descript dark hair, holding their guitars or sitting behind

---

14. As David was the one that put the Kon-Rads in matching outfits, this is quite a curious comment. I suspect either Patton is misremembering – which at fifty years distance no-one would judge her for – or she means 'same' as in 'same old', implying that David wanted to constantly freshen their image.
15. Although he was very much in favour of this as well.

the drums, while the fifth sported an immaculate, blonde quiff, mismatched eyes and a golden or creamy white saxophone. By dressing his band identically, David ensured that he would stand out, something that would be less likely had each member been allowed to express their own individual style.

For a while the Kon-Rads suited David/Jim/Jones/Jay/Bowie, but it couldn't last. His ambitions were just too high. The band had a reputation as a solid dance act, banging out covers of the current top twenty and guaranteed to keep the floor full, but David was always going to need to dig deeper. Like many kids his age, including the members of the Stones, Yardbirds and John Mayall, an exploration of jazz and R&B had led him back to the blues, the pure stuff, reeking of Mississippi mud. Muddy Waters, John Lee Hooker, Howlin' Wolf, Leadbelly – stuff the other Kon-Rads wouldn't go near. As 1963 progressed and Beatlemania bloomed across Britain, David saw for himself that a band could succeed by writing their own songs and establishing their own image, setting a trend rather than following one as the Kon-Rads were doing. Bowie's personal tastes were expanding well beyond the borders of both his hometown and the chart fodder he was performing night-after-night.

Shortly after taking his O-Levels (he failed everything but Art) David had started work at a commercial art studio, Nevin D. Hurst, a Yorkshire company (which would have pleased John) with a London office located on New Bond Street, a short hop from the square mile of Soho. He didn't especially thrive in the job, which saw him mostly making the tea and running errands, though he was occasionally allowed to help with pasting up designs. His teacher, Owen Frampton, had helped him secure the position, stepping in when a careers officer noted David's interest in music and suggested he find employment in a local harp factory. Bowie felt that if he *must* have a job – and his father insisted on it – he could probably do better than screwing harps together. He stuck with the advertising job for around a year, the only nine-to-five gig we would ever have, but didn't particularly enjoy it. A creative soul he may well have been, but commercial art and advertising is a very specific discipline and David's heart simply wasn't in it. He did, however, get three things from his time in New Bond Street, aside from wages and keeping his parents quiet. First of all he got proximity to Soho and a hipster boss, Ian, who was continually sending him down Charing Cross Road to buy music, particularly from the legendary Dobells Records, which specialised in importing deep-cut jazz albums and blues 45s from the States. Ian was a music nut and, as he did with pretty much everyone, Bowie soaked up his knowledge and took his recommendations, often buying two copies on his shopping sprees – one as requested and one to keep for himself. It was here that he discovered the work of Bob Dylan, who himself had spent many hours digging through its shelves not six months before, as well as a slew of blues and folk greats. David was no longer stuck in suburbia – like his brother Terry, he was now working in London-proper, with Soho as his playground. For someone as obsessed with clothes and image, working so close to Carnaby Street and its cheaper tributaries was a god-send, and the bookshops of Charing Cross Road meant access to more writers and more ideas, continuing the journey he'd begun with the Kerouac and the beats, and allowing him to discover and soak in William S Burroughs, JG Ballard, Alexander Trocchi, Alan Stilliti, Frederick Nietzsche. At first he would just carry paperbacks around so they could poke from his pocket and make him look intellectual – before boredom and curiosity eventually persuaded him to read them. Bowie was being bombarded with influences at a greater rate than ever before.

Secondly, it properly exposed Bowie to modernism, not in the trad jazz and mohair-sweater sense of the late fifties, but the real proto-Mods with a capital M. The pill-poppin', espresso-drinking, suit-wearing first wavers. He realised that he wasn't just a well-dressed kid – but that, like Marc, he was part of a broader subculture that had emerged independently across the country. It was on the train into work that Bowie saw the first person he recognised as truly a Mod. It was a handsome young man, possibly called 'Michael' or perhaps called 'Leslie' [16] (Bowie recounted this story a few times and always couched that fact with 'I think he was called …') who was not only sharply dressed, but also quite obviously wearing eyeliner, eyeshadow and mascara to enhance his features. Bowie was entranced. 'I'd never seen that before,' he told Dylan Jones. 'I thought that was really peculiar and I thought it looked rather good.' It was only once he'd breached London's inner life that David really embraced his mod side; it informed the clubs he would go to, the bands he would listen to (James Brown and Marvin Gaye became favourites) and the people he would meet.

Thirdly, and most importantly, it meant that for the rest of his career he could talk about how *he used to work in advertising*. It was the ice-breaker he used to start a conversation with Andy Warhol many years later; he would drop hints of his previous career into his interviews, telling *Rolling Stone*'s Cameron Crowe how much he'd hated it, for example. It simply became part of the Bowie mythology: 'Of course he knows how to market himself – *he used to work in advertising*'. Geoffrey Marsh, who curated the *David Bowie Is* exhibition at London's Victoria and Albert Museum in 2013, argues that the job was a crash course in 'maximising the effectiveness of mass marketing'. Writing in the accompanying text for the exhibition, he speculated that 'Bowie would have had the opportunity to pick up a wealth of ideas about how to influence audiences, in particular.' It's possible a lot of these ideas would have been there anyway – his father did work in PR, after all – but it makes sense that a year in the focused world of the ad men would have sharpened a mind already receptive to notions of branding, media and conceptualisation.

---

16. Equally possibly these could be two different people.

The more he soaked in all of this – the city, the music, the ideas – the keener he was to apply it to his own work. Alas, the rest of the Kon-Rads weren't always willing to gamble on their saxman's wacky concepts, feeling that he was too prone to fads and gimmicks. At his suggestion they'd already modified their name, overhauled their image, added a hand-painted backdrop (illustrated by one D. Jones of Bromley) and rigged blue stage lights which, when activated, contrasted with specially applied paint on their guitars that appeared to make them change colour. The other members could only be pushed so far. 'If we go out on a limb we're going to lose all of our local bookings', Hadfield told Paul Trynka in *Starman*, 'and lose what popularity we have'. For David it was endlessly frustrating, and he constantly considered throwing in the towel. However, the gigs were plentiful and fun, he was becoming a better performer with every show and, besides, there really did seem to be some buzz building around the group. In August 1963, an article in the *Bromley & Kentish Times* claimed they had a fan club numbering some 200 local kids.

It was around this time that David had the first of many near-misses with true musical success. A Bromley-based entrepreneur by the name of Bob Knight caught a Kon-Rads show at Orpington Civic Hall and was convinced that the band had potential. Knight worked as an assistant to Eric Easton, a variety performer-turned-agent who had recently started co-managing the Rolling Stones, then on the cusp of their own stardom after signing with Decca. Knight convinced his boss to take a meeting with the group at his Regent Street offices. The Kon-Rads were suitably wowed by the visit, in which they were introduced to Brian Epstein, the Beatles manager, and even Mick Jagger himself, who dropped in for a quick chat.

The beat group boom, powered by The Beatles' two massive, ubiquitous number one singles and number one album, was gathering an unstoppable head of steam. The next Beatles single, 'She Loves You', was due out in the coming weeks and Parlophone had already pressed up a quarter of a million copies just to meet the demand of pre-orders. The boom was only going to get bigger, and the industry was increasingly haunted by Dick Rowe's mistake eighteen months earlier. The Beatles had broadsided everyone and no-one wanted to miss the next big cash cow.[17] The Stones, the next great hope, had already had a minor hit for Decca with 'Come On', and their own buzz was building. Tin Pan Alley (the nickname given to Denmark Street where much of the London music biz was based) was now very keen to take some chances on pretty-boy guitar bands. Having already squeezed Merseyside dry, it was now looking in its own backyard. By the summer of 1963 there were an estimated five and half million teenagers in Britain, buying around fifty-five million records a year, hungry for

---

17. Though not as haunted as they would be just a few weeks later, when the success of 'She Loves You' turbocharged Beatlemania and created a wave the music industry is arguably still riding to this day.

the next Beatles – it was a beast that was going to need feeding: the Kon-Rads, if they worked out, were just more musical spaghetti to throw at the wall on the off-chance it would stick.

Easton arranged a demo session with Decca for 29 August in West Hampstead, promising to manage the band if the label took them on. David was the youngest of the group at just sixteen, but could justly feel that his steering of the good ship Kon-Rad had brought them to this point. Amongst the four songs that the band put down that day was at least one Bowie original – possibly a song entitled 'I Never Dreamed', co-written with Kon-Rads guitarist Alan Dodds. There's some dispute over who wrote the lyrics to this piece; David Hadfied remembers the song being written by David, about a plane crash he'd seen on the news. Such a theme would certainly sync with later ideas of a typical 'David Bowie' lyric. It's also borne out by an article in the *Bromley and Kent Times* which refers to the song as one of the group's most popular and confirms it as a Jones/Dodds creation. However, Kon-Rads singer Roger Ferris told *Mojo Collections* in 2001 that he himself had written the words, describing it as 'a typical upbeat love song of the time', and while this view is contradicted by his bandmate and the contemporary press, it's supported by, well, the words themselves, which were quoted from memory to Andy Barding, writing for the official Bowie website, exactly fifty years later. The lyrics Ferris quotes are all 'staring into blue eyes', caressing soft hair, captured hearts and tender smiles. There's no aircraft wreckage in sight. Those words also, tellingly, include the song's title. 'I Never Dreamed' was thought lost for many years. A few members of the band had acetates[18] from the session but had misplaced them over the decades. A copy finally surfaced in 2018, discovered by David Hadfield in his loft. A brief ten-second clip is all that has ever been made available to hear, but it absolutely confirms that the lyrics Ferris quoted were accurate[19]. Unfortunately, we don't know what other three tracks were recorded, so can't know if a Bowie-penned song about a plane crash was among them. Sixty years on, with spotty memories and no-one at the time thinking it was worth keeping accurate records, we're largely in the dark.

Whoever wrote the words, Roger Ferris' description of the song is bang on. It is absolutely a 'typical, upbeat love song of the time'. It could be by any of the poppier beat groups doing the rounds in 63. Apparently David's voice is backing up Ferris', but listening to the ten-second snippet it's difficult to tell. It could be David, but it could just as easily be literally anyone else. Regardless of who

---

18. An acetate is essentially the 'original' disc from which records are pressed – usually an aluminium disc coated in lacquer, with the grooves expertly cut by hand using a lathe. Acetates were the first stage in the manufacturing process once a song had been recorded and mixed, and in the case of unsuccessful recordings, the only version of a record that may be produced.

19. Roger Ferris was already hugely jealous of the attention David got in the band at the time, since he was the lead singer and could reasonably have expected to be the one getting the girls. Having his lyrics misattributed as well must have stung.

wrote or sang on 'I Never Dreamed', it wasn't enough. Decca turned the band down, and true to his word, so did Easton. The group were crushed, especially David, who had genuinely thought that this was his big break. Hadfield believes that Bowie's mind was set against the Kon-Rads from that point onward.

David would play his final show with the band on New Year's Eve, 1963, but put off officially leaving for a few months (though he did signal his disdain by simply not bothering to turn up for a gig in Petts Wood on 25 January.) The last straw had been the songs that they chose to perform – desperate for something sexier and cooler in their set, Bowie had suggested they cover Marvin Gaye's 'Can I Get A Witness'. The other Kon-Rads shook their heads and their fate was sealed. David's delayed departure was due to one last opportunity that had come the group's way – an upcoming audition for *Ready, Steady, Win!*, a talent-show spin-off of the popular pop programme *Ready, Steady, Go!* with a top prize of £1,000 worth of Vox amplifiers and a deal with Decca. Alas, it was not an audition worth hanging on for. According to Bowie biographer Paul Trynka, the band's hand-drawn backdrop, covers of chart hits and matching outfits made them seem cabaret-ish and hackneyed next to the group that won their round – the Trubeats – who played their own material and dressed individually. Making this sting even more was the fact that the Trubeats featured one Peter Frampton, the son of David's art teacher and an old friend. David, apparently, was mortified and handed in his notice shortly afterwards.[20] The Kon-Rads would need a new sax man. Bowie, meanwhile, was already moving on. He had blues to play, clothes to wear, coffee to sip and Soho to explore.[21]

---

20. There is some dispute over this – Paul Trynka claims the band performed an audition in person, but other sources say they merely submitted a demo disc, and it was once again 'I Never Dreamed' that failed them. If the latter, it's not really a surprise: Decca were offering a deal to the winners and that label had turned down 'I Never Dreamed' once already. A couple of sources also put the *Ready, Steady, Win* entry in 1963, before the audition at Decca, however press clippings at the time confirm that the show wasn't broadcast until the summer of 1964, with auditions held early that year.

21. The Konrads themselves (who dropped the dash in their name as soon as David was out of the door) stayed together for a couple more years and didn't do too badly, at one point opening on tour for the Stones and releasing a handful of singles. A year or so later Daves Hadfield and Jones ran into one another in the Wimpy burger bar in Bromley; David was clearly at one of his lower ebbs career-wise and looked despondent. 'How's the band doing?' asked the younger man. 'Great!' replied Hadfield. 'We're touring with the Stones.' Konrads – one, David Jones – nil. Most of the band stayed in the biz one way or another, except for Andy Dodds who became a vicar and is probably happier for it.

Chapter Five

The Magician, the Meek and the Madhouse on Castle Street

While David Jones and the Kon-Rads were keeping Kent moving with chart hits and matching jackets, Mark Feld was having a quieter but no less personally impactful year. He mostly spent 1963 reading books in his parents' house by day and roaming the streets of Soho by night, catching whatever live music was going down and smiling his best smile at passing girls. He also caught gigs more locally at Tooting Granada, where he saw The Beatles and the Stones, touring US acts like The Ronettes, and pretty much everyone else emerging at the time.

With no school mates or local gang to impress, the energy he had previously put into clothes was funnelled into a new-found love of poetry and literature – pretty much the only positive he got from his school days – and with bags of time at his disposal, Marc began to devour anything he could get his hands on. Naturally he related most to the nineteenth century Romantics, seeing himself as a Lord Byron figure, floating through life being clever and dashing. He read Wordsworth, Shelley, Keats and Byron, though his particular favourite was the dramatic French proto-surrealist Arthur Rimbaud ('When I first read him it felt like my feet were on fire,' he later said), leading to a fascination with and romanticisation of French culture – to Marc, his fantasy version of bohemian Paris represented the very height of sophistication. Francophilia would become a recurring theme in his life and art. Occasionally he'd give into pressure from his parents and head to the local labour exchange where, in those days, an abundance of manual work was available even for an unskilled school drop-out. Unfortunately, as the only situation he was prepared to fill was the invariably unavailable job of 'poet', these trips rarely led to anything. Instead Phyllis, as usual, indulged and supported her son who remained convinced that the future had something special in store for him, and that it was waiting just around the corner. 'I didn't want to have my head confused with a job I didn't really want to do,' he told the journalist Michael Wale in 1972 for his book on the music industry, *Vox Pop*. 'I didn't know what I wanted to do, I had no direction at all, just that I knew something was going to be happening.'

Marc was lucky – he was living at the first point in history where a working class teenager could be allowed to idle away a year or so, lazily soaking in life. A few years earlier he'd have been packed off to do National Service and a few years before that, sent away to one of the bloodiest wars in modern history, while before the war 'teenagers' weren't really a recognised concept, at least not for someone of Marc's background. You finished school, you got a job. It was just what you did. The breakthroughs in art and entertainment, widespread consumer culture, the rock 'n' roll dream and Americana made it more acceptable for kids like Marc to set their sights higher and refuse to settle, especially if their old mum was happy to indulge them with a hot meal and a few bob.

Mark Feld wasn't good for much, even he must have known that, but one thing everyone who knew him as a young man agrees on – aside from the fact he looked fantastic in *everything* – was that his self belief was bulletproof. He knew he was meant for *something*, and was pretty sure it was going to involve what he felt were his three core skills: poetry, music and looking great. Those unsuccessful trips to the employment exchange indicated that poetry was probably a blind alley, career wise, so he moved onto option two: be a pop star.

Marc knew that there was a playbook for this. If Cliff Richard could drag himself from the wrong side of Croydon to the top of the charts, if *Helen Shapiro*, of all people, could start off just down the road and end up as the nation's sweetheart, then there was no reason Mark Feld couldn't do it too. As an avid reader of the music press and an enthusiastic follower of the charts, Marc knew exactly whose door he should be knocking on. At some point in the first half of 1963, fifteen year old Marc made his way back to North London, not far from the three streets of which he'd been king. His destination was 304 Holloway Road, a flat above a haberdashery in which the maverick producer Joe Meek had built a studio out of egg boxes, bits of wire, spare parts and his genius.

Though his influence was rather eclipsed when the Beatles and Stones ushered in the beat boom, for a year or so Meek was arguably the most important and certainly one of the most interesting figures in British music; an entrepreneur, an innovator and a complete eccentric. He had done his National Service working as a radar operator, which was a logical step after a childhood spent soldering bits of wire together to see what they did, and gotten into the recording business as an engineer in the fifties, making his name when he produced 'Bad Penny Blues' for Humphrey Lyttleton, a huge hit in 1956. Meek was a genuine maverick, constantly trying new recording ideas and pushing the boundaries of what could be done with the limited technology of the time. It was Meek that had the audacity to push Lyttleton's trumpet back in the mix on the very-much-trumpet-led 'Bad Penny Blues', and instead foreground Johnny Parker's boogie piano riff, accenting the bassier sounds of the instrument to give it more swing and thump[1]. Lyttleton was distinctly unimpressed with being sidelined on his own record, especially when Meek insisted he simplify

---

1. This actually came about because of necessity – Lyttleton's saxophonist was unable to make the session, and Meek had to find a way to plug the sonic gap left by the instrument's absence. Paul McCartney would later borrow heavily from Parker's piano part on the Beatles' 'Lady Madonna'.

his trumpet part, but the results spoke for themselves.[2] The track was the first British jazz recording to become a genuine smash hit, and it put Meek's name on the map. Fancying himself a hit-maker, he set up his own production and artist management company, RGM Sound, building a studio from scratch out of a London flat and using every inch of the space. It wasn't unusual for string sections to be recorded in the stairwell, while vocalists took advantage of the natural reverb found in the bathroom. He was one of the first producers in the world to truly use the recording studio as an instrument in itself – a cliche phrase now, but extremely unusual then. He loved instrumental music and had several hits based around reverby guitar riffs and futuristic keyboard sounds, augmented with vary-speed tape effects, overdubbing, treated vocals and pioneering electronic noise. The most famous of these was 'Telstar' by the Tornados, a number one hit both in the UK and the USA; virtually unheard of for a British record at the time.[3] Between building his studio in 1960 and his death in 1967 he churned out over 700 recordings, writing 250 songs himself despite not being able to play an instrument, read music and being, according to several acts who worked with him, completely tone deaf.[4]

Meek was always on the lookout for new talent, and as long as a lad was prepared to do as he was told, he would give pretty much anyone a chance to audition. Many stalwarts of the late sixties and seventies British scene got their start playing on Joe Meek records – Chas Hodges, Ray Davies, Tom Jones, Richie Blackmore and Jimmy Page to name just a few. His ear did occasionally let him down, however: A band called The Raiders were taken on to record instrumentals, but their singer was told his services were not required. He would later change his name to Rod Stewart. Another band, The Senators, recorded a couple of tracks but Meek was unimpressed and summarily sent them on their way – their singer would shortly rechristen himself Tom Jones. He also advised Brian Epstein against signing The Beatles. Still, it was largely known that answering his adverts in the back of *Melody Maker*, or just knocking on his door, could get you in to see Joe and seeing Joe *could* make you a star. Doing so carried risks, however – Meek had a deeply troubled private life; he was gay in an era when, shamefully, homosexuality was still illegal, and was constantly in fear of blackmail as a result. He was bipolar in an era when the condition was barely understood and intensely paranoid with a prestigious drug problem that

2. I heard Humph play once, around a week before his death at the age of 86 in 2008. He was chairing a touring version of Radio 4's *I'm Sorry I haven't A Clue*, a role he'd had since the 1970s, and ended the show by playing a solo rendition of 'We'll Meet Again', with a beautifully pure tone that left no-one unmoved. Which is no mean feat when a 3,000-strong audience at the Hammersmith Apollo is playing along on kazoos – breaking the official Guinness world record for the most kazoos played in one performance. This is true.
3. The guitarist on 'Telstar' is George Bellamy, who passed on the combination of epic rock and space age themes to his son Matt, frontman of epic space-rockers Muse.
4. He claimed some of these were co-written with the ghost of Buddy Holly, his all time favourite artist, with whom he'd commune via a ouija board.

would only get worse. He would die in 1967 at just thirty seven years old, in a murder/suicide incident during which he shot his landlady. As a producer, he could be extremely volatile, screaming when he was unhappy, accusing rivals of bugging his studio to steal his secrets and, once, firing a gun at The Senators during a session – thankfully loaded only with blanks. He was also known to proposition his young charges, sometimes just in the form of a suggestive comment, sometimes a hand on the leg, sometimes worse – According to a 2009 interview in the *South Wales Echo* with the Senators' bass player Vernon Hopkins, a terrified Tom Jones, fresh from the Valleys, once literally fled from the studio, shouting 'He's just touched my bollocks! The bastard grabbed my balls!'[5]

Marc would have been well aware of Meek's reputation, or at the very least knew he had a soft spot for a young man with a shy smile, and wasn't above using his looks to make an impression. We know he presented himself on the doorstep of 304 Holloway Road in 1963, though whether he ever recorded with Meek is subject to debate amongst fans – Meek kept him dangling for several months, promising a shot at some point and asking him to come back. Marc likely went inside the studio at least once, as he later described the pet budgie Meek kept in his bedroom. That is, unfortunately, all we know for sure. The two never entered into a business arrangement together, but it's still possible that some demos were made. One track called 'Mrs Jones' that surfaced after Meek's death, is believed by some to feature a Bolan vocal, though the recording isn't clear enough for anyone to be able to say for sure. It's also possible that Marc recorded at least one number with The Tremeloes' George Bellamy, though this is all based on hearsay. After Meek's death hundreds of demos and recordings, known as the 'Tea Chest Tapes' after the boxes they were stored in, were salvaged from his studio and it's possible that among them is a recording that definitively features Mark Feld. The tapes were recently acquired by Cherry Red Records, a British label specialising in re-issues, so there is some hope for those searching for the holy grail of Bolan demos. [6]

With his music career a work in progress, Marc's next move was to try monetising his most concrete skill – looking great. Once again able to wind his mum around his little finger, he persuaded Phyllis to front £100 of family savings, a considerable sum in 1963, to pay for modelling lessons. Marc, a clothes

---

5. In 2017 Jones gave an interview to BBC Radio 5 where he talked about the sexual harassment he'd received from older men in the early days of his career, though he stopped short of naming Meek.

6. Meek also recorded The Kon-Rads, though it's likely the session took place after Bowie left – he doesn't seem to be on the recordings that have surfaced in recent years. Kon-Rad's drummer David Hadfield told Paul Trynka about visiting the Holloway Road studio with David on one occasion, however Bowie himself contradicted this on his website in 2008, saying 'I never worked with Joe Meek, never even met him … would have loved to have though. But, I believe The Konrads did do a track or two with him.' Two other future Bowie backing bands, The Riot Squad and the Manish Boys, would also work with Meek.

horse for whom showing off and posing came as naturally as breathing, took
to it straight away and was even briefly signed to an agency. Remarkably, and
presumably to everyone's surprise except Marc's, that £100 investment turned
out to be a worthwhile one. Marc booked a couple of relatively decent modelling
jobs (notably the Littlewoods catalogue and a brochure for John Temple, a men's
tailors, for which he modelled suits) and even a couple of walk-on TV parts.
Although he never earned anywhere close to the amounts he would later brag
about (he once claimed to have made £2,000 from modelling in a single week,
just to prove to his parents that he could – which was, to say the least, extremely
unlikely), his new career did generate enough cash to repay his parent's loan
and get them off his back about his 'layabout' lifestyle, with enough left over
the buy himself a new acoustic guitar – the first he'd had since he was eight
years old. Ultimately though, Marc found living purely off his looks to be an
unsatisfying way of paying the bills. He didn't particularly enjoy being styled by
other people, which is no surprise since his appearance had been his primary
form of self expression for years. He also found acting to be boring, because it
mostly involved waiting around. For someone who was so sure they deserved to
be a star that they'd thrown a tantrum when one acoustic performance in the
2 I's hadn't led straight to a record deal, walk-on parts in kitchen sink dramas
and modelling cheap suits in the Littlewoods catalogue were never going to
be enough.

Marc spent most of 1963 waiting for Joe Meek to call (he never did), reading
poetry, studying Bert Weedon's *Play In a Day* guitar manual and booking the
odd modelling job. Instant musical stardom had once again failed to materialise,
though this time he took it in his stride. It wasn't until the following year that
the wheels would really start moving on his career. Having failed at the bat-
your-eyelids-at-Joe-Meek-until-he-makes-you-a-star method of pop success,
it was becoming clear that he couldn't wriggle his way into the music industry
without help. What he needed – what all the great stars had – was a manager.
His own gentile Brian Epstein to believe in him, to put in the elbow grease, to
work their little black book and to do the maths. He would arguably spend the
rest of his life trying to find someone to fulfil that role properly.

Marc met his first manager, Geoffrey Delaroy-Hall, at a party in late 1963
or early 1964 (reports vary) when he was still aged just sixteen. Delaroy-Hall,
twenty-seven years Marc's senior, is a fascinating figure; an RAF hero who
had flown nearly fifty missions over Nazi-occupied Europe during the war,
for which he was awarded the Flying Cross. The former airman would have
made an immediate impression on Marc – he was a dashing man, mixed-race
and handsome with a dazzling, wide smile and a personable character, fond of
wearing a black top hat. As well as being a decorated war hero, he worked as a
barrister and owned property in Manchester Square, near Marylebone, which
he rented out – he was thus both clever and never short of a few bob. Just to add

a final sparkle to this attractive and accomplished man, he raced cars in his spare time.[7] Their relationship was short-lived but formative. Delaroy-Hall moved Marc into an unoccupied basement room in his rather run-down property, allowing him to live rent free in exchange for managing his music career, and fronted the money necessary for a professional recording. He was still involved with Marc over two years later, with records showing he was again covering his rent ('Landlord's a queen!' Marc wrote in his journal in 1966) – though their business relationship was long over – and would continue to take his former client and his friends out for lavish dinners, often inviting them to stay at his house afterwards ('Very generous to us younger guys; splendid dinners,' says Allan Warren, another teenager whom Marc would befriend later that year).

At just sixteen, Marc wasn't yet old enough to make legal commitments for himself[8] meaning that Delaroy-Hall would need one of his parents to sign the contract on their son's behalf. According to Caron Willans, a lifelong Bolan fan who knew Delaroy-Hall in his final years, Phyllis definitely had her suspicions about the nature of the relationship between this sophisticated older man and her cherubic sixteen-year-old son, but she wasn't about to start refusing Marc now, not when that man was promising to deliver everything he had ever wanted. Thus it was that Delaroy-Hall got his signature and Marc got a manager and, for the first time in his life, a place of his own.

Was Phyllis right about Delaroy-Hall's relationship with her son? Probably. We know from interviews with school friends that Marc's sexual exploits with girls went back to his late childhood, so we can assume that by the age of sixteen he was fairly experienced in that area, but he also had flings and sexual encounters with men, and he wasn't above using his good looks to get his way. This relationship with Delaroy-Hall is our first encounter with Marc's broader sexuality. It does, unfortunately, also cast a slightly unpleasant shadow over the whole arrangement. There doesn't appear to have been any harm done, at least as far as we know – the sixteen-year-old Mark Feld never seemed to let anything or anybody put him on the back foot – still, there's no getting past the fact that Delaroy-Hall at forty-three was *significantly* older than Marc, as well as far more worldly and experienced, which meant that he would likely have had the upper-hand in their power-dynamic. By twenty-first century standards the relationship would be seen as more than a little sinister. This was the sixties though, and the age-gap wasn't the only worry: sex between men

---

7. Delaroy-Hall would continue to be impressive. He was even mentioned in Parliament in 2000 by his local MP, Julian Lewis, after standing up to a racist next-door neighbour at the age of 79, making the local news. By that time he had retired to Yorkshire, but still gave free legal advice at a local volunteer centre. He died from cancer just two years later, still in possession of his contracts, photos and recordings from his time managing Mark Feld.

8. Something he'd be well aware of thanks to the Cliff Richard-starring music industry satire *Expresso Bongo*, in which a shady impresario must talk Cliff's mum into signing a contract. Being a Cliff fan always comes in handy.

would remain illegal for another three years. Delaroy-Hall, a respected barrister with a reputation as a war hero, was playing with fire. Still, Marc didn't do badly out of the arrangement, enjoying a rent-free pad, a professional recording experience and the invaluable knowledge that someone believed in him, while Geoffrey Delaroy-Hall walked away from their partnership none-the-richer. It was an early example of Marc using sex to get what he wanted, something that would become a pattern.

The role that Delaroy-Hall played in Marc's life also raises an interesting possibility: was this the root of the black magician he called 'The Wizard' and was so fond of talking about in later interviews? The tale of an older man who took him in hand during a trip to France and taught him magic could easily have been a metaphorical redressing of his relationship with his first manager. Delaroy-Hall doesn't appear to have had magic powers (or been French for that matter) but he seemed exotic and had bags of charisma, and if he was indeed Marc's first male lover, that could certainly map on to the idea of learning 'magic tricks'. It's an interesting bit of myth-making, with Marc taking a relatively ordinary experience and weaving it into something magical and strange; which would be another theme of his career.[9]

If Delaroy-Hall is indeed 'The Wizard', then it was probably his greatest contribution to Marc's career. In terms of getting him closer to the top of the charts, or even into record stores at all, his success rate was pretty poor. His one solid result was the creation of a good quality demo recording, though even that went largely unheard for nearly fifty years and really only benefited Marc by giving him his first taste of a professional recording studio. 'All At Once', a rather pleasant light ballad, was recorded on 28 August 1964 at IBC studios, where The Kinks had recently cut 'You Really Got Me'. Marc croons his way through a passable Cliff Richard impression and while it's not exactly a virtuoso performance, it's certainly good enough to make Jeff Dexter's claim the previous year that Marc 'couldn't sing' seem a bit harsh. His voice may lack power, but it has an appealing cuteness and when the key changes there's a hint of something with more guts hiding behind the simpering. The song itself is syrupy, true, but it also has a certain yearning charm and a lovely ascending guitar line – had it been tracked a few years earlier it could well have been a modest hit. Unfortunately, in the wake of the Beatles and the rattling excitement of the beat boom it was at best a throwback and at worst hideously dated. This was the sound of 1960, a million miles from the speeding, bleeding edge of the increasingly swinging 1964. Geoffrey Delaroy-Hall may well have been a sophisticated saviour who taught Marc 'magic', but he was still a man in his forties. It was perhaps optimistic to think that he'd be in touch with the sounds

---

9. Another of Marc's early managers, Simon Napier-Bell, believes the 'Wizard' story was an embellishment of an encounter in a Parisian gay club with a stage magician. We'll get to him later.

that excited a teenage audience.[10] He failed to gain any interest in either the recording or the singer, in fact there's no evidence that an acetate was ever cut, and shortly afterwards the Feld/Delaroy-Hall professional partnership seems to have fallen away.

Though Marc would always have a soft spot for Cliff-style crooning and presumably trusted his manager, it's still surprising that he'd agree to such an old-fashioned tune – and not just because the charts were full of Beatles, Stones, Pacemakers and Kinks. He'd flirted with the beat groups (although, tellingly, not enough to grow his hair out into a Beatle bowl) but he was never a paid-up devotee of R&B-inspired pop, nor had he developed the depth of love for the blues that so hooked David. Instead, Marc spent his modelling money on an acoustic rather than an electric guitar, inspired by a new musical inspiration, one that, ironically, electrified him in the way Bill Haley and Cliff had done back in the fifties: Bob Dylan.

We've looked at many artists that had formative impressions on the London boys throughout this book, but outside of Bill Haley and Little Richard, Dylan is probably the most important in terms of image, ideology and songwriting. Neither David nor Marc were Beatles obsessives (though both were fans – basically everyone was) and they absorbed the fab four's influence through the membrane of the music and culture changed by Beatlemania, rather than by specifically trying to be Lennon or McCartney. Dylan was different. The Beatles had changed music by supercharging pop and establishing the rock group as a creative force rather than mere performers, opening the door to rock 'n' roll being seen as more than a fad. Essentially, they future-proofed pop music. Dylan was the one that expanded the boundaries. It was Bob Dylan that brought the idea of "authenticity" into pop, along with seriousness, wilful outsiderdom and constant reinvention. It wasn't really until Dylan that pop could be considered both commercially *and* creatively substantive. He was also the first genuinely huge star without a conventional singing voice, whose musicianship was rudimentary. No-one had made a notable success combining lyrics, charisma and urgency without virtuosity before.[11] There's a very solid

---

10. There's some debate over who wrote 'All At Once', which certainly wasn't a Feld original. The tape containing the recording was handed to John 'Danielz' Wilan, the singer of a T.Rex tribute band, T.Rextasy, and his wife Caron shortly before Delaroy-Hall passed away in 2002. The writing credit on the label simply said 'Bellamy'. It's quite likely that this was George Bellamy of the Tremeloes, whom Marc would have met at Joe Meek's studio. Bellamy says he has no memory of the song, though at sixty-years distance and with a lot of water under the bridge, that doesn't necessarily mean he didn't write it.

11. This isn't to say that Dylan is a *bad* musician – he's absolutely not. His guitar playing is fine, his harp playing is fine, and his singing voice is, in its own way, pretty good. It's a voice defined by its imperfections though, not its range or accuracy. As my old English teacher once said, 'some people sing because they want to, or because they're paid to, Bob Dylan always sounds like he sings because he *has* to.'

argument that it was Dylan that pioneered the concept of the rock star as a creative outsider.

But before that, Dylan was first and foremost a folk singer and a poet. He'd been born Robert Zimmerman in 1941 to middle class parents of Eastern European Jewish stock living in Minnesota. In High School he'd caught the rock 'n' roll bug, performing Elvis and Little Richard tunes and briefly playing piano in teen idol Bobby Vee's backing band, before falling hard for traditional American folk as a college student in Minneapolis. He became, much like Lonnie Donegan at around the same time in the UK, a sponge for traditional music: blues, country, spirituals, folk, ragtime. The liner notes for his second album, *The Freewheelin' Bob Dylan*, claimed that he'd spent his youth living all over the country; North and South Dakota, Kansas, New Mexico and Minnesota, soaking up songs by Leadbelly, Jelly Roll Morton, Howlin' Wolf, Hank Williams and Woody Guthrie. It was mostly untrue. His home state aside, these travels didn't happen – at least, not in any sort of literal way. In another sense, though, they sort-of did. Zimmerman *had* toured his country via seeking out and learning its music, even travelling back in time. He was also a rabid consumer of poetry and literature, discovering the beat poets and – a particular favourite – Dylan Thomas, from whom he took his stage name. Now calling himself Bob Dylan, he moved to New York in 1961 and quickly went about absorbing every song performed in Greenwich Village's numerous folk clubs. He had a ravenous hunger for music, and his memory for it was extraordinary. By 1968 he had recorded over 250 songs, including those he'd written himself, and knew many more.

Dylan first came to the UK in the bitter winter of 1962, by which time a low-key debut album, *Bob Dylan*, had sold only moderately, but to all the right people. America's music press was gradually falling in love, and whispers that someone extraordinary was emerging had begun to cross the pond with import copies of the folk magazine *Sing Out!*. Dylan, therefore, wasn't a complete unknown during that first trip, though his fame existed in a very hipsterised, very serious folk community. Though he would later deny having any knowledge of the British scene ('I went to one of the clubs when I was in London in 1962 but didn't stop long', he fibbed outrageously to *Melody Maker* a few years later), Dylan had actually approached London in exactly the same way he had New York: he visited as many of the city's room-above-a-pub folk nights and coffee houses as he possibly could, learning traditional English songs like 'Scarborough Fair' and 'Lord Franklin's Lament', both of which would be re-tooled into original compositions on his next album, *The Freewheelin Bob Dylan*. Dylan, remarkably, was in the country to appear in a BBC teleplay called *Madhouse On Castle Street*, in which he was to play a student protest singer. However, as it soon became clear that he had absolutely no ability to act whatsoever, his contribution became almost entirely musical; opening and closing the show with a new song, 'Blowin' in the Wind' – only the fourth time that it had ever been performed.[12]

The folk scene in Britain was divided, snobbish and a little bitchy. Players often strove for some sort of imagined authenticity, connecting them to the musical traditions of ages past and Dylan, though an encyclopaedic expert on folk of all kinds, was seen by the genre's London gatekeepers as too modern, too idiosyncratic, too dangerously popular. Others, though, fell completely under his spell. As Dylan moved from club to club, coffee bar to coffee bar, he was leaving an imprint of himself on his audience, literally changing the scene as he passed through it. It was a reciprocal relationship – while Dylan sparked fierce admiration and inspiration in the British scene, rejuvenating it and bringing it out of the pub cellars, daring it to embrace new fangled ideas like microphones and denim and songs written in the twentieth century, London gave Dylan a deeper understanding of western musical tradition and some new colours to his palette in the shape of old English and Scottish folk songs. He returned to the US early in 1963, shortly before his appearance in *The Madhouse on Castle Street* was broadcast by the BBC, showcasing four original Bob Dylan songs. Many fans can trace the discovery of their idol to that broadcast. When he came back to the UK the following year, the seeds he had planted during that first winter had borne significant fruit. Performing at the Royal Festival Hall (at a show organised by future David Bowie manager Kenneth Pitt) he received the full-on Beatlemania treatment, with fans screaming and trying to rip hanks of hair from his head as he departed. That year, *Freewheelin ...* (which was already a year old) went to number one and the influence of Bob Dylan spread across British music. His lasting impact was assured when Lennon and McCartney heard his lyrics and suddenly realised that 'yeah yeah yeah' was not going to cut it any more.

Mark Feld, as usual, was aboard that particular train a little earlier. We don't know Marc's precise route towards Dylan, though we know it happened in 1963, and that it was almost certainly 'Blowin' in the Wind' that did it. Dylan's solo rendition both opened and closed *The Madhouse on Castle Street* and shortly afterwards the palatable American folk trio Peter, Paul and Mary covered the song to considerable success, reaching number 14 on the British charts. Marc couldn't have failed to be aware of it. 'Blowin' In The Wind' is perhaps the perfect encapsulation of Dylan's first phase, the one that initially grabbed attention and crystallised the idea of who 'Bob Dylan' was. It's a protest song, based on an old tune called 'No More Auction Block' sung by the freed African slaves who fled to North America when Britain abolished slavery in 1833. The African American socialist Paul Robeson had recorded it in 1947, though it

---

12. All known tapes of the piece have since been wiped by the BBC, in a move thought by director Philip Saville to have been deliberately malicious, since Dylan was a world-famous superstar by the time someone decided to destroy the recording.

was a spiritually profound fifties take by the civil rights pioneer Odetta that most significantly impacted upon Dylan. His rewriting broadens the song into an anti-war hymn that posits several deep questions about human nature and growth but dangles the answers just out of reach. Peter, Paul and Mary's version is more accessible and less urgent than Dylan's, but it still gets the point across, becoming the first explicitly anti-war song to ever be a hit single. The themes of the song resonated with Mark Feld who spent most of his spare time immersed in poetry and playing guitar, and he quickly fell under Dylan's spell. Dylan was doing everything that Marc was coming to find enchanting – he was a true poet, casting spells with a single guitar and, of course, he had become *famous* from it. Marc's love for Bob Dylan was absolutely genuine, but in him he'd also found a possible road to success that didn't involve hanging around outside Joe Meek's front door. He realised there was room for idiosyncrasy in pop, for unusual voices, for self-mythology, for world-building. Just as Cliff and Elvis had led Marc to an immaculate quiff, and the merest sniff of a mod walking past his front steps had led to more sharp suits and pairs of shoes than any twelve-year-old could possibly need, Dylan inspired the next great evolution of Mark Feld. By the end of 1964 he had acquired both of Dylan's albums, a new acoustic guitar, a harmonica that could be suspended in front of his mouth while he played, a stylish flat cap, all the chords to 'Blowin' In The Wind' and a new name.

Chapter Six

Dave's Red and Blues

While Mark Feld was undergoing a one-man folk revival, David Jones had gotten the blues. The beat bands were still dominating the pop charts, but a scruffier, harder scene was forming beneath them. Many young bands, getting themselves together in the wake of the Beatles, especially in London, were being inspired by the grittier stuff that had come out of Chicago, Detroit and the American south a decade or so back or more – John Lee Hooker, Muddy Waters, Howlin' Wolf, BB King, Huddy 'Lead Belly' Leader, Bo Diddley. It was tough music; working class, usually Black and drawn out of poverty and hardship. Compared to the chirpy tunes hanging around the British top ten, American blues felt somehow more real and more exciting. These teenage blues fans would probably have been listening to trad jazz had they been born ten years earlier, and prog if they'd been born ten years later – they were the kind of kids that took themselves and their music seriously, and therefore craved more serious sounds. Bowie and former Kon-Rad George Underwood, he of the right hook and good bone structure, were delving deep into the imported treasures dug up during David's lunch break visits to Dobell's record shop on Charing Cross Road. Like the Rolling Stones, the Pretty Things and the Yardbirds before them, they devoured the authentic sounds of Black America as only a pair of white, suburban teenagers from South East England could. Bruised from pounding youth club dance floors with the Kon-Rads, David was now desperate to establish himself as a more authentic artist, and it was in the songs of John Lee Hooker, Howlin' Wolf and Muddy Waters, as well as Bob Dylan, that he found the inspiration he was looking for. Jones and Underwood formed a new band with a local drummer, Viv Andrews, this time veering away from teenybopper floor-fillers and concentrating on hard R&B and blues. Initially they called themselves Dave's Red & Blues (which at the very least tells us who was calling the shots now) but soon changed their name to The Hooker Brothers in tribute to John Lee Hooker, the great Delta bluesman, and started hustling for gigs around the area. They only played a handful of shows, one of which was at the Bromley Court Hotel's Bromel Club, a mainstay venue on the orbital London jazz circuit, where they appeared during the interval at a gig by an established act called the Mike Cotton Sound. The eponymous Mike Cotton, an experienced jazz and blues trumpeter and band leader, watched the two skinny white youths filling in time during his break with the tough Black sounds of the Mississippi. His response, reportedly, was to raise an eyebrow and tell them 'You're very brave'.[1]

The duo's next move (their short-lived drummer Andrews vanishes from the story at this time, though he will resurface in our story tangentially as the drummer in the Pretty Things) was to expand their sound and repertoire and start taking their gigging seriously, utilising a tactic David would repeat a few times in the mid-sixties – joining someone else's band and making it his own. His next three projects were all established bands that took a chance on a well-spoken, talented young singer and suddenly found the words 'Davie Jones and the ...' prefixing their name. The first such were The King Bees, a trio from Fulham who had placed an ad for a singer in the back of *Melody Maker* and probably got more than they bargained for.[2] The now-five piece (David talked George Underwood into keeping him company, and the King Bees into taking him on too) got a set together of floor-filling but none-the-less credible hard R&B: Chuck Berry, Muddy Waters, Howlin' Wolf, Elmore James; gaining a small but vocal following playing venues like the Bricklayers Arms in Elephant and Castle. David, fronting a band properly for the first time, was apparently an edgy and nervous frontman to begin with, and such fans as they had at the time remember the real heart-throb of the band being George Underwood, a conventionally handsome, chisel-jawed specimen given a creative edge by the fact that he was now studying at art college. The other three, amicable enough and a little older than their precocious and ambitious new frontman (and his better looking friend), found the decisions being made for them as David and George toughened up their sound and introduced some reworked standards to the set: Muddy's 'Got My Mojo Workin' and 'Hoochie Coochie Man', and an old African American folk song, 'Lil Liza Jane'. Underwood has since said that he and David found the other King Bees' tastes a little safe and prosaic, with guitarist Roger Bluck being 'a bit Chet Atkins', referring to the cosy-as-an-old-cardigan Nashville star; though it should be pointed out in their defence that even before the appearance of Jones and Underwood, the founding members had named their band after a relatively hip blues rarity; Slim Harpo's 'I'm A King Bee', a song cool enough for the Stones to cover on their debut album. They were at least on the right track and the band quickly gelled into a functioning and musically lean unit.

It was the marketing moxie of professional PR man John Jones, David's father, that got things rolling for London's latest teenage bluesmen. The

---

1. Also in their repertoire was a cover of 'House of the Rising Sun', an old folk tune with origins possibly dating back centuries, which Bob Dylan had recorded on his debut album. David had wanted to take Dylan's version and make it heavier and louder. You can imagine how he felt when The Animals had a global hit later that year with the exact same idea.
2. True to both his mod pride and tendency toward myth-making, Bowie would tell the press that they'd met at the hairdressers.

old entrepreneurial spirit that drove him into club management and tour promotion as a younger man was still ticking away, and you do wonder if there was some part of him that was tempted to manage David's career himself. He certainly remained intimately involved with it until his death in 1969, keeping up regular correspondence with his son's managers and staying on top of his financial affairs. It was John that suggested that, like the Beatles, the King Bees needed a wealthy benefactor, a Brian Epstein, to see them as an investment and fund their endeavours. By now the Beatles' origin story was a modern rags-to-riches fable; it's not surprising that mimicking it formed the naive business template for both Bolan and Bowie's early careers. John suggested that David write to John Bloom, the canny businessman ('the Alan Sugar of the day' said George Underwood) almost single-handedly responsible for the expansion of washing machine ownership in late fifties homes. Bloom had made his fortune by striking a deal with a manufacturer in the Netherlands, selling his machines at half the price of his competitors and offering generous credit arrangements (back to the old 'never never' again). Within a few years he was a millionaire. He was also an expert at marketing his personal brand, inserting himself into his own adverts with a strapline declaring him to be, at twenty eight, 'Britain's youngest self-made industrialist'. By 1964 he was a household name, rubbing shoulders with the great and good of society and having tea with the Queen. The ideal person, therefore, to take a chance on this 'pop music' boom.[3]

John helped his son draft a letter to Bloom, the spirit of which – according to George Underwood, who was somewhat embarrassed by the whole affair – was 'Brian Epstein has the Beatles, you can have us'. 'If you could sell my group the way you sell washing machines', the letter went, 'you'll be onto a winner', before promising Bloom that he would certainly 'make another million' for himself. Bloom, as it turns out, had absolutely no interest in the music industry but still admired the sheer chutzpah of the request (he reportedly called David a 'cheeky sod'). He was someone who believed in pulling yourself up by your bootstraps, in asking for what you want and seizing opportunities. One of his favourite phrases was 'it's no sin to make a profit', a term he'd stolen from the judge at a trial years before, when one of his competitors attempted to sue him for deliberately undercutting their business in order to steal lucrative government contracts. He got a kick out of David's letter and, having little knowledge of the pop market himself, passed it on to his friend, Leslie Conn, a show business type who, like Bloom, was a Hackney-born hustler from Jewish stock. Conn promptly brought the boys in for an audition at his London flat – no doubt to the delight of his neighbours – and was impressed enough to book the King Bees for a try-out show at no less prestigious an occasion than John Bloom's

3. Unfortunately, 1964 was something of a watershed year for Bloom as his rivals collectively slashed their own prices, ending his dominance in the marketplace and collapsing his business. David and John got to him before this, though.

wedding anniversary party at the Jack of Clubs in Soho. In front of luminaries ranging from Vera Lynn to Roger Moore to Lionel Blair to Adam Faith to Shirley Bassey, the band managed to get through two loud, filthy-sounding Muddy Waters tunes, 'Got My Mojo Workin' and '(I'm Your) Hoochie Coochie Man', before Bloom, sensing his middle-aged and well-to-do guests were either baffled or incensed by this unseemly noise, politely booted them off stage – leaving David in tears. The band assumed that they'd blown their chance, and in front of a prestigious audience at that. Bloom's guests, meanwhile, were placated by Vera Lynn singing 'White Cliffs of Dover'.

The gig was almost, but crucially not quite, a disaster. Although they had enraged their host, they had impressed at least one person that night: Les Conn possessed more imagination than the King Bees had given him credit for, and saw potential in their singer, at least. With the permission of the protective Mr and Mrs Jones, he signed David up to a five-year management contract, while also taking on the rest of the King Bees as a separate unit.

Like John Bloom, Les Conn was a hustler; a would-be impresario who had been all round the Tin Pan Alley block and then back again, trying his hand at various backstage music biz gigs. Pop music was still a new phenomenon, not even a decade into its cultural life, and the conventional entertainment industry was still figuring out where to fit it in. It was a landscape that a fast talking grifter with an air of confidence would find easy to exploit.[4] Conn talked a good game, and despite a lack of star-making success thus far, his little black book of contacts was solid. He worked as a plugger for Dick James, a former-crooner[5] and previously-small-time music publisher who had gotten incredibly lucky in 1962 when George Martin, a producer he'd worked with in his performer days, put him in touch with the manager of a certain young Liverpool band that he had just signed. James thus became majority owner of Northern Songs, a company formed exclusively to publish the works of John Lennon and Paul McCartney. Within a few years he was a millionaire.[6] Part of Conn's brief was to bring in the next big thing. It's indicative of how small a pond London's pop industry still was in 1964 when you consider that David's first major shot at a record deal, with the Kon-Rads, came via someone with a direct link to the Rolling Stones, while his second, with the King Bees, came via an associate of The Beatles.

---

4. I always imagine Les Conn as the Laurence Harvey character in the fifties pop movie *Expresso Bongo*, exploiting Cliff Richard for all he was worth.
5. Most famously he sang the theme to the classic adventure series *Robin Hood*, a show David would base some of his mid-60s looks on.
6. He sold his share of the Lennon/McCartney catalogue in 1969, much to the annoyance of the Beatles who'd have rather liked to buy it from him themselves. By that point he'd already acquired the rights to the work of a couple of new songwriters – Elton John and Bernie Taupin. He died in 1986; a very wealthy man indeed.

Conn, with the support of Dick James and – amazingly, considering his reaction at the party – £400 of John Bloom's money, moved quickly, calling in a favour with Decca records who agreed to a one-single deal. David's letter to John Bloom had been posted in March, the disastrous performance at Bloom's anniversary do had taken place in April, and it was less than a month later that the King Bees found themselves in a Decca recording studio cutting their debut. The record was in the shops by 5 June.

The single was 'Liza Jane', an almost unrecognisable reworking of the African-American spiritual 'Lil' Liza Jane', the origins of which could be traced back to the cotton fields of Louisiana and the days of slavery. Everyone from Fats Domino to Bing Crosby had taken it on; Nina Simone's 1960 version is probably the most definitive, though it was Huey Smith's rollicking R&B take that had inspired David and George. None of these bear much of a resemblance to the likeable racket knocked out by the King Bees that spring day in Decca's West Hampstead studios. Despite the Jones/Underwood commitment to authentic blues, the band's arrangement of the song sounds like an exact midpoint between the early Beatles and early Stones. The lead vocal has virtually no trace of the David Bowie of just a few years later, but sounds a great deal like both John Lennon *and* Mick Jagger in places; (which, when you think about, it is no mean trick: the two voices are not especially alike) the throaty yell of the opening line is Lennon at his most belting, while the way David sings 'liiiiiitle Liza Ja-ayne' so perfectly replicates Jagger's Mississippi-via Moorgate delivery it would fool his own mother.[7]

While the loose swagger gives a certain rattling Rolling Stone charm to the a-side, the b-side, a cover of Paul Revere and the Raiders recent single[8] 'Louie Louie, Go Home' (recorded on Dick James' orders) was pure Beatles, with David sounding for all the world like John Lennon singing 'Twist and Shout'. 'Louie' was originally slated for the a-side, but Les Conn, who introduced himself with 'Conn by name, con by nature' with good reason, had other ideas; 'Louie' had officially recognised writers and publishers (by staggering coincidence the record was published by the Dick James organisation) that would need paying, whereas 'Liza' was a completely reworked version of a trad number. Realising that further lining the pockets of Paul Revere with radio royalties benefited no-one useful, Conn chose to flip the release and make 'Liza Jane' the focus track. For good measure he gave himself the sole writing credit and listed himself as the song's 'music director and producer'[9], apparently as part of his deal with

---

7. David was an excellent mimic in any case, but his Mick Jagger impression was absolutely uncanny. There's a brilliant example available on YouTube taken from a late-90s interview with Michael Parkinson.

8. *Very* recent – it had only come out in March. Pop moved quickly in those days.

9. The producer on the day was actually the dapper Glyn Johns, who would go on to work with The Beatles on *Let It Be*.

Bowie. Conn maintained until his death that he'd arranged the song based on a jam the band was toying with, while George Underwood claims that he and David had worked the arrangement out in his mum's kitchen.

Leslie Conn is the early 60s British pop industry in microcosm; flying by the seat of his pants, throwing stuff at the wall to see what stuck, taking chances where he could and talking loudly and quickly to cover the fact he didn't really know what he was doing. Grabbing the sole writing credit to David Bowie's first single was a perfect example of his opportunism: Not only did it mean he'd get the royalty, it also ensured that Dick James was deprived of the contractual right to publish any future Jones/Bowie compositions that he would have received had the credit been given to the band. Not that it did Conn much good – the single completely flopped and had a fairly poor history of re-releases, probably because it sounded nothing like anything else Bowie sang on. The song was re-recorded in the early 2000s for *Toy*, an album in which David revisited his earliest material, which might have netted Conn a few bob had Bowie not scrapped the project before release.[10] The original recording was finally included on a 2014 Bowie compilation, *Nothing Has Changed*. Alas, Conn had died in 2009; just five years before his nifty bit of accreditation back in 1964 might finally have borne fruit. He's quoted in his obituary in the *Independent* as saying he was 'the only guy in the music business to have started at the top and worked his way to the bottom'.[11]

The record was released with a moderate splash of publicity. A press release 'from the office of Dick James' was issued, telling a more-or-less accurate account of the John Bloom party debacle, a much air-brushed version of David's life thus far, and a completely fabricated history of the band ('Davie met up with his four-member backing group the King-Bees when he visited his local barber shop … between clips he got chatting to the four lads, also there to be sheared, about their musical interests, and before you could say "Short back and sides", they decided to join forces.') The press release doesn't mention anyone else in the band by name, but goes into giddy details about 'Davie Jones', who is described as 'a handsome six footer with a warm and engaging personality' and lists his favourite singers as Bob Dylan, Little Richard and John Lee Hooker – these were canny choices: a fashionable current star, a beloved rock 'n' roll idol and an authentic Delta bluesman. None of the three are especially represented on the King Bees' debut single, but they were exactly the right names to drop. The document goes on to tell us that among David's interests are American Football, baseball and 'collecting boots', while his dislikes, rather curiously,

---

10. *Toy* finally saw the light of day in 2021, though the sultry new version of 'Liza Jane', which sounds far more like the Rolling Stones of the 90s than the 60s, wasn't included.

11. The original pressing of 'Liza Jane' is now, naturally, a much sought after collectors piece that can fetch thousands. Its scarcity was dramatically increased when boxes and boxes of unsold copies stored in Conn's garage were thrown out by his mum when he moved abroad in 1966.

include 'Adam's apples'[12]. The press release was issued with some new shots featuring David and George in matching calf-length suede boots, with David sporting a brown leather waistcoat and a voluminous bouffant hairstyle; a strange attempt to meld the shaggy scruff of the Stones' Mick N' Keef with the elegant styles of the mods. It's probably the worst haircut he would have in his entire career. It's clear who Conn considered the focus of the project – Davie Jones is a smiling buccaneer and George Underwood a chiselled heart-throb in blue jeans. The rest of the band look like they've walked out of Mark Feld's Littlewood's catalogue.

Les Conn and Dick James' campaign resulted in a few pieces of low-key press: a middling review in *New Musical Express*, an appearance on BBC 1's *Juke Box Jury* (the song was declared a 'miss' rather than a 'hit', before David was asked to awkwardly shake the judges' hands), and some local news pieces (including one in the *London Evening News*, the result of David's father calling in a favour with one of his contacts – despite admitting that he thought his son sounded awful). The highlight of the whole campaign was a live performance on the pop show, *Ready, Steady, Go!*, something which must have been particularly satisfying for David after his failure to get on the show's spin-off talent contest, *Ready, Steady, Win!*, with the Kon-Rads just months earlier. Also filming in the same studios that day were The Crickets and, of all people, legendary blues hero John Lee Hooker, the very person who had inspired Jones/Underwood's first attempt at hard R&B and blues with The Hooker Brothers. David called his bandmates down to the studio floor to study Hooker's fingerboard technique.

'Liza Jane', sadly, would vanish without a trace. The single failed to inspire TV viewers or radio DJs and got very little support from Decca, who had banished it to their lightweight Vocalion Pop imprint and only agreed to its release in order to placate James and shut Les Conn up. Few of the 3,500 copies sold, and the song failed to dent the weekly music paper's charts. Bowie's first release tends to get short shrift from biographers and fans, probably because out of all David's early singles it's the one that sounds the least like 'David Bowie'. Looking at it now though, 'Liza Jane' isn't actually a *bad* record; it's breezy and likeable, it goes along at a lick, it sounds hurriedly recorded but it's catchy enough and it's built around a solid, garagey blues riff. The real problem was that it sounded like every other single recorded by a young beat band that year. Without any real marketing oomph it had no way of standing out from the crowd. Had Decca put the might of their record plugging, advertising and PR teams behind it, it could have been a modest hit. Still, even with all the good will and major label cash in the world, the slight 'Liza Jane' was never going to set the pop landscape alight by sticking so rigidly to the '64 beat group playbook. In a way it had a

---

12. If this was a way of underlining his exclusive heterosexuality then the old saying 'the lady doth protest too much' definitely springs to mind.

similar problem to Mark Feld's 'All At Once', recorded just a few months later. Marc was crooning the soppy sound of 1960, while David was knocking out something much more up to date but completely generic, both artists allowing their managers to steer them into tried, tested and over-saturated directions, rather than towards risk or originality. In David's view, the Kon-Rads had failed because they played it too safe. Now the King Bees had done the same thing.

It was time to reflect and take stock. David was now a professional pop singer, but that was out of necessity rather than as a result of his success – his employers' patience with an office junior who turned up with dark rings around his eyes from gigging into the early hours of the morning had finally been stretched to snapping point and he'd been given the boot.[13] David's mother, Peggy, was livid, but John stood by his son's ambitions and offered to help him out financially. Being a musician was now Davie Jones' full time career, and he took it very seriously – however, in his opinion, the rest of the King Bees – including George – did not. That month he told his four band mates that he was leaving, having already found a new group to front.[14] David was not resting on his laurels – he never would, really – and he had the arrogance and breathless enthusiasm of youth added to the whirling momentum of 60s London on his side. Between January and July of 1964 he had left the Kon-Rads, joined the King Bees, scored a manager, released a single, appeared on television, split up the King Bees and found a new band to join – the Manish Boys.

As luck would have it, just before David told his manager that he was considering departing the King Bees' hive[15], Conn had taken on a new group who were in need of a singer. British R&B's most prolific hermit crab was ready to inhabit a new shell. The Maidstone based Manish Boys, some of whom really *did* meet in a barber's shop, put out just one single with David; a cover of Bobby Bland's 'I Pity The Fool', released on Parlophone records. It was a serious-sounding, atmospheric, mid-tempo blues record with some enticing horns and great licks from Parlophone's go-to session player, one Jimmy Page (using one of the first fuzz pedals available in Britain). More interesting for a

---

13. As anyone who has tried to keep a day job while attempting to make it as a performer will tell you, it's not so much the gigs that get you as the travelling home afterwards. Playing a gig at 9pm in Reading wouldn't be a problem if it didn't mean getting to bed at 3am in Bromley.
14. Shortly before David's departure Les Conn had the band audition for Mickie Most, one of the top producers of the day. He was unimpressed with Bowie, but agreed to sign George Underwood, who was rechristened Calvin James. Most brokered a deal with Columbia that resulted in a few singles (Les Conn managed to snag a writing credit on the b-side of the first, naturally),with Conn co-managing his career with former 2 I's doorman and future Led Zep manager Peter Jenner. Alas, neither single did any business. Bowie was livid that his friend had apparently jumped over him for a record deal and the whole affair put a bigger dent in their friendship than Underwood's fist had back at school. The pair were estranged for a few years. During that time George endured a period of poor mental health and spent some time in psychiatric care with David's brother, Terry. He gave up music as a full-time pursuit and eventually established a career for himself as an artist. It's not the last we will hear of him.
15. Which really must have stung.

Bowie scholar was the b-side, 'Take My Tip'; the first David Jones original to make it out into the wider world, a sort of finger-snapping bluesy swing draped around a walking bassline. It's not a bad little number either, despite a title only a sniggering seventeen-year-old would find funny. It couldn't be more of its time, but crucially it's at least a version of '64-vintage R&B that doesn't sound hacked together from spare parts found in the bins behind the Pretty Things' rehearsal space. The vocal style on both songs is also, for those of us listening from the future, recognisably that of 'David Bowie'.

The other career milestone achieved during David's time as a Manish Boy was his first real tour – Conn managed to get the group added to the final leg of a package tour featuring Gerry and the Pacemakers, Gene Pitney, Marianne Faithful and the Kinks. Also on the bill were the Mike Cotton Sound, the band that gave David and George a spot during the interval of their show in Bromley back in January – again underlining how far and how fast David's career had developed. Touring was hard work, unglamorous and involved being crammed into a smelly coach with a dozen or so other musicians and, apparently, being forced to wait hand and foot on Gene Pitney. The band would take the stage as the audience were still filing in, and made little to no impact on most nights. Still, as a 'paying their dues' experience it was perfect. Sitting next to Ray Davies and Gerry Marsden as they rumbled through the English countryside, it must have felt to David and his bandmates like they were finally on their way, and not just to the ABC Theatre in County Durham.

This was all formative stuff that would serve David well as he developed his craft and learned about his business, but it was still more of a rock 'n' roll apprenticeship than any kind of real career. David got some good contacts from this period (Ray Davies, Marianne Faithful, producer Shel Talmy, who'd recorded 'I Pity The Fool', venues like the Marquee and the Eel Pie Island Jazz Club), played some decent supports (the Gene Pitney/Pacemakers/Kinks tour, Manfred Mann, The Moody Blues, James Brown[16]) and generally cemented himself as a boy-about-town on London's beat circuit. 'I Pity The Fool' did better than 'Liza Jane', though not by much, and by the spring of 1965 David again felt like he had outgrown his surroundings and was ready to skuttle to his next shell; disillusioned by a lack of gigs, furious that the single had been released, against his wishes, under the name 'The Manish Boys', not 'Davie Jones and the Manish Boys', and bored to tears with having to spend so much time in Maidstone where the rest of the band were based. It was time to go. All in, the Manish Boys would barely figure in our story – if it wasn't for The Society For The Prevention of Cruelty To Long Haired Men.

---

16. Well, sort of. The band's unreliable Bedford van broke down on the way to the gig, and they arrived just in time to see Brown take the stage. The storming show was apparently worth the trouble.

In many ways the Britain of the early sixties wasn't that different to the one we know today; people did their best to get by, they went to work and school, they watched the telly at night, they had sex with their partners and argued with their neighbours, they got buses and went to the cinema and had a few drinks at the weekend. It was, for the most part, a world we would recognise. Until you get to the subject of men's hair. When the Beatles first emerged they were revolutionary not just for their sound and humour but also, in a way that seems utterly alien now, for their haircuts. Each had a fluffy, shaggy mop-top; at its shortest down to their ears, at its longest brushing their collars, fringes ending just above their eyebrows and swooping slightly to the side as if caught in a breeze. It was clean and relatively tidy, and it flew about appealingly when they shook their heads and went 'wooooooo!'. In an off-hand gag in the first Beatles movie, *A Hard Day's Night*, which has become strangely accepted as serious by some sources, George Harrison named this haircut 'Arthur'.

Arthur had continental roots – Lennon and McCartney had nicked the style from the hipster art students, Klaus Voorman and Jürgen Vollmer, they met in their Hamburg days. During their time in Germany, they allowed Voorman's girlfriend, Astrid Kirchherr, to brush the Brylcreem out of their teddy boy quiffs and re-form their locks into what was then known as the 'French style', the shaggy cut later made famous as the 'Beatle hair'; though they were too shy to carry the style back home. A little while later, Lennon and McCartney met up with Vollmer in Paris and asked him to recreate the style for them, which he duly did, there and then in his apartment. This time they were feeling more daring, and the new hairdo stayed. When they returned to Liverpool their bandmates followed their lead[17]. People went potty. By today's standards the Beatle-cut is a fairly unremarkable, every-day do, worn by people of any gender. In the early sixties it was somewhere between utterly comical and completely anarchic. To some it made them look untidy and unprofessional, for others it was tantamount to cross dressing. It became part of their gimmick, like the suits and the shaking heads and the music hall-style wisecracks, they folded it in and used it until it became normalised and ubiquitous. A 1963 appearance on the *Morecambe and Wise* show saw the group playing up to the popular comedy duo's schtick: 'It's the Kaye Sisters!'[18] says Eric Morcombe. 'No, it's The Beatles!' Ernie corrects. Paul chips in with 'So you're the one with the little fat hairy legs', setting up George to land the punchline: 'Well we're the ones with the big fat hairy heads'.[19] November of that year saw the first documented case of a

---

17. At least Harrison did; current drummer Pete Best kept his teddy boy do. It probably didn't have a bearing on his firing, at George Martin's suggestion, in 1962; but it's worth noting that when Ringo joined he wasted little time in making an appointment with Arthur.

18. A vocal trio who achieved fame as cabaret stars in the 50s, who sported identical haircuts.

19. It's a genuinely funny bit actually, and well worth seeking out. The band also do some fantastic live cuts – 'I Want To Hold Your Hand' is great.

headmaster sending a pupil home to get his hair cut after he came in sporting a Beatle barnet. The most common question asked of the band when they went to the States in 1964 was 'When did you last have a hair cut?' ('Yesterday' replies Lennon.)

Eventually the public came to accept Beatle hair as part of their cheeky charm. Their immaculate songcraft and scampy Scouser personas were enough to win over parents and teachers and MPs, and soon shaggy bowlie styles were everywhere. The rate at which something that initially seemed unacceptable to normal values achieved cosy ubiquity was genuinely astonishing. By the end of 1963 the *Daily Mirror* was reporting 'The Beatles are wacky. They wear their hair like a mop — but it's WASHED, it's super clean. So is their fresh young act.'[20] On the one hand it was *just hair*, but on the other it's representative of something much wider – the boundaries of acceptability. The Moptops had proven that pop musicians could have a huge impact away from music. By the end of 1963 you could buy novelty Beatle wigs.

Just when these follicle forms had started to settle into a new normal and things had calmed down, the Rolling Stones turned up. Mick Jagger's hair trickled down past his collar at the back, Keith Richards' was even longer, and Brian Jones' fringe draped down past his eyes ('With this hairy curtain' quipped the *New York Times*, 'it is fortunate for them that reading music is not an essential requirement for a pop group ... you almost expect them to have white canes alongside their guitars'). In 1964 the *Mirror* reported that one headmaster in Coventry had sent every kid with a 'Mick Jagger' haircut home and told them not to come back until they had 'cut their hair properly – like The Beatles'. Then came The Pretty Things, Bromley's other R&B obsessives (featuring one former Rolling Stone and David and George's Hooker Brothers drummer) who overtly made long hair into a statement. The group's Phil May proudly claimed the longest hair in rock 'n' roll. Headmasters upped their game – there were reports of one bringing in an army barber to buzzcut the boys, while others made any long-haired lad sit with the girls.

People were genuinely appalled and not a little intimidated by this sudden craze for untidy hair. The Stones themselves were absolutely demonised and regularly thrown out of fancier clubs and lounges or refused entry to various establishments due to their appearance. Bass player Bill Wyman reports being accosted on a train home from a gig by a much straighter-looking type telling him that 'Yobs like you shouldn't be allowed out in public'. 'I'm being paid to look like this', Wyman snapped back. 'What's your excuse?'[21] The Stones and the Pretties were both constantly accused in the press of having 'dirty'

---

20. The piece goes on to say they 'don't need to make jokes about homos', which proves at the very least that the writer spent very little time in private with the foursome.

21. This comes from Wyman's own autobiography, *Stone Alone*, so it's entirely possible that this witty retort should be taken with a pinch of salt.

hair, something Brian Jones in particular was livid about, since he spent so much time cleaning and brushing his genuinely beautiful blond mane that his bandmates had given him the nickname 'Shampoo'. Editorials in the classier newspapers went into a sort of frothing moral panic; though not as panicked as the barbers trade, which reported huge losses as the amount of men letting their short-back-and-sides grow out began to accumulate. The Rolling Stones, now becoming huge stars, copped much of the blame for this. 'The Rolling Stones are the worst for it', said a representative of the National Federation of Hairdressers (again reported in the *Mirror* which seemed to have a thing for rock star hair stories), 'one of them looks like he's got a feather duster on his head'[22]. The Stones responded by putting an advert in the final *NME* of the year wishing 'Happy Christmas to starving hairdressers and their families'[23].

Within three years, longer hair on younger men would become fairly common, though not universally accepted, among the general population and practically a requirement for rock musicians; hippy boys with locks flowing down their shoulders would come to be a fixture of the scene, but back in 1964 it was still a statement of utter non-conformism. It was seen as a deliberate two fingers stuck up to convention, a stake in the ground that said 'I reject you'. Up until that point, the only young men to have longer hair were those that had avoided their national service[24], or a small band of beatniks and arty jazz types. It was a style connected either with effeminacy or uselessness: sissies or layabouts. A shift, however, was probably inevitable; the first pop generation of the sixties was also the first in twenty years that didn't have to join the army, *and* the first to have much more access to further education; universities, polytechnics and art schools, with their microcultures and social bubbles. These attitudes were still alien to the average man on the street though, especially older people and those far away from London's simmering cultural cauldron. Those young men that grew out their hair often found themselves either feared or ridiculed. The fact that it was a style now associated with sexy, successful rock stars rather than lazy dropouts, and thuggish rebellion rather than simpering campiness was causing something of an identity crisis in British society as well as baffling the media.

David was no stranger to these issues. As a dandified mod with both a preoccupation with the theatrical and his own blown-out bouffant, he was more than familiar with having jibes and cheap shots directed at his appearance, although as he was image conscious to the point of obsessiveness, he felt looking fabulous was worth the risk. But where others saw offence or inconvenience, David and Les Conn saw an opening. Towards the end of 1964, John Jones

---

22. This could be any of them, but it's probably Brian.
23. Since the drop in trade resulting from so many men having their hair cut less often genuinely *was* hitting barbers hard, it's unlikely that anyone in the trade reading this would have seen the funny side. It was also likely to earn Mick Jagger a clip round the ear – his mum was a hairdresser.
24. In the US long hair on men was associated with draft dodgers and pacifists.

called his friend at the *Evening News*, Leslie Thomas, an old Barnardo's boy who was always willing to do the organisation a favour. Thomas ran a piece entitled 'For Those Beyond The Fringe', about one David Jones of Bromley who had formed an organisation, The International League For The Preservation of Animal Filament, which provided support and representation for men with long hair. 'It's time we united and stood up for our curls', David told Thomas, who reported the piece with his tongue very firmly in his cheek. 'Everybody makes jokes about you on the bus, and if you go past navvies digging in the road it's murder!'

Of course, the preposterously named 'League For The Preservation of Animal Filament' (a phrase that tries so hard to be clever it ends up being essentially meaningless, something smart teenagers are especially prone to) didn't actually exist. The whole thing was just an excuse to get David's name in the paper and spark a little interest in his group by piggybacking on a subject that had weirdly fascinated the media.[25] The tactic was more successful than anyone could have expected: a few weeks later David, who had by now wisely changed the name of his fictional activist group to the more self-explanatory 'The Society for the Prevention of Cruelty to Long-Haired Men', a handful of Manish Boys and handsome old George Underwood found themselves engaging in some light debate on BBC Two's *Tonight* programme, a newsy magazine show hosted by the genial Cliff Michelmore. This wasn't David's first TV appearance, he'd already appeared briefly on Juke Box Jury to awkwardly thank the judges for saying they thought his record was a miss[26], and performed with the King Bees on *Ready, Steady, Go!*. This was different though. Here, the young Bowie is in his element – he's likeable, charming, clearly clever, funny and looks like someone who knows more than everyone around him. The other boys in the group do some talking, but it's David that pulls the attention, David that steals the show; arguing what is essentially a completely fictitious activist position with surprising elegance. He comes out of it very well. Years later the *NME* journalist Nick Kent would remember seeing the programme as a thirteen-year-old pop fan. 'You could tell it was a bit of a put-on,' he told Dylan Jones, 'but I remember thinking, now, this fellow we'll probably be seeing again.'

As Conn started to gear up the publicity machine for the release of 'I Pity The Fool' a few months later, the easy wins of the long-hair coverage presented too juicy an opportunity to ignore. The band were booked to perform on BBC Two's pop show *Gadzooks! It's All Happening* and Conn cooked up a publicity scheme with producer Barry Langford, announcing in the press that the BBC wouldn't

---

25. Oddly, Phil Lancaster, the drummer in David's next band, The Lower Third, believes his friend was absolutely sincere in this operation. 'He was deadly serious when he set it up', he says in his memoir *At The Birth of Bowie*, 'earnestly wanting to highlight the plights that he, and other guys with lengthy tresses, faced.'

26. In fairness, they were absolutely right about this.

allow the group to perform unless David and co cut their hair. The band were going to make a stand and refuse to sacrifice their image for the establishment. Conn even planned a protest around Television Centre with 'Be Fair to Long Hair' placards. It worked like a charm. The press, who knew a bit of easy outrage when they saw it, took the bait. The first piece about the group 'banned by the BBC' for their hirsute heads, ran in the *Daily Mail*, then as now a barometer for reactionary Britain. David happily hammed it up for the paper – 'I wouldn't have my hair cut for the Prime Minister, let alone the BBC'. Similar pieces ran in the *Daily Telegraph* and *London Evening Standard*. The *Mirror*, always happy to prompt some outrage at the expense of the apparently unkempt, followed a few days later, reporting that the BBC had backed down on the condition that the band would donate their fee should any complaints be made by viewers. The paper made its stance on the issue very clear – long hair on men was 'nauseating … evidence of a sickness in the air'. Ahead of the performance on 8 March the *Evening News and Star* sent a photographer to a hair salon where David was getting a set and blow-dry ahead of the performance.[27]

As press campaigns go, it was a doozy. The Rolling Stones had already laid the groundwork for hair-based press outrage the previous year, and Conn knew the papers would see a 'BBC ban' as an easy win. No-one seemed to question it either, accepting that a long hair ban was a totally natural move for a pop show, despite it having already featured Dave Dee, Dozy, Beaky, Mick & Tich, the Animals and Long John Boudry that year – all of whom had fairly shaggy cuts. Perhaps they thought 'enough is enough'? The British Safety Council even wrote to Langford to commend him on his stance, saying that they were 'concerned with the effects of accidents caused by unduly long and effeminate hair styles'. The stunt got David more press than he would receive for many years, and was so powerfully effective that the idea of the Manish Boys being 'banned for their long hair', and David being a 'long hair activist' are still occasionally reported as fact in articles and biographies sixty years later.

The problem was, of course, that as effective as the fabricated hair scandal was at gaining column inches, it was a dismal failure at selling records. The *Mirror*, *Daily Mail* and *Evening News* are all very well, but absent from the publicity list are *New Musical Express*, *Melody Maker*, *Record Mirror* or any other pop paper. The single got some short notices in the music press, but made absolutely no real impact. It was a fine enough blues number, but no-one was getting excited. When 'I Pity The Fool' finally hit the shops on 5 March 1965 it was roundly ignored. Gigs were drying up, the press weren't especially interested, a proposed season at Hamburg's Star Club, where the Beatles had done their apprenticeship, fell through and the band's van finally broke down beyond

---

27. Oddly the fictional excuse Langford gave for insisting on a cut was that, rather than offensive, long-hair was simply outdated, telling reporters 'kids today just simply don't want this long haired business any more'.

repair, limiting their movements. The Manish Boys, without really discussing it, began to wind down.

David was already eyeing his next move, preparing to audition for a mod outfit called The Lower Third, getting himself into the audience and in front of the cameras on pop shows like *Ready, Steady, Go!* and the *Five O'Clock Club*, and generally hanging around in Soho, becoming a face on the scene, nursing a coffee for hours in the 2Is or Denmark Street's La Gioconda cafe. He was, however, broke. Sacked from his job, with little royalties and no gigs, things were beginning to feel stretched, although Les Conn did his best for his client. Having recently parted ways with Dick James, who saw no future in Davie Jones, Conn was setting up on his own and had acquired office space at 23 Denmark Street. He threw his client a few bob to paint the new premises with the help of another struggling young act that Conn had been helping out and was considering taking on, and the two got on with the job over a couple of days, arguing about clothes and music and comparing career notes. That was the day that David Jones met Mark Feld.

Chapter Seven

Toby Or Not Toby

arc's route to holding a paintbrush in Les Conn's office meandered somewhat through the back end of 1964 and into 65, and his career in the months since recording 'All At Once' with his dashing gentleman manager had nowhere close to the same velocity as David's. While David was appearing on *Ready, Steady, Go!* and inventing fictional follicle activism, Marc was busking Bob Dylan songs and easy-to-learn three-chord tricks on the Charing Cross Road and practicing his rudimentary harmonica skills. He was still on the scene though, still a smart face. His occasional TV extra work brought him into the orbit of other young actors, including one, who thanks to his role on a kids show called *The Five O'Clock Club*, had one foot at least tangentially in the music biz.

The Five O'Clock Club was a tea-time music and entertainment show broadcast by ATV, one of the franchises that comprised the still newish ITV channel, with a remit pitched younger than the station's flagship pop show, *Ready, Steady Go!*, featuring comedy puppets and skits alongside the pop performances ('Like *Blue Peter* but much racier', as one of its hosts describes it). Youth TV, of course, often comes with a youth presenter. Plugging the gap between the puppets on the one hand, and the adult hosts like Muriel Young on the other was fifteen-year-old Allan Warren, a jobbing actor who had been in the game for a few years after graduating from the Drury Lane theatre's stage school. Warren's life was *fun*. In those days, before the entertainment industry was paying any attention to child labour laws, and when social services didn't see fifteen year olds as their problem, Allan Warren was basically doing whatever he liked. '*The Five O'Clock Club* only took up a day per week to do two shows' he says, 'so I was filling the time up running around London doing bit parts for different TV series for the same studio, doing a cough and a spit here and there, "He's gone up that way guvnor", and that would pay me thirty quid. Because I was on tap I could easily get the part. I was earning a ridiculous amount of money, the national average wage in those days was between nine and sixteen guineas[1] and I was making a hundred guineas.' Embracing the entrepreneurial spirit of the time and encouraged by his mother, the cultured and well spoken Warren rented his own place, a rather plush flat at 81 Lexham Gardens in Kensington, with

---

1. The national weekly average was actually something like nineteen guineas, a guinea being an old term for one pound and one shilling.

wall-to-wall carpets and full central heating – mod cons that were unknown in much of the city. The young actor took full advantage of his new wealth; as well as his rather fine pad, he would book cabs to take him into town and leave them waiting for him outside, and pay a hairdresser to pop round and give him a trim while he was still in bed. Like any fifteen year old living on their own for the first time would, he started throwing parties and inevitably the waifs and strays of the scene drifted in for a night's drinking, hung around afterwards and simply didn't leave. 'When you're young you don't realise that they all move in', he says. 'They come in for dinner and three weeks later they're still sitting there. They'd never heard of rent, and I'd never heard that you were supposed to charge them. So any spare rooms they took over, and if that wasn't good enough, the living room floor was.' Such a one was Mark Feld, still just sixteen years old, though looking younger, cherubic and charming. One day he turned up at Lexham Gardens for a party, with only a carrier bag and a guitar, and having vacated both his business and living arrangements with Geoffrey Delaroy-Hall, didn't leave for several months.[2]

Marc was given his own room, but that was more a place to play the guitar while sitting cross legged in front of the fireplace. He mostly slept in his host's bed. If Marc's unconfirmed sexual relationship with the forty-something Delaroy-Hall feels a little uncomfortable to modern sensibilities, his entanglements with Allan Warren were far more wholesome. The two boys didn't exactly begin a relationship so much as they enjoyed a tactile and playful friendship, both young enough to be exploring their sexuality together. It was sex, yes, but there was an innocence to it as well. Whatever behaviour the pair indulged in, be it debauched on the one hand, or businesslike on the other, that innocence ran through their entire relationship. They were boys playing together as much as they were anything else. The cultured, decidedly camp Warren and the naive, dapper and also rather camp Mark Feld were well matched. Both were oddballs in their own way; Marc was working class but aspirational, self-assured to the point of arrogant but somehow extremely likeable with it and image conscious to the point of absurd, with an innocent quality that drew people to him. Warren, meanwhile, was a boy out of time who couldn't stand rock 'n' roll, more interested in the music of the 30s than the 60s, fond of Noel Coward, Ivor Novello and Jack Buchanan. He was both old beyond his years, and also boyish and playful. Neither boy had any real grasp of how the adult world worked, and had fortunately found themselves in a situation whereby they could put off finding out.

---

2. Oddly, though a few Bolan biographies claim that Marc did extra work on the *Five O'Clock Club*, Warren doesn't remember meeting him on the show; 'He was just one of the people who drifted into my life for the parties' he says. 'He was literally just someone who came and squatted, he had no role in the show at all.'

Warren had landed on his feet in several ways, not least in his mother's attitude to his new playmate. In an era where homosexuality was still vilified and illegal, Mrs Warren really didn't give a hoot. Allan is fond of telling the story of how his mother, staying at Lexham Gardens one day, found him and Marc in bed together. Her attitude, standing there in her fluffy slippers and her hair in curlers, was 'Two teas this morning is it?'. 'I said "Listen you, I have women around but occasionally I like boys."' he says. 'She looked at me and said, "Well I've had eleven kids, one of them's got to be." And that was the whole sexual lesson between mother and son – it was my business and get on with it.' Whether that was an example of a wider loosening of attitudes, or merely one posh mother's briskly realistic view is up for debate.

It could hardly escape Warren's notice that his new lodger had a passion for music. 'He never stopped playing this blasted guitar,' he says, 'his acoustic guitar, and to me he looked like a baby-faced Cliff Richard crossed with Tweetie Pie, with his big, round face and bow lips. He did a Cliff Richard impersonation when he spoke.' Since Warren worked on a pop show, and his new housemate wanted to be a pop *star*, the pair decided they would try to launch Marc's career by getting him on the *Five O'Clock Club*, and that Allan would be his manager. To an extent this was more grown-up role-play from the two teenagers. The apartment came with a huge desk, which Warren equipped with several telephones – only one of which actually worked – because he felt it was the sort of thing a pop manager would have. To his credit though, the fifteen-year-old took his new role seriously enough to have a contract drawn up, guaranteeing him a generous 25% of any income, and arranged for a demo recording session and professional photoshoot.

Warren appears to have paid for two recording sessions, one in late 64 at Regent Sounds studio on Denmark Street, during which Marc possibly laid down a cover of Dylan's 'Blowin In The Wind' (a song he had been torturing Allan with for weeks), and perhaps also a Bolan original, 'The Perfumed Garden of Gulliver Smith', which would make the latter the first of Marc's own songs to be committed to tape. However, as records are scant and no tape appears to have survived there's very little we can say for sure about the session. A second set of recordings were made in early 1965 during a short session at Maximum Sound studios, resulting in an acetate which Warren could use to try to get Marc a deal. 'Blowin' In The Wind' was again attempted, as was an old Dion b-side, 'The Road I'm On (Gloria)'[3], the two displaying the twin prongs of Marc's taste in music: Bob Dylan and classic rock 'n' roll. A tape of the recording survives thanks to studio engineer Vic Keary, and serves as evidence of the extremely raw early Bolan. While the previous year's 'All At Once' had been a carefully

---

3. Engineer Vic Keary also believes a version of 'The Perfume Garden of Gulliver Smith' was attempted, which implies that Marc felt this one of his strongest songs. He was still recording versions of it two years later.

produced effort with Marc simply required to sing the melody, the Maximum Sound records are an unfussy and unfussed *with* representation of his gifts at the time. Those gifts aren't, alas, particularly abundant. The tracks are basic, to say the least, featuring rudimentary and slightly out-of-tune guitar playing and less-than-rudimentary harmonica. Marc's voice, however, though occasionally struggling to find its pitch, certainly does have *something*. He's still reaching for Cliff's croon, even on the Dylan cover, but he can more than carry a tune. The distinctive singing style Marc would adopt a few years later has not yet fully emerged, but the seeds of something different, something compelling, are already there.

Perhaps the most interesting thing about this session isn't the recordings themselves at all, but the box in which they would be found. On the label the words 'Mark Felds' [sic] have been crossed out to be replaced with a different moniker: Toby Tyler, a name taken from a 1960 Disney movie, *Toby Tyler or 10 Weeks With the Circus*, which was based on an 1880 children's book. There's two questions here for which we don't know the answer – firstly 'Why Toby Tyler'? It's as good a name as any, alliterative, and memorable, the two-syllable 'Tyler' is reminiscent of 'Dylan', and Marc was absolutely pitching himself at the gap in the market labelled 'British Bob Dylan' but other than that, it appears to have no special significance. A more interesting, equally unanswered question is 'Why not Mark Feld'? Since his earliest serious performances, when he and Stephen Gould renamed themselves 'Rick and Ellis', Mark seemed to feel instinctively that he needed a new name, that plain old Mark Feld was never going to cut it. He knew that Harry Webb became Cliff Richard, that Thomas Hicks became Tommy Steele and that Reg Smith became Marty Wilde, while more recently Robert Zimmerman became Bob Dylan. The new breed of pop stars, the Beatles, Stones and Kinks, might be using their real names, Ringo aside, but Marc's idea of what a star should be like had been hardcoded into him before they came to light. Rock 'n' roll stars had rock 'n' roll names. It's just how it worked, and he would try on many different tags before he found the one that fitted most snugly. As his friend Riggs O'Hara later said, 'He was just trying to find the right name that would get him through the door'.

With the Toby Tyler demo and some smart photos featuring Marc looking every inch the earnest protest singer in his peaked cap with his guitar held to his chest, Allan went to his bosses at the *Five O'Clock Club* who were, perhaps understandably, unimpressed. However the two boys' enthusiasm was undimmed, and Warren was able to arrange a meeting with Barry Green, an A&R man at EMI, who invited both boys into his office, served them tea and politely listened to their acetate. 'He was really sweet to us.' says Warren. 'He had this big grand office, and he had a lovely tea set out for us. He played the record and was very polite. Though he didn't take him on, he couldn't have been nicer.' The boys got a second bite of the cherry in February 1965 when Marc was invited to audition for A&R man John Pearson. During a fifteen minute session he cut a cover of Betty Everett's 'You're No Good To Me' at EMI's Abbey Road studios. Again the company passed, though did indicate that if he came to them with a good enough original song, they may reconsider.

For much of 1965 Marc bounced around between friends, living with different people at different times, returning to his parent's Wimbledon prefab when he had no other options. Allan Warren was soon replaced as an unofficial landlord by Riggs O'Hara, an actor to whom Marc became extremely close. The pair met at one of Warren's numerous affairs and quickly connected, with Marc moving into O'Hara's large flat in Barnes. O'Hara was present at the Abbey Road session ('Betty Everett was fabulous – he got that from me' he told *Record Collector* in 1997), and Marc was so fond of his new friend that before deciding on the name Toby Tyler he'd briefly toyed with 'Mark Riggs'. It was with Riggs that Marc finally fulfilled his self-bestowed prophecy and went to Paris for a long weekend, during which the pair did all the usual touristy stuff, apparently having a blast ('His eyes were on stalks the whole time' says O'Hara).[4] Marc mythologised this trip, as we know, and folded it into his own origin story, expanding it to a three-month, five-month, six-month, eighteen-month or four-year stay (depending on who he was talking to and when), during which he was supposed to have met the famous 'Wizard'.[5] As we've established, 'the Wizard' was possibly a metaphorical version of Geoffrey Delaroy-Hall, the worldly older man who taught him 'black magic', but Riggs O'Hara is also in the mix. O'Hara knew Paris already and was excited to show his new friend around. He was well-connected, talented and likeable, and opened Marc's eyes to a world of culture and celebrity – together they attended opening nights of plays, went to fancy parties and ate in restaurants – the kind of lifestyle a working class Hackney lad would be swept away by. O'Hara reckoned at the time that Marc 'didn't know a lot of people', going on to say that 'anyone that he met, he met through me. It was a period of education for him.' Bolan biographer Mark Paytress cites this era of Marc's life, and the Paris visit in particular, as a turning point in his development as an artist. 'The Paris episode marks a critical point in the young singer's life, career and, above all, mythology,' he says in his book *The Rise and Fall of a 20th Century Superstar*. 'It was the moment Mark

---

4. According to Harry Feld, Marc found a slug in the bath of their hotel and was so revolted that he came home early.

5. Another story goes that Marc met a fortune teller called Bobu in Paris who predicted that he wouldn't live to see his thirtieth birthday. He also apparently became transfixed with a painting in the Louvre called 'The Sixteenth of September' – spookily, of course, the date of his death. The painting is of a tree and features a crescent moon, the same phase the moon was in on the fateful night of Marc's accident, a coincidence which seems so far-fetched I had to double check it (it's true – at least as regards the phase of the moon). Bolan biographer Paul Roland makes much of this creepy coincidence, though there is one slight flaw in the story: despite persistent rumour, Marc's death wasn't caused by his car hitting a tree – it hit a steel reinforced fence post first.

Feld ditched his dreams of becoming Cliff or Dylan or even Toby 'troubadour' Tyler and instead switched to the fantasies that grew inside his head'.

This was fortuitous, because Marc's plan to become the 'British Bob Dylan' had just taken a knock: someone had beaten him to it. Pye Records released 'Catch the Wind', the debut single by the Scottish folk singer Donovan in March 1965, and the press immediately applied the 'British Dylan' tag, which hung around poor Donovan's neck for the next several years. He's certainly a better candidate for the title than Marc, who was less a Bob Dylan equivalent and more a Bob Dylan fan. Donovan, on the other hand, had put the work in. Like Dylan he had crisscrossed the folk clubs of his homeland, absorbing old songs and regurgitating them, falling in love – as Dylan had – with Woody Guthrie and Ramblin' Jack Elliot. It paid off – 'Catch the Wind' was a huge hit in the UK and even a minor one in the US. The music press loved him. Marc had missed his window, and would spend the next few years chasing Donovan's coat tails, something he deeply resented. 'He used to hate Donovan', says future Bolan manager Mike Pruskin. 'He always said he was kind of a diluted Dylan. Marc also wasn't keen that Donovan wore similar clothes to himself – the mosquito boots and the like'. [6] In a strange way, however, the popularity of Donovan would ultimately free him. Rather than the 'new Bob Dylan', he could develop 'the first Marc Bolan'.

By the Spring of 1965, Marc was already in need of another manager. Warren had done all that he could within the frame of his limited experience, and their role-play game of 'pop manager and star' had petered out after those initial failures. Warren had also fallen upon hard times. His gig at *The Five O'Clock Club* had finished and his income had dropped substantially. The predictable outcome of a financially independent fifteen-year-old was lots of fun memories and absolutely no savings. 'I got a note that I owed three months rent,' he says. 'Nobody had taught me that if you have all the money going out, you need to have it coming in'. Warren's landlord was a handsome property tycoon called David Kirch. ('A very tall man, about six foot four, waves of blonde hair, like James Fox the actor and I thought "god he's good looking" … of course he wouldn't go near me. I was sort of vamping around him, not the other way around' says Warren, never one to leave out an important detail.) Kirch was surprisingly understanding about the whole business, moving Warren into a cheaper flat and asking him if there was anything he could use to settle his debt. The only thing poor Allan had that was of any potential value at all was

---

6. Donovan endured perhaps the most mortifying moment of any British pop singer ever, when he finally met Bob Dylan during a 1965 tour. The press had been pitting them as rivals, but they got along fairly well. Hanging out in Dylan's hotel room, the pair played each other some of their new discoveries and compositions. Donovan offered up a new song, 'Tangerine Eyes' which he'd modified from what he'd assumed was an old trad folk song. Unfortunately that 'old trad folk song' turned out to be Dylan's own 'Mr Tambourine Man'. Dylan is reported to have said that it 'was not an old folk song … yet'

his contract with Mark 'Toby Tyler' Feld, which was offered up in lieu of the roughly £200 owed.[7] 'He knew nothing about pop music, had no interest in it, or in being a pop manager,' says Warren, 'he was a property manager. He just took it because there was nothing else'. As it was, Kirsch's time in the pop game came to an end fairly abruptly. 'About three months later Marc's mother, who was a Jewish lady, quite tough, she marched into this friend of mine's [Kirch's] office.' explains Warren. 'Now at the time, you have to understand, homosexuality was illegal, she was saying "What have you been doing with my son?" He said "I've never done anything with your son", and she said "Exactly! Show me the contract!" and she tore it up right there in front of him'. Marc was now free to pursue new management.

Luckily, new management would pop up within a few weeks in the form of 18-year-old publicist Mike Pruskin, then working for Surrey beat group The Nashville Teens and Van Morrison's first band, Them.[8] Pruskin was the cousin of the celebrated Lionel Bart, now more famous for his writing of the hit *Oliver!* than for the terrible paint job he had done on the basement of the 2 I's back in the mid 50s. The young and relatively green Pruskin was impressed enough by the even younger singer, bursting with ideas and energy, to throw his lot in with him, walking away from his job as a junior Denmark Street PR ('They were a bunch of creeps anyway' he told T.Rex superfans Caran Thomas and John Willans for their book *Wilderness of the Mind* – one of the few interviews he ever did on Bolan's career). The pair hit it off spectacularly – Pruskin was one of the few people in the industry who could match Marc for puppyish excitement. 'He is the antithesis of what the opponents of the pop men imagine as the cynical middle-aged manipulator in the camel-haired coat', the legendary

7. Kirch, who was awarded a KBE for philanthropy in 2013, is a man keen to do good deeds. In 2006 he gave every pensioner living in Jersey a £100 Co-Op supermarket voucher, and has apparently continued similar acts of generosity toward the island's elderly ever since. Those looking for musical connections might be briefly excited to note that he is known to have once possessed 'one of the world's largest collections of Zeppelin memorabilia'. Unfortunately this refers to the type of airship, not the rock band named after them.

8. It's not entirely clear how Pruskin came into Marc's orbit. Bolan megafan John Bramley in his book *Beautiful Dreamer,* traces the link back to Phil Solomon, who managed the band Them and founded the legendary pirate station Radio Caroline, and whom Marc apparently 'sought out'. Bramley isn't clear on how Marc was introduced to Pruskin, but since the latter was handling Solomon's biggest client we can assume some sort of professional introduction was made. Unfortunately Bramley neither cites his sources, nor tells us how Marc came into Solomon's orbit in the first place. Every other telling of Bolan's life story, including Paul Roland's *Metal Guru,* Mark Paytress' *The Rise and fall of a 20th Century Superstar,* Lesley-Anne Jones' *Ride A White Swan,* Cliff McLenehan's *Marc Bolan 1947-1977 Chronology,* Caran Thomas and John Willans *Wilderness of the Mind* and Chris Welch's *Born To Boogie* fudges Pruskin's entry into Marc's career just a little, keeping the actual mechanism of their introduction vague. Since Solomon died in 2013 and Pruskin, who went on to become an art dealer and gives very few interviews, has faded from public view, there's very few people left to ask. After Phyllis Feld forcibly ended Marc's association with David Kirch and Allan Warren the trail, frustratingly, goes cold until we pick the story up with Pruskin's assumption of managerial duties.

Observer columnist and jazz musician George Melly said of him. 'The only trouble is that by the time I, in my middle-aged sloth, have lumbered forward to investigate what he has brought to my attention, he has usually turned violently against it.' Pruskin and Feld got along so famously that they ultimately decided to get a place together where they could mastermind their careers, winding up in a flat on Manchester Street. Since we know Marc's rent was again being paid by a man named 'Geoffrey', that according to his journal his landlord was 'a queen', and since Marc had enjoyed free digs in that same street the previous year, it's not a huge stretch to assume that he had once again thrown himself onto the generosity of Delaroy-Hall, whom we know from Allan Warren was still a part of Marc's life, taking the young men out for occasional posh dinners.

Pruskin was Marc's first genuinely effective manager, and made several key introductions that would finally advance his client's career. The most significant move was to take Marc's latest song, a short, surreal piece called 'The Wizard In The Woods', to his Denmark Street neighbour; a freelance agent who worked with Beatles associate Dick James. The man's name was Leslie Conn, and he in turn made an introduction to a young American studio engineer, Jim Economides, who had recently left Capitol records in LA to find his fortune in London. It was Economides who made the necessary introductions at Decca, where beleaguered exec Dick Rowe, having missed out on both the Beatles and the 'British Bob Dylan', was now on the lookout for a 'Decca Donovan' and eyeing young men with acoustic guitars. That August, Mark Feld signed to Decca Records for a one single deal.

It was 'The Wizard' that did it. Decca's Dick Rowe was happy to take chances on anyone with potential at this point, just in the name of seeing what stuck (that 'man that passed on the Beatles' tag was starting to sting), but wasn't sure what to do with Marc once he had him. It was left to the far more discerning Mike Leander, the label's in-house arranger, to work out the details. Leander was impressed with the song, finding Marc's lyrical voice to be refreshing and pleasingly weird. Marc was still working under the shadow cast by the by-now giant Dylan, but with 'The Wizard', or 'The Wizard in the Woods' as it was still titled, there was a genuine sense of a creative breakthrough. In another three years or so rock music would be full of fantasy, psychedelia and whimsy as the hippy era began to gain real cultural clout, but back in 1965 pop narratives were still rather straightforward. Admittedly change was in the air – across the city, a band called The Pink Floyd Sound were getting together a set of R&B covers, The Beatles were writing *Rubber Soul*, their most progressive record yet, while on the other side of the Atlantic, Brian Wilson was working on the songs that would become *Pet Sounds*. Dylan himself had released *Bringing It All Back Home* just that summer: classic records all. But for all the emotional honesty, clever chord changes and winding narratives of 'Wouldn't It Be Nice', 'Norwegian Wood' or 'Maggie's Farm', none of them are about a man in a pointy hat who creeps silently through the forest followed by dark shadows, before melting into the sky. Seventeen year old Mark Feld had out-weirded all of them. By late 1967, post *Sgt Pepper's Lonely Hearts Club Band* and Pink Floyd's *The Piper At The Gates of Dawn*, you couldn't swing a purple cat in London's underground scene without hitting a whimsical song about a talking frog sitting on a magic toadstool, but back in the summer of 1965 there was nothing in pop like Bolan's latest lyrics. What's more, any proto psychedelic moments that were happening in the brains of Floyd's Syd Barret, John Lennon and one David Jones were happening independently of Marc. He had arrived at this moment by himself – the first time in his creative life that he was forging his own path, not approximating someone else's. One thing you can absolutely say for 'The Wizard' is that Cliff Richard could never have done it. After working with Marc over several evenings to arrange his two-chord fantasy ditty into a decent pop format, Leander greenlit some studio time, scheduled for early in the morning of 14 September with an eye on a November release. Things, at long last, were finally happening.

In the meantime, Marc still needed to eat. Though Pruskin had managed to sell Marc's publishing, it generated paltry amounts. 'We got £15 a time for one thing we did, and then sixpence for something else,' he said in *Wilderness of the Mind*. 'We didn't make any money out of it.' The big labels had learned that they could give their banner headline bands some creative and commercial autonomy, but when it came to solo acts, especially *young* solo acts, they were still ready to crack the whip. There was a machine in place at Decca, EMI and the rest. You put a hardworking youngster with big dreams into one end, and a pop sausage was produced from the other. It was a system that had grown in Tin Pan Alley from the days of Larry Parnes and his stable in the late fifties. Young stars were to be stacked high and sold cheap; acts like Marc were for making money *from*, not giving money *to*. While he waited for the chart dominance he *knew* would come, Marc was going to need some pocket money.

Luckily Les Conn, still involved and always keeping an eye on his young charges, was happy to help. Having recently parted ways with Dick James, who saw no future in David Jones or Mark Feld, Conn was setting up on his own and had acquired office space at 23 Denmark Street. He threw his client a few bob to paint the new premises with the help of another struggling young act that Conn had taken on the previous year, and the two got on with the job over a couple of days, arguing about clothes and music and comparing career notes. That was the day that Mark Feld met David Jones.

Chapter Eight

Young Dudes

'So there's me and this mod whitewashing Les's office,' Bowie explained in a lengthy interview with *Mojo* in 2002. 'And he goes, "Where d'you get those shoes, man?" ... We immediately started talking about clothes and sewing machines.

"Oh I'm gonna be a singer and I'm gonna be so big you're not gonna believe it, man."

"Well I'll probably write a musical for you one day then, 'cos I'm gonna be the greatest writer ever."

"No, no, man, you've gotta hear my stuff 'cos I write great things. And I knew a wizard in Paris," and it was all this. Just whitewashing walls in our manager's office!'

For fans of both artists, the day the pair spent painting Les Conn's new gaff ('a shitty green colour' according to the man himself) has achieved the status of modern myth, to the point that it was even the subject of an episode of Sky Comedy's *Urban Myths* in 2018, an entertaining half hour comedy-drama starring comedian Jack Whitehall as (a suspiciously tall) Mark Feld, Luke Treadaway as David Jones and the *Young Ones'* Ade Edmondson as Les Conn. It's a decent enough bit of speculation, with a script regurgitating some of the better known anecdotes from both stars' lives, but it very definitely shouldn't be taken as gospel.

We only really have David's account of that day to go by, however, and David is not always the most reliable narrator of his own story – for example, in the 2002 *Mojo* article he describes his 1965 self as 'a sort of neo-beat-hippy,' which is a fairly accurate description of the Bowie of 1967 but not really of 1964 or 65, when he was still very much in his sharp-suited mod phase, having just left the Manish Boys and joined his next band, the Lower Third. In this case, however, the account is probably not a million miles from the truth. The two boys *were* both obsessed with style, and they were both, to quite a remarkable extent, absolutely certain of their abilities. Allan Warren remembers Marc talking about himself endlessly. 'Marc was one of those people that would say, "I've had enough of talking about me. Now, what do you think of me?" I'd think, God, another three hours talking about him!' David, meanwhile, had walked out on two bands because his bandmates didn't match his ambitions, and a third for not properly crediting him on a single – not the actions of a man lacking either entitlement or self-belief. They'd both started to pick up steam in their career too, and would certainly have compared notes and engaged in a game of industry top trumps. Marc was working with Mike Pruskin at this point, and was already in talks with Decca, while David had released two singles (glossing over the fact that both had flopped), toured with Gene Pitney and the Kinks and played the Marquee. David was probably the one winning on bragging rights, but both would have been in full peacock mode. The fact that Bowie references Marc's preposterous 'wizard' story suggests his new friend was already laying it on thick with the self-mythology.[1] 'They were very similar', Les Conn is quoted as saying in Paul Trynka's *Starman*. 'They totally believed in themselves, both of them. It was me that brought them together, and they both had exactly the same attitude which was "we are going to make it"'.

When did this famous meeting take place? And was this really the first time that the pair had met? The answer to the second question is 'probably', though there are some claims that they had been in each other's company before. An old school friend of Marc's, Richard Young, reckons that he and Marc met David with Geoff McCormack in a soul and R&B club called Le Bataclan in Soho, a favourite hangout when bunking off from school trips, in '61 or 62'. However, it's possible that the intervening half a decade has muddled some of these memories – Le Bataclan didn't open until 1963, by which time Marc had moved away from the school he shared with Young. Young also claims that they were both expelled on the same day for bunking off, which doesn't quite work either as Marc was expelled from an entirely different school. It does tell us, however, that the two young mods were orbiting the same venues and people.

Les Conn, meanwhile, told Bowie biographers Peter and Leni Gillman that he took both Marc and David, together, to see his boss, Dick James, only to have them roundly rejected, with James apparently telling Conn 'you're wasting your time'. An obituary of Conn printed in the *Independent* in 2009 goes further, claiming that James had called the two young hopefuls 'long-haired gits'.[2] This is interesting, because it was Dick James' rejection of Bowie that prompted Conn to strike out on his own – the very reason he had a new office that needed painting in the first place. If true though, this means that the doomed introduction to Dick James would have been the lads' actual first meeting. Of course, what we have to bear in mind here is that literally every person involved in this story was a yarn spinner with a knack for self mythology on a fairly grand scale; never knowingly delivering a story unpolished, and all are now

---

1. Bolan didn't reserve the Wizard story for press interviews – he told it to almost everyone he met. Helen Shapiro would run into Marc for the first time in years, much to her surprise, at an event for *Fabulous* magazine in December. She was given the same story. 'He told me he'd been living in Paris with this wizard,' she told Mark Peytriss. 'He was very enthusiastic about it, but I didn't really know what he was going on about.'
2. The Gilmans, in their book *Alias David Bowie*, quote the genial and well-spoken Dick James as denying this, apparently saying 'I wouldn't dream of addressing anyone like that'. It would not, of course, be out of character for Les Conn to have embellished the story, just a little.

dead, which means that we can't check the details. The only calm voice involved in the whole affair is that of the gentlemanly Kenneth Pitt, who would assume Bowie's managerial duties within a year, who says in his book *The Pitt Report* that 'it was in Conn's office that Jones-Bowie first met Feld-Bolan' and this, juicy stories and mythologising aside, is all we can say for sure.

As for the 'when?' – we can be relatively confident that the painting incident happened in the late spring or early summer of 1965. The very latest it could have taken place would be 27 July – one of the few absolutely solid markers that we have. It was on this day that a fan of David's spotted him on Denmark Street in the company of Marc and asked for an autograph – creating one of the very few pieces of paper in existence to bear the signature of both London Boys. We also know that one of the songs Pruskin approached Les Conn with was 'The Wizard', which wasn't written until after Marc's famous trip to Paris with Riggs O'Hara in the Spring of 1965. David would have been most in need of the money and willing to pull on some overalls after the breakup of the Manish Boys in late April/early May. We can, just about, with a bit of wiggle room, put a pin in the timeline for that day of painting and decorating being in either May or June 1965.[3]

Regardless of the exact date and circumstances of that meeting, this was the day that their friendship began. It was a friendship that would endure in various stages for the next twelve years. A lot has been made of that friendship, which has grown its own mythology of sorts.[4] A widely accepted view is that they were best friends and bosom buddies through the sixties but this is not quite the case. They were absolutely friends, that's undeniably true, and would regularly meet to compare notes and idle away some time at Denmark Street's La Gioconda coffee bar, a cafe that became something of a clubhouse for the music industry and was usually full of out-of-work musicians, business types doing deals, band meetings and *NME* journalists on the hunt for some gossip ('That was the place you would go if you wanted something like a backing singer or a bass guitarist,' singer Dana Gillespie, a contemporary of Marc and David and occasionally the latter's girlfriend, told Dylan Jones) La Gioconda, essentially, became business premises for anyone that didn't have an office. David would be there most days, nursing a coffee between meeting his managers or working in Shel Talmy's demo studio next door. His next band, the Lower Third, owned a converted ambulance for carting gear between shows, and it was invariably kept

---

3. The Sky Comedy show places the story in 1964, the date that tends to crop up in Bowie biographies, including Kevin Cann's usually impeccable timeline *Any Day Now – David Bowie: The London Years 1947-1974*. Most Bolan biographies, however, place the meeting in 1965. The latter is the more likely date – however much you play with the timeline, it's almost impossible for the chain of events that brought Mark Feld to Les Conn's office to have happened in 1964, while a meeting in 1965 comfortably fits the stories of both men.
4. Hence this very book.

parked up by the cafe, with a few of the band kipping inside most nights, while using La Gioconda as a combination of office, living room and bathroom.

For most of the sixties the Bowie/Bolan friendship took the form of shooting the breeze in La Gioconda, eyeing up each other's successes and failures, talking about clothes and music, people they knew that were doing well (whose careers were enviously analysed and torn to shreds) and people they knew who weren't (whose careers were happily analysed and also torn to shreds). They were part of a scene of young musicians who were all in the same boat and their friendship was neither unique nor exclusive within this group – Elton John, Steve Marriot, Rod Stewart and more lived similarly intertwining lives and even the more famous names like Pete Townshend, Ray Davies and Phil May used Denmark Street as their base of operations and mingled with the up-and-comers. The pop industry was not a large scene in those early days, everyone knew everyone, London Boys all. In 2011, around thirty seconds of handheld footage of Denmark Street were uploaded to YouTube, filmed by a man on a visit to the West End in 1965. As he tries to focus on his wife, the shot is blocked by a swaggering blonde youth with an immaculate suit and haircut who flashes an unmistakable grin and heads into the nearby La Gioconda; 18-year-old David Jones. Either someone got incredibly lucky with this footage, or Bowie walked that street so often every day that if you pointed a camera anywhere there was a fifty/fifty chance you'd catch him.

Not that sipping cappuccinos was all that Marc and David did. 'Marc took me dustbin shopping,' Bowie told an audience during an appearance at the BBC Radio Theatre in 2000. 'At that time, Carnaby Street, the fashion district, was going through a period of incredible wealth. And rather than replace buttons on their shirts or zippers on their trousers, they'd just throw it all away in the dustbins. So we used to go up and down Carnaby Street and go through all the dustbins, around nine, ten o'clock, and get our wardrobes together.' The pair would be at the same parties, at the same gigs and in the audience of the same TV shows. Their relationship would deepen over the years, as their careers began to mirror one another's and their rivalry became more intense, but at the beginning David and Marc were also Marc and Elton, and Rod and Steve, and Dana and David and, well, whoever else happened to be around. Lower Third drummer Phil Lancaster, in his memoir *At the Birth of Bowie*, claims to have rarely seen the boys knocking about together in those very early years. 'I can't remember ever seeing Marc around or hearing Dave mention him' he says. 'We certainly didn't share any billing with Marc or any of his groups.'[5] However, a close friendship would develop as the sixties progressed and the boys' lives became more intertwined through mutual friends and scenes. Ken

5. Probably because Marc didn't join 'groups' until after Lancaster and Bowie had parted ways – his gigography is relatively scant in the early-mid sixties.

Pitt remembered their relationship as being very involved. 'David idolised Marc for a while', Pitt wrote. 'He was going around to his flat night after night, playing songs, listening to songs, talking about music, and then he'd come back here and we'd talk about our own projects and David would say, "Well, Marc says this" or "Marc says that ..." Bolan had a tremendous influence on him at that time, and David considered him an authority.' What became significant about their friendship over the years wasn't so much its day-to-day detail, but simply that – for the next twelve years – they were there to bear witness for each other as they traced remarkably similar paths. At the beginning, however, they were merely two well dressed teenagers with central London as their backyard.

Soho and the surrounding streets, containing the 2 I's, Tin Pan Alley, Carnaby Street, Covent Garden, the Marquee and more, are absolutely essential to the story of the London boys, and it's worth taking a minute to get our heads around the geography. When people refer to Soho they're generally talking about a square mile in the centre of London cornered by Oxford Circus in the north east, Tottenham Court Road station to the north west, Leicester Square to the south west and Piccadilly Circus to south east, bordered by four iconic London roads: Oxford Street, Charing Cross Road, Shaftesbury Avenue and Regent Street. Back in the mid 60s, just as it is now, Soho was London's flashiest shop window. It contained most of the theatres, Chinatown, Little Italy, the covert gay bars of Old Compton Street and Piccadilly and sex shops of Wardour Street, the fashion centre of Liberty London department store and nearby Carnaby Street and the movie screening rooms and studio offices of Soho Square itself. Berwick Street had a bustling, multicultural market, while stately Regent Street housed offices and the apartments of socialites. Just outside the square mile, across the Charing Cross Road, was Denmark Street, aka Tin Pan Alley, home to innumerable music shops, publishing companies and recording studios. Until the final nail of gentrification in the mid 2010s, Soho contained numerous legendary live music clubs, though most have now closed. Back in the fifties and sixties it was the heart of the UK's music and movie industries. By 1965 it had become Marc and David's personal stalking ground.

Soho had long been something of a village, hidden inside the grand metropolis of central London. For a couple of hundred years it had been the area of the city in which European immigrants tended to settle, giving those streets an abundance of Spanish butchers, Italian cafes, Greek restaurants and Swiss chocolatiers that are still in evidence today. It wasn't just European immigration either – a small Chinatown had built up in the very heart of Soho. By the early 20th century there was already a uniquely cosmopolitan atmosphere to that handful of streets which attracted poets, writers and artists in much the same way as Montmartre in Paris, or New York's East Village had. It created a reputation for bohemian creativity which was still very much in place by the mid sixties. Adam Faith, one of Britain's earliest pop stars, wrote of his first visits to the area in his 1961 autobiography, *Poor Me*, 'It was fascinating to walk along the pavement through this medley of all nations. To see newspapers and magazines on sale in a dozen different languages and watch the waiters from the Indian, Chinese and Italian and Turkish restaurants gathered on the corners out of hours.'[6]

Spiritually, Soho was the centre of what was rapidly becoming (and would the following year would be labelled by *Time* magazine as) 'Swinging London'; a little package of creativity, fashion, art, music, commerce and clubbing centred in that hallowed square mile of the West End that seemed to set the cultural tone for the era. In the future, when people thought of Britain in the 1960s, they weren't thinking about the typhoid outbreak that blighted Aberdeen in 1964, or the 430,000 cattle culled due to an explosion of foot and mouth disease in Wales and the Midlands in 1967. They were thinking of Mary Quant miniskirts, of Michael Caine as Alfie, of John and Yoko, Carnaby Street, pop art and pop music. They were thinking, whether they knew it or not, of Soho. It was an area with a perfect storm of cultural elements. On the one hand you had the creative industries: the music business in Denmark Street, the movie business on Soho Square and the fashionistas of Carnaby Street. On the other hand, it was also the setting for industries profoundly outside the social mainstream – Soho had been the home of everything gloriously indecent in London for literally hundreds of years and was a traditional hub of brothels and other sex work, pornography and the more vulgar end of vaudeville, from which the strip clubs had evolved. By the time Marc and David were painting Les Conn's office they were within a ten minute walk of nearly a hundred strip clubs and a couple of dozen sex shops. The area was studded with discreet notes and postcards advertising personal services, often thinly veiled under terms like 'French lessons'. London's first dedicated porn cinema, the Compton Cinema Club, opened as a private members club on Old Compton Street in 1960. Naturally, the sex trade went hand in hand with organised crime, and throughout the 19th and 20th centuries, the area was constantly divided up and shared between gangsters and criminal factions, who controlled the sex and drugs available on the streets.

The coffee bar culture of the 50s and early 60s, itself largely a product of Italian immigration, had a knock-on effect that reverberated into the 'Swinging London' era – venues with no alcohol licence and thus no age restrictions attracted young people in their droves, contributing to the feel of Soho as the centre of a 'youth quake'. Even when the coffee bars were gone, the young people remained – providing an audience for the blues and rock venues that had grown out of the jazz clubs, skiffle cellars and Espresso bar rock 'n' roll of the 50s. The less-threatening atmosphere of the 'Expresso' bars also made them a more

---

6. The fact that Adam Faith had written an autobiography aged just 21 gives you some idea of the speed at which the music biz moved in those days.

comfortable hang out for gay people, particularly as the queer-friendly pubs and bars dotted around Piccadilly and the 'Dirty Square Mile' had tightened their rules in the face of government crackdowns. In an interview published in *QX Magazine* a scene regular known as 'Amber' remembered a number of covertly gay bars in the fifties, including The Alibi, the Huntsman, Take 5, The Apple, No. 9 and the Casino – 'You didn't have to go 100 yards. We had more places then than now'. Soho's queer tradition continued below the surface in the lean years between the crackdown of the early 50s and the decriminalisation of same-gender sex in 1967, both in shabby back alley encounters and the more salubrious private members clubs about which the establishment would often simply look the other way. The Colony Club, established in 1948 and still going strong in the mid 60s, operated by the glorious and notorious proprietor Muriel Belcher (a 'theatrical Portuguese Jewish lesbian' according to Sophie Parkin in her 2013 history of the club) and venues like it provided a home for the oddball creatives and establishment deviants who gathered behind a closed door beyond which they could be themselves. Over the years its membership included Francis Bacon, Peter O'Toole, George Melly, E.M. Forster, John Hurt, Dylan Thomas, Lucian Freud, Tallulah Bankhead, Mary Kenny and Lady Rose McLaren to name but a few. In a 1964 interview with BBC Radio's *The Third Programme* Quentin Crisp, the former rent boy and general raconteur, called Soho 'the reservation', saying of the area that 'we [queer people] are now able to live there protected, no longer shot at as though we were big game. We can do as we please.'

Below the often traditional and certainly more overtly capitalist practices of the creative industries and clubland that was perhaps the most public face of the area, London's underground and counterculture were also sparking. Better Books on Charing Cross Road was practically the headquarters of the UK beatnik scene. Roughly around the time Marc and David were getting acquainted with the stiff end of a paintbrush, Allen Ginsberg was giving a reading at Better Books. The scene around the shop directly led to the famous Albert Hall poetry event in June 1965, often seen as a year zero for the British underground. The tying together of youth culture, drugs, poetry, revolutionary politics, underground press like *International Times*, radical art and psychedelic music that would become counterculture London all has its roots, more or less, in Better Books.

When the journalist Simon Jenkins, then working for the London *Evening Standard*, was showing American friends around the area in the mid 60s they were, as he wrote in his *A Short History of London* many years later, 'amazed by the shortness of girls' skirts and the sight of same-sex hand-holding in the street.' Back at the turn of the century, Arthur Ransome, the author best known for the *Swallows and Amazons* books, said of Soho in his book *Bohemia In London* that it was crammed with 'adventurous young Englishmen from conventional homes determined to live in any way other than that to which they have become accustomed'. Sixty years on, the area's character could scarcely be better summed up. All of this came together to create a unique flashpoint, an otherwise impossible socio-chemical reaction that created the conditions in which 'Swinging London' could flourish.

Only a handful of people were lucky enough to be directly involved in Soho's day-to-day and night-to-night business of commerce, creativity, nightclubs and vice but it was enough to generate enough buzz and energy to seemingly power the youth culture of the whole city. David and Marc, between them covering pretty much every bohemian and pop-cultural artform and most of its vices, were exactly where they were supposed to be. They were not yet driving the new pop culture, but they were being dragged along by it, swimming toward its centre. It makes them our perfect guides to the era.

Both London boys had some evolving to do, together and apart, before either hit upon a form and formula that would make an indelible mark. And in truth, London wasn't yet ready. David and Marc were very much of the city, but the city was not yet of them. They would need the expansion of the underground and its blending with mainstream pop culture to truly find their place; an evolution probably best exemplified by the post-*Revolver* image and music of The Beatles – as the loveable moptops who had re-energised and future-proofed pop music as a cornerstone of popular culture grew their hair, discovered psychedelics and merged with the hippified underground of peace and love, sex and drugs. The mainstream had already accepted the Beatles, and so would eventually allow them to take it by hand and lead it off into the Lewis Carroll theme-park of the hippy years.

Not that any of this made a blind bit of sense or difference once you got more than ten miles away from Piccadilly Circus. 'Swinging London was tiny', the ever quotable Nik Cohn told *The Independent* in 2011. '500 people and three nightclubs. In Muswell Hill it was still the 1950s.' The historian Dominic Sandbrook, in his book *White Heat: A History of Britain in the Swinging Sixties* quotes a young woman who reckoned that 'everything reached Hull about five years after it reached everywhere else'. Outside the West End bubble life carried on more or less as it had done for the last decade. Much of the country lived in poverty and embedded social norms were still recycled by the education system. The slow recovery from the economic and literal devastation of the war, now twenty years in the past, was still far from complete. 'Apart from a few pockets of affluence and new money, London was not much different from what it had been at the end of the war,' legendary London photographer David Bailey told *GQ* in 2020. 'Everything was grey, dirty, cheap, miserable. Especially anywhere east of Tottenham Court Road. London was …like a different planet, because up in Liverpool or Manchester or Newcastle there was nothing happening at all.' In Wimbledon, Sid and Phyllis Feld saved, scraped and scrubbed. One of their sons was diving into bins behind Carnaby Street shops and setting short stories about wizards to music, but the other was a lorry driver, as his father had been. Down in Bromley, John and Peggy Jones were keeping up appearances in the curtain twitching world of suburbia, while their son was manufacturing fake scandals about his haircut and going through backing bands like Roger Moore's character in *The Saint* went through disguises. The bright colours of Soho were the stuff of pop magazines, faintly baffled reports on late night TV, Radio Caroline and the odd Sunday Supplement. It would take a while for that vibrancy to spread. Most of the country was far better represented by *Coronation Street* than by the swinging scenes of movies like *Blow Up* and *Alfie*.

Yet even outside of the elitist and outsider bubbles of Soho, 1965 was definitely a year in which Britain had begun to change, culturally, politically, ideologically and symbolically. Winston Churchill's death in January felt huge. The former prime minister had been a living symbol of wartime Britain, an era that was starting to become romanticised even then. He had come to adulthood while Victoria was still on the throne, had been a high profile, Harrow-educated politician before the First World War, and had led the country through the second. Now, with much pomp and ceremony, he was paraded through London and laid to rest. With him went the old paradigm: there was now an entire generation of young adults who didn't remember the war at all. The Labour government elected (albeit narrowly) the previous year was starting to affect its promised liberal reforms, just as the post-war government had. In November the death penalty was abolished, and that same month it was made illegal to refuse service to someone on the grounds of race, ethnicity or nationality – modern, progressive values enshrined in law. The government was already moving toward the huge milestones of legalising homosexuality and abortion and reforming divorce laws, all of which would pass into law in the coming years. At the end of the year the Beatles played the final show of their final British tour[7], effectively bringing the curtain down on the beat band era. During a BBC TV debate about censorship in the theatre, the writer Kenneth Tynan became the first person to say 'fuck' on British television.[8] The times, as Bob Dylan had predicted only the previous year, were a-changing.

These were the values and norms of a younger generation, and Britain *was* younger – younger than it had been since Roman times, in fact. In 1965, forty percent of the population was under twenty-five. The youth voice, culturally, commercially and politically was the loudest it had ever been. Attitudes toward everything from hair length to abortion and sexuality were being taken into account by a government aware it had youth to thank for its power. This was,

---

7. Though they would limp through some more gigs abroad in 66, apparently hating every second of it.
8. There is some dispute over this, admittedly. He's probably the first person to use the word deliberately and in full knowledge of the fuss it would cause, and the first person anyone actually seemed to *notice* saying it.

in a very real sense, Marc and David's world. They were young men who shared these liberal views[9], and were both themselves experimenting with sexual and stylistic norms. They were the perfect example of a generation that understood the power of escapism and fantasy, the blending of Black and White culture and the importance of the media. Britain wasn't just the youngest it had been in centuries, it was the most progressive that it had been too.

It's become a cliche to say that the 'swinging sixties' happened to about five hundred people attending clubs in Leicester Square, and everyone else heard about it later – but it was also true. Many of those at the eye of the storm knew that they were living through extraordinary times of change and excitement. 'From the very start of the Sixties I could see myself at seventy-five on television telling people about that time,' Michael Caine told David Bailey for his book *Goodbye Baby & Amen: A Saraband for the Sixties* in 1969. 'It was the time of my time. I will never have so much fun again, ever.' David and Marc were at the heart of an extraordinary explosion of colour and life, and though they were not yet strong or significant enough to influence that tide, it powered them all the same. As both sat nursing a cappuccino in La Gioconda, talking about this or that bird, this or that group, this or that new tailor off Carnaby, both were readying themselves for what they were sure would be their big break and ticket to pop immortality – David's debut with the Lower Third, 'You've Got A Habit of Leaving Me', and Marc's first single 'The Wizard'. Alas, both had a long way to go yet.

---

9. Allen Warren says that one of the reasons he and Marc ultimately parted company was over political differences. Warren had a very old fashioned, conservative (and indeed *Conservative*) outlook on life – and still does – whereas Marc, despite some iffy quotes in *Town* magazine when he was just fourteen, was by now a committed liberal.

Chapter Nine

Cowboys and Umlauts

A s the two future pop icons – a label that would surprise both of them only in that it would take so long to be proven true – became acquainted, David was already deep into his next doomed assault on the charts. Having awkwardly disentangled himself from the Manish Boys,[1] he had recruited a new backing band, The Lower Third, this time from a chance meeting in La Gioconda. Like the Manish Boys and the King Bees before them, the new group, who had formed in Margate before moving to the city to seek their fortune, wrongly assumed that *they* were recruiting *him*. Different again from the more blues-orientated Manish Boys, the re-christened 'Davy Jones and the Lower Third' were a bracingly loud mod rock band, with an obvious debt to The Who (with whom they would share some dates later in the year). Townshend and co's raucous toughening of the beat group formula had gained them a solid live reputation and would yield spectacular results later that year with 'My Generation', one of the great singles of the era.

That summer, the band recorded a new song of David's, 'You've Got A Habit Of Leaving', again with Shel Talmy, the producer of 'I Pity The Fool', at that point most famous for working with The Who and the Kinks. Talmy was not exactly stretching himself with the recording which, though solid enough, sounds like a grab-bag of spare Pete Townshend riffs, but then the raw material he was working with wasn't exactly swimming in originality either. The Lower Third were very much following The Who's lead, down to David's Roger Daltrey-esque swinging and bashing of his microphone, the use of squealing feedback and their insistence that bass player Graham Rivens stayed rooted to the spot as the rest of the group created chaos around him. The point was underlined the first time Bowie met Pete Townsend, during a soundcheck when the Lower Third opened for the Who in Bournemouth. Drummer Phil Lancaster recounts the story in his book *At the Birth of Bowie*: 'When we finished the number, he approached the stage to say hello and asked whose song it was that we were playing, to which Dave replied "It's mine". "That's a shame," said Pete, "sounds like my stuff."' Still … clinging to the coattails of the coolest group emerging that year never did any unknown band any harm, and David and co, playing

---

1. His departure from the group was only confirmed for the rest of the band when two of them ran into him in producer Shel Talmy's office, having popped by unannounced and found him there to talk to the producer about his new songs. David, sheepishly, was forced to admit that he was no longer interested in being a Manish Boy.

gigs at the Marquee and the 100 Club on Oxford Street began to acquire a solid following and a reputation, as Lancaster puts it, as 'the second loudest band in London'.

In the years since young 'King of the mods' Mark Feld had made it into *Town* magazine, the mod subculture had exploded, and with the Lower Third, David was very much leaning in. The press knew the term 'mod' now, if not from the fashion-focused Who fans popping pills in Soho, then from the running battles at weekends and on bank holidays between gangs of sharp dressed boys and their arch enemies, the greaser 'rockers' that had terrified locals in seaside towns throughout 1964 and 1965. As Nik Cohn neatly summarised in *Awopbopaloobop*, 'mods thought rockers were yobs, rockers thought mods were ponces.' The early mods, true modernists, had been an unconnected, largely working class group of exceptionally well dressed, aspirational youths, but things had moved on. By 1965 'mod' was a movement, fuelled by dancing and dextroamphetamine and stolen Vespas. Mods weren't just a bunch of well dressed lads now. They were an *audience* – The Who had seen to that. David moved the Lower Third into full-on Mod mode fairly quickly. The band had their hair cut shorter and neater, David teasing his into a small beehive (his 'Animal Filament' principles having apparently evaporated), and acquired herringbone shirts and rope-soled corduroy shoes with skinny ties, handmade by drummer Phil Lancaster's mum. The new single was accompanied by a press release in which David had his cake and ate it by claiming to be 'Bromley's first Mod' who 'has since changed his philosophy to become a Rocker'. In truth, though David was absolutely a mod in the classic sense of the pre-64 sharp-dressed modernists, he wasn't really running with the pack when mod became a mass youth subculture, except in the sense of being a well-dressed young man hitting the clubs at the weekend. He certainly wasn't clobbering greasers on Brighton beach, and there is – thankfully – no known evidence of him wearing a khaki parka. Mod was, quite literally, just another suit he wore. It was a look that would see him through the next few years.

In August, Parlophone records released the debut single by the Lower Third, which was credited, much to the disappointment of the rest of the band, to simply 'Davy Jones', who may have been overcompensating for the debacle around 'I Pity The Fool'. 'You've Got A Habit of Leaving' was a likeable enough piece of mid-sixties mod noise, released once again to the deafening indifference of critics and record buyers alike ('lots of wailing, very offbeat' shrugged *Record Mirror*, 'a rather boring noise' harrumphed the *Aberdeen Express*). The failure of the record was the final nail in the coffin for several elements of David's career. Shel Talmy decided that this was as good as it was going to get for David Jones (or 'Davy Jones' as he was credited for this release only) and succumbing to pressure from his EMI bosses, booted the group off the Parlophone label. Les Conn, too, was now ready to part ways with his young charge after a year of banging their collective heads against a wall. He was getting fed up with Mark Feld too, feeling that whatever effort he was putting into supporting his two young hopefuls, the chances of profiting from either seemed to be vanishingly slim. 'I was going broke looking after them', he told Paul Trynka. 'And I was getting very depressed with the music business – I had to say goodbye'. Conn stuck it out with Marc for a few more months before quitting Tin Pan Alley for good. He left the country shortly afterwards, moving to Majorca where he finally made his fortune (and presumably had a much happier time) running dance parties on the beach.

David, characteristically, was not long without representation, having already met his next manager while hustling for gigs with promotor Terry King. Working for King was Ralph Horton, a wily booking agent who had previously represented the Moody Blues. Horton is a key figure in David's early development. It was Horton that pushed the band further into the trendy mod scene, distancing David from the long-hair pseudo Pretty Thing of the previous year. He was well connected and knew booking agents, stylists and promoters; he vowed to get the group signed again quickly. He was also, alas, haphazard when it came to money and was occasionally guilty of a rather poor attention to detail. It was also very clear to the rest of the Lower Third that it was always going to be David, not his bandmates, for whom Horton would make time.

Horton himself quickly realised that booking gigs for a band and managing an entire career were very different disciplines, and he found himself almost immediately in need of help. One of his first moves was to consult a contact of his, a genial booking agent by the name of Ken Pitt, to see if he'd be interested in helping. Pitt himself said he was too busy – he managed Manfred Mann at the time and was currently organising a tour for Bob Dylan, among numerous business interests – but did offer some advice: the name 'David Jones' (or Davy, Davey or Davie) was too commonplace and would have to go. Pitt could think off-hand of a couple of other David Joneses, including one young performer that he was sure was going to make it big within the next year,[2] and another who literally worked in his office. A summit was quickly held and David agreed that a change of name was necessary. Fortunately he'd been carrying around a spare in his back pocket ever since the days of the Kon-Rads, inspired by a real life figure, Jim Bowie, portrayed by Richard Widmark in the 1960 western *The Alamo*. On 17 September 17 1965 Horton wrote to Ken Pitt to thank him for his advice, informing him that 'I have now changed David's name to David Bowie'. It would not be the last time that Pitt heard the name.

Mark Feld was also due a re-christening. On 9 August, he fulfilled the ambition of a lifetime and signed a recording contract with Decca records,

---

2. He was right. Former child actor Davy Jones had already gotten a Tony nomination for his portrayal of the Artful Dodger in Lionel Bart's *Oliver!* on Broadway and would soon join a manufactured Beatles-style pop band called The Monkees.

a one-single deal based on his song 'The Wizard'. Decca announced their new signing in *NME* on 10 September, which reported that 'songs by Burt Bacharach and Sonny Bono (of Sonny and Cher fame) are being considered for Marc's first disc which will probably be issued around mid-October.' None of these claims would turn out to be accurate.

Comparing David and Marc's experiences that year gives us a fairly rounded look at the entry-level of the music industry in 1965. The Lower Third were a beat group, meaning they were self-contained and an absolute doddle to capture on tape. They were simply chucked in a studio with Shel Talmy, who – more or less – set up some microphones and pressed record. The group spent a few hours ripping through the A and B sides, songs they had gigged-in and rehearsed, did some limited overdubs, and then everyone went to the pub. Marc's studio time was very different. As a solo artist, Marc got to experience the full sausage factory approach that Decca applied to its pop prospects, spending days sitting with arranger Mike Leander[3] who 'put him in the same light folk category as Marianne Faithfull', as he told Mark Paytress. On 14 September, Leander and Decca A&R Jim Economides took him to the label's West Hampstead studio – the same room, in fact, where David had cut 'Liza Jane' the previous year – and introduced him to the band, basic orchestra and back-up vocalists, the Ladybirds (the vocal trio would go on to be in the in-house backing singers on both *The Benny Hill Show* and *Top of the Pops* and would appear alongside Sandi Shaw when she won the Eurovision Song Contest in Vienna two years later[4]). Marc would later say that he was brought back down to earth from the glamour of his first big recording experience by the sight of his backing singers 'talking about corsets and knitting'. The size of the ensemble and the complexity of the instrumentation meant far more takes and a far more involved recording process than would be necessary for a band like the Lower Third. Engineer Mike Hirst did most of the actual work of balancing the sound, operating the gear and working with the musicians – though it was Leander and Economides who would get the production credit.

The resulting record was undeniably good. It was weird, true, coming in at under two minutes with no real chorus to speak of and surrealist, fairytale lyrics, but as a piece of music, as a reflection of the craft of recording and arranging, it has plenty to recommend it. Hirst had done an excellent job with Leander's arrangement and Marc's two-chord, two-minute skeleton song. The track sounds remarkably lush and full, the flutes and strings and the backing

---

3. Leander would go on to achieve huge success in the 70s as the man behind Gary Glitter's music, creating the genuinely remarkable 'rock 'n' roll Part 2' almost entirely on his own in the studio.
4. The Ladybirds shouldn't be confused with another all-woman pop band in the 60s, also called the Ladybirds, from Denmark, whose main gimmick was performing topless. This second Ladybirds shouldn't be confused with yet another band called The Ladybirds, from the US, also all women. Remarkably this other Ladybird's main gimmick was *also performing topless*. All three bands were totally unaware of each other.

vocals contributing to a Phil Spectorish sound, but with a flowering oddness of its own. Marc acquitted himself well with the vocal, too. His voice is strong, and has an urgency to it not present on any of his earlier recordings. He'd not yet developed the distinctive vocal tics that would characterise his later work, but there is undoubtedly something here. The fact he achieves a compelling midpoint between Dylan's raw sincerity and Cliff's pleasing croon is, in itself, pretty impressive. It was the best record that either of the London boys had yet made. Alas, like the three Davey/Davy/Davie Jones records that preceded it, it would make very little impression.

Aside from the trivial detail of recording music, another equally vital process had taken place that summer, this time one of metamorphosis: Mark Feld had officially become Marc Bolan, or rather 'Marc Bölan' – the umlaut would come and go over the next few months. The first known use of his new name was in the *New Musical Express* article on 10 September, announcing his signing to Decca. Remarkably, that means that the newly christened 'David Bowie' and 'Marc Bolan' were introduced to the world exactly a week apart. While the origins of 'Bowie' are fairly clear, the inspiration for Marc's stage name is much, much harder to pin down. Mike Pruskin, who was the closest person to Marc at the time and thus probably our most reliable witness, has a pretty straightforward explanation: 'We were trying to find a more catchy name for Marc, and came across a French fashion designer called Marc Bohan,' he says in the book *Wilderness of the Mind*, 'so we changed it around a little and put an umlaut on top of the 'o' ... It was Marc and I who decided on the name, before Decca got involved.' Pruskin is quick to remind us that this is 'contrary to any other stories you have heard.' This explanation makes sense, especially given Marc's obsession with all things French. At the time, during an interview with Maureen Cleave of the *Evening Standard,* Pruskin explained that they included the umlaut for similarly francophile reasons. 'One admired them for hanging on to it even when it looked less French', Cleave tactfully observed of this very specifically *Germanic* affectation[5].

Pruskin's explanation seems solid enough, but it's just one of a myriad of origin stories produced over the years. Marc's school friend Richard Young claims that 'Mark once told me that the name Bolan came from two names: "Bo" for Bowie, and "lan" from "Dylan".'[6] This one is more unlikely, not least because Marc's adoption of 'Bolan' actually precedes David's of 'Bowie', by at least a few days. A similar and more plausible theory posits that Marc found

---

5. Maureen Cleave, who died in 2021 (coincidentally during the writing of this chapter) was a fantastic, witty and informed pop writer who expertly chronicled the unfolding culture of the sixties. It was from her interview with John Lennon that the infamous 'more popular than Jesus' quote came, later taken out of context and plastered across the US in a blaze of controversy. More impressively, she also helped Lennon out by polishing one of the verses to 'A Hard Day's Night' for him. A good pop journalist is a treasure.

6. Taken from his interview in Dylan Jones' oral history *David Bowie.*

'Bolan' by conflating the far ends of 'Bob' and 'Dylan', taking the 'Bo' and the 'lan' and simply slicing out the 'b Dy'. Meanwhile, Marc's former flatmate Riggs O'Hara – he of the Paris wizard trip – is sure that he took his surname from the other occupant of their flat, the actor James Bolam, at that point gaining fame as one of the two stars of the TV sitcom *The Likely Lads*. 'Jimmy got very offended and thought it really outrageous that Mark would take his name,' he told *Record Collector* in 1997, ' so Mark just changed the 'M' to an 'N', as simple as that. Nothing to do with Bob Dylan'. Marc, apparently, was baffled that Bolam would have an issue with someone encroaching on his personal brand. 'He couldn't understand why Jimmy was upset,' O'Hara explains. 'He thought it was absolutely ridiculous that Jimmy would think he was going to be as big as Mark was'. The 'James Bolam' theory is supported by an off-hand comment made in the September edition of *London Life* magazine, where Marc reveals he had originally considered 'Bolam' as a stage name. The autograph signed in the presence of David in July also appears to read 'Marc Bolam', and it's this version that Marc's brother, Harry suspects is most likely.

Yet still the theories keep coming – biographer Lesley-Ann Jones reckons that Marc's interest in eastern religions in his early teens led him to reading about the end of British rule in India in the year of his birth, 1947, and the colonial-era railway line that went across the country, entering what is now Pakistan via a valley known as the 'Bolān pass'. She speculates that the name could have been noted on some level and mentally filed for later use. Future Bolan manager Simon Napier-Bell claims that 'Bolan' comes from François 'Francy' Boland, a Belgian pianist, who guested on an EP by the legendary jazz horn player Chet Baker called *Chet Baker Sings*. The record was apparently a favourite of Marc's, who liked to carry it around with him, and he had spotted Boland's appealingly gallic sounding name while poring over the sleeve. 'I had it in my record collection too,' he told Jones in her book *Ride A White Swan*. 'He saw it in my flat. He happened to mention in passing one day that it had been the inspiration for the name he had chosen. I didn't twig at first, but then I got it.'

The one voice largely silent on the subject is Marc's own, who knew better than to puncture his own mystique with mundane truth. 'He understood the game, you see.' says Napier-Bell. 'An important aspect of stardom is the ability to keep them guessing. Once your fans know everything about you, once they realise that you are only as human as they are, they start losing interest.' One of the few times Marc came anywhere close to explaining his stage name was during an interview for Michael Wale's 1973 exploration of the music industry, *Vox Pop*. 'The first record I put out was under Marc Bolan, but it was spelt M-A-R-K B-O-W-L-A-N-D,' he explained, 'and it was totally a Decca fabrication. I thought, "Who's that?" you know. I didn't know it was my record because they'd stuck this name down!' Marc's attitude here is characteristically dismissive, and the idea of being callously re-named on the whim of a record exec, as so many young hopefuls before him had been, would have appealed to his sense of rock 'n' roll romance. There are, however, no documents listing a 'Mark Bowland' on Decca at the time. The *NME* announcement uses 'Bolan', and the single came out with 'Bölan' on the label (though curiously the umlaut is missing on one of the two sides). Pruskin says that even early acetates of 'The Wizard' were labelled 'Marc 'Bölan'. It's possible someone, somewhere, at some point in the organisation misheard the word and wrote down 'Bowland', but if that's the case then it was corrected fairly swiftly.

Marc's explanation – that his new surname was foisted on him by his label – is the only version in which he didn't decide on his name himself. However, given his stubborn self-belief, and the fact that Decca was happy for his wizardly creative vision to be presented as he told it, it's hard to believe that something as important as a stage name would have been decided without his input. There are so many versions and theories by this point that we cannot know with any certainty which is true – Perhaps it was a combination of all of them? Perhaps Marc encountered these similar sounding names again and again, until he finally took the hint from the universe and put his own twist on them? (Interestingly, among Bob ~~Dylan~~, Bowland, Bolam, Boham and Boland, there is no straightforward 'Bolan' in the list of potential inspirations.[7]) It's delightfully typical of his silver tongue that the least likely of all of these accounts, is Marc's own.

To give the execs at Decca their dues, legitimate effort was put into promoting 'The Wizard' and the label pulled out all of the stops that they hadn't bothered with for David's 'Liza Jane' the previous year, which had been snuck out on the lesser Vocalion Pop imprint. An intriguing press release declared that:

> 'Marc Bölan was born in September 1947. After fifteen years had passed he travelled to Paris and met a black magician called The Wizard. He lived for eighteen months in The Wizard's chateau with Archimedes, an owl, and the biggest, whitest Siamese cat you ever saw.'

It goes on to claim that Marc had travelled to Rome to 'find himself', before coming back to London to write about his 'magicians pact' with the 'great god Pan', acquiring a magic cat along the way, it was accompanied by a drawing of a particularly groovy looking black moggy. You have to admire Decca for leaning so far into Marc's strangeness. Three years later such surreal whimsy would be so commonplace as to feel a little lightweight and twee, but in the mod-sharp, bluesy world of 1965 pop, the company was taking a big swing by buying in so absolutely to Marc's tale.

---

7. There is the 'Bolān pass' theory posited by Lesley-Anne Jones, but with the exception of the 'Bowie + Dylan' suggestion, this feels like the least likely of the various possibilities.

In terms of press coverage, it seemed to work. Marc was featured in a lengthy piece in *The Observer* written by the great George Melly, of whom he was a huge fan. Melly had attended the recording of 'The Wizard' and had been won over by Marc's originality. 'The end product was certainly commercial, but the original impulse was not and something of this comes over' he wrote. 'Bolan's voice seems from the same stable as Donovan's. It's derived from Dylan and Guthrie. His songs, however, are his own.'[8] Maureen Cleave had visited the Bölan-Pruskin residence for a witty piece in the *Evening Standard* entitled 'Knit Yourself a Pop Singer', which Pruskin would later say they regretted, but contains some absolute pearls. Whereas Melly had made only the briefest mention of the 'black magic' angle, being presumably somewhat embarrassed by it, Cleave makes it the centre of her piece, letting Marc very much dig his own grave ('I learned about the black art but being evil didn't particularly appeal to me' says Marc. 'It's all true' adds Pruskin.) The most fascinating thing about the *Evening Standard* piece is how naked and upfront Marc is about his ambition. Despite his slightly dippy tales of Parisian black magic, his idea of what stardom is and could be was absolutely on the button, and perhaps even rather ahead of its time. 'The prospect of being immortal doesn't excite me,' he tells Cleave, 'but the prospect of being a materialistic idol for four years does appeal.' The quote could have come from the Marc Bolan of 1974. His reason for wanting this fame is clear: 'I'm sick of modelling and living off wizards,' he says.

On top of the press, Decca managed to land some fairly solid TV appearances for their new signing, though none of them apparently went very well. The most prestigious of these was also the most frustrating. *Ready, Steady, Go!*, like the BBC's slightly more staid *Top of the Pops*, was a rite of passage experience for a young pop star, especially one that had grown up on *Six-Five-Special* and *Oh Boy!*, the show for which *Ready, Steady* was a natural successor and which Marc had watched being recorded every Saturday in Hackney. David had played the show the previous year; it was one of the few bits of TV he'd achieved with 'Liza Jane'. Now it was Marc's turn. Again highlighting the small scale of the music industry at that time, Marc had a link to most of the acts performing – Tom Jones, like Marc, had been a Joe Meek hopeful, Nashville Teens had been working with Mike Pruskin until just a few months earlier and The Small Faces were fellow Carnaby Street mods – singer Steve Marriot was very much part of Marc and David's Soho circle. Just as David had felt when he found himself sharing studio space with John Lee Hooker and The Crickets, Marc could legitimately feel that he had, in some way, made

---

8. The rest of the feature is devoted to zeitgeisty mods the Small Faces, whose singer Steve Marriot had auditioned for the Lower Third alongside David. David himself was briefly a member of the Small Faces in their earliest days.

it.[9] The taping, alas, was nothing to be proud of. As a solo singer with no band, Marc had been thrown together with in-house players who had little rehearsal time with the material and made something of a hash of the live performance. 'The band played in the wrong key and missed the intro out,' Marc told Michael Wale. 'It was a terrible disaster the whole thing'. Unfortunately – or perhaps fortunately – no recording of the show survived. Marc performed 'The Wizard' on a handful of other pop shows, including *Five O'Clock Funfair* and *Thank Your Lucky Stars*. Again no recordings have survived, and though neither were as disastrous as *Ready, Steady, Go!*, neither would they provide Marc with an electrifying television moment that would enthral the watching audience – something that he would make his speciality in the early 70s. The biggest disappointment of the whole campaign was a televised charity gig at the Wembley Empire Pool, the 8,000-capacity north-London arena, with a fairly starry bill which included The Who, Georgie Fame, The Hollies and Wilson Picket. The show, a 'Glad Rag Ball' organised by students at the London School of Economics, was originally meant to be opened by John Lee Hooker and headlined by the Kinks, two loud and thrilling live acts. However, both pulled out and were replaced with Marc Bolan and Donovan, young men with acoustic guitars. Neither fared well that day, but Marc had it worse. He was still green as a live performer, and struggled to hold the attention of audiences in small clubs, let alone 8,000 rowdy students. He made it through his three-song set, but was greeted by boos and jeers as he left the stage. His performance was edited out of the television broadcast altogether, which in retrospect was probably for the best. The show had taken place on the day his debut single, 'The Wizard' was released. It was not a good omen.

Poring over the music papers the following week would have been a disappointing experience for Marc. After all the fuss, TV appearances, press and some relatively decent reviews he could be forgiven for expecting a chart showing for his debut. Alas, even *Record Mirror*'s modest prediction that the disc would have 'enough appeal to hit the lower reaches of the charts at least' proved to be wildly optimistic. In fact, most of the press the song generated, features and reviews alike, seemed to have called it wrong. Almost every journalist and critic to cover Marc, from the high brow George Melly in the *Observer* right down to pop specialist Penny Valentine at *Disc Weekly*, had talked up the song's potential and written about his 'bright future'.[10] Of all of 'The Wizard's' reviews, only Judith Durham, the singer with Australian folkies The Seekers, seemed

---

9. Also performing that day was soul legend Wilson Pickett and French singer Sylvie Vartan. Marc had no direct connection to Pickett, but he would definitely have danced to his tunes. Vartan, meanwhile, established her Bolan connection that very day – he was able to charm her into taking a copy of 'The Wizard' home to France, and she ultimately ended up recording a cover of the b-side, 'Beyond the Rising Sun'.

10. Suggesting that pop critics are either incredibly perceptive fortune tellers seeing further into the future than they could know, or else are making it up as they go along.

to have it right when she cast an eye over the singles in *Melody Maker*'s weekly 'Blind Date' column and called it 'a bit too raucous for the hit parade'.[11] 'Too raucous' seems a little uncharitable in the year when The Who were probably the coolest breakthrough band in Britain, but she was bang on about the song not being chart friendly. Despite terrific prospects, 'The Wizard' joined David's first three singles as another London boy flop.

The failure of Marc's debut needs a little unpacking. There are straightforward reasons for why *David's* first three singles flopped: 'Liza Jane' was technically a major label release, but Decca had done the absolute bare minimum to support it and the song was so generic that it struggled to get noticed in a crowded market. David didn't yet have the charisma to sell any old brand of snow back to the Eskimos. His next label, Parlophone, was equally half-hearted in its marketing; 'I Pity The Fool' was a much better song than 'Liza Jane', but its main publicity came from a manufactured scandal that had everything to do with hair and nothing to do with music, focusing on one band member whose name didn't even appear on the label. 'You've Got a Habit of Leaving Me', meanwhile, had basically no promotion at all. It was a decent enough tune, but had nothing to help it stand out from the pack. 'The Wizard' was different. Someone at Decca clearly believed in Marc's record, and its marketing department had put the requisite hours in. It had even received favourable notices from critics and radio; yet that record, too, sank without a trace. Why? Partly the blame is with Marc himself. You can put an artist in front of an audience, work hard to get them on TV, or on the bill at a prestigious event, but as soon as they open their mouth or hit their first chord then it's entirely up to them. The blunt truth is that Marc simply wasn't ready – his TV appearances had been either disastrous or forgettable, and at the solo acoustic gigs he played at the time, he came off like a shy, amateurish Bob Dylan[12], not an image that gelled with his brash interviews or imaginative music. The song itself, meanwhile, was perhaps, with its trippy imagery and fantastical tone, a little ahead of its time. Critics and DJs who lived and breathed the shifting trends of pop might have dimly sensed something of the near future in it, but the general music-buying audience wasn't quite ready. Forward-looking, progressive records need mass playback, rave reviews and ideally a following or a movement – a fandom or a subculture to sit within. Alas, the mild interest 'The Wizard' received from the media wasn't enough to pique the curiosity of the marketplace.

In the rather clinical music business of the 21st century, a record like this would be focus-grouped; different PR and marketing firms might pitch innovative campaigns, specialist receptive media would be schmoozed, radio pluggers

---

11. Marc himself would get to be the *Maker*'s 'Blind Date' during his 70s pomp, where he dubbed new discs by Elvis and Billy Fury as unworthy of their glorious pasts, but enjoyed offerings from Neil Young and Randy Newman.

12. Probably because he *was* a shy, amateurish Bob Dylan.

would enthuse to sympathetic DJs and words like 'soft launch' and 'teaser track' would be thrown around. The music business of 1965 had not yet developed such sophisticated tactics. Pop was still a new game, and those gatekeeping it at the commissioning level often had little to no cultural relationship with their customers. Again, execs were throwing everything at the wall to see what stuck, and any artist not immediately found to be sticky enough would be lucky to get another chance to find a receptive surface on which to adhere. An episode of ITV's documentary series *World In Action*, which aired toward the end of 1964, examined the music industry of the era – it portrays a business in which almost every record exec, plugger and manager seems to be a besuited man in his forties, looking far more like a used car salesman or branch manager of a high street bank than someone controlling one of the engines that drove youth culture at one of the most exciting times his (and it *is* always 'his') industry will ever go through. Marc Bolan, umlaut or not, was a product that no-one knew how to market. The industry's usual tactic for dealing with a failed product was to toss it into the reject pile and start again on the next pliable and potentially sticky star and that's more or less what happened here. Marc was asked to come up with a solid follow-up single, and cut some scratch demos with Mike Leander in December 1965 but Decca didn't feel any of them were strong enough, and promptly shoved Marc down the chute to the reject pile. This would be the pattern for both London boys throughout 1966 and into 67 – secure a deal, release a few singles, see them flop, get dropped, get up, dust themselves off, find a new label, repeat to fade – flop, drop and roll.

Chapter Ten

Loose Change

David's new manager, Ralph Horton, though a little haphazard, quickly proved that he meant business. By the end of 1965, three achievements in particular were to prove key as the newly christened, shorter-haired David Bowie emerged, blinking onto the scene. Firstly, David Bowie and the Lower Third were signed to Marquee Artists, a booking agency working out of the now-famous London venue, The Marquee. MA were a national and international live booker and were able to start filling the band's diary – which was badly needed, as work had started to dry up in recent months, and money was becoming increasingly tight. Cash flow would become an increasingly sore point for the Lower Third. For now, though, things were looking up; the band even played a run of shows in France, including a New Year's Eve gig in Paris with Arthur Brown, a show which drummer Phil Lancaster considers among the best received they ever played. More important, though, were the gigs at the Marquee itself. David had played the venue with the Manish Boys – his sometime-girlfriend Dana Gillespie met him after seeing them there in 1964 – but after signing with MA it became something of a second home. The Lower Third played a regular Friday night residency at the club, allowing them to start building a true following. Later they would be the house band for a Saturday afternoon show produced for the pirate station Radio London and sponsored by Inecto Shampoo, and would play live, unbroadcast sets between chart stars of the day; The Who, Stevie Wonder, the Kinks and more. Horton also secured work outside London, with regular gigs in Bournemouth and on the Isle of Wight, opening for higher profile headliners like The Who, Pretty Things, Them and Johnny Kidd and the Pirates. These gave David and the band much needed stage time as they developed into a tight, reliable live act and arguably the best live band Bowie would have in the whole decade. It also meant that David felt comfortable enough to start pushing at the musical edges of what a pop band in the mid sixties could and should be. The band added an instrumental, show-stopping version of the classical piece 'Mars, Bringer of War' from the *Planets* suite (and more significantly from Bowie favourite *The Quatermass Experiment*, a terrifying sci-fi show first broadcast in the early fifties), as well as a raucous take on 'Chim Chim Cheree' from Disney's *Mary Poppins*. Alas, no recording of either has made it into the world, so we can only speculate at their style and quality. He suggested that the rest of the band start wearing makeup, enhancing their classic-mod credentials ('Not fucking likely' was bass player Graham Rivens' response – the idea was quickly taken off the table.) Not only was David starting to assemble the building blocks of theatricality he would eventually use to build his 70s career, he was – as ever – something of a canary in the coalmine for emerging pop trends. The beat era was coming to an end, and newer bands like The Small Faces, of whom Bowie was very briefly a member, and The Kinks were learning lessons in storytelling from Dylan and in sonic expansion from The Beatles and Beach Boys, finding that combining the two created a sound and image that chimed with London's own cultural heritage of Music Hall and musical theatre. Bowie's insertion of classical themes, theatrical presentation and *Mary Poppins* alongside his increasingly impressive original compositions and contemporary covers – the Third were known to sling in songs by the Kinks and James Brown, among others, to keep their audience on side – was very much in the spirit of the time. British pop was growing beyond four chords, shaggy hair and Chelsea boots.

Horton's second big win as Bowie's manager was, alas, less useful for the band themselves, though that wasn't really his fault. As with Marc's appearances to promote 'The Wizard', management can hardly be blamed for their client's performance once the music started. That November, Horton arranged an audition for the band with BBC radio. At the time the BBC was falling way behind the commercial pirate stations – London, Caroline and Luxembourg – in pop music clout. While the pirates were free to play whatever they liked[1], the BBC's hands were tied by its 'public service' remit and national broadcaster status. Vinyl had replaced sheet music as the medium of choice for popular songs and the Musicians' Union had started to panic about loss of revenue for its members. In order to keep everyone happy, an agreement was made between the union, the copyright authorities and the BBC which limited the amount of records that could be played on air to eight songs across a two hour broadcast – a quota known as 'needle time'. The only way around this for pop-focused presenters like Brian Matthew, the host of the popular *Saturday Club*, was to invite bands in to play live, or pre-record renditions of their latest hits (or indeed other people's – the corporation would regularly bring in jobbing musicians to bang out hits of the day rather than pay the stars themselves). As these were real, live musicians performing real, live music, the union was kept happy. The limited needle time made getting a pop record played on BBC radio an absolute nightmare. It was all well and good for The Beatles to develop a cosy relationship with *Saturday Club* and pop in every few months to play their new tunes and some golden oldies, but less-known bands had to face an uphill battle that started in front of an audition panel.

---

1. Technically they were breaking the law both by broadcasting records and broadcasting without a license, but there was very little anyone could do about it.

David and the band headed to the BBC's Broadcasting House, located then as now at the terminus of Regent Street in central London, to perform three songs: Bowie's own 'Baby, That's a Promise', James Brown's 'Out of Sight' and, rather bravely, the quartet's cover of 'Chim Chim Cheree'.[2] It did not go well. 'There is no entertainment in anything they do,' said one of the corporation's panellists, going on to describe them as 'very ordinary, too ... [with] a singer devoid of personality'. Another called the band a 'routine beat group' with an 'amateur-sounding vocalist who sings wrong notes and out of tune'. Perhaps most damning of all was the panel member who saw absolutely no future for the group – 'I don't think the group will get better with more rehearsal' they said. 'What we heard will always be the product.' The tape of the session has never been made available, and it's doubtful – though possible – that it has survived the intervening half century or so. It would be a fascinating listen, and not just because there are no other known recordings of two of the numbers performed that day, 'Chim Chim Cheree' and 'Out of Sight'. A tape of the session would answer the one burning question we're left with here – 'could they really have been *that* bad?'

As tempting as it is to picture the BBC's selection committee as elbow-patched stuffed-shirts still stuck in the 1950s, the fact that there seems to be a consensus across the board of panellists suggests that the Lower Third were not at their best that day. It *is* curious though. By all accounts, the band were reliable performers and there's plenty of evidence from the time that Bowie was already a competent vocalist, by now fairly used to working in the studio, having cut 'You've Got A Habit of Leaving' earlier that year and demoed several tunes since. Perhaps they were just having an off day? Perhaps nerves got the better of them? It's also likely that the choice of material worked against them. The sole original piece, 'Baby, That's A Promise', had been knocking about in the band's repertoire for a few months, but by the standards of David's material of the time, it was pretty tame stuff; a beat-group-by-numbers track which the band had demoed a few months prior. A tape of those demo sessions has survived, but 'Baby, That's A Promise', unlike other recordings made in the same session, has never received an official release – which in itself speaks volumes.[3] We don't know what the Lower Third's version of Brown's 'Out of Sight' was like, and the BBC panel didn't seem to think it warranted a mention one way or another ... which leaves 'Chim Chim Cheree'. The inclusion of a reworked Disney song was a ballsy move, which apparently backfired spectacularly. Several of the panellists mentioned the song directly or referenced the group's 'odd choice

2. Bowie himself would later say that another number, then called 'Now You've Met The London Boys' was also played, though as the song isn't mentioned in the various retellings by other band members or in any of the BBC feedback, it's possible he was misremembering this.
3. It has been bootlegged numerous times of course, and is easy to track down online if you want to judge for yourself.

of material' as a mark against them, with one singling it out specifically. 'The treatment of Chim Chim Cher-ee kills the song completely' they said. 'Instead of being bright and gay the song becomes a sad ballad.'[4] Though we can't hear the Third's version of the tune (which drummer Phil Lancaster describes as 'raucous' in his memoir), it's a fairly safe assumption that if the tone of the original was changed to be less 'bright and gay', the effect would have been absolutely intentional. Either these apparently out-of-touch, square panellists missed the point, or else the point wasn't being made well enough – either way, the disappearance of the song from Bowie's post-Lower Third sets does suggest that he was stung by the experience.

The third and most significant of Horton's contributions to Bowie's career came with his fulfilling of a promise to find the band a new record deal, introducing David to Tony Hatch, the in-house producer/A&R (in those days the two roles were essentially the same thing) for Pye records. Pye was home to hot-right-now names like The Kinks and Sandi Shaw, as well as skiffle legend Lonnie Donegan, and seemed on the surface to be a good fit for a delighted Lower Third. However, Hatch, who would be producing the group, wasn't much for rock 'n' roll. A Burt Bacharach devotee, his taste was for smart, tasteful pop. He'd written Petula Clarke's huge 'Downtown' and Bobby Rydell's 'Forget Him', and had previously worked with the super-safe likes of Pat Boone and Connie Francis.[5] His only brush with the beat boom had been writing and producing The Searchers; Merseybeat contemporaries of the Beatles. It's telling that where George Martin had polished The Beatles into their best selves, Hatch had rather sanitised the Searchers[6]. Still, Pye had the exciting rattle and hum of The Kinks, suggesting the label would know how to handle a racket like David Bowie and the Lower Third.[7]

Hatch, as it turned out, could take or leave the group as a stage-shaking rock experience. He was, however, extremely interested in David Bowie as a songwriter. Sourcing songs for the various artists under his care was a time consuming business, and in David he hoped to have an act that could generate his own material in the way The Kinks did, and perhaps also provide songs for

---

4. The same panellist goes on to say that Bowie is a 'cockney type' but 'not outstanding enough'.
5. He would go on to write TV theme music, including the themes to *Crossroads*, *Emmerdale* and – perhaps most famously – the intro music to the Aussie soap *Neighbours*.
6. The two groups make for an interesting case study. Both had similar backgrounds, and had arrived at the bright lights of London via the clubs of Liverpool and Hamburg, where they played largely the same sets of rock 'n' roll standards. Those years provided both bands with much of their early repertoire, however George Martin was able to keep some of the raw energy of The Beatles' club sets in their recordings, while Hatch drained a lot of the life out of The Searchers. For evidence, compare and contrast both bands' versions of 'Twist 'N Shout', 'Some Other Guy' and 'Money (That's What I Want)'.
7. On the other hand and with no small irony, it had been David's previous producer, Shel Talmy, rather than Tony Hatch that recorded the Kink's breakthrough hits, and that under the close direction of Ray Davies.

other Pye signings. Hatch may not have been a rock aficionado, but he knew quality song-writing when he heard it and his faith in David's work, or at the very least in his potential, tells us how fast Bowie was growing as a writer. The first song the band attempted with Hatch was a prime example of that flowering talent – 'The London Boys' (then still called 'Now You've Met The London Boys') had been part of the group's live set for a while by that point, and was apparently a fan favourite: Phil Lancaster remembers audiences cheering when they recognised the intro. It's arguably the best of David's mid-sixties lyrics, a mid-tempo, faintly melancholy slice of mod life, all 'flashy clothes', pill taking and Soho. There's more depth here than Bowie simply sticking his head out of the door of La Gioconda and writing down what he saw. The 'London Boys' of the story are lonely, unfulfilled, too young to appreciate that their lives are essentially empty. Being a 'London Boy' doesn't feel like it's very much fun. This was Bowie reflecting on his own life and seeing the gaps rather than the glow. It's a remarkable piece of writing for someone not yet nineteen.

The song wouldn't emerge until the following year, entirely re-recorded and given a much more downbeat feel. According to the Lower Third's Phil Lancaster, the original version was a tougher, livelier beast, which Hatch was apparently quite happy with in the studio but appeared to cool on soon after. Pye would eventually decide that any controversy resulting from the edgy lyrics would probably not be worth the effort, and the session was consigned to the vault where it remains at the time of writing.[8] Instead the label opted for another Hatch-produced, Bowie original – 'Can't Help Thinking About Me', released just after the new year in 1966, a week after David had turned nineteen. Along with 'The London Boys', 'Can't Help Thinking' shows the stellar ground David was already covering as a lyricist and as a singer. Listening now, it's hard to believe that just a few months before it was recorded, the BBC's accreditation committee was dismissing Bowie as an unexceptional writer and poor vocalist – it's an excellent, full-throated performance of an intriguing and layered lyric. Even its title betrays an askew version of pop traditions – most stars addressed their songs to someone else, a sweetheart, a brother, a fantasy but David Bowie was already thinking mostly of himself. The quality of the writing didn't go unnoticed, either. Pop mogul Jonathan King[9], writing in his column in *Music Echo*, evangelised about it. 'The tune is catchy,' he says, 'the performance impeccable and the lyrics outstanding … this is a disc which does not deserve to die'.

Pye gave the release a decent enough promo campaign, taking out adverts in the music press, including half of the front page of the *NME*, and securing reviews, airplay and TV coverage, with the obligatory spot on *Ready, Steady,*

8. The masters of the session turned up in 2016 so it's likely the first version of 'The London Boys' will see the light of day at some point. You may already have heard it.

9. Now, of course, the *disgraced* pop mogul Jonathan King.

Young children during the Blitz in London. David and Marc would have spent their childhood surrounded by sites like this. (*New Times Paris Bureau Collection, Wikimedia Commons*)

Stoke Newington Common where Marc was raised, as it is today (*Author's collection*)

The house on Stoke Newington Common in which Marc lived until his teens. (*Author's collection*)

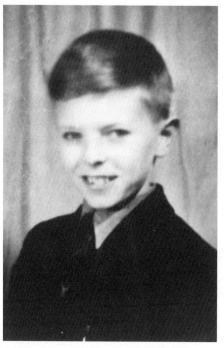

A young David Bowie, aged around seven years old, roughly 1954. (*Pictorial Press Ltd / Alamy Stock Photo*)

The plaque marking the house on Stoke Newington Common in which Marc lived until his teens. (*Author's collection*)

David's hero Little Richard, 'The Innovator, Originator, the Architect of Rock and Roll,' pictured on a Topps gum card in 1957. (*Wikimedia Commons*)

One of Marc's heroes, Cliff Richard, from his first US television appearance on *The Pat Boone Chevy Showroom* in 1960. (*Public domain*)

Bill Haley, the decidedly square bandleader who kicked the door open for rock 'n' roll as a mainstream force, and changed Marc Bolan's life. Pictured with his band The Comets in the 1954 *Universal International film Roundup Of Rhythm*. (*Public domain*)

The plaque dedicated to David, adorning the Plaistow Grove house. (*Wikimedia Commons*)

The house at Plaistow Grove in Bromley, where David Bowie lived with his family from 1955 until he moved in with Ken Pitt in 1967. (*Wikimedia Commons*)

The crowded interior of the 2 I's coffee bar at 59 Old Compton Street, London, about 1958. (*Alamy*)

'All they did was break things, windows, and locks and bones. There was nothing else to do.' – Teddy Boys pictured in Gateshead in the early 60s. (*Mirrorpix/Reach*)

'Where is the goal toward which he is running as fast as his impeccably shod feet can carry him?' Mark Feld and friends, pictured in *Town* magazine in 1962. (*Don McCullin/Camera Press*)

A Grafton alto saxophone identical to the one David received for Christmas in 1961 and played in the Kon-Rads. (*Wikimedia Commons*)

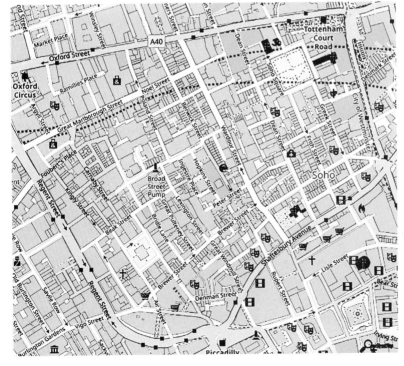

The square mile of Soho as it is today, note Denmark Street in the upper-right. (*Wikimedia Commons*)

Bob Dylan, who changed the game for both London boys in 1963, performing at St. Lawrence University in New York. (*Public Domain*)

'David Jay' with his Conn Sax in a photoshoot for the Kon-Rads, 1963. (*Avalon*)

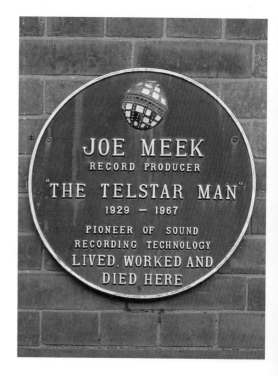

The blue plaque at 304 Holloway Road, marking the location of Joe Meek's studio. (*Public domain*)

Davie Jones and the Manish Boys, pictured outside BBC Television centre before their performance on *Gadzooks! It's All Happening*, March 1965 The performance was the subject of an entirely manufactured controversy over the group's long hair. (*Trinity Mirror / Mirrorpix / Alamy Stock Photo*)

The fearless leader of the definitely-real activist group The Society For The Prevention of Cruelty To Long Haired Men, pictured March 1965. (*Trinity Mirror / Mirrorpix / Alamy Stock Photo*)

Marc, shortly after cutting 'The Wizard' in 1965. (*Trinity Mirror / Mirrorpix / Alamy Stock Photo*)

Swinging Londoners cutting a dash on Carnaby Street in 1966. (*Wikimedia Commons*)

David Bowie and The Buzz appear on Ready, Steady, Go! In 1966. (*Pictorial Press Ltd / Alamy Stock Photo*)

Trade ad for David Bowie's single 'Love You Till Tuesday', 1967. (*Wikimedia Commons*)

Bowie photographed on the rooftops of the city near Paddington, 1968. (*Tracksimages.com / Alamy Stock Photo*)

a first LP that is different

DAVID BOWIE

Ⓢ SML 1007   Ⓓ DML 1007   12" stereo or mono LP record

another great new sound on **DERAM**

Deram Records Decca House Albert Embankment London SE1

A music press Ad for David Bowie's debut album, as it appeared in *Disc & Music Echo*, 1967.

Anthony Newley, one of
David's biggest influences
during the early part of
his career, pictured with
Tom Jones on American
televisions, 1969.
(*Wikimedia Commons*)

Adverts for both the Dury Lane
Arts Lab (where David would
appear many times) and the
Middle Earth club in Covent
Garden, where Tyrannosaurus
Rex played several gigs, appeared
in *International Times*, 1967.
(*Reproduced with kind permission
of International Times*)

A newspaper advert for upcoming shows at Middle Earth. Note Tyrannosaurs Rex opening for the Jeff Beck Group. (*Reproduced with kind permission of International Times*)

A newspaper advert for one of Tyrannosaurus Rex's biggest headline shows, with David Bowie (as a mime) supporting. (*Reproduced with kind permission of International Times*)

Newspaper advert placed in the music press by
Ken Pitt showcasing Bowie's mime shows.

An advert in *International Times* introducing David's first appearance in *Studies Toward An Experiment into the Structure of Dreams* sometime in 1968. (*Reproduced with kind permission of International Times*)

A newspaper advert for the debut Tyrannosaurus Rex album, 1968's *My People Were Fair and Had Sky In Their Hair … But Now They're Content To Wear Stars on their Brows.* (*Regal Zonophone/ EMI, reproduced with kind permission of International Times*)

A newspaper advert for the second Tyrannosaurus Rex album of 1968, *Prophets, Seers and Sages: The Angels of Ages.* (*Regal Zonophone/ EMI, reproduced with kind permission of International Times*)

A 1969 newspaper advert for the third Tyrannosaurus Rex album, *Unicorn.* (*Regal Zonophone/ EMI, reproduced with kind permission of International Times*)

A newspaper advert for Tyrannosaurus Rex's 1969 single 'Pewter Suitor'. (*Regal Zonophone/ EMI, reproduced with kind permission of International Times*)

Contact sheet from a Tyrannosaurus Rex photoshoot, featuring Marc Bolan and Steve Peregrin Took, by Tony Gale at the Pictorial Press offices in Salisbury Court, Fleet Street, London on 28 August 1968. (*Pictorial Press Ltd / Alamy Stock Photo*)

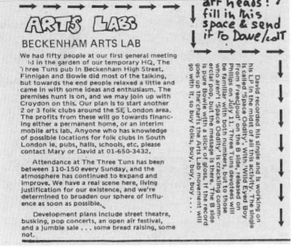

A short article by David Bowie and Mary Finnegan advertising the Beckenham Arts Lab in 1969 which ran in International Times. (*Reproduced with kind permission*)

A press advert for 'Space Oddity' as the publicity machine finally kicks into gear, September 1969. (*Philips/Mercury*)

David and Angela Bowie on their wedding day in 1970, accompanied by David's mum, Peggy Jones. (*Kent News, Pictorial Press Ltd / Alamy Stock Photo*)

Marc Bolan with new recruit Mickey Finn circa 1970. (*Pictorial Press Ltd / Alamy Stock Photo*)

Bowie in 1970, around the release of 'The Prettiest Star'. (*Pictorial Press Ltd / Alamy Stock Photo*)

Go!. Horton, however, wasn't content to let the label get on with things, and did his best to grease the song's way to the top. He hired his own publicist who immediately tried to drum up interest from the press – unsuccessfully as it turned out – by having the band pose in Hyde Park with a trans woman who had recently undergone gender confirmation surgery, presumably because gender transitions were still relatively rare and had some sort of novelty value in the press. The pictures featured the four lads holding her, according to Phil Lancaster, 'like a rolled up carpet'. The shots, alas, got absolutely no traction and appear to have been lost to time. Horton also organised a launch party at a bar near Hyde Park, The Victoria Tavern, inviting any music hack or photographer who could be tempted along, most of Pye's staff and the odd bored-looking rock 'n' roller. The only famous name anyone seems to be able to recall being there was Alfred 'Freddie' Lennon, John Lennon's estranged, vagabond father, who had recently signed a deal with Pye; the label hoping to benefit from a little second-hand Beatle cache.[10] David spent the evening failing to engage journalists, but charming the girls from the Pye office. The fact that Tony Hatch, the band's producer, who was relatively famous in his own right and would at least have supplied a decent photo op, failed to attend suggests that no-one high up at the label was taking Horton's efforts particularly seriously.

All of this extracurricular marketing was funded by Horton's friend Raymond Cook, who like John Bloom before him was an appliances mogul charmed by David into venturing some money in the pop market. Bloom loaned Horton, David and the band £1,500 in return for an almost absurdly generous ten percent of earnings, so long as Bowie's income topped £100 per month. Horton would go back to Cook, cap in hand, several times, and the money essentially bankrolled Bowie and Horton's plans. Eventually Cook would cough up £250 – not exactly chump change in 1966 – for a decidedly dodgy attempt to 'buy' 'Can't Help Thinking About Me' into the charts. It helped the single limp into the very lower end of the *Melody Maker* top forty, peaking at thirty-four, but Cook put his foot down about funding any more nefarious record buying and the song slipped out of the chart the next week. Poor Ray Cook would never see a penny returned on his investment.

It's worth a short note here on the way the 'charts' worked during this era ... in that they basically didn't. The modern idea of the pop chart had been pioneered

---

10. They needn't have bothered. Despite apparently respectable sales, Freddie's one single, 'That's My Life (My Love, My Home)' – which is actually kind of charming in a syrupy, nostalgic way – mysteriously vanished from the charts, killing his career stone dead. Rumours have swirled for years that Brian Epstein had pulled some strings at a mortified John Lennon's request, and managed to get the single buried. On the day of the Lower Third's launch party, a rumour went around that John himself would be popping in – alas, inviting Freddie almost guaranteed that his son was never going to turn up. Bowie, already displaying solid media savvy, was the only member of the Lower Third to duck out of a photo with the older Lennon, rightly assuming that the association would do him no favours.

by the *NME* in the early fifties – the paper's co-founder, Percy Dickens, would call around twenty or so music stores, mostly in London, and ask them which records were selling best, compiling the results into a chart published in the following week's edition, correctly assuming that a weekly chart would drive both sales and advertising, and increase the paper's power. Other papers, notably *Record Mirror*, *Melody Maker*, *Disc* and *Record Retailer*, soon followed suit, and by the mid 60s the BBC also had its own top 30 chart[11]. Crucially each chart had a different methodology and used different sources in different ways to measure success, meaning there was usually some disparity between them. It also meant the charts were easy to rig if you knew which shops were being used as a source by which papers. 'There wasn't anything to stop you putting a load of girls in taxis, telling them which shops to go to, especially on Thursday and Friday,' Andrew Loog Oldham, the manager of the Rolling Stones, told *Q* Magazine. 'We'd send them back in on a Saturday to re-order when there was no stock there, so that you got big re-orders on the Monday morning.' Tony Calder, who along with Loog Oldham would go on to form the UK's first independent music PR firm, IMAGE, admitted in the same interview to spending £500 per week on bribing key shop staff to fiddle the numbers.[12] Don Arden, who managed The Small Faces and The Nashville Teens, had a network of housewives spread across the country on £10-per-week retainers, charged with buying specific records in specific shops at specific times, and Brian Epstein was rumoured to have purchased 10,000 copies of 'Love Me Do' upon its release, ostensibly to sell in his own shop, and claimed he'd sold the lot – getting the single into the top ten within weeks. Simon Napier-Bell, who managed The Yardbirds and would go on to manage Marc, claimed he could just call up a guy known as 'Gerry' and negotiate any chart placement you wanted.[13]

Eventually, in 1969, an 'official' chart was launched, using written records from many more shops than any of the individual papers had access to (around 250 at first). All official chart data prior to this usually comes from the *Record Retailer* Top 40, which was retrospectively declared the most reliable – being an industry paper with less commercial clout, it was generally considered less subject to rigging and hyping. Even so, it means that analysing any music charts from before the launch of the UK Top 40 is far from an exact science.[14]

---

11. Hence why, to this day, we say a single gets in the 'charts', plural.
12. A tactic that backfired spectacularly when an error with dates took the Beach Boys' 'Help Me Rhonda' to number one before the record had actually been pressed, much to the surprise of the band's label, EMI.
13. 'Gerry' would then sting you for more cash to continue to keep the record in the charts so that it fell out of the top 40 naturally, rather than plummeting like a stone after a week and giving the game away.
14. Any pre-69 chart positions mentioned in this book will be from the *Record Retailer* chart unless otherwise noted.

However it was achieved, the brief incursion 'Can't Help Thinking About Me' made into the bottom few inches of the *Melody Maker* chart wasn't, by any stretch of the definition, a success, though Tony Hatch remembers Bowie himself being fairly pleased with the result, which seems odd given his towering self-belief and ambition. Perhaps he thought it was a necessary stepping stone? Perhaps he had faith in Horton's vision for his future? Still, it's unavoidable that this was David's fourth single and fourth flop. He was also on his fourth band in four years. The songs were getting better, but something wasn't working.

David's inevitable split with the Lower Third happened barely a week later, and though this time it wasn't directly linked to the failure of the single (the rest of the band staged a mutiny after Horton claimed he had no money to pay them) the break did mark a watershed in his career. The Lower Third were the last real rock 'n' roll band that David would join for many years and their replacements, The Buzz, were under no illusions about their roles on Team Bowie. David had been a collaborative band member in the Kon-Rads, King Bees, Manish Boys and The Lower Third. Though he'd managed to float his name to the top of the bill in three out of the four groups, those bands all considered themselves democratic units, to a greater or lesser extent ... the Buzz, however, were specifically formed to back a solo artist, which they did quite literally – David told them firmly that the front of the stage was his territory alone. As usual Bowie moved fast: the split with the Lower Third had happened on 29 January and David Bowie and The Buzz, hired via a *Melody Maker* advert and some asking around in Tin Pan Alley, made their stage debut on 10 February.[15]

It wasn't just a matter of a change in backing musicians. The departure of the Lower Third essentially brought about the final death of David Jones, the R&B wannabe. Since leaving the Kon-Rads David had been keeping pace with pop trends, always in step with the zeitgeist, though not yet at its cutting edge. The wording on his singles had varied[16], but he'd still always fundamentally been the singer in a band. David Jones had been, more or less, a team player. Future singles would be credited to 'David Bowie' alone. Musically things were changing too. The Buzz were a tamer bunch, missing the Who-ish fizz and boom of The Lower Third and with substantially less chemistry. Gigs became a showcase for David himself, hence a run of Sunday afternoon shows at the Marquee advertised under the banner of 'The Bowie Showboat'. In the

---

15. Jimmy Page, the young guitarist who had added his skills to the Manish Boys' 'I Pity The Fool' auditioned for the Buzz, but was beaten to the gig by John 'Hutch' Hutchinson who would go on to be a Bowie collaborator on and off into the 70s. Despite this knock back, Page ended up doing alright for himself.

16. 'Liza Jane' was credited to Davey Jones and the King Bees, 'I Pity The Fool' merely to The Manish Boys, 'You've Got A Habit of Leaving' to plain old Davy Jones, while 'Can't Help Thinking About Me' was credited to David Bowie *with* The Lower Third. Technically all four singles had been credited to completely different artists, and almost all of them had caused an internal row of one sort or another.

studio, Tony Hatch was taking things in a more, well, *Tony Hatch* direction, less concerned with harnessing the knockabout punch of a band's live sound, and more interested in achieving a palatable sonic polish.

David's next single, April's 'Do Anything You Say', was the first to be credited to 'David Bowie' alone (an uncredited Buzz provided the backing) and though musically still in the mod/R&B mould, was a less raucous, less punchy channelling of the Pete Townshend template. It was the beginning of a transition process. By the time we get to David's final Pye single, June's 'I Dig Everything', the mod rock was fading and a groovy, lighter pop was taking its place. Both singles were flops, but were at least important stepping stones as Davy Jones retreated further back into his locker and David Bowie began to find himself as a solo artiste. He and Horton's plans were getting ever more elaborate, with David himself losing interest in being a mere rock 'n' roller, and eyeing up wider roles in the entertainment world – acting, writing, theatre, cabaret. Horton, who was in-thrall to his young charge, merely nodded and promised he'd make it happen.

On the business side, it was becoming increasingly apparent that Ralph Horton didn't have the skills or the capital to get David over the various hurdles littering his route to the top. Ray Cook had finally turned off the money tap and was hoping that at some point his ten-percent cut was going to start rolling back toward him (David's next manager was to spend a long time untangling that particular arrangement). Despite Horton's big ideas, his E-Type Jag and his book of contacts, even he was beginning to understand that he was out of his depth. He liked the idea of being an Andrew Loog Oldham, a Kit Lambert or a Brian Epstein but didn't seem to have the savvy or the organisational skills necessary to get there. The solution was to look for a co-manager. As 1966 began, Horton would approach several known and unknown figures about co-managing David (technically alongside his silent partner, Ray Cook.) One such was Simon Napier-Bell, the manager of the Yardbirds, who remembers visiting Horton's Belgravia flat. Napier-Bell claims that Horton literally offered sex with David as a sweetener if they went into business together, an offer he says he rejected. Whether this is actually true or not is up for debate.[17] Horton was also hopeful that he could reel in Kenneth Pitt, the manager who had suggested the previous year that David would need a new name. Pitt was tempted; he had no intention of taking on a rock band, but the departure of the Lower Third and Horton's assurances that David had the potential to be an 'all round entertainer', not just a pop singer, certainly piqued his interest. David, however, wasn't the only wannabe vying for Ken Pitt's attention. In January 1966, Pitt had been contacted by a teenage manager called Mike Pruskin, wondering if he could

---

17. 'Consequently, I neither slept with Bowie nor managed him,' Napier-Bell later told his friend, the journalist Lesley-Ann Jones, 'In retrospect, I admit that both things might have been worth doing.'

help him with a young artist he was working with, who had just released his own debut single through Decca. Pitt found himself trying to decide between managing two young unknowns, both with bags of potential – David Bowie and Marc Bolan.

With his fairly typical knack for self-mythology, Marc would later tell the writer Michael Vale that he had 'spent a year trying to get away from Decca,' saying that they 'wouldn't record me'. Even by the standards of Marc's bare-faced fibbing, this one was an absolute whopper. As 1966 dawned, Decca records couldn't wait to get shot of him. An unsuccessful demo session over Christmas 1965 should have spelled the end of his time with the label, however Jim Economides, the young engineer/would-be A&R who had been instrumental in signing Marc in the first place, pushed for more songs. He responded with one of his best yet, 'The Third Degree', a solid rocker with a loping groove and lyrics that, though compelling, were unarguably less out-there than 'The Wizard'. To Economides it sounded like a hit, but his paymasters at Decca had no interest in maintaining an act that, as far as they were concerned, had blown his chance. Instead Economides funded studio time and session players himself (including future Led Zeppelin bass player John-Paul Jones) and was able to convince Decca to licence the single back from him to release, which since they no longer had to stump up for a recording session, felt like a reasonable compromise. Unfortunately, as the label had very little stake in the record's success it was given only a fraction of the attention and publicity that 'The Wizard' had enjoyed, and subsequently did no better than its predecessor had. It's a shame, because 'The Third Degree' is an excellent little rocker, on which some of the pouting, preening boogieing Bolan of the seventies first shows his face. Like 'The Wizard', it was ahead of its time. Its failure was the final nail in the coffin for Marc's time at Decca – his biggest champion at the label, Economides, quit town unexpectedly and fled back to the states having apparently run up huge debts in London. Decca's interest drifted away, as did Mike Pruskin's, who found he'd done as much as was within his power for his client. The two were forced to leave their Manchester Street flat after being unable to cough up the rent (Geoffrey Delaroy-Hall had presumably lost interest in accepting payment in kind). Pruskin eventually moved to New York, where he struck up friendships with beat poets Allen Ginsberg and Diane di Prima, hanging out in Woodstock (the town, not the festival), before returning to London many years later to begin a career as a very successful art and antiques dealer. Marc went back to his mum and dad's prefab in Tooting and started reading *The Hobbit*.

For both London boys 1966 was a year of manoeuvring and transitioning. Another set of flop, drop and rolls, another year of singles no-one bought, and another year of musical growth that would set up their next evolution. Both wrote some of the best material of their early periods around this time ('The London Boys', 'Can't Help Thinking About Me', 'Rubber Band' from David,

'The Third Degree', 'Jasper C. Debussy' and 'Hippy Gumbo' from Marc), even if few people actually heard them.

1966 was, arguably, the pinnacle of the decade, the year when the version of London that had been concentrated in Soho went truly overground; Mary Quant, Michael Caine, David Bailey and the Beatles clambering out of the Sunday supplements and into the living rooms of the nation, the waves of the youthquake rippling across the country, fainter and watered down, but still felt. Even in Hull. A famous piece in an April edition of New York's *Time* Magazine (those ripples had somehow crossed the Atlantic before they'd even got to the Midlands) declared London 'The Swinging City ... buzzing with minicars and telly stars, with half a dozen veins of excitement'. London's secret was out. It celebrated by playing *Revolver* and winning the World Cup at home.

By the end of 1966, neither David nor Marc had much interest in what David Bailey would later call the 'theme park' of Swinging London. To them, this version of Soho was a particularly stylish jacket that they'd both been wearing for a while, which suddenly everyone else was getting off the peg in Burton. Both would turn at right-angles to the *Alfie*-isation of British culture, finding managers, record labels and styles that allowed them, for the first time, to start to tailor new (metaphorical) jackets[18] less connected to those worn by everyone around them. Neither was a mover of their scene yet, but both were, by increments, beginning to separate themselves from the conventions they had ridden thus far. They were becoming originals. In essence, 1966 marked the year when both would stop being products of their culture and start to become creators of it.

Instrumental here was Kenneth Pitt, who already showed an interest in both boys – it was Pitt who had advised Horton to change David's name, while Marc Bolan and Mike Pruskin lived literally across the road from his Manchester Street flat. Pitt is a fascinating and often misunderstood figure, and a mass of contradictions that defy stereotypical views of the sixties. Those who met him often mentioned his 'beautiful manners' (Angie Bowie) and 'witty, cultivated' personality (George Tremlett), finding him 'a gentleman' (Tony Zanetta) and a man of 'imperceptible graciousness' (Paul Morley). He was well into his forties at the point he enters our story, had studied fine art before the war and had been through the terrifying ordeal of the Normandy beach landing on D-Day. Afterwards he was posted to Palestine, where Buzz guitarist John 'Hutch' Hutchinson believes he may have been working covertly for British intelligence[19]. Such a man, knocking on the door of middle age, belonging to another time, feels out of place in the youth-orientated, buzzy world of Swinging London. 'There's no doubt there was a square-ness about Ken's approach,' wrote *NME* legend and Bowie obsessive Paul Morley in his own book, *The Age of Bowie*, 'rooted in

---

18. And this being David and Marc, also literal ones.
19. 'More the Roger Moore than the Sean Connery type, mind you' he says in his memoir, *Bowie & Hutch*.

the simpler 1950s, when show business was not tangled up with spiralling anti-establishment alternative energies.' That's not all there was to Pitt, though. He'd found his way into the music industry after the war and become one of the UK's first dedicated music publicists. Though he worked with the more traditionally showbiz likes of Sinatra (who called him 'my man in London') and Liberace, he'd also promoted shows in the fifties for Jerry Lee Lewis, Duke Ellington and Louis Armstrong, all achingly cool artists. More recently he had booked tours for Bob Dylan – probably the most cutting edge pop act in the world at that point – and was currently managing Manfred Mann, a band so cool they were literally used as the theme music for *Ready, Steady Go!*. It was Pitt that persuaded the Manfreds to record the Jeff Barry/Ellie Greenwich tune 'Doo-Wah-Didi', which became their first number one. In 1966, during a trip to New York, he was bewitched by the Velvet Underground, a band so cutting edge they transcended both pop and art, and dedicated himself to (unsuccessfully) booking them a London residency. He was also gay, or at least bisexual (he always refused to put a label on his preference) and, what's more, an overt supporter of the de-criminalisation of homosexuality. Despite Angie Bowie's continual reference to him as an 'old queen', he approached his own sexuality quietly and privately, a fact exemplified by his chosen form of queer activism: joining the Conservative Campaign For Homosexual Equality.

Modest as he was, Pitt would still have admitted that he was a relatively influential figure on the scene, though it's unlikely he could possibly be aware of the implications for 'pop history' (his own words) that hung on his decisions in the early months of 1966 as he considered the promising but, thus far, unsuccessful prospects put before him by Ralph Horton and Mike Pruskin respectively. Ultimately he turned down Marc; he never gave a reason as to why, though a former assistant remembers him saying that he thought David had more staying power, a comment Pitt himself had no memory of. Whatever the reason, the decision certainly set events in motion for both London boys. Had he taken Marc on, it's unlikely he'd have given Horton and Bowie the time of day when they came calling a few months later. With one teenage charge to mould from pop hopeful to all-round entertainer (something Marc – who wanted to be famous by any means – would certainly have gone along with) Pitt would have had no interest in acquiring a second. Having passed on Marc, however, he still had an opening on his books when Horton again contacted him to ask about co-managing David. The older man agreed to pop along to one of the 'Bowie Showboat' nights at the Marquee. That Sunday night Ken Pitt, by all accounts, fell head over heels in love, and pop history was set in motion.

Chapter Eleven

How Queer?

'Throughout the 1960s, Britain was punch drunk,' wrote the Conservative's conservative, Mary Whitehouse, in her 1977 book *What Ever Happened To Sex?*[1]. 'A continual stream of advocacy in favour of premarital sex, abortion on demand [and] homosexuality.' Whitehouse, a teacher who had become shocked into activism by the declining morals of her pupils, had become the public conscience of a certain kind of buttoned up small-c conservative little Englander. Her crusade against the plummeting standards of society made her a figurehead, but she was hardly alone. Regardless of who was in government, regardless of Mick Jagger pouting and preening on TV, regardless of the camped-up performances of Kenneth Williams and Liberace, regardless of how many knee-tremblers and hand shandies were dispensed in the back alleys of Soho, Britain was still very much a country that regarded sex between two men as, at the very worst, an unnatural abomination or a mental illness and at best something alien, odd, a little icky and distinctly un-British. Which is, of course, nonsense, there is a grand tradition of British queerness, of queer figures in the public eye, of absolutely accepted camp. To the public though, such mincing antics had their place – on the television (preferably after 9pm), on the stage or down in 'that London.' Anywhere else was pushing it.

Some of this innate homophobia manifested in a fnah-fnah 'backs against the walls lads' humour; for better or worse always present in British comedy from Shakespeare to the music hall to the *Carry On* movies. Sadly it was also common for it to develop into hate crimes of violence and murder. A study by the contemporary anthropologist Geoffrey Gorer, published in 1971, examined the sexual attitudes of men and women aged between sixteen and forty-five and found that the most common attitude toward homosexuality was disgust and the second most common was pity – to be gay was to be either unacceptably degenerate, sinful even, or in the very best case, mentally ill. The previous five years of what we now think of as Swinging London's atmosphere of free love, rampant, joyful debauchery and gender bending had scarcely made a dent in those statistics, though Gorer noted that sympathy or even acceptance of gay people was far more common in the younger subjects he interviewed. When Gorer's study was published sex in private between consenting men had been

---

1. A question she asked often and never seemed to find a satisfactory answer for.

legal, in England and Wales, at least[2], for nearly four years. Even its legality was scarcely evidence of acceptance; the MP David Owen, one of the most outspoken supporters of de-criminalisation, made a speech in Parliament during a campaign for legalisation in the fifties in which he declared that 'no Honourable Member, whatever viewpoint he or she put forward, has condoned homosexual behaviours'. A decade later and views had scarcely improved. No-one in Parliament was arguing that being gay was healthy or normal – merely that as a private sexual activity, it shouldn't really be the business of the state.[3]

In 1966, when David Bowie found himself under the care of Ken Pitt, and Marc Bolan was taken on by his next manager, Simon Napier-Bell, both of whom were gay men, sex between men was still very much illegal.[4] Neither David nor Marc were what you'd call straight, and both, to a greater or lesser extent (probably much lesser in the case of Bowie and Pitt), were involved sexually with their new managers, as they had both been with previous managers. All four were playing with fire. While there had been points in history where the media and police would look the other way, in the years following the war it had been open season on queer men. The media, especially the conservative media, had been gunning for closeted gay men in the establishment since the fifties. In 1952, just fifteen years earlier, *The Sunday Pictorial,* the country's best selling tabloid at the time, had run a damning three-part series entitled 'Evil Men', intent on weeding out high profile gays in prominent positions. 'The chief danger of the perverts is the corrupting influence they have on youth,' one editorial raged. 'Most people know there are such things – "pansies" – mincing, effeminate young men who call themselves queers. But simple decent folk regard them as freaks and rarities ... If homosexuality were tolerated here, Britain would rapidly become decadent.'

The press found a sympathetic ear in the police. By 1954, 1,069 men were serving time at Her Majesty's pleasure after falling foul of assorted pieces of

---

2. Scotland and Northern Ireland were *very* late to the party, not de-criminalising gay sex until 1980 and 1982 respectively. Quite astonishingly, Marc Bolan wouldn't live long enough to see a United Kingdom in which private sex between consenting adults was legal for everyone, everywhere.

3. Though 'homosexual acts' taking place in private between two men were legalised in 1967, there were many, many caveats – those men had to be over the age of 21, only two could be present and anal sex, a fairly common element of male/male coupling, back then rather charmingly referred to in official documents as 'buggery', would remain completely illegal until 1994, and still illegal if more than two people were involved after that. The offices of *International Times* were raided in 1972 after they ran classified lonely hearts ads for gay people – still bafflingly illegal. It wasn't until the year 2000 that the age of consent and the full panoply of consensual sexual practices, including 'buggery' with multiple-partners involved, were finally equalised legally across the genders. It took until 2010 for these rules to become standard in all areas of the British Isles, with Guernsey the final crown dependency to bring the age of consent into line. Modern Britain, finally, has no laws around sex or relationships that discriminate based on gender. Legislatively speaking, it took nearly six hundred years to completely erase all traces of Henry VIII's buggery laws from the statute book.

4. Curiously, there has never been a British law banning sex between women, though the common tale linking the exclusion of women from a 19th century sexual offences act to Queen Victoria's belief that lesbians weren't actually a thing, is almost certainly nonsense.

homophobic legislation; modifications and updates of laws dating back to the time of Henry VIII. In the previous year, 600 men had been arrested in London alone.

The police focus seemed to intensify at the end of the fifties after the first serious political maneuvers to legalise gay sex began in government – in 1957 an official parliamentary committee looking into vice surprised MPs by returning a recommendation for de-criminalisation. The paper was known officially as 'the Wolfenden Report', after the committee's chairman, but the press had another name for it: 'The Bugger's Charter'. Wolfenden's recommendations met initial resistance, yet their very existence in the country's seat of power meant that homosexual emancipation was now probably an inevitability. This was partly due to an increase in genuinely progressive values, but mostly because homosexuality was common enough to mean that powerful people, in possession of state secrets, were at risk of blackmail. At the height of the Cold War, this risk was unacceptable. Still, the powers that be were not going to come quietly, and as often happens when people start to sense that illiberal laws have had their time, the authorities kicked back hard while they still could[5]. Raids on queer spaces, particularly the clubs and pubs of Soho and Piccadilly, intensified. These tended not to end with arrests, but names would be meticulously taken down and warnings issued. Entrapment was a common police tactic right into the sixties: undercover officers would install themselves near the areas known to be frequented by gay men, usually public toilets[6], flirt knowingly with likely suspects and switch to 'you're nicked, sonny Jim' mode as soon as their target showed an interest. These sting operations were ostensibly meant to curb the sex trade, but often targeted lone men who were neither buying nor selling. The tactic was devastatingly effective, and landed the likes of Wilfrid Brambell (TV's Albert Steptoe, who had co-starred with The Beatles in *A Hard Day's Night*) and Brian Epstein himself, during his days as a young drama student, in custody. Anyone found guilty of homosexual acts could be fined, imprisoned, subjected to chemical castration via the administering of female hormones (as the codebreaker and war hero Alan Turing was, leading to his probable suicide) or forced to endure electric shock therapy, in which they were shown sexually provocative pictures of men and women and given painful shocks if they responded to what were considered the 'wrong' images. It was excruciating and humiliating, and that was before one considers the public shame that came with the sentence. Naturally, with the stakes so high,

---

5. We have very much seen this with the rise of right wing governments in the 21st century.
6. The relationship between casual gay sex and public conveniences has been long established and continues to this day, to the point that though not exactly *accepted*, it's certainly unremarkable. It's worth stopping and thinking on that for a while – gay sex was so unacceptable, so shameful, that men were forced to use *actual toilets* as places to meet and have sex with prospective partners. It's something queer culture doesn't reflect on nearly enough.

blackmail was common even for the man on the street, and many gay men lived in fear and loved in secret.

Amid this hostile environment the music industry became something of a safe haven for queer men: a culture in which same sex love was, if not openly embraced, at least considered par for the course. Both Pitt and Napier-Bell, though very different in almost all respects, had been able to thrive because they were part of a lineage largely created by other gay men. As John Gill, one of the very few openly gay music journalists working in the 1980s wrote in his excellent book *Queer Noises;* 'Clever, talented and ambitious gay men inevitably gravitate to the professions where they are most likely to find acceptance and fulfillment.' As Gill points out, the music industry as we know it was the product of queer men, who were also middle class and often Jewish. Gill singles out four of them as being instrumental in creating the archetype – Larry Parnes (the manager of Billy Fury, Tommy Steele and Joe Brown[7]) Brian Epstein, Joe Meek and Kit Lambert (the manager of The Who). To this list we could probably add Parnes' associate, the solicitor David Jacobs, who was able to help Liberace, of all people, successfully sue the *Daily Mirror* for libel after it had the temerity to suggest that his onstage flamboyance meant that he might be gay,[8] Lionel Bart, EMI's chief exec Sir Joseph Lockwood, Robert Stigwood – the manager of Cream – the latterly-disgraced Jonathan King and, if you're feeling generous, Simon Napier-Bell. Gay men like Parnes had been able to harness their own instincts, tastes and values and repackage them as palatable pop products, thus carving themselves a niche in which they could thrive. As the pop historian Jon Savage wrote in an *Observer* piece accompanying his 2006 compilation album of the queer pop of the sixties and seventies: 'The music industry was one of the few places where gay men could be themselves, and indulge their sexual predilections in a way that was economically viable'.

In 1964 Parnes had tried to loop together the elite of London's music management into an organisation he called 'The British Impresario's Guild', compromising ten men – almost all gay, including Parnes, Epstein, Jacobs and Stigwood – who between them managed or represented around ninety percent of Britain's pop market. The plan was that the group would pool money, resources and influence to help steer and maintain their industry, which many worried had reached saturation point. The official organisation lasted for just two meetings before collapsing, but is a remarkable example of the power of a group of men that what would occasionally, out of ear-shot, be nicknamed 'The Gay Mafia' or, more poetically, 'The Velvet Mafia'.[9]

---

7. Brown was presumably bunking off the day Parnes' famous off-the-cuff renaming of his artists took place – it was for the best: Parnes wanted to name him 'Elmer Twitch'.

8. It did and he was.

9. This latter also being the title of Darryl W Bullock's excellent book on the history of rock 'n' roll's gay impresarios, from which much of this information is taken.

'It's no secret that most of the best managers are gay', writes Simon Napier-Bell in his book *Black Vinyl, White Powder*. Napier-Bell argues that well-to-do gay men were the perfect bridge between the out-of-touch record company executives, mostly in their forties and older, and the teenaged and twenty-something artists and audience they were too hopelessly old fashioned to understand. 'It was gay managers, and their friends in fashion and media,' he said, 'who were chiefly responsible for creating the image of British youth culture that was being sold around the world.' Pete Townshend – who would himself later come out as bisexual – told Napier-Bell that he liked having a gay manager, feeling that gay men 'were scornful of conventional behaviour; they mixed more easily with young people, and seemed to understand them.' Napier-Bell also argues that as most gay men had 'got used to playing a two-faced game', maintaining their separate closeted and 'out' lives, they already had the ideal training needed for the weird duality of artist management, in which they must be stern and business-like with executives, and familial and even fatherly with their acts (It is perhaps this duality that leads John Gill in *Queer Noises* to declare that 'managers are necessarily unpleasant people.') Though Parnes' attempt to formalise what was essentially a queer industry cabal had failed, the 'Velvet Mafia' still provided a network of contacts, agreements and mutual support for London's gay elite. When Joe Meek's career was on its uppers in the mid sixties it was fellow gay mafioso John Lockwood who came to his rescue, offering him a job as EMI's go-to in house producer.

It's not that surprising that Marc and David, both completely soaked in rock 'n' roll myth, had many of their earliest same-sex experiences with men who managed them. In sleeping with the very interface between themselves and the music industry, they were taking their fascination to its logical extreme. Sex played a huge role for both at all stages of their early careers. It was a means to an end, a way to win people over, a bargaining chip and a method of control. It was also a lifestyle choice, a rejection of convention, a thrillingly outlawed pursuit and, of course, an end in itself. We can over analyse both men's relationships, and the way they used sex to blend their personal and professional worlds, but ultimately we can't lose sight of the fact that sex is, well, *fun*. That two attractive and charismatic teenagers moving in circles of recreational promiscuity would end up in bed with so many, many people, sampling the full buffet of genders available to them, isn't a massive shock, whichever way you slice it.[10]

Neither David nor Marc had a big, emotional 'coming out' moment that we know of. Instead, queerness was simply part of their lives, and had probably been floating around in their social circles ever since they were old enough to understand the concept. Alan Dodds, the guitarist in the Kon-Rads remembers

---

10. Freud once said that 'sometimes a cigar is just a cigar', meaning that not every phallic object was a subconscious penis replacement. This works the other way, too – sometimes a penis is just a penis.

David talking openly about being bisexual as early as 1963, while still at school. Both London boys were, after all, linked to the first flourishings of mod, and though later that subculture became synonymous with loutish thugs and fighting, its first flowering was dandyish and inherently queer, if not always openly and flamboyantly gay. As Jon Savage says with a characteristic twinkle in his 2006 *Observer* piece, 'mod's hint of mint was not entirely in the heads of hostile observers'. Young mods and gays shopped at the same Carnaby Street stores, danced in the same clubs to the same music and did the same pills. Mods wore makeup and feminine hairstyles – just observe David's 65-vintage bouffant/mini beehive. As the gay writer Haydon Bridge observed in an article in *QX* magazine, the predominantly-gay mod club Le Duce, was set up as 'a queer version of the nearby straight mod club, The Scene. Like their hetero counterparts, queer mods wanted to dance non-stop (and had the drugs that enabled them to).'[11] The two clubs essentially catered to the same clientele and played the same music. The only real difference was that Le Duce had the good sense to keep the predatory older men and industry types out.

Perhaps this is why neither Marc nor David ever seemed to show any level of discomfort over their sexuality. It was something to revel in, enjoy, even flaunt. With very few exceptions – the likes of Quentin Crisp for example – the generations preceding them rarely felt so comfortable in their skins. Gay men were, after all, living lives they had been told were immoral pretty much since birth. In his book *The Velvet Mafia*, Darryl Bullock quotes the songwriter Ed Hamilton, who knew both Brian Epstein and Joe Meek, as saying that he didn't think either man was 'happy being gay … they didn't want to be creeping around backstage doing things that were untoward. Brian wasn't brought up like that'. Though there were other factors involved – drugs and mental health problems – their shame would arguably be a factor in both men's premature deaths in 67 and 68 respectively. At Paul McCartney's twenty-first birthday party a drunk-out-of-his-skull John Lennon was so incensed when a friend accused him of having slept with Epstein, he beat him very nearly to death. This was one of the most unfortunate episodes of Lennon's life, and one he would express deep regret for. 'I must have been frightened of the fag in me,' he later told his biographers Peter McCabe and Robert D. Schonfeld. On another occasion he admitted that the rumours were actually true, and that there had been a one-off sexual encounter with Epstein on holiday in Spain. In a 2015 interview with *Vulture*, Lennon's wife Yoko Ono confirmed that John had been bisexual, living in a time when he felt he couldn't act out on those desires.

Had John been a few years younger and growing up a London mod rather than a Scouse rocker, perhaps things would have been different. Both Marc and

11. This, as with most aspects of 'Swinging London' was largely restricted to the trendy Soho scene. If you suggested to the average parka-wearing Who fan in Southend or Solihull that they were taking part in queer-coded culture you'd likely get mown down by an angry thug on a Vespa.

David seemed to treat campness as a bit of a laugh and were basically happy to go where it led them. The singer Mike Berry, one of Joe Meek's stable, was close with David around this time, and told biographer Paul Trynka that the pair did have an innocent, fumbling sexual element to their relationship. Both were happy to say that they liked both boys and girls and so both were quite naturally comfortable with letting that spill over into their friendship. It recalls the relationship Marc had with Allan Warren, when they had been playing at pop star and manager a few years earlier.

After meeting Ralph Horton, however, David's immersion into Soho's gay life became more pronounced. Horton, a closeted gay man, was far more clued into the scene and though not quite a paid up member of the velvet mafia, was certainly hanging around somewhere on its lower rungs.[12] Horton was completely besotted with David, who quickly learned to twist him around his handsome little finger. It wasn't just flirting to get what he wanted, however, their relationship does seem to have been genuinely sexual. Lower Third guitarist Denis Taylor remembers sleeping in the freezing cold in the band's converted ambulance one night close to Horton's Warwick Square pad and hammering on his door to be let into the warm, only to be told that (according to drummer Phil Lancaster) 'you can't come in, Ralph's in bed with David'. Taylor had appeared on a night that Horton was hosting what Phil Lancaster calls a 'gay party', complete with cardboard taped to the windows to avoid passers-by getting an eyeful. The Lower Third, working class lads from Margate, were all a little shell-shocked by the discovery. 'I'm not sure we even knew much about bisexuality' wrote Lancaster, 'you were either straight or "queer[13]", there was no sexual middleground, so to speak'. David was also, even then, a notorious womanizer. The plain-speaking lads of the Lower Third could just about get their heads around the idea of men that liked other men, but having a foot in each camp was simply strange. Not that the boys were especially homophobic – speaking to Paul Trynka, bass player Graham Rivens was very specific that his loathing of Ralph Horton wasn't 'just because he was a poofta', though the use of the word 'just' there does suggest at least *some* prejudice. Likewise, Taylor's immediate assumption upon hearing that his singer was a-bed with their manager was that the band was over, which doesn't suggest the most progressive of outlooks.

Soho's queer scene by now *loved* David. Horton knew the right places to go and who to introduce him to – among his admirers were apparently a *Melody*

---

12. The 'mafia' part of the nickname is, of course, not meant to be taken literally. Most music managers weren't gangsters, although there was a surprising amount of crossover between London's genuine criminal underworld and the queer end of the music industry, much of which could be traced back to the infamous Kray twins – Ronnie Kray was bisexual, and since both twins liked moving in the circles of the rich and famous his escapades helped blend the two worlds.

13. The word 'gay' would gradually rise to prominence to mean 'homosexual' during the sixties. It had previously been used as something of a covert or slang term, however as Lancaster shows here, it hadn't quite penetrated yet.

Maker journalist and a Radio London DJ, both of whom gave Bowie far more coverage than his profile warranted at that time, and at least one famous actor. Also buzzing around was Lionel Bart, ever alert to the beautiful young things on the scene, who absolutely adored David (David's future girlfriend, Mary Finnigan, is sure the two had some sort of fling while she and David were seeing each other.) Paul Trynka quotes Simon White, a gay man working at the Marquee around the time of the 'Bowie Showboat' gigs, who describes the typical audience as 'six girls at the front and half a dozen of us queens at the back, with Ralph hanging on his every move'. Whether David genuinely reciprocated the feelings of his many male admirers is up for debate. To use a modern phrase, he could certainly do better than the likes of Ralph Horton, a prematurely-aged man ten years David's senior, reportedly chubby with thick rimmed glasses who wore leather gloves indoors as a rock 'n' roll affectation. Still, whether he meant it or not, Bowie knew when to turn on the camp when it was required, amping up his queening to impress his captivated audience, even if that audience was just one person. More and more, he made effete camp part of his persona, finding to his delight that when blended with his good looks the whole package was catnip to girls as well.

It was on 17 April 1966 that Horton finally convinced Ken Pitt to attend a David Bowie performance at the Marquee. David certainly gave Pitt a show. Horton and Bowie had discussed in advance how important and useful it would be to have Pitt onboard, and David and the Buzz seemed to have tailored their set specifically to meet his interests, closing with an intimate and spot-lit rendition of 'You'll Never Walk Alone', knowing that while much of his teenage audience would associate the song with Gerry and the Pacemakers, Ken Pitt would be thinking only of Judy Garland. It was a move calculated to appeal to Pitt's queer instincts and bring him onside. It worked spectacularly. Pitt's description of the show in his memoir, *The Pitt Report*, is that of a man absolutely entranced: 'From my favourite position, leaning against the wall at the back of the club[14], I could see that he was wearing a biscuit-coloured, hand-knitted sweater, round-necked and buttoned at one shoulder, its skin-tightness accentuating his slim frame.' It was, as Ralph and David had planned, the Judy Garland moment that clinched the deal. Pitt describes the number as 'daring and delightful', saying that he immediately 'began to think of Ralph's unyielding doors and the keys that could unlock them.'

Pitt was a consummate businessman and brought badly needed professionalism to Bowie's operation. He was the first real grown up to take charge of David's affairs. He was also, undeniably, and arguably for the rest of his life, absolutely smitten with David Bowie. Buzz guitarist John 'Hutch'

---

14. Which according to Marquee staffer Simon White, remember, is where the 'queens' habitually stood.

Hutchinson, who witnessed all of this first hand, admits in his memoir that Pitt's own descriptions in *The Pitt Report* made for 'uncomfortable reading'. Various acquaintances of David, from Hutch to Angie Bowie, and almost every biographer have speculated about Bowie and Pitt's relationship, though none can ever say for sure whether it became explicitly sexual. George Tremlett, the music journalist who was to write the first serious biography of Bowie (1974's *The David Bowie Story*), observed the pair living together at Pitt's Manchester Street flat and is fairly sure that their professional relationship spilled into the sexual, at least early on, though is at pains to point out this this would 'never have been as important to Bowie as it was to Pitt'.

Marc's relationship with his next manager, Simon Napier-Bell, then representing the Yardbirds, ran along fairly similar lines. It was Marc that made the first approach at the suggestion of Vicki Wickham, the producer of *Ready, Steady, Go!* whom he'd met when he appeared on the show to (disastrously) perform 'The Wizard'[15]. Bolshy as ever, Marc called Napier-Bell at home, declaring that he was 'going to be the biggest star ever' and that he 'just needed a manager to make all the arrangements'. Napier-Bell made an attempt at fobbing him off with a request for a demo tape. Instead Marc offered to come round and play him some songs. As it turned out, and by absolutely no coincidence, he was just around the corner. Minutes later, Marc was sinking into an armchair with his acoustic guitar, now affecting a kind of camp bohemian look, (a 'Dickensian urchin ... but scrupulously clean', Napier-Bell later told Lesley-Ann Jones) launching into an hour's worth of his latest numbers – a remarkably accomplished set of songs that genuinely impressed his host. Napier-Bell took him straight to a recording studio that very evening to knock out some proper acoustic demos. According to one of Napier-Bell's numerous memoirs, *You Don't Have To Say You Love Me*, he then took him out for a posh Chinese dinner, where they discussed Marc's theory that sleeping with people, and especially kissing them, was an effective way of transmitting skills and creativity between minds; after which they put the theory to test – but only after Marc swore he wouldn't steal Simon's brain. 'If I do, I promise once I've had a look I'll put it back', flirted Marc. 'Plus twenty-percent of yours', said the always-working Napier-Bell. The two would continue a semi-sexual relationship for the rest of their short association ('it was mostly kissing and cuddling, if we had sex it was never penetration, just an extension of the kissing and cuddling').

To Simon, Marc's sexuality was tricky to pin down. 'Gay, straight, bisexual? He was none of those really' he told Lesley-Ann Jones. 'Just available to anyone who was intelligent, worth knowing, who fancied him and found him cute ...

---

15. Wickham and Napier-Bell had co-written Dusty Springfield's instant classic 'You Don't Have To Say You Love Me'.

and clever.' Though the most commonly used word to define Marc and David's sexuality was 'bisexual', Napier-Bell's description actually lends itself to a more modern term – 'pansexual'. While bisexuals are sexually and romantically attracted to more than one gender, to be pansexual is to be attracted to people *regardless* of gender. According to *Gay Times* 'many pansexual people are only attracted to people based on their personality, meaning they can be attracted to people who are male, female, non-binary or any other gender', a description that fits in with many accounts of Marc in the sixties.[16] Allen Warren, another manager, another lover, has a view that backs this up. 'If he went to bed with a man it was because he had some kind of affinity with that person' he says. 'Some understanding, liking, caring. If he happened to feel that way for you, then that was fine.'

Jeff Dexter, a long-standing friend of both Marc and David, doubts that Marc actually had queer tendencies at all. 'A few men have said, written and implied down the years that they shagged Marc. I know they didn't,' he told Lesley-Ann Jones. 'He wasn't into blokes! Put it this way, I slept with him enough times … nothing went on. If ever it did, there was always a bird in between!' According to Dexter, Marc's queerness was an act to impress the velvet mafia, a calculated campness, laser targeted at those with the power to help him. It's a view that's supported if we list the men that we know Marc had some involvement with: Geoffrey Delaroy-Hall, Allan Warren, Simon Napier-Bell, all professional as well as personal relationships. Keith Altham, a former music journalist who knew Marc well in the sixties and would go on to be his publicist in the seventies, has a similar view. 'If you were hustling to get somewhere in the industry, it was all part of the game: flirt a bit, lead them on, let them think they were onto a good thing with you … Old queens love nothing more than to be seen out with pretty young boys.'[17]

It's true that as far as we know, based on those that have gone on the record, Marc never had what you'd call a boyfriend. But then he didn't have all that many girlfriends either. He did, meanwhile, have a *lot* of sex. In the closeted world of the sixties, either side of legalisation, relationships and encounters with men weren't widely broadcast, while ones with women involved easily grasped, dialled-in social ritual and expectations that were totally palatable to the public. Mixed-gender encounters were public domain, same-sex ones were secret, therefore there's much we simply can't know. Jeff Dexter, however, is adamant about Marc's heterosexuality ('He would lead people on when it suited him, sure, but he would definitely never go that route, [but] he loved women. He

---

16. The journalist Simon Reynolds, in his excellent book on glam rock, *Shock and Awe*, uses the phrase 'Peter Pansexual' to describe Marc Bolan. Ever since I read it I have been seethingly jealous that he got to that pun first.
17. Again this from Lesley-Ann Jones *Ride A White Swan*. Jones, a former tabloid journalist, has a knack for getting great quotes from her subjects.

might have given the odd bloke here and there a hug, but he wouldn't have held his cock'.) As close as he and Marc were, his view doesn't quite hold up. We *know* Marc had 'sex' with men. True, we don't know the ins-and-outs, the who-did-what-to-whoms, but we don't really need to. The accounts from Warren and Napier-Bell alone are enough. Having a preference for women, and being able to sleep in a bed with your mate without trying it on, are not workable definitions of heterosexuality. Marc himself flipped back and forth on the issue, at one point saying that he'd had one gay encounter, as a fifteen-year-old, just to see, but never again. However when asked if he was heterosexual in a 1975 interview with *Popswap Mirror*, he replied 'No, bisexual, but I believe I'm more heterosexual 'cos I definitely like boobs.'

What's clear is that as far back as the mid-sixties, both of our London Boys were happy to play with sexuality, image and gender roles, something they would both become famous for in the seventies. Both used their sexuality as a tool: to be liked, to be talked about and to curry favour.

In 1948 the American social biologist Alfred Kinsey developed what became known as the 'Kinsey Scale'. His theory was that human sexuality was not static or binary, but fluid. That we have different tastes, urges and impulses at different times of our lives and about different things. On the Kinsey Scale, being exclusively heterosexual gives us a score of zero, while being exclusively homosexual scores a six. Everything in between arguably puts you in the bisexual/pansexual zone, and anything over a zero puts you on the LGBTQ+ spectrum somewhere. David and Marc would score somewhere between one and three: they both leaned more towards women for preference, but neither could be said to be *exclusively* heterosexual. In those days, in that scene, basically nobody was.

Allen Warren is one of the few people who has spoken openly about sexual encounters with both London boys, though his experience with Bowie was less cute than his early fumblings with Marc:

'I came across Bowie a couple of times. He was working as an extra on a small show I was doing on television. He used to do extra work and he would do non-speaking parts and sit there in the dressing room, strumming his guitar. He was very reclusive. I used to think he was sort of odd looking, with his milky white skin. The next time I saw him was on the bed of an agent's bedroom down the Fulham Road in Battersea. My friend came to me and said: "Come and look at this beautiful boy, he fancies you, come in" – and he went in and there was this beautiful, porcelain white naked boy lying face down on his bed and I thought, "he is beautiful, he's right", and then he turned and as he turned he flashed these two different coloured eyes, which freaked me out and I ran back up the stairs. It was like a cat! That's the nearest to romance we ever got.'

As Simon Napier-Bell told Mark Paytress in his *Marc Bolan: Rise and Fall of 20th Century Superstar*: 'The sexual borders had completely collapsed by that time ... in the sixties, it was pretty difficult to have any sort of relationship with someone without it being sexual. There was a feeling that you were not entering into the spirit of what that decade was about.' It's a sentiment echoed by Allan Warren, as quoted by Daryl Bullock in *The Velvet Mafia*: 'In the sixties it was practically compulsory to be bisexual! There were orgies practically every weekend, and you didn't mind who you slept with: their sex didn't come into it. If you weren't at least a little bit bisexual then you were not very trendy.' Whatever else they might have been, the David Bowie and Marc Bolan of 1966 were always, always on trend.

Chapter Twelve

Metamorphosis '66

Between the failure of 'The Third Degree' in June and his impromptu audition with Simon Napier-Bell in November, Marc had been on one hell of a creative spree. He had fallen in love with fantasy, CS Lewis's Narnia books and Tolkien's *The Hobbit* especially, and their imagery seeped into his own. He wasn't restricting himself to music, either. He wrote plays, short stories, film ideas, poetry, and rambling, surrealist diary entries. His work was populated with elves, faeries, gnomes, talking animals, and strange beasts either swiped from mythology via Tolkien, or else wholly born out of his imagination. One story, *Pictures of Purple People* features a villain called 'Scenescoff', a term he used for the buzz-killers and squares who were the enemies of his own scene. Scenescoff would reoccur as a character several times in Marc's work over the coming years.

Although London's expanding underground[1], which was growing alongside but still apart from the counterculture in the US, was fuelled by the beat poetry of Ginsberg and Burroughs, it was also beginning to ingest the imagery and some sense of the idealism found in the British fantasy of the early twentieth century. JRR Tolkien's *The Lord of the Rings* was the worst offender, although Lewis' *The Lion, The Witch and the Wardrobe* and its sequels, Michael Moorcock's *Elric of Melniboné* stories and Mervyn Peak's *Gormenghast* trilogy all played their part in injecting fantastical language and imagery into the beating heart of Swinging London. Within a couple of years a shop called 'Gandalf's Garden' had opened in Chelsea, catering to the truth-seekers and spiritualists of the hippy crowd.[2] It would later spawn a magazine of the same name. The Middle Earth club in Covent Garden – which later relocated to the Roundhouse in Camden – took its name from Tolkien and would play a vital role in Marc's success. A charitable interpretation of this fascination with fantasy was about idealism: Tolkien's masterpiece champions a simpler way of life, rejecting mechanisation and living in harmony with nature. His High Elves are personifications of art and beauty, threatened by the evil of man. As much as Tolkien himself would have hated it, it's possible to read all sorts of allegory into these stories[3], especially during the

---

1. The scene, not the tube train network.
2. Gandalf's Garden was opposite the achingly cool boutique Granny Takes a Trip, which was far more fashion focused. Between the two they perfectly represented London's underground scene.
3. Tolkien always said that any allegorical meaning the reader might take from his work would be unintentional. He preferred to think of his themes as having 'applicability' with meaning bestowed by the reader not the author, saying he 'cordially disliked allegory in all its manifestations'. Which is a hell of a statement from a Roman Catholic.

divisive political and geo-political climate of the sixties. And of course there's all the business with magic and healing. Less charitably, and ultimately more likely, it probably had a lot to do with the drugs. LSD use had been gradually on the increase for the last couple of years and by 1966 had reached something of a tipping point, with the Home Secretary even bemoaning its use in Parliament. Psychedelia had arrived in London; mind expansion, tuning in and dropping out were becoming increasingly popular pastimes in the capital's never-still youth culture. The works of Tolkien and Lewis, in which animals spoke, trees talked, magic rings were wielded and characters enjoyed mushrooms and 'pipe weed' were in happy sync with the psychedelic era.[4]

Marc, as usual, was bang on trend. He'd been writing songs about wizards before it was cool. His taste for mystical surrealism, which was more whimsical than it was psychedelic, reverberated nicely with the growing energy of the in-coming hippy era; the next great evolution of Soho subculture, which saw sharp threads and union jacks supplanted by love beads and an aesthetic dominated to an almost ludicrous degree by flowers. Through the middle of '66 he soaked this stuff up, reading and writing and reading some more, busking on the Charing Cross Road whenever he could be bothered, before heading back to Tooting so his mum could get his tea on the table. Fantasy was a natural fit for Marc's worldview – he had, after all, lived in a fantasy of his own devising, one way or another, for years; creating himself as a character in his own Narnia, his own Middle Earth. That was as true of Mark Feld, the pre-teen ace face, stalking Hackney in search of handmade winklepickers, as it was of late sixties Bolan, who placed a statue of Pan, which he called 'Poon', on his mantlepiece[5] for creative inspiration. Marc projected an other-worldliness. The word 'Elf' is used to describe him consistently throughout his career ('elfin', 'the bopping elf') and he leant into a version of himself as an ethereal nether-being, a fey creature from the faerie realm. It meant that he fitted snugly into the emerging era of flowers and crystals just as well as he had into the suited and booted beat boom.

If it seems like his head was in the clouds during this time, it's worth noting that Marc never stopped hustling; hanging around in La Gioconda with David, always on the lookout for someone that could help him. *NME* journalist Keith Altham would regularly bump into him in the Brewmaster, which was situated above Leicester Square station and was the boozer of choice for Denmark Street music hacks, where he'd be bothering the assorted critics, trying to foist his demo tapes and telling them he'd be 'more popular than Presley, bigger than the Beatles'. According to Atham's memoir *The PR Strikes Back*, the general response was 'Shut up Marc, have a Coca-Cola and come back when you're

---

4. Especially the bit in *The Fellowship of the Ring* with Tom Bombadil, oddly left out of Peter Jackson's movie version.
5. This had been gifted to him by his former flatmate Riggs O'Hara, and would appear on the rear cover of his first album.

old enough to drink'. Still, his charisma and tenacity were enough to make him stick in the minds of the drinkers, even if they didn't have any music to peg it to.

Had they actually heard any of that music they might have started to take this tiny, charismatic urchin more seriously. The songs he'd recorded for Decca the previous December had impressed nobody, but since then his writing had come on in leaps and bounds. His acoustic guitar playing was rudimentary, but it was also rhythmic and compelling and his lyrics were completely unique; with their fantasy worlds and all. Many of them were nonsense, of course, but he had developed a knack for juxtaposing imagery, for lurching from the straightforward to the whimsical, for using words and phrases for their percussive power as much as for their meaning. Most startling of all though was his voice. The evolution hinted at in 'The Third Degree' had continued – the Cliff Richard croon and Eddie Cochran snarl had been significantly reduced and replaced with a completely unique, trebley bleat. Marc had pitched his voice higher, and highly stylised his delivery, making it both camper and more exciting. It matched, focused and amplified the strange imagery and odd flexes of his words, making his hooks catchier and his lyrics jump out. No-one else sounded like this. Almost no-one else ever really would.

Marc was never especially straightforward about the origins of his very stylised delivery, which was a world away from the smooth crooning he delivered on 'All At Once' or the folky twang on the demos he recorded as Toby Tyler. There's still a little Cliff in there, it's true, and certainly some Dylan, but there's also Little Richard, Johnny Ray and Gene Pitney, and something else that seemed to be entirely Marc's own. Bolan himself would claim that his vocals were an attempt to mimic the trilling of his guitar – a suitably Bolanesque answer, that somehow manages to make absolutely no sense whatsoever while also feeling about right. In *You Don't Have To Say You Love Me*, Simon Napier-Bell says that Marc arrived at the distinctive bleat 'by playing [baritone jazz singer] Billy Eckstine 45s at 78[rpm]', and practising the vibrato heard on old Bessie Smith blues records. Whatever the inspiration, the voice simply *worked. That* voice, coming out of *that* person and singing *those* words triple-reinforced the Bolan mystique.

When this whole package was unloaded for Napier-Bell, live and in person in his front room, he was floored. 'I was enraptured with what I saw and heard,' he told Lesley-Ann Jones. 'I thought the whole world would be too.' That night Marc demoed fourteen acoustic tracks, all original, all previously unreleased. Among them were 'Hippy Gumbo', 'Hot Rod Mama' and 'Cat Black'. Afterwards, Marc genuinely assumed that they'd just recorded his first album. According to Napier-Bell, he was already absolutely certain that he was about to become a megastar, that the manager of The Yardbirds just needed to click his fingers and create instant success, apparently forgetting that the full might of Decca's marketing department had already failed to make 'The Wizard' anything but a blip on the chart landscape. 'It took me a month to persuade him that he wouldn't become an instant superstar simply by announcing that he existed and was ready for public consumption,' wrote Napier-Bell, as it gradually dawned on him that he had now pledged himself to 'the expansion of an ego already in danger of devouring the universe'.[6]

While Napier-Bell couldn't quite click his heels three times and make Marc a star, he was at least a professional with some leverage. As the manager of the hard blues act The Yardbirds,[7] still one of the biggest bands in the country, people would at least take his calls. He was able to call a favour with EMI, the Yardbirds' parent label, and get the new Marc Bolan single released on its Parlophone imprint. Simon and Marc decided on the mesmerising, hypnotic 'Hippy Gumbo' from the pile of demos they had made on the night they first met, and the song was recorded again, this time slowed down with a dark and rich string part giving the tune a seductive, almost witchy vibe, Its pace was slow and sticky, like molasses dribbling from a spoon, its lyrics enigmatic to the point of meaningless[8], yet odd enough, mystical enough to trick the brain into thinking it was hearing something profound. It was Marc's third strong single in a row, and comfortably his best yet. Arguably it's one of the best things he would ever write.

Unfortunately, the praise wasn't universal. The track got some good notices; in his book *Marc Bolan – Beautiful Dreamer*, T.Rex super-fan John Bramley pulls a great one from the press clippings that he kept at the time: 'This one could easily make it because of the unusual, tense, dramatic voice used this time by Marc, sort of wavering ... like an old jazz singer,'[9] but other critics were left cold. Another quote from Bramley's clipping collection describes Marc's voice as 'a crazed mixture of an incredibly bad female Negro blues singer and Larry the Lamb'. Much like Decca with 'The Third Degree', Polydor made no particular effort to market this strange little record, and it was left to Simon Napier-Bell to work his little black book to get the word out. The only notable TV appearance he could scrounge was *Ready, Steady, Go!*, acquired via his close

---

6. As you can see, Simon Napier-Bell, though occasionally guilty of a maddening smugness of tone, has a hell of a turn of phrase. This is from *You Don't Have To Say You Love Me*, but all of his books are equally entertaining.

7. At this point the Yardbirds had just recruited Jimmy Page, one-time Manish Boys session guitarist, beginning the chain of events that would eventually see Page put together 'The New Yardbirds', featuring one-time Marc Bolan session bass player John Paul Jones. Eventually they would change the group's name to Led Zeppelin. You may have heard of them.

8. June Bolan, Marc's future wife, claims the song was about a man Marc was in love with, while Simon Napier-Bell assumed the lyrics were about Marc meeting someone with his own face and thus were an exercise in pure narcissism. When you think about it, they could both be right.

9. Bramley didn't keep records of who the quotes were taken from. Some digging around has so far proved inconclusive. The quote could have come from a dozen or so local and national papers, music-focused and otherwise.

friendship with producer Vicki Wickham. Marc appeared on the 13 December edition, the second-to-last ever filmed.

Also on the show was an American guitarist recently discovered playing in a Greenwich Village café by the Animals' bass player Chad Chandler. Chandler brought him back to the UK, set him up with a drummer and bass player and unleashed him on the London scene. The Jimi Hendrix Experience played their first shows in the winter of 1966 and quickly proved themselves to be an astonishingly compelling live act.[10] Jimi and his band were on *Ready, Steady, Go!* To promote their debut single, 'Hey Joe', a deafening performance of which is all that anyone watching that evening was probably going to remember. Marc and Jimi, two supernaturally charismatic, slightly otherworldly but – somehow – still oddly cute stars struck up a friendship that night, each complimenting the other's performance ('They were really heavy vibing each other,' says Marc's future publicist BP Fallon, who was at the recording, in *Marc Bolan, A Tribute*, an oral history of Marc's life published shortly after his death.) According to Marc, Hendrix had told him that he was going to be a big star. The two would be on nodding terms for the next few years, during which Marc introduced him to his cousin, Stephanie Kays, who worked for her father in an electronics shop near Marble Arch, after the fresh-off-the-plane guitar legend told him that he didn't have a stereo. Hendrix was smitten with Kays and, much to Marc's glee, pursued her for a few months, though as she already had a boyfriend she was – extremely regretfully – resistant to his charms. Stephanie, Jimi and Marc would often have a pub lunch together during the former's dinner break. That the two stars knew each other fairly well speaks to how small the rock and pop scene in London really was, even at the Swinging zenith of the decade.

Alas, a friendship with Jimi Hendrix, though admittedly something to be treasured, was about all Marc got from the release of 'Hippy Gumbo', which despite Napier-Bell's best efforts died a death after not making any of the UK's assorted singles charts and picking up little to no attention. It's not a huge surprise – it was a patently uncommercial release, thrown out into a singles market already groaning under the weight of a number of pop masterpieces. Released within a couple of weeks either side of 'Hippy Gumbo' were The Beach Boys' 'Good Vibrations', The Four Tops' 'Reach Out (I'll Be There)', The Supremes' 'You Just Keep Me Hangin' on', Wilson Pickett's 'Mustang Sally', Jimmy Ruffins' 'What Becomes of the Broken Hearted', Donovan's 'Sunshine Superman' and other hits by The Troggs, The Who, The Kinks, Cream, Manfred Mann, Cilla Black and Marc's beloved Cliff Richard. 'Hippy Gumbo' was a gorgeous piece, but with little promotion and no big name, it was lost among all the pre-Christmas noise. Marc and Simon went back to the drawing board.

---

10. According to Andrew O'Neill's excellent *A History of Heavy Metal*, Hendrix's arrival on the London scene ended a long-running game of one-upmanship between Pete Townshend and Eric Clapton, who buried the hatchet in order to concentrate on a mutual jealous loathing of the new star.

Seeing Jimi play 'Hey Joe' on *Ready, Steady, Go!* had shaken Bolan out of his acoustic dream as he witnessed the power of a fully armed and operational Fender Strat blasted through a Marshall stack. He was ready to make some noise, and his manager knew exactly where he could do it.

1966 was a transitional year on London's bleeding edge. While the rest of the country was catching up with Carnaby cool, the London scenes were already moving on. For many, this would be a sideways step into weirder worlds as the influence of Britishness began to loosen its grip on pop, and the pendulum swung back to America. The two countries' scenes had established a game of cultural volleyball ever since the US first punted Bill Haley and Elvis across the Atlantic; the UK serving an ace a few years later in the shape of the Beatles and Stones. Now it was America's turn once again, spiking the ball back with west coast rock and album-focused psychedelia. With it came not just music and fashion, but ideals and values. The British counterculture had thus far been a small scene of beatniks – it was about to get a turbocharge. The UK underground had grown out of the pre-pop trad jazzers and the hairy sweater set, and had galvanised around a handful of people almost all connected, in one way or another, to Better Books, the Soho bookshop that had hosted readings by Ginsberg back in 1965 and other 'happenings', a term synonymous with tuning in and dropping out, and groovy, druggy, art-focused events – although ultimately it seemed to be used to describe any gathering of three or more people with long hair during which a joint was smoked. The first big happening had been the 'International Poetry Incarnation', a massive poetry reading held at the Royal Albert Hall in the summer of 1965, co-organised by Better Books' Barry Miles (usually known as simply 'Miles') and his wife Sue Miles, among others. The Miles' co-founded Indica, an art gallery synonymous with the underground, with the artist John Dunbar in 1965. It was in Indica, in November 1966, that John Lennon, a friend of Dunbar, first met Yoko Ono. The following year, alongside the photographer John 'Hoppy' Hopkins, Sue and Barry also co-founded the *International Times* newspaper which pretty much became the bible of the London underground movement. The paper was launched at a huge happening at Camden's Roundhouse featuring a performance by The Pink Floyd, quickly becoming the house band of the scene. Hoppy would also co-found the UFO club with the producer Joe Boyd, who recorded The Floyd's earliest material. This handful of well-connected individuals, mostly middle class and well educated with links to the liberal press, the music industry and, specifically, The Beatles, had a disproportionate impact as the beatnik scene hit the mainstream, as underground went overground and the 'beats' became 'hippies'.

The Soho notion of 'cool' was fragmenting as it accommodated new influences and embraced older ones. It was within this environment that David Bowie was finally weaning himself away from mod, away from conventional sartorial sharpness and away from the established idea of 'cool', a concept he had followed to the point of obsession for most of his teenage years. Ken Pitt was absolutely essential in the process of breaking David away from being just another Keith Relf or Brian Jones wannabe in a good jacket.[11] One of the many common misperceptions about Pitt is that he wanted to make the previously cool David into an 'all round entertainer'. It's true to an extent – but overlooks the fact that David himself was also losing interest in becoming a straightforward rock 'n' roll singer. He had been banging his head at that particular door for five years now and his success had been limited. As Pitt comments in the closing passage of his book, *The Pitt Report*, 'David was keen to establish himself as an all-round entertainer. Those who … take as their yardstick rock and roll, fail to understand that David never was a devotee or exponent of rock and roll. Whenever he rocked and rolled he did so … as an actor'. David's own words and much of his work have backed this up. Pitt was just giving a spit and polish to something that was already there.

In 1961 David had been taken to the West End by his parents to see *Stop The World, I Want To Get Off*, co-written by and starring Anthony Newley. It was a watershed moment for him. Newley, a Jewish lad from Hackney like Marc Bolan, was one of David's prime inspirations, and an influence that ran concurrently to his love of rock and jazz. Not only was he a successful stage and screen actor, writer, director and recording star with a genuinely global career, he also wrote his own material, sang in his own accent and seemed to have carved out a niche in the entertainment world that was uniquely his own and not subject to trends or fashions. In 1960 he created a television series, *The Strange World of Gurney Slade*, for ITV. It was meta, melancholy, strange, *massively* ahead of its time and alienated its audience to the point that the network shunted it into a graveyard slot mid-run and cancelled it after just one series. The show, which is fantastic by the way, opens with Newley in a traditional sitcom setting, complete with nagging wife and gossiping next door neighbours, sitting in silence as the action happens around him – before standing up, and walking toward the camera, which pans back to reveal the set of a television show. Newley walks out of the studio and through London, musing to himself as he goes. [12] Bowie was a huge fan of the show. Between *Gurney Slade*, his chart hits as a crooner, his film career and his respected career as a stage actor, Anthony Newley's very existence was a lesson in what was possible for David. He also built Newley's Cockney-inflected singing style into his own delivery, an element that would

---

11. Bowie was often mistaken for both The Yardbirds' Relf and the Stones' Jones during his early career, and would absolutely play up to it if he was in the mood. Especially if there was a girl to impress.
12. Newley recorded a special commercial for the series when it was repeated in 1963, which saw him addressing a tattered poster of the show with his own face on it. 'Well, it was a noble effort, wasn't it?' he says. 'You tried. I give you that, you tried. But the public is no man's fool, you know. The public knows what it wants, and you had no right to even try and suggest something different.'

become more and more noticeable over the next year or so of recordings, and would never entirely depart.

Ken Pitt, who had once handled publicity for Newley, was someone well placed to help David capture some of that energy and broad appeal. The two discussed films, theatre, musicals and television in the same breath in which they planned David's pop career. Later many critics and fans, not least David's wife Angela, would accuse Pitt of pushing David into an unfocused career as an all-rounder, someone who could play the cabaret clubs as well as have chart hits. This is largely unfair – David was completely complicit in this. As late as 1969 he was telling *NME* readers that 'I'm determined to be an entertainer, clubs, cabaret, concerts, the lot ... There is too much false pride within the pop scene, groups and singers decrying cabaret without ever having seen the inside of a northern nightclub.' Under Ken Pitt's tutelage, that process began in 1966. Pitt took his young charge to as many plays and concert performances as he could manage, showing him 'the good, the bad and the indifferent', from Frankie Howerd and Cilla Black at the Prince of Wales Theatre, to the Palladium's Christmas pantomime, *Aladdin*, with Cliff Richard in the lead role, to Joe Orton's dark satire, *Loot*.

It wasn't just his showbiz instincts that made Pitt a tremendous asset to Operation Bowie. David was also badly in need of a business professional to rescue his affairs. Though much of the detail had been kept from David, Ralph Horton had increasingly been making a mess of his financial situation. Ken Pitt spent much of his first year as manager sorting out the debtors that regularly came knocking, not least of which was Ray Cook, who was yet to see a penny on his investment in the Lower Third the previous year. By the end of his first month, Pitt had forked out £630 on various debts, including court orders, and the purchase of a replacement ambulance for touring. David's income that month was slightly shy of £150. Things had got so bad that when Pitt headed on a business trip, first to the US (where he met Andy Warhol and acquired an acetate of the debut Velvet Underground album), and then to Australia and Singapore, Horton – with David's agreement – informed the current members of the Buzz that there was no longer any available cash to pay them and that the band was going to be broken up as Ralph felt that the income generated from gigs was not enough to make further dates worthwhile. The band offered to stay on and back David for nothing, prompting Bowie to burst into tears and run out of the room. Horton had to gently explain that, even with the musicians performing for free, there simply wasn't enough work to make keeping the band together worthwhile.

Horton's hope was that signing David to a publisher would fill the gap that live work no longer could, and he resumed the negotiations that Ken Pitt had begun earlier in the year with David Platz at Essex Music. Eventually he agreed on a deal that would put an advance of £500 straight into his outstretched hand. David badly needed the money, both to settle business debts and simply to live on, and he and his father (whose approval was needed since David was still not yet twenty-one) gladly signed on the dotted line. Horton called Pitt, now in Singapore where his client Crispin St. Peters was performing, to give him the good news. It came as something of a shock. There were two very good reasons for this – first of all, when negotiations began with Essex, Pitt had been discussing an advance double the one that Horton had agreed to. Secondly, and far worse, Pitt had actually decided against signing with Essex, having secured a far more lucrative deal with a firm in the US. He was returning to London with a contract in his briefcase for David's world-wide publishing rights with an agreed advance of $30,000, with $10,000 to be paid immediately – providing David with financial security for the foreseeable future. Since he was supposed to be handling the business end of David's affairs, with Horton handling the creative side, he had no inkling that his partner would be taking meetings and making decisions in his absence. Ken quickly called John Jones, David's father, who was as shocked as Pitt – he had believed the Essex deal was done with Pitt's involvement. The two agreed that no good would come of telling David that his friend and manager had torpedoed his financial security, but needless to say Horton's days were numbered. Within the year, Pitt would be in sole control of Bowie's career.

Even before Horton's departure, and despite his golden publishing deal being cruelly cut down, Pitt was more than pulling his weight, and things were moving even before he departed for his US trip that November. Following the tepid reception of Bowie's third (and least satisfying) Pye single, 'I Dig Everything', David had come to Pitt privately and poured his heart out about his dissatisfaction with the label. Pye execs were pushing for him to record some of Tony Hatch's songs rather than his own, which he had no interest in doing and the label's initial rejection of the 'The London Boys', a song David felt was one of his strongest, still stung. Pitt left Horton to disentangle the Pye contract, which proved to be no great hardship – after three duds in a row, Hatch and Pye were content to let David walk away, with their best wishes, even waiving their rights to any future recordings of unrelease Pye-era demos'. This was important – Pitt had adored 'The London Boys' when David played him the earlier recordings, and felt it was perhaps the best representation of Bowie's songwriting and style. He quickly funded a day's recording during which David, with the help of the departing Buzz and some session horn players, laid down a new, more melancholic, affecting version of 'The London Boys', a quirky, upbeat new number called 'Rubber Band' and a spoken word piece David had recently completed called 'Please Mr Gravedigger'. Free of Tony Hatch's more muzaky instincts and given the sonic colours (specifically a tuba, oboe and trumpet) he needed to paint the picture in his head, David produced his strongest set of recordings so far. 'Rubber Band' brought the influence of Anthony Newley truly to the surface for the first time, with an excellent vocal (including an impressive octave jump in the second verse) held aloft by a music-hall influenced musical frame that was almost entirely removed from the mod rock 'n' roll of almost all of Bowie's previous recordings. There's no audible guitar to be found – though one might be buried in the mix – with the tuba providing the bassline, and the brass section giving the song its primary identity. Lyrically David was already in sync with the whimsical story telling that would mark British psychedelia (though you'd be hard pushed to describe any of these songs as psychedelic), all stiffly waxed moustaches and tea and scones. There's something of the quirky charm of early Pink Floyd in the words, and a direct line to a genre of songs Paul McCartney was writing for The Beatles – 'Penny Lane', 'When I'm Sixty-Four', 'Obla-Di-Obla-Da' – that John Lennon would dismiss as 'granny music'. Of his contemporaries, you can hear far more of the storytelling and Englishness of Ray Davies than the Who or the Stones. It also predated the Small Faces throwback masterpiece *Ogden's Nut Gone Flake* by a clear two years.

Even better was the new version of 'The London Boys'. Again, David makes exceptional use of the brass instruments, creating a warm, almost Salvation Army band feel, which alongside a swirling organ and a sophisticated arrangement by David and Buzz bass player Derek 'Dek' Fearnley, who had become his main musical foil in the band, as well as the best studio performance David had yet turned in as a vocalist, resulted in an absolutely exquisite musical moment.

It was what Ken Pitt had been waiting for. With the new recordings in hand, he was able to find David a new deal, this time with Decca's new imprint, Deram, established as a showcase for new British talent that might not sit as comfortably on the rather fusty label's main rosta.[13] Not only did the label agree to put out the recording of 'Rubber Band', with 'The London Boys' as the b-side, Pitt was also able to sell Bowie as an album artist. This was virtually unheard of at a time when acts almost always had to prove themselves with a hit single before they were given the chance to make a long player. However, Pitt was able to argue that Bowie already had the songs, the vision and the talent to support an entire record. That December, 'Rubber Band' followed Bowie's previous six singles into pop obscurity, matching the lack of progress shown by Marc's 'Hippy Gumbo', released just a week earlier, no doubt giving the pair something to grumble over cappuccinos together in La Gioconda that Christmas. It scarcely mattered. 1967 was dawning. There was technicolour change in the air, and David Bowie had an album to record.

---

13. 'Deram' came from 'Deramic Sound', which was itself an abbreviation of 'Decca Panoramic Sound', the company's newly developed studio technology which favoured creating stereo recordings. It's why all of the music Bowie recorded on Deram was released in stereo; which was not always guaranteed in those days.

Chapter Thirteen

Petals and Flowers

S imon Napier-Bell didn't just manage The Yardbirds and Marc Bolan. In the summer of 1966, exhausted by the rigours of keeping Jeff Beck and Keith Relph on stage, on time, and on the right drugs, Napier-Bell had rewarded himself with a break in St Tropez in the South of France. There he ran into John Hewlett, a handsome British kid who'd wandered into the bar with an apparently quite distinctive-looking local prostitute, causing Napier-Bell, tactful as ever, to drunkenly hurl abuse at the couple until they joined him and proceeded to get hammered. Hewlett (who'd funded his holiday via a friend with a knack for stealing cheque books) and Napier-Bell got along like a house on fire, and the talk soon turned to music, at which point Hewlett revealed he played bass in a band called The Silence. His new friend was drunk enough to promise to come and see him play – and that is how, as he wrote in his memoir, Simon Napier-Bell 'got stuck with the worst group in the world for the next two years'.

When Napier-Bell, true to his word, eventually saw The Silence he was appalled. They were a messy, play-by-numbers mod group with a lousy sense of tempo who only got away with ripping off other people's songs because they played them so badly that nobody noticed. In a way they were hugely ahead of their time – had they formed in *1976* instead of *1966* they'd have slotted right into punk's bracingly neanderthal first flourish. As it was, despite the high energy performance of singer Andy Ellison, The Silence were too raw, too sloppy and too damned loud to really be of interest. The story doesn't end there, however. Napier-Bell made the mistake of joining them for a drink after the gig … and woke the next day to find that he'd agreed to manage them.

John's Children – Napier-Bell changed their name as a way to protect John Hewlett from being sacked once someone worked out that he couldn't really play his instrument – are, in their own way, a perfect case study of the mid-sixties rock scene. Napier-Bell, almost despite himself, became genuinely fond of the four Leatherhead lads, and persisted in his intention to manage them even after he'd properly sobered up and taken some aspirin. Over the next six months he would throw every trick in the book at the band in an attempt to make them famous, reasoning that this would actually be easier and quicker than waiting for them to get any good. First he paid for LA's finest session musicians, including members of the famous 'Wrecking Crew',[1] to cut a song

---

1. Including Hal Blaine, the legendary drummer who had played the unforgettable and much-imitated beat on The Ronettes' 'Be My Baby', arguably the most perfect pop song ever recorded.

he co-wrote with Hewlett called 'Smashed Blocked', thickening the intro with a recording of an Arsenal football crowd and schooling singer Andy Ellison through the vocal part line-by-line. Mixed by Napier-Bell himself, who had a habit of getting overly creative in the studio, 'Smashed Blocked' is something of a lost classic; a lurching slice of weirdness that alternates between a gorgeous ballady verse and a psych-rock chanting chorus. There was very little around in the English scene that sounded like 'Smashed Blocked', which predated Pink Floyd's debut single by a good six months. Napier-Bell claims that he coined the term 'psychedelic' to describe its heady brew, though as that word had previously been used to label the rock music coming out of San Francisco, it's more likely that he had simply tuned into something that was already in the air (the debut album by The 13th Floor Elevators, for example, was called *The Psychedelic Sound of the 13th Floor Elevators*, and came out in the same week as 'Smashed Blocked'). Despite some exceptionally good reviews, the single bombed in the UK (where it was released on Columbia under the tamer name of 'The Love I Thought I'd Found'), but Napier-Bell was able to utilise a range of hyping techniques to create a minor and largely artificial hit in the United States, mostly by using clothes, records and sweets to bribe school children to call radio stations. It was enough for White Whale, the band's US label, to request an album, which Napier-Bell provided by recording his boys playing live in a studio, dubbing over the hysterical audience screams from the Beatles' *A Hard Day's Night* movie and claiming it was a concert recording, thus passing off the band's lack of studio polish as vigorous live energy. The album was to be called *Orgasm* and managed to accrue 35,000 pre-orders in the US alone before being predictably pulled from sale due to the nature of its title.[2] For his next trick, working closer to home, Napier-Bell used British session musicians to record the group's second single, 'Just What You Want – Just What You'll Get', and then called his friend 'Gerry' to buy the track into the lower reaches of the top-30 for a couple of weeks, thus increasing their value as a live act. He made sure their live show was unforgettable, dressing them all in white, buying state of the art Jordan amps (allegedly louder than anything on the market in Britain and, so Napier-Bell claimed, developed in Houston by NASA)[3] and encouraging the band to whip themselves with chains, howl, smash their gear, fall off the stage and generally behave like rabid thugs. In the end it was all too

---

2. *Orgasm*, like 'Smashed Blocked', is worth digging out. The playing is rudimentary, but by this point the group's song writing was getting pretty good, even without Napier-Bell's intervention.

3. This 'NASA' claim is tenuous at best and likely some trademark Napier-Bell myth-making. Jordan Electronics, which made the amps, was a division of the Victoreen Instrument Company, a firm which primarily manufactured equipment used to measure radiation. Some of its products were indeed used by the US space programme, but there's absolutely no evidence that the subset of the business dealing with amplifiers and effects pedals and the department that made Geiger counters for astronauts were closely connected. Both Jordan and Victoreen were based in California, rather than Texas. This doesn't seem to have stopped Andy Ellison repeating the NASA claim in interviews as recently as the 2010s.

much for guitarist Geoff McClelland, who had a catalogue of stress-induced health issues and was already bitter after being unceremoniously replaced by Jeff Beck on the b-side to 'Just What You Want …' despite being promised that he could finally appear on one of his own records (he utterly failed to nail his guitar solo and Napier-Bell lost patience and called in one of the world's greatest lead guitarists instead). John's Children were in need of a guitarist, ideally one with charisma to spare, who could write songs and sing. Fortunately, there was one hanging around.

Napier-Bell's idea to parachute Marc Bolan into John's Children was a stroke of genius. The band had some profile thanks to the success of 'Smashed Blocked' in the US and were a fantastic, if primitive, live act, but their song-writing was, at best, merely acceptable, and there was nothing especially cerebral or compelling about the group's personalities. Marc Bolan, on the other hand, wrote fantastic songs and gave excellent quote, but was inexperienced as a live performer and had little profile of his own. The hope was that Marc would fulfil a similar role to the one played by Pete Townshend in the Who: to be the musical focus and to bang out some hits. The only slight drawback was that Marc was only a marginally better guitarist than the one he was replacing. He'd been stunned by the magic Hendrix had generated before his eyes back in December, but had no real idea of how to achieve it himself. Before joining John's Children, Marc had never even *played* an electric guitar.[4]

Marc and Simon hadn't quite given up on the idea of a solo career, and had already recorded what they hoped would be his next single, a boogie-woogie groover called 'Jasper C. Debussy', the closest he had yet got to the sound that would make him a huge star a few years later. Alas, after three flops in a row no-one was willing to take a chance on releasing it. Napier-Bell hoped that a stint in John's Children would sharpen his stagecraft, improve his musicianship, raise his profile and generally put him in a better position for solo stardom. That John's Children, a band he seemed to keep on his books as some sort of experiment or hobby or personal challenge, would benefit from Marc's excellent songs was an added bonus. The band were gradually convinced to accept the new arrival via a campaign of subliminal marketing, in which their manager would leave photos of his protégé lying around his office and the recording studio and play Bolan demos loudly whenever the band were about to arrive. Eventually Andy Ellison was dispatched to Tooting to bond over mushrooms on toast and hear some of Marc's latest songs, among them a tune called 'Desdemona' and a half-written piece called 'A Midsummer Night's Scene'. He was impressed with what he found, and Marc was accepted into the band, just in time for the promotional duties for 'Just What You Want – Just What You'll Get'.

---

4. An occasionally repeated story that Simon considered placing Marc into the Yardbirds, a band whose whole schtick rested on having a virtuoso lead guitarist – Clapton, Beck, Page – is unlikely to the point of laughable.

Though it took him a while to warm into the raucous, carefully choreographed anarchy of the John's Children stage act (he couldn't perform without downing bottles of red wine before his first few gigs), Marc immediately embraced the titanic levels of volume he could get out of the Jordan amp and his newly-acquired Gibson SG. For a while, before he finally began to adapt to the subtleties of his new set up, the band found they had replaced the untutored fumbling of their previous guitarist with a sledgehammer of feedback and noise, as if Marc was trying to manifest the sound of Hendrix or Townshend through sheer force of will. He often didn't even bother to tune his instrument, and got offended when drummer Chris Townson tried to sneakily do it for him before shows.[5]

John's Children gigs were far more about spectacle than subtlety ('forty-five minute happenings' is how Marc described the band's performances to *NME*). What Bolan lacked in virtuosity, he made up for in songwriting. The band quickly recorded several Bolan originals – 'Desdemona', 'Hippy Gumbo', 'The Perfumed Garden of Gulliver Smith', 'Sara Crazy Child' and 'Hot Rod Mama' among them, with Marc's 'The Third Degree' added to their live set. The noticeable lurch in quality was enough to interest Kit Lambert, a friend of Napier-Bell and the manager of The Who. Lambert had just launched his own record label, Track, ostensibly as a vehicle for The Who, but also as a recording home for The Jimi Hendrix Experience, who he immediately saw were bound for stardom. Possibly as a velvet mafia favour for his friend, possibly because he sensed Bolan's star potential, and possibly just for the hell of it (Lambert was fond of tossing such grenades into the business, just to see what would happen), John's Children were also brought on board and almost immediately packed off to mainland Europe to open for The Who.

The John's Children tour of Germany in support of Messrs Townshend, Daltrey, Entwistle and Moon has become the stuff of rock legend. Lesley-Ann Jones quotes John Entwistle reminiscing about the shows: 'Mad, they were … Out-Who'd The Who, the bastards. Keith [Moon] was not thrilled. [He] kicked ten weeks of shit out of their gear one night and nearly wrung their flamin' necks, not that it stopped them … Gore. Chains. Chairs. Feathers. Pillow fights gone mental. Crowd went nuts for it.' In truth, John's Children's time on the tour lasted for just five shows. Napier-Bell's plan was, as he admits in *You Don't Have To Say You Love Me*, to bring The Who's audience, desperate to be driven into a frenzy by their heroes, to 'premature ejaculation – all over John's Children'.[6] He wanted to see if this group, which he had carefully crafted

---

5. This is especially evident if you listen to the very few live recordings of John's Children, particularly a BBC radio session done for *Saturday Club* that June. You can find a version of Marc's 'Hot Rod Mama', featuring dual lead vocals and extremely out of tune guitar on YouTube if you poke around a bit. Almost a decade later, producer Tony Visconti was still having to tune Marc's guitar on the sly in the studio.

6. Like I said, Napier-Bell has a hell of a turn of phrase.

into a parent-baiting, orgiastically violent rock 'n' roll freak-out that made the Pretty Things look like the Ladybirds[7], could indeed 'out-Who the Who'.

The shows would go like this – Marc, bass player John Hewlett and drummer Chris Townson would come out first, playing a thumping, driving beat. As the audience, mostly in 10,000+ seater sports arenas, started to pay attention Andy Ellison would run on from the wings, jump from the stage and dash through the crowd, tossing duck feathers into the air so they streamed behind him as he ran, a comet with a snowy white tail, doing a quick circuit of the arena before making it back to the stage to launch into the opening number.[8] A few songs later, Ellison and Hewlett would strip to the waist and start to wrestle, which was Marc's signal to unleash a wave of screaming feedback, leave his guitar lying across his amp so the squealing noise expanded and continued of its own accord, and then start whipping his bandmates with an iron chain, until Townson smashed the hell out of his drum kit (carefully so as to make sure that he could use it the next night) signalling the end of the set. The Who were livid, partly because they felt the audience was getting too excited, too early and were not quite as prone to the wow-factor of their own set as they normally would have been; partly because feedback and smashing stuff was absolutely *their* thing, and this was encroaching on their territory, and partly because the feathers, which they asked the band to stop using every night only to be ignored, remained in the air and played havoc with Roger Daltrey singing. It's no wonder that John Entwistle called them 'bastards'.

The band were eventually forced to make a sharp exit in Napier-Bell's Bentley during the fifth show of the tour, when an incensed audience stormed the stage after Ellison smashed some lights. The venue security were mobilising and the fire brigade were apparently called out to attack the band with a high pressure hose[9] as they fled the scene. With the band crammed into his car, Simon put his foot down and the Bentley took off screaming onto the autobahn, that expensive allegedly-NASA-patented gear left behind forever. Each member was in a different degree of physical or emotional distress, all blood, feathers, bruises, black eyes. 'I think,' Simon Napier-Bell allegedly announced, 'that the stage act is coming together quite well'.

This final show was reviewed by the German Newspaper *Mannheimer Morgen*, and its critic did a good job of relaying the essence of the band's performance: 'The stage wasn't capable of containing the fit of raving madness of these ecstatic musicians. Amps fell down, making nerve-killing sounds and the stage lighting also collapsed … So, these are John's Children. 'Poor John!''[10]

---

7. The backing singers from 'The Wizard', not one of the topless ones.
8. Marc's notes at the time suggest this was 'The Third Degree'.
9. This detail comes according to Simon Napier-Bell and should probably be viewed with suspicion.
10. This translation is taken from Cliff McLenehan's excellent book, *Marc Bolan 1947 – 1977: A Chronology* .

All five knew that they'd blown their chance with The Who, but that was okay. Pulling out the stops for that final show was a deliberate decision; they'd reached a point where their headliners weren't going to allow things to continue in the same vein. It was either tone things down or accept they would be thrown off the tour, and no-one in John's Children wanted to tone down *anything*. By now Marc was completely absorbed in the chaos, playing his part to the letter. As he thrashed across the stage at that final show in Germany, walloping his amp, his bandmates, the stage, anything, the figure of the tiny, elfin Bolan sat in Simon Napier-Bell's plushest armchair strumming 'Hippy Gumbo' seemed a long way away.

By joining John's Children, Marc was, as ever, placing himself right in the thick of the zeitgeist, just as the innocent, monochrome mod days of Beatlemania, beat bands and the blues were retreating into the rearview mirror and the more raucous end of R&B started to collide with the acid-frazzled tunes coming out of California. The scene was retrospectively dubbed 'Freakbeat'[11], which is as good a name as any for super-charged R&B groups like John's Children, The Pretty Things and the Action as well as the wilfully weird, tuned-out psyche rock of The Crazy World of Arthur Brown, Soft Machine and of course The Pink Floyd. Freakbeat wasn't really a genre, more a way of describing those transitional bands who seemed to contain both halves of the sixties at once as if split between the two hemispheres of a single brain.

1967 was the year that the hippies finally arrived in London, or at the very least the year that people outside the underground scene started to notice that something was going on. That the term 'Hippy' was starting to be used at all was a symptom of that volley-ball effect between British and American youth culture. Hippies were an American phenomenon, the term originally an abbreviation used to describe the beatnik hipsters of Greenwich Village, those determined to live a life outside of conventional values. The movement had been given a huge injection of sunshine as it spread to the opposite coast and blossomed in San Francisco, notably in the area known as Haight-Ashbury. The counterculture became less uptight, less concerned with intellectual cool, and more interested in hallucinogenics and free love. 'Hippie' (as it tended to be termed in the US) came to be associated with the free-spirited flower children of the 'Summer of Love' and the sweeping trend for love beads, outdoor music festivals and pot that swept the US in 1967. This sea-change in youth culture and its tipping point into the mainstream was marked, as usual, by *Time* magazine. The summer of 1966 saw the famous 'London Swings' issue, July 1967 saw a cover dedicated to 'The Hippie'.

---

11. The phrase was coined by Phil Smee in the 80s, an occasional journalist who lovingly assembled several reissues of overlooked sixties bands. He was also the man that designed Motörhead's iconic logo.

The word gradually creeped into the British vocabulary across 1965 and 1966 (Marc, after all, had written his 'Hippy Gumbo' the previous summer), and by 1967 was becoming commonplace. In both the US and the UK, hippy culture had a central core of genuine firebrands with fiercely held ideas, but then blurred into the mainstream as an aesthetic rather than a lifestyle. 'Flower power' became the catchphrase of a scene that proclaimed itself dedicated to 'peace and love'. The hippy values and aesthetics piggy-backed into the mainstream via The Beatles, who had given up touring for good post-*Revolver*, traded in their matching suits and matching haircuts and allowed themselves to grow out their hair, grow beards and moustaches and, in Lennon's case, wear eye glasses. Their era-defining masterpiece, 1967's *Sgt Pepper's Lonely Hearts Club Band* was monstrously successful and sneaked several psychedelic techniques and ideas into homes across the country. It was followed just a month later by the band's most explicitly hippy moment – a performance of 'All You Need Is Love', seen by 500 million people around the world as part of the *Our World* satellite broadcast. The band played Lennon's hymn to peace and love surrounded by flowers and with fans and friends sat cross-legged on the floor. It was a happening all of its own.

As 1967 went on, the flower power aesthetic was really starting to take hold. Fashion formed a big part of it, but at its nucleus was a genuine counterculture, fuelled by mostly middle class intellectuals but theoretically open to anyone. Its natural home was in Notting Hill, Ladbroke Grove and Portobello Road, where a mish-mash community of students looking for cheap digs, West Indian immigrants, former beatnik hipsters, left-wing revolutionaries, social justice campaigners and crystal-waving new age types had created a uniquely flavoured corner of the city. While the mods had been about pills, late nights, sharp suits and scooters, this underground scene had a spiritual aspect with ideas taken from Indian mysticism, Hinduism, Buddhism and Hari Krishna as well as Wicca and Paganism, with trips out of the city more likely to be headed for Glastonbury Tor or Stonehenge than Brighton Beach. There were real ideas here; poetry, literature and art. There was also drugs. Pot had become widespread to the point of compulsory, and psychedelics, LSD and magic mushrooms, were finding a market with the promise of 'freeing the mind'; something that synced neatly with hippy idealism.

When those drugs met the freakbeat bands, spectacular things could happen, either as a direct result of their immediate consumption, or else in terms of trying to capture or replicate the effects of taking acid through an audio-visual experience. Sometimes this was done through lengthy freakout jams, and sometimes by the guitarist buying a sitar and giving it a go. The American psyche rockers had been funnelling acid into rock 'n' roll for some time, but something about the British character gave it a narrower, more nostalgic twist. The album was king in America, and labels were prepared to take a chance on a longplayer from unproven bands, who often took advantage of the extra vinyl space to noodle tediously for what felt like hours. The British industry wasn't built like that. It's why Ken Pitt's deal with Deram, which secured an album contract for David regardless of a hit single, was such an impressive move. Instead, London's burgeoning psyche scene had to condense its ideas and experiences into palatable 45 rpm singles. This restriction made for more creative, more exciting and substantially weirder hits than could ever emerge in the US. It's why John's Children's 'Smashed Blocked' felt so authentic. British psychedelia, as pop historian Bob Stanley puts it in *Yeah Yeah Yeah*, was the sound of rock 'n' roll 'with a child's kaleidoscope pressed tightly to its eye'.

By the spring of sixty-seven, the kings of English psyche rock were The Pink Floyd, an art student four piece under the command of another elfin guitarist, Syd Barrett. The Floyd had been another of London's many slingers of club R&B, but singer/guitarist Barrett and keyboard player Rick Wright kept pushing the envelope in terms of the texture, volume and length of their interludes. Barrett was also proving himself to be a hell of a songwriter, with an ability to blend character pieces, twee Englishness and psychedelic imagery into compact pop packages, as he admirably displayed with the group's first two singles, both now considered classics; 'Arnold Layne' and 'See Emily Play'. The pop singles were just the sweetener though – Pink Floyd's speciality was in long, extended, free-forming jams, like their space-rock centrepiece 'Interstellar Overdrive'. It made them the perfect band to soundtrack the launch of *International Times*, the counterculture newspaper founded by many of the key names in London's scene. As *IT* reported in its review of its own launch party, the band 'did weird things to the feel of the evening with their scary feedback sounds, slide projections playing on their skin, spotlights flashing on them in time with a drum beat.'

Both David and Marc were huge fans of Floyd, seeing in them aspects and gleams that they'd wanted to include in their own music. Both worshipped at the altar of Syd Barrett, who had a similar impact on them as Bob Dylan had, with the added bonus of almost being a contemporary. In David's case it was all about the lyrical themes. Barrett had an interest in Victorian and Edwardian imagery, in Englishisms and tweeness, that chimed very much with Bowie's own. Barrett also sang in his own accent, which was still a rarity in the British scene.[12] For Marc, it was all about the presentation. Those feedback-drenched freakouts with John's Children were partly an attempt to summon the sheer power of Jimmy Hendrix (as was his occasional habit of playing the guitar on the back of his head), but they were also a mirror of Barrett's long, meandering sonic poems. Barrett was an extremely creative guitarist, using his instrument to create shapes and tones unusual in rock 'n' roll.

---

12. In many ways it's a rarity even now.

On 29 April, shortly after returning from Germany, Marc finally shared a bill with Syd Barrett, with both John's Children and the Floyd booked to play the now legendary '14-Hour Technicolor Dream' event at the Alexandra Palace. The show had been organised to raise funds for *International Times*, whose offices had been raided by the police, though hapless mismanagement meant that despite several thousand people attending, the event barely broke even. It was the first *huge* happening of the hippy era, and probably the most important event in London's burgeoning counterculture since the poetry reading at the Albert Hall two years earlier. There was art, and films projected on fluttering bed sheets. A full-sized Helter Skelter stood in the middle of the huge hall, absorbing the sound coming from two stages set up at either end and running concurrently, meaning that anyone enjoying the slide did so amid the din of duelling psychedelic rock. All of London's psych rock and freakbeat players were there: Arthur Brown, his head literally on fire as usual, Soft Machine, the Pretty Things, the Move and dozens more, headlined by a performance from an exhausted Pink Floyd, having hot-footed from a gig in the Netherlands earlier that evening. The sets by the Floyd and John's Children, though very differently anticipated and performed at very different points of the event, did have a curious similarity: both involved guitarists who seemed to have checked out from reality altogether. Syd Barrett, a prolific acid user, was starting to come apart at the seams. Taking the stage as the sun rose over London, Syd barely played a conventional chord, instead unleashing distracted experiments on his guitar, slowly detuning and returning his strings, scraping things across the pick ups, creating weird tones and textures that had little semblance to the notes on their records. For Pink Floyd it was the beginning of the end of their first great phase – within a year Syd's erratic behaviour and unravelling mind meant he was out of the band, one of the greatest acid casualties of British rock.[13] Though Marc didn't have acid as an excuse (he barely touched drugs in those days), the performance that day by John's Children was remarkably similar. Marc wandered, almost blank eyed, around the stage, his guitar hoisted behind his head, letting the feedback ring, hardly playing a clear note at all. In fairness most of the extremely stoned crowd barely noticed, but to the rest of the band it felt as if Marc – who had seemed disenchanted ever since the group had returned from Germany – had lost interest completely. He would stay with John's Children for another three months, contributing to the recording of a planned album, playing some shows and doing a BBC session, but everyone else in the band at the time felt that his heart was no longer in it.

---

13. In his biography of Barrett, *A Very Irregular Head*, Rob Chapman has a much more sympathetic view of the show, describing the 'delicate glissandi' floating from Syd's guitar as the sun rose. He quotes Soft Machine guitarist Daevid Allen who thought the band sounded like 'the music of the spheres'. Members of Pink Floyd themselves have been less complimentary of the performance ('A great gig – though God knows what it actually sounded like' wrote Nick Mason in his autobiography.)

It's to the eternal regret of his bandmates that Marc chose to lose interest in the project at a crucial moment for John's Children, when their ascension to the mainstream hung just out of reach. The week after the Alexandra Palace event, the band's first Bolan-penned single, 'Desdemona', was released – a superb pop slice that was by far the best thing anyone involved had done so far, either together or independently. Marc's playing is rudimentary, as it usually was in those days, but his decision to modulate the song's key at the end of every verse gives an unusual texture to his ringing, Townshend-style power chords. The whole thing was raised aloft by the only member of the band with real technical proficiency: drummer Chris Townson, who unleashes a storm of fills and runs throughout the song. Despite the clear influence of Messrs Moon and Townshend,[14] Marc's quirks as a writer mean that 'Desdemona' sounds less like The Who than you'd think, and not just because of his bleating backing vocal. It had the most potential of any song released by either London boy thus far – simultaneously modern and classic sounding – and received rave reviews in the music press, with Marc's backing vocal and Chris Townson's drumming rightly praised. Alas, BBC radio took objection to a line in the chorus – 'lift up your skirt and fly' – essentially making it impossible for it to be the huge hit it deserved to be. It became Marc's fourth non-starter in a row.

The band, including their disillusioned guitarist, ploughed on with their plans. Track records were still interested in a John's Children album, and several songs were laid down throughout May and June of 1967, including Marc and Andy's 'Midsummer Night's Scene', which was intended to be the group's next single. A July release was pencilled in, and test pressings and promo 45s (somewhere between twenty and fifty) were produced (backed with Marc's 'Sara, Crazy Child'). They would never reach record stores. Marc hated what Napier-Bell, who produced the tune, did to his song. 'We did one take and it sounded good, really tight but very raw. I felt like it was going to be huge. It was much better than we were', Marc told NME's Danny Holloway in 1972. 'The next day, and it was a totally different thing. Simon had overdubbed all these oo-bee-doos. He had to edit everything. And I heard it and I quit the next day.' Napier-Bell was indeed a tinkerer. Andy Ellison reckons his pre-music biz background in film editing was partly to blame – he was happy to work alone into the night, slicing and splicing tape. In much the same way as he'd messed around with 'Smashed Blocked' and the *Orgasm* album, Napier-Bell attempted to make 'Midsummer Night's Scene' into the ultimate Summer of Love anthem, looping its 'petals and flowers' refrain to add a trippy, hypnotic texture to the verses. Copying and pasting musical passages, locking them to a groove and creating new effects is substantially easier to do in the twenty-first century, though it still takes

---

14. Chris Townson would actually cover for an injured Keith Moon for a handful of Who gigs later in the year.

skill to do well; In 1967 it was a painstaking, difficult process that required the delicate touch of an expert. The Beatles had created endlessly inventive editing solutions with the limited technology of the day, but Simon was no George Martin. He didn't exactly 'butcher' 'Midsummer Night's Dream', as Marc occasionally claimed, but his attempts to create psychedelic vibes certainly felt hamfisted. The band were sure they had a dead cert number one hit, and though that might have been optimistic, 'Midsummer Night's Scene' was still a fine song that could well have caught the spirit of the time ... had their manager been able to leave it alone. It spelled the end of Marc's short but extremely formative time with John's Children. There was no big bust up, no storming out (Napier-Bell even pulled Townson and Hewlitt in to play on a new song that was intended as a Marc Bolan solo release), he simply drifted away from the band. Track cancelled the release of the single before the record went properly to press and the handful of early pressings that made it out into the world are now extraordinarily valuable – a copy sold at auction in 2002 for £3,700. It is legitimately one of the most sought-after 45s in the world.

Napier-Bell would continue to throw every gimmick he had at his disposal in order to promote the remaining members of John's Children – within a few weeks pictures of Ellison, Hewlett and Townson, naked but for some petals and flowers, were plastered on walls across London, as he attempted to make them literal poster children for the flower-power generation. Alas, John's Children would never be anything but a cult band. As for Marc, he had several options available to him. He had a manager, he had the attention of Track records, the label of Hendrix and The Who, and he had songs. A solo career still seemed to be on the cards, and Napier-Bell was already looking into it. Marc wasn't quite ready to give up his electric dreams though, and wanted a band of his own. He was still an artist that straddled two worlds – he was absolutely part of the hippy trend and understood what the underground meant; he would later be accused of faking his hippy values for credibility, which is a little unfair – he genuinely did have a spirit that resonated with the counterculture. He loved poetry and surrealism, and was a largely gentle and sweet soul who had taken part in CND marches a few years earlier. However he also, nakedly, wanted to be a star, and no amount of meditation, trippy lighting and happenings could entirely quench that fire. Both of these elements were in his mind when he advertised for a new band. The 30 June edition of *International Times*, the parish newsletter of the British underground, carried a notice on page fifteen alongside an advert for a 'mauve day glow coffee table,'[15] requests for 'contributions for anthology of new multiple conscious L S Delirium way out writing'[16] and a plea for a 'lawyer for drug busts and youth harassment'. It read:

---

15. '... and the wood shows through? How? For quick info call BAY 7694.'
16. It also requested 'astral country runner space parapoetry'.

'FREAKY LEAD GUITARIST, bass guitarist and drummer wanted for MARC BOLAN'S new group. Also any other astral flyers, like with cars, amplification and that which never grows in window boxes. Phone WIMBLEDON 0697: 9 am to 3 pm'.[17]

Covering his bases, a second advert ran in the far more conventional classifieds section of *Melody Maker* on 1 July, this time simply saying:

'FREAKY lead guitarist wanted – Wimbledon, 0697 9am-3pm).'[18]

Two weeks later the news of Marc's departure from John's Children was announced in a short piece running in the 15 July edition of *Melody Maker*:

'A new John's Children single called "Come And Play With Me In The Garden" will be released on Track on July 21. Singer and songwriter Marc Bolan recently left the group to form his own group, Tyrannosaurus Rex.'

---

17. Curiously, the same issue of *IT* carried a listing offering John's Children for live gigs, at the cost of £40-£60 per show.
18. Much shorter, probably because *IT* charged a mere sixpence per word for its classified ads, whereas the *MM* 'Musicians Wanted' section asked for a shilling – twice the price.

Chapter Fourteen

Haven't You Got A Gnome To Go To?

David Bowie, the music obsessive who had pored over records since his childhood, who had absorbed music through his pores, who had come to appreciate the album as a supreme artform, approached the end of 1966 indulging a fantasy that he had been chasing for the last five years. He was recording an album that would be the ultimate representation of his creativity and a distillation of his musical personality, his worldview, his dreams, everything. It was a lot of pressure to put on a couple of months of on-off recording. Deram, his new label, were supporting him in his vision, and staff at the label and at its parent company, Decca, seemed to be genuinely excited about their new signing. Here was an artist consciously echoing an established showbiz star, Tony Newley, who was at the same time still a teenager – a genuine generational representative, someone who seemed to understand the cutting edge. And he wrote his own songs, some of which had genuine hit potential, particularly the punchy, none-more-mid-sixties 'Love You Till Tuesday' and a late edition added in the new year – a ballad called 'When I Live My Dream'. This was a kid fizzing with ideas.

It could, of course, have been very different. It had taken the contacts and charm of Ken Pitt to get David in front of Deram, and it's supremely unlikely that anyone at Decca realised that this was the same kid that had flopped with 'Liza Jane' on their Vocalion Pop imprint just two years earlier, or had once been a member of failed auditionees the Kon-Rads. By the time Bowie began the process of recording his debut album, he had already morphed through five different incarnations, each slightly shifting his music in one direction or another. Had the stars aligned otherwise, had different opportunities come along, he could easily have made his debut album for Parlophone with Shel Talmy and the Lower Third, delivering a mod rock thriller to file alongside The Who and The Action. He could certainly have made a commercial pop LP with Tony Hatch at Pye. Both would have been very different debut albums to the one he ended up making. The sophisticated, quirky and genuinely palatable songs that would make up *David Bowie*, the eponymous debut that would become the most overlooked and undervalued corner of Bowie's back catalogue, created a snapshot of an artist that seemed unable to keep still.

Even as he finished making it, he was already moving forward– and at speed. Ken Pitt had returned from the US with more than just a now-useless contract for a $30,000 dollar publishing deal (which David wouldn't learn about for another four years in any case). During his time in New York, Pitt had met Andy Warhol and been introduced to his proteges, The Velvet Underground, whose potential he had immediately recognised – something which is often forgotten when people talk about what a stick-in-the-mud showbiz throwback Pitt could be.[1] He'd been given an acetate of their debut album, *The Velvet Underground and Nico*, still four months away from its release, which he'd excitedly passed on to David who devoured it whole, listening to it late into the night, letting the needle find the middle of side two and then flipping it over to play again.

There's a case to be made that *The Velvet Underground and Nico* is the most influential rock album of the 1960s. As Bob Stanley puts it in *Yeah Yeah Yeah*: 'There is a point on ['I Heard Her Call My Name'] where you can actually hear a tear in the space–time continuum. This was 1967, but it was also 1977. And 1987. [Lou] Reed and [John] Cale had somehow created a noise so brand new that it tore a hole in pop's natural state of progression'. It would take a few years for the pure signal to dissolve into the London scene, and its influence would be felt most strongly in the seventies, but for David the future was now. Hearing the Velvet Underground was very nearly as important as hearing Little Richard. That first Velvets record, which even now sounds more exciting and more contemporary than probably anything else released in the mid sixties, was a new perspective on rock. Lou Reed's grown-up take on rock storytelling, approaching lyrics like a novelist or an essayist rather than a poet or a songwriter, led to a fundamental lurch in the way David looked at music. He found himself knocked for six. Anthony Newley would loom large on his debut album, but the Velvet Underground loomed over his entire career.

'I'd never heard anything quite like it,' he would tell PBS in 1996. 'It was a revelation to me ... the nature of his lyric writing which for me just smacked of things like Hubert Selby Jr, *The Last Exit from Brooklyn* and also John Rechy's book *City of the Night*. Lou's writing was right in that ballpark. It was Dylan who brought a new kind of intelligence to pop songwriting but then it was Lou who had taken it even further and into the avant-garde'. In 2003, Bowie would pen an editorial for *New York* magazine in which he went further. '"I'm Waiting For the Man,"' he wrote, was 'the linchpin, the keystone of my ambition ... This music was so savagely indifferent to my feelings. It didn't care if I liked it or not. It could give a fuck. It was completely preoccupied with a world unseen by my suburban eyes.' David, as we have seen, had always been on-trend. It was a key part of his personality. With his new devotion to the Velvet's classic debut, which scarcely anyone else in Europe had heard,[2] he had, as he later noted himself, achieved the ultimate mod dream of being into something unspeakably cool

---

1. Even David was guilty of downplaying Pitt's interest, often saying he was given the record because Pitt wasn't interested in it, and glossing over the fact that Pitt came home from his trip determined to book a UK residency for the band. David's enthusiasm only sharpened an idea that he already had.
2. Or hardly anyone in America for that matter. VU were always a cult prospect.

before anyone else even knew what it was. Pitt had gifted David this treasured early Christmas present on 16 December. The following night, David Bowie and The Buzz played their last ever gig, at Lewes Town Hall in East Sussex. The band encored with 'I'm Waiting For The Man', a song David had heard only twenty-four hours earlier, becoming one of the first bands anywhere in the world to cover The Velvet Underground.[34]

What's fascinating is how removed an album like *The Velvet Underground and Nico*, with its sparse, fuzzed out, very grown-up art rock, was from the music David was making by day. They're barely in the same universe. Work resumed on the Deram album after Christmas, while 'I'm Waiting For The Man', 'Heroin' and 'Venus In Furs' were still echoing around David's head. These were difficult influences to incorporate into a record of light pop narratives, and you can't hear a great deal of the Velvet's influence on, say, 'When I Live My Dream', one of the later additions to the album, though it does crop up here and there. Future Bowie guitarist Carlos Alomar is convinced that 'I'm Waiting For The Man' – a song which can be considered the blueprint for the next forty years of credible indie rock – was channelled directly into a tune David had written over the Christmas break, a novelty pop ditty which he called 'The Laughing Gnome'. It is, admittedly, a bit of a stretch to find much musical common ground between one of the coolest pieces of music ever recorded and a comedy song that many Bowie fans try very hard to pretend doesn't exist, but Alomar does have a point. He's not talking about the theme or spirit of the record, nor its melody, but the simplicity of its chord progression – both songs, stripped of everything else, revolve around a pulsing two chords and a pounding 4/4 beat. Of course, what you build on top of that makes all the difference, but in that underpinning structure, that frame, the influence of the Velvet Underground was already seeping in. It would only become more profound. Further evidence of this can be found over two decades later, when Bowie embarked on a greatest hits tour and asked fans to vote for the setlist via a phone in. He was surprised to see a strong showing for 'The Laughing Gnome' – unaware that an *NME* campaign called 'Just Say Gnome' was cheekily encouraging fans to vote for it. David started to seriously think about how he could present the song in a modern rock 'n' roll show, and told *Melody Maker* that he'd considered playing it 'in the style of the Velvets or something'.[5]

David and Marc Bolan were still very much in lockstep, and both faced a similar dilemma in 1967 – the tension between their pull towards the avant-

3. We don't know who the actual first band ever to cover it was, although a solid guess would be The Yardbirds, then featuring both Jeff Beck *and* Jimmy Page, who already had it in their set earlier that year, having encountered the Velvet Underground on tour in the US.
4. Less well known is that Pitt also gave David a copy of arch beatniks The Fugs' eponymous 1966 album, which he also enjoyed. The band's 'Dirty Ol' Man' also made it into the setlist that night.
5. Alas when he got wind of the *NME's* plan to rig the vote it was booted off the setlist for good.

garde and the underground, and their blunt desire for fame and fortune. It would take both a while to find a way to balance these two sides – arguably, Marc never really managed to do so. Like Marc advertising for musicians in both *Melody Maker* and *International Times*, David found himself wanting to make more 'out there' music, inspired not only by the Velvets but also by Pink Floyd, whom he'd seen several times at the Marquee and other new stars of London's art rock scene, but without scuppering his Anthony Newley all-rounder dreams or his chance of becoming a household name. Which is why, at the same time as he was readying the release of 'The Laughing Gnome' and putting the finishing touches to the *David Bowie* album, in the same month in fact that Marc put aside his solo recording career in order to join the circus with John's Children, David joined a band called The Riot Squad.

Old habits, as it turns out, died hard and with the Riot Squad, David once again employed the hermit crab technique that had got him into the Kon-Rads, The King Bees, The Manish Boys and The Lower Third. This was less about his ambition to make it to the top however, and he never – as far as we're aware – pushed to have marquee billing in the group. In fact, he kept his membership of the band relatively quiet. He'd officially parted company with Ralph Horton earlier that year, and though Ken Pitt was continuing to undertake the duties of a manager, the pair hadn't actually updated their legal arrangement, and it would be another few weeks before Pitt signed on the dotted line with David and his father. During this period, when he was technically not obliged to run his ideas past anyone, Bowie had an opportunity to explore some creative avenues that lay outside the grand plan that he and Pitt had put together. While Ken was busy putting him forward to co-write musicals[6], write radio and teleplays[7,] star in films and – genuinely – present children's TV[8], David was engaging in freak-out art happenings on stage in elaborate theatrical make up and, in his own words, 'interesting trousers', whipping his bandmates at the climax of songs, using police car lights for stage lighting and covering Frank Zappa and the Velvets. It was not a million miles away from what Marc was doing in John's Children at exactly the same time.

This was a far less official affair than other bands that David had joined. The Riot Squad had been around for a couple of years by that point, with a relatively fluid line up. They had previously been managed by the former impresario and journalist Larry Page before splitting up and being completely

---

6. Including one provisionally titled *Kids On The Roof*, an idea that David had brainstormed with Tony Hatch while he was at Pye – the two had planned to write it together. A few of the songs on the 1967 *David Bowie* album, including 'Join The Gang', were originally intended for this project.

7. David's *The Champion Flower Grower*, about a Yorkshire gardener called 'Woody' who moved to London, loosely based on his father, Heywood. It remains, to this day, frustratingly unproduced.

8. This was a show called Playtime, and involved some stuffed toys called Nana The Bear, Spot The Dog, Katy The Doll, and Snod The Kitten. Pitt sent them a copy of David's song 'There Is A Happy Land' as evidence of the sort of thing he could do. He didn't get the job.

re-formed from scratch by sax player Bob Evans.[9] The group had also been one of the last acts to work with Joe Meek before his suicide earlier that year, which had obviously left them reeling, with half the band walking away. Evans, another London boy on the scene (although a slightly older one – he was apparently thirty-six by this point and wore a wig in the hope that no-one would notice) had run into David by chance and the pair got acquainted over coffees in La Gioconda. David was gabbling through his ideas about performance art and the new cutting edge music from the US he was listening to, while The Riot Squad needed someone new to freshen up their act – an obvious solution presented itself. Bowie did a handful of gigs with the band, pushing them into more theatrical directions and was happy to finally find a group that would take risks with their presentation and stage act, something that The Lower Third refused to do and The Buzz didn't suit. Bowie even talked the engineer working on his album, Gus Dudgeon, into staying after hours at Decca to record a few songs. Inevitably, the group laid down a faithful version of the Velvet Underground's 'I'm Waiting For The Man', as well as a new song of David's, 'Little Toy Soldier', which seems to be about an innocent child before crashing creepily into the 'Whiplash girl child in the dark' verse from the Velvet's 'Venus In Furs'. There was also a rough version of David's 'Silly Boy Blue', the recording of which was intended for use in their set.

Bowie played several gigs with the band, one of the first of which, amazingly, involved opening for Cream, and they even appeared in a feature in *Jackie* magazine, where he was listed as 'Toy Soldier'. The name 'David Bowie' was successfully kept away from the project. The tracks recorded at Decca were kept in the can until the Acid Jazz label released them as the *Toy Soldier* EP in 2013. It's telling that none of the early biographies of Bowie so much as mention The Riot Squad, including Peter and Leni Gillman's 1986 book *Alias David Bowie*, otherwise one of the most comprehensively researched books on David's life you'll find. Even Ken Pitt, who was around at the time, only mentions The Riot Squad once in *The Pitt Report*, and only in passing as a support act at the 'Laughing Gnome' launch party. The Riot Squad was an experiment, a diversion, the scratching of an itch. It was nonetheless valuable, however: baby steps towards the theatricality, showmanship and blizzard of cultural influences that he would master in the 70s, especially in the shows performed in character as Ziggy Stardust. It also shows us that despite the arch pop of the *David Bowie* album, David was as clued-in to the free-form creativity of the freakbeat and

---

9. Evans has had a fascinating career. After the Riot Squad he had some success in Venezuela with a band he describes as a 'Riot Squad tribute act', later he joined the Bonzo Dog Doo-Dah Band and, under the name Bob Flag, had a successful career in musical comedy, even playing the opening night at the legendary alternative club The Comedy Store in London. Most bizarrely, a giant close up of his face was used to represent 'Big Brother' in Michael Radford's movie version of *1984*. In the 70s he worked with David's wife Angela in a satirical review called *Krisis Kaberet*. He now lives in Japan.

burgeoning psych rock era as anyone else and that his swerving of that whole slightly grubby scene was a specific choice. David and Ken Pitt were betting on cleaner, more wholesome fare. It was time to get to work.

'The Laughing Gnome', which was recorded complete with sped-up gnome voices and a barrage of groan-inducing puns, had been earmarked, at his own suggestion, as David's next single, a decision which can seem baffling in retrospect. With half a century's hindsight, it's easy to laugh at 'The Laughing Gnome' and, honestly, many have, and not kindly. It's often wheeled out as evidence of Bowie's fallibility, his misguided grasping for anything that might bring him a hit and the point at which his Newley obsession overtook his good sense.[10] It's also been read as a channelling of the Velvet Underground, a metaphor for mental illness (with the chattering gnomes being manifestations of the narrator's psychosis) and a representation of David's own relationship with his talent. Art, after all, is subjective. What tends to be overlooked is that when 'The Laughing Gnome' was first released, quite a lot of people liked it and expected it to be a hit.

Firstly we should get one thing out of the way – 'The Laughing Gnome' isn't a *bad* song. It is by no means a *great* song, but it's far from terrible. It has that propulsive Velvets underpinning, it has Bowie in his chirpiest Tony Newley mode, it has a lot of deceptively clever studio trickery and it's catchy as all hell. A modern audience might struggle to grasp how anyone could have expected it to be a hit, but that's partly because the novelty song has faded from sight in twenty-first century pop music, save the occasional stab at a cash-in hit at Christmas. In the mid sixties, however, it was far from uncommon. The Ivor Novello awards even had a 'best novelty song' category. The past decade had seen helium-voiced hits for Pinky and Perky and The Chipmunks, while Bernard Cribbins' Cockney schtick had charted highly with comic songs like 'Right Said Fred' and 'Hole In The Ground' and Newley himself had released a swinging version of 'Pop Goes The Weasel'. Ronnie Hilton's 'A Windmill In Old Amsterdam' had sold more than a million copies in 1965. Pop songs aimed at children, or that played for broad laughs were not only fairly common, they were more than capable of selling in big numbers. Even outside of pure novelty, this was a record released into the newly-hippified scene of 1967, where oddball and childish storytelling was actually rather fashionable, from The Kinks' 'Dedicated Follower of Fashion' and The Beatles' 'Yellow Submarine' the previous year (they would also release 'I Am The Walrus' later in 1967) to almost everything Syd Barrett ever wrote. Trippy lyrics were in, and though 'Laughing Gnome' leans on the side of silly rather than surreal, the concept is as weird as anything emerging from the acid-frazzled minds of the hippy acts.

---

10. This is a little unfair. Anthony Newley never recorded anything as uncool as 'The Laughing Gnome'.

Mike Vernon and Gus Dudgeon who had produced and engineered the song (and the album) thought they had a sure-fire hit on their hands, as did execs at Deram and their bosses at Decca. 'The Laughing Gnome' was also well reviewed, especially by *NME* ('A novelty number chock full of appeal. This boy sounds remarkably like Tony Newley, and he wrote this song himself. An amusing lyric, with David Bowie interchanging lines with a chipmunk-like creature.') and just a few months earlier *Disc & Music Echo*'s Penny Valentine had predicted stardom for three artists in 1967: Jimi Hendrix, The Pink Floyd and David Bowie. It felt like something was primed to happen. We now think of 'The Laughing Gnome' more as a laughing *stock* but back in the spring of 1967 almost everyone around Bowie thought it was the record that would finally push him over the top. The only problem? Nobody bought it. 'The Laughing Gnome' was David's ninth single in four years ... and his ninth flop in a row.

As disappointing as this was, it wasn't a death blow. Pitt had, after all, sold David to Deram as an album artist, and the album was still the main focus. Unfortunately, interest at Decca, Deram's parent label, seemed to be cooling. The album was scheduled for release on 1 June, three months after recording had completed – a relatively long wait in those days. More worryingly, at the start of May the music press announced 1 June as the release date for the new Beatles album, *Sgt Pepper's Lonely Hearts Club Band*, comfortably the biggest release of the year and a bona fide cultural event that would practically guarantee that *David Bowie* got lost in the noise. While several people at the label, including in-house producer Mike Vernon, believed they had someone special in David, and that they had made a fine album with him, there was a worry that a general lack of interest at Decca was going to sink their work. Deram boss Tony Hall, a friend of Pitt's and a champion of David, had moved on from the Decca organisation entirely in the spring, and been replaced by Selwyn Turnbull, whom Pitt believed only mildly tolerated his client. There was already a feeling that Bowie's debut didn't have the momentum it deserved. Two weeks prior to the album release, Pitt wrote to Decca's artist manager, Hugh Mendl – another great believer in David, who found his hands tied by the limited visions of his label – with a laundry list of worries about the record, including the lack of a proper marketing plan, the lacklustre efforts around 'The Laughing Gnome' and the war he'd had to wage to get David included in Decca's advertising. These were legitimate concerns – a few months later he and David were hunting for Bowie's music in a record store and enquired where it could be found. The assistant took a while to locate his work, because their catalogues didn't list a 'David Bowie' signed to Decca Records. Eventually she found the source of the problem, confidently telling her two customers that they had been mistaken – David Bowie was signed to Pye records, not Decca. The label's sales team had neglected to include the album in the release lists sent out to shops.

Decca's creation of the Deram imprint had been intended to drag the label into the modern era. Despite being the home of the Rolling Stones, who were signed in a post-Beatles, let's-not-miss-another-one rush, Decca was the most old fashioned of the 'big four' labels that dominated music in the 50s and 60s, the others being EMI, Pye and Philips, who between them and their various imprints (EMI had HMV, Columbia, Parlophone and Capitol, Decca had Warner, Vocalion, RCA and Atlantic, Pye had Reprise and Chess and Philips had Fontana and Polydor) accounted for the vast majority of the market. The label's ethos was very much directed from the top down. Decca's boss, Sir Edward Lewis had built the company up from nothing in the thirties and forties, first as a maker of gramophones and radiograms, then as a manufacturer of discs themselves, before eventually getting into catalogue management and recording, ruthlessly acquiring other businesses as he went. The company's success had been founded on classical music and light crooners like Bing Crosby and Judy Garland. Lewis was a man of his time, and tolerated pop music as a necessary nuisance, rather than embracing it as the thrust of the modern business as his rivals had done.[11] The combination of his micromanagement of the label's direction and his personal lack of interest in pop music meant that the company was always going to struggle to keep its market dominance, especially given EMI's willingness to try new things, and the growth of upstart independents like Track. Tony Hall's abandonment of his post at Deram was a blow to the label's pop wing – Hall would go on to work with Hendrix, The Who, Black Sabbath, Scott Walker and The Zombies, hardly safe musical territory, while Decca, still dominated by the formidable but pop-illiterate Sir Edward, lost control of the pop game, even losing The Rolling Stones after refusing to let them use a picture of a graffiti-covered toilet wall (a Porsche dealership restroom, defaced by Mick 'n' Keef themselves) for the cover of *Beggars Banquet* in 1968. Lewis didn't relinquish his control of the label until selling his majority share in 1979, just days before he died from cancer. By then Decca was hopelessly behind in the pop realm. Lewis's lack of interest in commercial acts, especially the weirder end of the market, meant that the pop wing of the label was never quite supported in the way its classical, jazz and light departments were. Mike Vernon, David's producer, was convinced that his boss didn't even know who David Bowie *was*, and certainly wouldn't have the enthusiasm for his work that was necessary to greenlight the marketing campaign they needed. The days of Decca pulling out the stops for oddball ideas, like Marc Bolan's 'The Wizard' a few years earlier, were long over. Pitt's hope in signing David to Deram, was that

---

11. One of Decca's first directors was the businessman and politician Sir Sigismund Mendl. He took the job over another he had been offered, at Smith's Crisps, after his wife convinced him that fried potato chips had no commercial future; being something one's servants cooked fresh, rather than something one purchased. His grandson was Hugh Mendl, the Decca A&R man instrumental in signing Bowie.

the new imprint would mean fresh ideas and enthusiasm. His disappointment at finding he was dealing with the same old Decca, 'still deeply entrenched in the halcyon days of the fifties', as he wrote in his memoir, was palpable.

David's debut album, *David Bowie*, was released, as feared, to a frustratingly minimal fanfare on 1 June. Predictably, the papers were going potty over *Sgt Pepper*, The Beatles' technicolored, groundbreaking conceptual masterpiece, dedicating double-page spreads to track-by-track guides and vox-popping fans on the street. *Disc & Music Echo* even had enough column inches to spare to be able to phone around all of the army bands in Britain on the hunt for a 'real' Sgt Pepper, who might actually have a 'lonely hearts club band' ('Are you sure you don't mean Sgt Perkins, one of our trumpeters?' asked the secretary of the Coldstream Guards, while a Ministry of Defence press officer in Whitehall scolded the paper, saying they had 'rather more important matters on their hands right now – a possible war for example'.) There was a smattering of press for *David Bowie*, but you had to look hard to find it. *Disc & Music Echo*, whose Penny Valentine was an early champion of Bowie, was probably the most effusive – holding back the write-up until a week after *Sgt Pepper's* release in order to make *David Bowie* the lead review and running Valentine's assessment alongside a dapper picture of David (the only contemporary album review to do so) under the headline 'Hear David Bowie – He's Something New'. The review calls the collection a 'remarkable, creative debut ... full of abstract fascination'. In common with other reviews, it also gives the 19-year-old props for writing his own songs, noting that he had serious potential, 'if he gets the breaks and the right singles'. *NME's* Allen Evans was also positive, again being impressed that the record was self penned by someone so young. He goes on to call the album 'refreshing' and Bowie a 'very promising talent', though seems to miss some of the album's subtlety ('He sings about ordinary things like a rubber band and uncle Arthur'). Inevitably, the Tony Newley comparisons loom large.

If we're looking for evidence that David's label didn't really understand him, it's right there in what little marketing they put around his album. The 3 June edition of *Record Mirror* carried a large spread displaying four of Deram's latest releases. Under Bowie's it reads 'Debut LP from a very original talent – humorous often, very sympathetic always. He already has two widely-famed singles to his credit'. Leaving aside the claim of two 'widely-famed' singles (precisely which of David's nine successive flops are they referring to?), it seems unlikely that 'humorous often, very sympathetic always' was going to tempt many people in, just as it was also unlikely that David's teenage potential audience, getting into The Pink Floyd and Jimi Hendrix and enjoying freak outs in parks, were going to be turned on by references to Anthony Newley who was more likely to be their mum's favourite singer than their own. An advert placed in the 10 June edition of *Disc & Music Echo*, optimistically situated above a chart in which the album does not appear, proclaims *David Bowie* to be 'a first LP that is different', which tells us very little as marketing goes. Pitt's fears that Decca would drop the ball on promotion had been well founded.

David had spent the previous five years switching his musical formula, trying and discarding ideas and identities as often as he tried and discarded backing groups. Until signing to Deram, he had been letting the musical landscape dictate his own style, from beat group R&B to blues to mod rock to lighter pop. It took five years of trying and failing (all, remarkably, before he was nineteen) to gain the confidence to take such an admirably big swing, coming out with a record that blended disparate influences, that told small stories and created characters ('Uncle Arthur'), shot side-eye at his own scene ('Join My Gang'), was astonishingly weird ('Please Mr Gravedigger') and dealt in both dramatic balladry ('When I Live My Dream') and cheeky pop ('Love You Till Tuesday'). Musically it had little connection to the work he'd done during his attempts to be both mod *and* rocker with The Lower Third and The Buzz, but without that initial apprenticeship (and it's hard to think of Bowie's 1960s as anything but an apprenticeship) it's unlikely he could have arrived at this point.

David Bowie, the 1967 album, has not gained a great deal of respect as the years have gone by. Bowie fans, both serious and casual, and critics alike have seen it as lightweight, or if they feel like being generous, of value only to rake through for signs of later promise. That's a little unfair – David's debut can be removed entirely from the context of his later work and enjoyed on its own terms. There are gems here; smart writing and warmth brushing against playfulness and cool. In many ways it defines the era in which it was made by its very opposition to it. David *was* embracing the hippy creativity of the mid-to-late sixties ... just not through its typical sounds and styles. Instead, he was making himself the outsider – in some ways that's a much purer interpretation of underground thinking than psychedelic freakbeat. It was an important lesson for David: to trust his own instincts and reinterpret the energy of the era, rather than blindly following. What's especially impressive is that he would, more or less, continue to do so, despite the initial attempt ending in failure.

There is, of course, an irony there. Had David made a Lower Third mod record or brought in Tony Hatch to steer him into the groovy pop in which he specialised at Pye, then it's likely that his label would actually have known how to market it. A more predictable record, probably a worse one, could actually have given David the hit he wanted. As it was, he stuck to his artistic guns, which is worthy but dangerous. Even Mike Vernon, the album's producer, who adored the work he and David had done together, was convinced that the album wasn't commercial enough to actually sell. In that he was correct. David's first attempt at a serious body of work was met with indifference by the record-buying public; its potential audience distracted by love beads and Beatles. It would be another two years before he was able to make another album, and by then the world would be a different place – the Beatles were imploding, the hippy dream was souring and Marc Bolan was the king of the underground.

Chapter Fifteen

Tony Visconti's Bathtub

On 29 April 1967, the same day that Marc was refusing to play proper chords on stage at the 14-Hour Technicolour Dream and a week or so after David had released 'The Laughing Gnome', an American musician called Tony Visconti arrived at Heathrow on a flight from New York. Visconti was from Brooklyn, of Italian stock, and had grown up in the fifties on a street with Italian Americans at one end and Puerto Ricans at the other.[1] As a child, he'd shown a natural aptitude for music, delighting his family with his ukulele skills as a small boy and then graduating to guitar just in time to discover Elvis. Over in the UK, at around the same time, Mark Feld's parents were struggling with the idea of their son as a pint-sized, precocious rock 'n' roll fan – Visconti's were a little more supportive and ensured that he studied music, setting him up with the respected classical guitar teacher Leon Block. He never lost the rock 'n' roll bug though, and played guitar and bass in various bands, while also getting a solid education in classical music at school, playing in both the orchestra (double bass) and marching band (tuba), taking extra music theory classes and learning how to write string parts on his lunch break. By the time he was sixteen, he was playing gigs with Fats Domino and sitting in on bass in wedding bands, hotel lounge acts and jazz trios. By the time he was nineteen, he'd already both developed and kicked the New York jazz musician's practically-compulsory heroin habit[2]. By the time he was twenty-two he was married, had scored a minor local hit duetting with his wife on a fairly dreadful composition of their own called 'Long Hair', got into NYC's acid scene, become a professional songwriter and found an aptitude for recording and arranging music. A chance meeting with the English producer Denny Cordell, fresh from recording Procol Harum's classic 'Whiter Shade of Pale' led to a job offer in London as his assistant. Cordell had recently set up his own production company, Straight Ahead/New Breed in partnership with David Platz, the president of Essex Music, who handled the publishing for, among others, David Bowie. The pair had jumped ship from their partnership with Decca/Deram in favour of its rivals, EMI, which had revived an old imprint, Regal Zonophone, to release Cordell's production. A couple of weeks after meeting Denny Cordell

---

1. Gangs of each would meet in the middle, clicking their fingers, engaging in surprisingly balletic fights and trying to avoid the local cops.
2. He used his last ever fix to get himself disqualified from a draft into the US Army, narrowly avoiding the horror of Vietnam.

in New York, Visconti was walking into Essex Music's Oxford Street offices, within a day he had produced Manfred Mann, within two he had met Brian Jones and seen The Jimi Hendrix Experience. His life had changed forever, and he hadn't even met the two artists that would define his career.

Seeing the London of 1967 through Visconti's eyes is fascinating. On the one hand, the rock 'n' roll scene was everything he had wanted; wild, exciting, fast moving, endlessly creative. Miniskirts were more mini than anything he could ever have dreamed of and the pot was stronger than any he'd ever encountered. The studio technology was better (although he was surprised at how rare stereo mixing was compared to even the scrappier studios he had worked in at home) and the creativity wilder. When Tony and his wife, Siegrid, moved to Elgin Avenue near Ladbroke Grove, the epicenter of British hippiedom, they found themselves surrounded by *their* people – the longhairs, the weirdos and the beatniks of the London scene. In one sense, Visconti was living his dream. There was another side to London though, and the new arrival was shocked by the generational divide in the city. The gap between younger and older, and indeed between the 'square' and the 'turned-on' communities, seemed huge to him. Four years on from David's 'Society for the Prevention of Cruelty to Long-Haired Men', Visconti still found his shaggy locks being sneered at in the street by older or straighter Londoners. In his memoir, *Bowie, Bolan and the Brooklyn Boy,* he remembers a walk into the city with Pretty Things drummer Viv Prince,[3] that developed into a full on generational confrontation, with one side staring and tutting at the yellow-haired, dandified musicians and the other – represented by Prince alone, and much to the horror of a mortified Visconti – shouting and jeering back, at one point trying to terrify one old man with a rubber spider ('They don't frighten me, I've seen 'em before you git!' was apparently the response). To a newcomer to the city, elements of the rubble-coloured world of fifties London were still very much apparent – the food was terrible, the coffee 'like mud' and the money, still in pounds, shilling and pence, archaic and confusing. The television and radio were disappointing too – three black and white channels that all ceased broadcasting before midnight came as a shock to someone used to the hyper-commercial, hyperactive TV of the USA, while the radio was surprisingly conservative. The BBC was safe and uninspiring, and commercial stations like Radios Caroline, Luxembourg and London had poor reception and were hosted by cheesy DJ's, that 'sounded old and had a patter like vaudevillian comedians'. Visconti had been raised in the era of the great New York rock DJs, of Alan Freed, Jocko and Murray the K, of the AM rock radio giants; the super-pop of WABC[4], the ultra-hip WINS, and

---

3. Not to be confused with a previous Pretty Things drummer, Viv Andrews, who had also played in the short lived Davy Jones/George Underwood R&B project Dave's Read And Blues,

4. The most popular top 40 station in the US, which would rename itself 'W-A-Beatle-C' during Beatlemania.

the hyper-active, hundred-mile-an-hour blasts of chat between the songs on WMCA. To suddenly be confronted with a cutting edge that consisted of Tony Blackburn, Jimmy Saville and *Saturday Club* was disorientating, especially when compared to London's otherwise thrilling and fast-moving musical landscape. The only ray of light was John Peel – also newly arrived from the US, though a native Liverpudlian – who began his late night Radio London show, *The Perfumed Garden*, a show both *of* and *for* the growing underground, at around the time that Visconti first arrived in the city, playing cutting edge psychedelia, freakbeat and folk late into the night.[5] He would be parachuted into Radio One by the BBC when it launched later that year.

One record Visconti worked on, The Move's classic 'Flowers In The Rain,'[6] underlined the conservatism that was still at odds with pop's cutting edge. The song was an exciting blast of pop-psychedelia which suffered the indignity of being kept from the number-one spot by the cheesy crooner Engelbert Humperdinck.[7] The underground scene in London might have felt all encompassing, it might have led fashion and influenced pop, but the wider public still had safer tastes. The British establishment was still extremely powerful – when The Move's manager, Tony Secunda, released an advertisement for 'Flowers In The Rain' that featured Prime Minister Harold Wilson in bed with his secretary, Wilson successfully sued for libel. The court ordered all royalties for the track to be donated to charity for as long as its copyright remained in place. At the time of writing, no-one involved in 'Flowers In The Rain', including Visconti, earns a penny from it. Rock 'n' roll might have ruled in Soho, Portobello Road and Notting Hill Gate, but the upper echelons of British society were still very much set against it, while the wider public erred on the side of musical caution.

Like a psychedelic Ebenezer Scrooge, there would be three spirits of English rock that would visit Visconti and change his life. The first had been Denny Cordell and in the summer of 1967, 'the Summer of Love', he met the second. Deram had recently released the next single by their precocious young Newley-alike, David Bowie; a re-recorded version of 'Love You Till Tuesday' – one of the most obviously commercial moments on the *David Bowie* album. This 'piece of world-weary cynicism masquerading as a paean to free love' (according to Nicholas Pegg's *The Complete David Bowie*) had been made tighter, bouncier and, well, *groovier* with a new vocal and a new orchestral part arranged and recorded under the direction of Ivor Raymonde, the writer and arranger of Dusty Springfield's 'I Only Want To Be With You'. The new

---

5. Often at the wrong speed.
6. The first song to be played on the aforementioned Radio One, trivia fans.
7. The Move were in good company – Humperdinck's classic 'Release Me' had kept the double-a side of 'Penny Lane' and 'Strawberry Fields Forever' off the top spot earlier in the year, breaking the Beatles' four-year run of number ones.

version had more in common with the slightly cheesier work Bowie had done for Pye than the likeable charm of his Deram album, but there was no denying how solidly catchy it was. Bowie and Pitt obviously believed in the release – the re-recorded version would be part of David's promotional package for the next several years as well as being released in the US and the Netherlands, re-recorded in German, included in a promotional film Pitt put together two years later, and be part of the cabaret auditions on which David would soon embark. Decca's Hugh Mendl and Mike Vernon had both earmarked 'Love You Till Tuesday' as the album's most obvious hit, and the hope was that this would be the kick that would finally get things moving. The reviews backed this up, with solid and enthusiastic write-ups in all of the main music papers, most of which highlighted how much the track deserved success. 'Could easily make it,' raved *Record Retailer*, 'Deserves instant recognition,' declared *Melody Maker*, 'A stand out single,' enthused *Record Mirror*. *Disc & Music Echo*'s Penny Valentine, however, by now a seasoned Bowie watcher, seemed resigned to the fact that the song would likely go the way of 'The Laughing Gnome' and the *David Bowie* album before it. 'It would be nice,' she sighed, 'if more people appreciated him.' Valentine, one of the sharpest critics of the day, had it exactly right. David's most commercially appealing single yet, the one everyone had pinned their hopes to, sank like a stone. It would be his last release for two years.[8]

David was now desperate for a hit, though his manager was a little more sanguine about the matter. To Pitt, a short term, potentially flash in the pan success was less valuable than a firmly established reputation as a reliable performer or the accumulation of a body of work and a multi-strand career in several different media. (As Pitt wrote in his memoir: 'My years of experience had taught me that real lasting success would only come after a gruelling apprenticeship ... David would become a star, it was all a matter of time and meanwhile one had to prepare a firm foundation to carry the weight of that stardom.') That David was still very much in his Anthony Newley phase – the very definition of a respected all-rounder – suggests that their interests, for now at least, were aligned and Bowie was happy to go along with Pitt's plans. To Bowie though, a hit single was still an intoxicating goal and he made a concerted attempt to write something commercial for his next release, or as he put it to Pitt while watching TV one night, he needed to 'write some top ten rubbish.' It was also clear that they would need someone new in the producer's chair. Pitt offered the job to Denny Cordell, Deram's star producer, whose work on 'Whiter Shade of Pale' was sitting at the top of the charts while David was

---

8. Perhaps the most stinging critique of all came from Pink Floyd's Syd Barrett, a specific influence and hero of David's, who was acting as guest reviewer in *Melody Maker*'s weekly 'Blind Date' column. 'Yeah, it's a joke number,' he said. 'Jokes are good ... but I don't think my toes were tapping at all.' David should be grateful he wasn't Barry Fantoni, whose 'Nothing Today' Barrett dubbed: 'Very negative ... morbid. I don't want to hear it again'.

failing to enter them. Cordell, despite juggling more artists' projects than was probably healthy[9], agreed to check out David's work but found it wasn't for him. He did, however, know a man with substantially weirder tastes than his, all of twenty-three years old and recently arrived in the city from Brooklyn, who might be up for the job.

The first time Tony Visconti heard the name 'David Bowie' he was in David Platz's office at Essex Music, Cordell having suggested to his business partner that his new apprentice might do something interesting with Deram's oddball prodigy. He was blown away by what he heard, though he had some reservations about the style:

> 'From the speakers came an amazingly mature voice, the phrasing and subtlety was something you'd expect from a seasoned stage or even a cabaret singer. The songs were humorous and dark; the backing was imaginative … What was this? … Although it was all over the place, I liked it.'[10]

Unusually, David himself was waiting in the wings for Visconti to deliver his verdict.

It's worth noting at this point that Ken Pitt always claimed that he met Visconti in advance of the playback session to discuss David's work, while Visconti claims the meeting in Platz's office was his first encounter with Bowie's music in any form. Pitt told the story many times and kept meticulous records (we know, for example, that the meeting took place on 24 July 1967). It's possible that half a century's distance has understandably fudged the details for Visconti, and that the earlier meeting simply didn't stick in his mind – Ken Pitt, for all his charms, would not have made the same impression as the twenty-year-old David Bowie.[11] It's equally possible that he simplified the tale for the sake of sharper storytelling. In the grand scheme of things it's not hugely important.[12]

---

9. At this point he was producing records for The Move, Manfred Mann, Procol Harum and former Moody Blues frontman Denny Laine pretty much simultaneously, often working with two bands on the same day.

10. From Visconti's memoir, *Bowie, Bolan and the Brooklyn Boy.*

11. Visconti and Pitt were never fond of one another – one was a left-leaning and outspoken New York hippy, while the other was a refined, well mannered middle-class Tory in his forties. In an interview with George Tremlett in 1974, a still-bitter Pitt calls Visconti a 'typical New York draft-dodging anarchist', an accusation Visconti repeats in his autobiography (misquoting it as 'pinko draft-dodger'), claiming he'd taken the quote from Pitt's own memoir, *The Pitt Report.* It's an out-of-character sentiment for the normally faultlessly polite Pitt, especially in print, and despite Visconti's claim, he seems to have calmed down by the time he wrote his book in 1983 – the phrase 'pinko draft-dodger' wasn't in either of the editions that I checked.

12. Tony Visconti declined to be interviewed for this book – quite understandably, given how much he's asked about this stuff – and an earlier interview I'd done with him for *The Guardian* didn't cover this detail, so I was unable to clear up this maddening if inessential discrepancy. Kenneth Pitt himself died in 2019, outliving his most famous client by three years, so was also unavailable for comment, though it should be said that he gave interviews about David throughout his life, including his last years, and his story remained consistent.

Visconti and Bowie hit it off immediately, finding they had a ton of musical middleground. Visconti was impressed when Bowie name-dropped The Fugs, The Mothers of Invention and Ken Nordine's spoken-word *Word Jazz* album ('We must have been two of a dozen people who had bought it'), and even more so when he realised they had a shared interest in eastern philosophy, Buddhism and European avant-garde cinema. They spoke for hours, took their conversation on a lengthy walk around Soho and ended their day catching a new Roman Polanski film. Both felt that they had made a firm friend, and were absolutely keen to work together. Deram and Essex gave the duo the go-ahead for a short session – just three hours – to produce a new potential single. Visconti chose 'Let Me Sleep Beside You', one of David's 'top ten rubbish' attempts; far from a cynical try at hit-making, Visconti thought the song extremely credible and cool. Bowie had originally envisioned it as a Dylanish country-folk number; under Visconti's eye it morphed into something far more sophisticated with a dash more rock 'n' roll. It wouldn't have sounded out of place on Bowie's next record, still two years away – an early example of the mesh of influences that Bowie and Visconti would combine to great effect in the early seventies.

Unfortunately, their efforts were for nothing. Deram were spooked by the sexual connotations of a song called 'Let Me Sleep Beside You'[13] and were convinced the BBC would never play the track. It remained in the vaults until 1970, when the label were cashing in on Bowie's more recent successes with a cheap as chips compilation of his work there. The stereo version, slaved over by Visconti in the limited window he had to work on the song, wouldn't be released for another forty years. The number itself, however (and its excellent proposed b-side, 'Karma Man') are beside the point. Bowie and Visconti had begun a personal and professional relationship that would flourish, on and off, right up to Bowie's death in 2016, just days after his late-era masterpiece *Blackstar*, his final collaboration with Visconti, had been released. Bringing the two men together as friends and colleagues was easily worth three hours of Deram's studio time. For the next four years, their lives would be intensely intertwined.

Platz and Cordell were impressed with Tony Visconti. He had got his job through an incredible act of blaggery; seizing his opportunity to impress Denny Cordell on a day that he happened to be in the same room and somehow turning that into the offer of a lifetime – it was sheer New York chutzpah meeting the 'Yeah, why not' experimental spirit of sixties London. That in itself showed tenacity, creativity and quick thinking. What impressed them more was his work, though. His contribution to The Move's 'Flowers In The Rain' was the magic ingredient that had made the record special: a woodwind quartet score (which he suggested be recorded at half speed in order the create a strange,

---

13. Decca had only just shaken off the fuss caused when the Stones had released 'Let's Spend The Night Together', so you can see why they'd be jumpy.

pixieish effect. He seemed to be able to turn his hand to anything they threw at him, quickly and competently getting on with the job. Young he may have been, and a chancer, definitely, but he had also proved himself to be a professional. As the blissful summer of love turned into another bitter sixties winter,[14] Cordell charged his apprentice with bringing in a band of his own, scouting someone from scratch, developing them for the label and producing them. Visconti loved the idea, and was immediately convinced he was going to discover 'the next Beatles'[15]

Unsure where to start, he resorted to scouring the pages of the underground bible *International Times*. According to his memoir, he saw the name 'Tyrannosaurus Rex' several times in adverts, a name which jumped out at him and lodged in his head, meaning that when he saw it advertised on a poster later it nudged him to check the group out. There's a few problems with the timeline here – Visconti says he discovered the group in 1967, however the band doesn't appear in a single advertisement in *IT* that year, and barely feature in the small print of gig listings. Tyrannosaurus Rex were, however, mentioned in almost every single one of John Peel's 'Perfumed Garden' columns, which would seem enough to whet any good hippy's interest. There is a slight snag there, though, too – in Peel's columns the band are described more than once as being signed to Track Records, which potentially meant they'd be of little use to Visconti, Cordell and Regal Zonophone.

What we can say for sure, is that at some point in the winter of 1967 or, at the latest, early spring the following year, Tony Visconti saw a poster that advertised Tyrannosaurus Rex at Middle Earth in Covent Garden. The club had opened in August 1967, and was actually a rebranding of an existing club night – The Electric Garden, held in the same space, opened in 1966. This was Covent Garden as it had been for centuries, a bustling fruit and veg market that catered for the restaurants, shops and hotels of the capital, opening at three or four in the morning, and ruled over by the dreaded market porters, men who were up before the crack of dawn and in the pub by nine, part-man, part-wagon, carrying heavy baskets of produce on their heads and thumping anyone who caused any bother. The bustling market was a feature of the West End dating back to the seventeenth century.[16] The Electric Garden was housed in a basement warehouse at 43 King Street, and would open late at night and

---

14. The cold in December reached -15C (3.9F) at one point. In January 1968, heavy snowfall and plummeting temperatures actually froze Big Ben's clock face. It was a doozy of a winter.

15. When you consider Marc Bolan's early 70s career, you could argue that in a sense he actually did achieve this, at least in terms of creating knicker-wetting, screaming teenybop mania unseen since 1964.

16. It's now a rather plush tourist hotspot, featuring a lovely piazza where you can get some very overpriced coffee, and a market full of stalls selling badges that say 'I Love London', phone cases with pictures of Amy Winehouse on them and hand-tooled leather belts. The porters themselves moved on when the old fruit and veg market was relocated at 'New Covent Garden Market', confusingly situated at Nine Elms, near Vauxhall.

kick its punters out in the early hours of the morning, just as the market was getting underway. It was, by Soho standards, just another rock club, albeit with a self-conscious hippy twist. Far more appealing, and opening at roughly the same time, was UFO on Tottenham Court Road, run by the same heads that had started *International Times*, Better Books, the Indica gallery and the Drury Lane Arts Lab – essentially the founding pillars of British underground art. Electric Garden was fine, it had bands and DJs and all the usual stuff, but UFO was something else. Taking its cue from the *IT* launch party at the Roundhouse, it featured far-out light shows, art films projected onto smoke, and projectors shining through glass slides full of bubbling wax crayon, ink and bodily fluids. The Pink Floyd were the house band, Hendrix played there, Soft Machine were in all the time, and outside you might find Pete Townshend stripped to his waist declaring that 'cold is just a state of mind.' It was briefly *the* place to be for the swinging hippy in the know. Unfortunately it couldn't sustain its reputation. Hippies tend to make poor businessmen, and the enterprise was barely able to stay afloat. Situated in an Irish club that rented out its function room on Wednesdays, the space was tiny and incapable of holding the amount of ticket holders necessary to fund a club with that level of prestige. Eventually it folded under the weight of its own reputation.

Meanwhile the Electric Garden had seen a change of management and been rebranded as Middle Earth, proudly announced in an article in the 16 August edition of *International Times*. With UFO gone, Middle Earth – which deployed much of the same psychedelic tricks but was much larger and thus able to accommodate a decent paying crowd – became the number one underground hotspot in the capital, carrying on UFO's tradition of blending rock gigs with art happenings, installations and dancefloor freakouts. DJ duties were provided by recovering mod Jeff Dexter (the man who once told Marc Bolan that he couldn't sing) and John Peel, lately of Radio London and now the host of BBC Radio One's *Top Gear*. Punters would head down the stairs, out of a busy London street and into Wonderland, all incense and trippy lights. Visitors might have to crawl through a tunnel to enter, or sit down to find that their chairs were situated on a giant inflatable that filled with air and deposited them near the ceiling. Dexter, who knew a thing or two about dancefloors, would spin the latest British and American tunes to keep people on their feet, treading the line between psychedelia, rock and soul. Peel, on the other hand, would play to people's minds, specialising in gentle, pastoral folk like The Incredible String Band or the mind expanding psychedelia of Frank Zappa and The Velvet Underground.

It was into this space that Tony Visconti descended on a hunt for a new band to sign. He walked into a hush. The audience sat in near-silence, smoking joints and letting the sound wash over them. In the middle of the stage sat two tiny men, one on a stool with a scrappy goatee beard and sunglasses, rapping on bongos with dextrous finger tips, the other cross legged on the floor, his his hair grown out into what his cousin refers to as a 'Jew-fro', corkscrew curls springing down his boyish face. He had a raggedy acoustic guitar and a trembling, completely unique voice, part warbling lamb, part angelic terror. His lyrics were full of hippy nonsense, all dwarves and unicorns and fawns, but musically they were percussive and robust. They were great songs. The duo, dressed like underground urchins, had chemistry, the audience was rapt, and Visconti was enchanted. After the show he enquired if the band had a record deal. Their singer, whose name was Marc Bolan, told him that John Lennon wanted to sign them[17], but he was open to offers.

Visconti was excited. This was a band with a small but expanding underground following, who were played regularly on Radio One by John Peel and who had a completely unique sound that felt both modern and like something out of the distant past. They also had a singer with the charisma of a pixie Elvis[18]. Their names, as they told Visconti that night, were Steve Peregrin Took and Marc Bolan. 'These were very poor, working-class lads who had a Beethoven symphony in their heads,' Visconti told *the Guardian* in 2013.[19] 'What I saw in Marc Bolan had nothing to do with very high standards of artistry; what I saw in him was raw talent. I saw genius. They were a folk duo, but I saw a potential rock star in Marc – right from the minute, the hour, I met him.'

Marc's journey from John's Children to Middle Earth had been an eventful but surprisingly fast one. He had walked out on the band in July and played Middle Earth for the first time as *Tyrannosaurus Rex* in September. By October he was recording a session for John Peel on Radio One and appearing on Dutch television. Everything, for once, was more or less going right. At first Simon Napier-Bell, still his manager, seemed keen to pursue Marc's relationship with Track records and exploit him as a solo star, and had therefore hustled up studio time (on Kit Lambert's dime) to record a new Bolan song, 'The Lilac Hand of Menthol Dan', which he hoped would be the single to relaunch him. Marc, though, still wanted his own rock band – a version of John's Children built around *him*, rather than one where he was simply the guitar star. His new band, recruited from the pages of *International Times* and *Melody Maker*, made their debut at the Electric Garden on 23 July, opening for Pandemonium[20], and billed due to a typo as 'Marc Bolland and Tyrannosaurus Rex'. Apparently, Marc was still auditioning band members on the day of the show. The four piece band[21] took to the stage to play a barely rehearsed set of Marc's songs, some of

---

17. He didn't.
18. You could say he was an Elvish impersonator.
19. Technically he told me, but I was representing *The Guardian* at the time.
20. The previous night the venue had played host to Riot Squad, though it's unknown if Bowie was still performing with them at that point.
21. There is some suggestion that it might have been a five piece, though Steve Took is quoted in Fee Warner's biography, *A Trip To Ladbroke Grove*, as saying there were only four.

which were Bolan numbers culled from the John's Children set. The gig was, apparently, a fiasco. The band hadn't rehearsed enough and had a guitarist who smoked a pipe and attempted to windmill like Pete Townshend despite having no sense of balance, regularly smashing into, and eventually knocking over the drum kit. To Marc it was a disaster and an embarrassment. Simon Napier-Bell, who due to his loathing of the hippy underground had neglected to attend, was left with a client now determined to abandon pure rock 'n' roll. Napier-Bell remains sure the blow to Marc's ego scared him off performative, flashy rock for a while, sending him scuttling to a very different musical form, one much easier to control.

There have been various claims that Marc's inspiration to 'go acoustic' dates from John's Children's legendarily messy tour with The Who. With time to kill in Germany after speeding away from the final gig, Napier-Bell and the band had taken in a show by Ravi Shankar, the beloved Indian musician who popularised the use of the sitar in rock circles during the sixties. He performed sat cross-legged on the stage with his instrument, his only accompaniment was from a tabla, the melodic Indian hand drums played with the fingertips. Apparently Marc sat rapt through the whole performance. It's a convenient narrative – Marc was a sucker for eastern mystique, Ravi Shankar was a hugely respected name and ultimately, Marc did end up performing cross legged with a bongo player. On the other hand he'd already reinvented himself as a serious folky once before – the Marc Bolan of Tyrannosaurus Rex was as much an extension of Toby Tyler as the Marc Bolan of T.Rex was of the bopping guitarist in John's Children. Whether seeing such an evocative, stripped down set as Ravi Shankar's had such a powerful impact as has been claimed is open to interpretation.

One good thing did come from the disastrous gig that 'Marc Bolland and Tyrannosaurus Rex' played in Covent Garden that summer's night: the arrival into Marc's life of his drummer, Steve Peregrin Took. Born Stephen Porter, Took was another London Boy and just seventeen at the point he joined forces with Bolan. As with Bowie, Took and Bolan were the same but different. Both were the younger of two children, Marc was working class, his family poor as church mice, Steve from a seemingly middle class background. Marc was a treasured child, indulged and pampered by his parents, charismatic, energetic and boisterous and the product of a tight-knit and loving family and community. Steve's father was a gambling addict who went to prison for embezzlement, leaving the family always short of money. His parents divorced shortly afterwards. He was also dyspraxic and suffered from asthma and painful eczema which meant he was bullied at school. It turned him into an introvert and an outsider, happy to be lost in his own worlds. In this respect you can see why he and Marc were drawn to each other – both outsiders, both living in fantasy worlds of their own creation, both feeling they were different. Marc's route to outsiderdom, however, had been a much happier one. He had more or less chosen it for himself as a product of his ego – he thought he was different not because he thought he was inferior, but because he believed he was *special*. Steve, meanwhile, absorbed the bullying and insults and felt inferior. He would always be on the back foot. After leaving school he played in bands, discovered drugs, ravenously consumed Tolkien and fell head-first enthusiastically into the hippy life, at which point he answered an advert in *International Times* looking for freaky musicians and astral flyers.

The pipe smoking guitarist and the mystery bass player didn't work out, but Marc and Steve found they instinctively got on. Took had to sell his drum kit in order to make his rent – but by this point it didn't matter. Tyrannosaurus Rex weren't going to need a full drum kit. Instead, Steve assembled a bag of makeshift percussion instruments and toys, including a 'pixiephone', a small glockenspiel he'd purchased from Hamleys toy shop on Regent Street. It helped that he was a superb musician. He played bongos (which Marc insisted on calling 'tabla') not with the flat of his hand, but with his individual fingertips, creating a dextrous web of tones and counterpoint melodies rather than merely keeping the beat. He could also sing instinctive falsetto harmonies and was an excellent arranger. It all suited the vibe the two realised they could create together – childlike and mystical, taking their cue from Marc's distinctive voice and fantastical lyrics. It synced nicely with the hippy dream, which was underlined when Steve took a new stage name ripped straight out of Tolkien.[22]

Track, however, soon lost interest – Kit Lambert had wanted Marc as the sexy, thrashing Pete Townshend type, not sitting on a rug and reeking of incense. The label did pay for some aborted sessions with Joe Boyd, who had produced the first two Pink Floyd singles, but weren't happy enough with the results to proceed any further. Simon Napier-Bell also fell away as 1967 progressed – he hated the hippy vibe, and felt that a bread-head businessman driving up the prices was probably the last thing Marc needed in his corner if he was to play the authentic flower child. Fortunately, the duo had another champion waiting in the wings.

John Peel had spent the better part of the sixties thus far in the US, trading off his Brit credentials in the wake of Beatlemania, and latterly soaking up the increasingly psychedelic counterculture rock coming from the west coast; the likes of Love, Country Joe and the Fish and the Grateful Dead. As a result he was probably the most progressive and switched on DJ working in Britain, miles ahead of the game. Peel had taken the midnight slot on Radio London, establishing a show he eventually re-named, with faultless hippy credibility, *The Perfumed Garden*. The fact that Marc had already written and demoed a song

---

22. It's probably telling that rather than call himself 'Frodo', 'Bilbo' or 'Gandalf', Steve went with 'Peregrin Took', a character who has a wide-eyed naive charm, and is a faithful companion.

called 'The Perfumed Garden of Gulliver Smith' appears to have been a genuine coincidence – neither admitted to being aware of the fifteenth century Arabic sex manual of the same name.

Peel had come across Marc during his time aboard *The Galaxy*, the ship from which Radio London was broadcast. Hearing that he had played 'Desdemona', Marc sent him copies of his first three solo singles, all of which Peel loved and played on air, with 'Hippy Gumbo' being a particular favourite. The two fell into correspondence, with Marc sending Peel any acetates, sessions or demos he cut as Tyrannosaurus Rex started to gain ground. They quickly became firm friends. Peel was a true believer in Marc's writing, playing his work regularly on his radio shows, first at Radio London and then on the *Top Gear* programme on Radio One, mentioning the group in literally every 'Perfumed Garden' column he wrote for *International Times* in 1967 and a lot of 1968, and bringing the band along to his DJ gigs, where he would invariably manage to get them onstage. It was through Peel that Tyrannosaurus Rex were able to play Middle Earth so often, a venue in which they would perform constantly throughout the next two years. He was instrumental in building their fanbase, to the point that *Melody Maker* journalist Bob Dawbarn joked that Peel was likely to be 'awarded the MBE for his services to Tyrannosaurus Rex'.

When Peel joined Radio One as one of several rotated presenters of *Top Gear*,[23] a Sunday afternoon show aimed at the fringes of the pop world, he insisted on bringing Tyrannosaurus Rex in to perform.[24] Took and Bolan recorded a session, broadcast on 5 November 1967, which would double as the band's 'audition' for playlisting on the station – much as David had done with the Lower Third two years earlier. Peel loved the session, but responses from the BBC panel were mixed ('Crap, and pretentious crap at that,' said one exec). The panel did eventually pass the band with six votes to two, although noted that they were 'suitable only for specialist programmes such as *Top Gear*', and Peel's bosses were livid at him for bringing these weirdo outsiders with only niche appeal onto BBC airspace. It was decided that John Peel's time as a presenter at BBC Radio One had come to an end. Fortunately *Top Gear's* producer Bernie Andrews, was fond of Peel and keen to keep him employed as long as he could. With only a small window of time available to act, he quickly booked him as the show's regular host for the next twelve weeks. It was a near thing. Peel's championing of Marc Bolan could have ruined his BBC career, and presumably quite drastically changed the shape of British indie music for the next three decades. Fortunately, the reverse happened: Peel's extended period

---

23. Which had absolutely nothing to do with cars.
24. This technically makes them one of the first groups to record a 'Peel Session', the legendary showcase of cutting edge bands for which Peel would become famous in later years. However, at this point most BBC shows had bands 'in session', recording special performances, so it doesn't have quite the kudos it would come to have in the seventies and beyond.

hosting the show meant that listeners got to know him, and bosses who were on the verge of firing him had to do an about turn when audience research showed that he was a firm favourite with music fans. Meanwhile, the DJ's compulsive patronage of Tyrannosaurus Rex was paying off for the band – Radio One had a large, captive audience since the pirates had been forced off the air by the Marine Broadcasting Offences Act (1967), which outlawed unlicensed off-shore stations. Radio One exposed Marc's music to a bigger audience than he had thought possible just a few months earlier. In a very real sense, John Peel and Marc Bolan had each other to thank for their future successes.

The day after Visconti had met Tyrannosaurus Rex, he received a phone call at the Oxford Street offices of Essex Music. It was Marc Bolan, asking if he could follow up on their meeting the previous night and meet Denny Cordell. Having tried the phone-up-from-round-the-corner-and-then-barge-in-with-a-guitar approach successfully once before with Simon Napier-Bell, Marc thought it was worth another go. A few minutes later, he and Took were unfolding a Moroccan carpet and unpacking a bag of toy percussion instruments, Marc tuning his by-now battered acoustic guitar with a pair of pliers as it was missing a tuning peg, before playing their entire set through for an audience of two – Tony Visconti and Denny Cordell. Fortunately, Cordell had a soft spot for weirdo acoustic acts; he loved The Incredible String Band, who had a superficial similarity to Tyrannosaurus Rex, and was a fan of folk music in general. He also saw the value of having a token 'underground' band on his books, giving his label some hippy credibility. Soon afterwards, Tyrannosaurus Rex were signed to Regal Zonophone and Marc was finally being given the chance to make a record.

He and Visconti became fast friends, and as the producer had already developed a close bond with David, the two London boys were drawn even closer together:

> 'They were younger than me by three years and living with their mums, I was their big American cousin in Earls Court. They'd come and visit me and we'd have jam sessions. They'd be together at my place quite often, it was neutral ground, there was no battle going on then. We just got on great. We'd have maybe one bottle of wine between ten people, it's all we could afford, copious amounts of tea, we'd just jam and listen to records. It was a great time.'

Not that either would be living with their mums for much longer. As 1968 drew on, David would finally leave Bromley and his parents, moving into Ken Pitt's Manchester Square pad, while Marc and his new girlfriend, June Child, found a cheap flat in Notting Hill. This gave them another reason to visit the Visconti residence – he had a bath, and they didn't. Once a week both would make the trip to Earls Court, where Tony had moved earlier in the year, to wash their hair. Visconti got close with Steve Took too. 'I loved him,' he says. 'He stayed over my house a lot. When he was homeless he would sleep at my place, I actually had a close relationship with him. I've got some nice photos of him looking fresh as a daisy after he had a bath. My famous bathtub! It should be in the Guinness Book of Records or something.'

The London boys had found their kingmaker. It was time to clean up.

Chapter Sixteen

Full of Mysterious Promise

In 1978, the Palestinian professor Edward Said, working out of Columbia University in the US, wrote a book in which he redefined the term 'Orientalism'. Previously an art style that ostensibly paid tribute to Eastern cultures, Said argued that the term was better applied to a particularly patronising form of cultural racism. Western intellectuals, Said opined, had fetishized the East since ancient times and sought to own, control and appropriate its culture. In his book *Orientalism* he stated that 'a white middle-class Westerner believes it his human prerogative not only to manage the nonwhite world but also to own it, just because by definition "it" is not quite as human as "we" are. There is no purer example than this of dehumanised thought.' To Said, the West saw 'the Orient' – a loose term that tends to be used in the UK to describe China and Japan, but can be widened to include all of Eastern and South-Eastern Asia, notably the Middle East and India – as a byword for cultures that are exotic, dangerous, uncivilised, novelty or somehow 'other'.[1]

Fascination with the 'Oriental' world was not a specifically 1960s phenomenon – the Victorians had enjoyed a preoccupation with China as well as the wider spirituality and spiritualism of 'the Orient'. Eastern religions and Eastern spirituality were seen as secret wisdoms and the likes of Aleister Crowley gained a large following by blending astrology, tarot, Egyptian, Tibetan and Indian theology, Christianity and the occult. His work is still widely read. The East was also, of course, where tea, spices and opium came from, the first two being the very definition of parochial exotica, while the latter reinforced the idea of China and India's connection to mind-expansion and bliss as well as decadence and debauchery. This carried on well into the twentieth century – the novels of Agatha Christie, for example, are full of 'Oriental' mysticism. The opening up of the world in the post-war era and the rise of modern international travel only magnified this.

By the mid-60s, the Orientalist idea of the East as a centre for spiritual truth was a widely-accepted one, especially within hippy circles. A better educated, more widely read and more worldly youth was drifting away from what you might

---

1. 'Orientalism is rightly thought of as racism in most countries now, particularly the unironic use of the term 'Oriental' to refer to something East Asian. It is considered offensive to describe an Asian American as 'Oriental' for example. Britain is one of the few exceptions, where backstreet Chinese takeaways called 'Taste of the Orient' and supermarket gins that promise hints of 'Oriental Spices' are still bafflingly common.

call 'active Christianity' (attending church on a Sunday or at Evensong, regular prayer, reading the Bible) though a more traditional and passive interaction with religion (weddings, funerals, christenings, church schools and nativity plays) still hung on, more tied up in habit and tradition than any particular passion or faith. Spirituality, however, did persist, and by 1968 a fascination with oriental mystique, be it the rise in Buddhism, the teachings of Indian gurus or the popularity of the Hare Krishnas, new age occultism and Scientology as well as the more sinister international cults of Bhagwan Shree Rajneesh and Sun Myung Moon. It was all, as the famous slogan for Fry's Turkish Delight chocolate bars said, 'full of Eastern promise'.

As with almost everything in sixties Britain, these ideas were brought into the mainstream and made palatable by The Beatles; initially through George Harrison's interest in Indian music and the use of a sitar and drones on songs like 'Norwegian Wood' and Sgt Pepper's 'Within You Without You', and adding a specifically spiritual aspect to Revolver's more generally psychedelic 'Tomorrow Never Knows'. The Fabs didn't just bring Indian mysticism into their music though – their time studying with the Maharishi Mahesh Yogi, a famed guru who taught transcendental meditation, is perhaps the most famous example of sixties culture's intersection with Indian-influenced spirituality. It culminated with the foursome and their partners (alongside Donovan and the actress Mia Farrow amongst others) joining the Maharishi in a retreat near the banks of the Ganges in February 1968. Ringo Starr, who according to legend took a suitcase full of baked beans to India because he was worried about the food, left after just ten days, finding that the lifestyle was not for him – the others stuck it out for several months. The group spent the time leading a simple and spiritual existence far removed from the trappings of swinging London (though another interpretation would be that they went on holiday for three months and wrote The White Album.[2])

The Beatles' adventures in India are the most celebrated and analysed aspect of the decade's fascination with the East, but they were far from the be all and end all of the phenomenon. Among London's hip underground, mysticism and spirituality could be found almost everywhere. International Times published pieces on Aleister Crowley, a guide to Hindu gods, the link between sex and yoga and the influence of ancient Babylonia; the Gandalf's Garden shop hosted talks on meditation and enlightenment, while at Apple – the company set up by the Beatles after the death of Brian Epstein in 1968 – every day began with

---

2. At one point Lennon took a helicopter ride with the guru and apparently asked him to 'slip me the answer'. In the recent series Get Back, which documents the band's 1969 recording of Let It Be, you can hear Lennon and McCartney discussing the trip, and the pair are under no illusions about the Maharishi's attitude to worldly goods – 'I wish I had his money,' John says. Harrison was far more serious about his spiritualism; at the start of the film you can see one of his Hare Krishna friends hanging around the recording.

the throwing of the I Ching, the ancient Chinese method of divination.[3] The counterculture invited you to 'turn on, tune in and drop out', but with that seemed to come a yearning for something greater than simply getting out of one's tree on mushrooms and listening to Frank Zappa. Donovan, who accompanied The Beatles to India, told Mark Paytress (in *Marc Bolan: The Rise and Fall of a 20th Century Superstar*) that he thought the flower power generation were 'searching for our own indigenous religion, which is Celtic, but which had disappeared in the face of the Christian teachings.[4] We looked to the East, because we felt that we could enter the secret world only through meditation which wasn't taught in the West.' Lama Chime Rinpoche, the Buddhist monk that mentored David Bowie and Tony Visconti, made a similar observation when he arrived in the UK in 1965. 'What I discovered,' he told *The Telegraph* in 2020, 'is that people in the West, they have a house, money, a television, a car, but they feel something is missing, and that's what they are trying to find.' It's put more bluntly by Jonathan Park, an activist in the sixties who went on to design sets for Pink Floyd, when he was quoted in Jonathan Green's oral history, *Days In The Life*: 'The era was tremendously godless, and the stress and strain of life does drive you to a point where you want to seek relief. There are two forms of relief: one is called heroin and one is called God. And a lot of people got into one or another.'

Modernity happened quickly and as we have seen, the speed of social and cultural change that ran from the Second World War to the end of the 1960s was extremely disorientating for many people. The old ways didn't seem to make sense any more, the local vicars and the convent nuns didn't fit with this new world of loud music and sex and television and James Bond. For some people, youth culture filled the gap left by the departing God; the one that Nietzsche had declared dead at the start of the century. For others this mass exposure to the profane highlighted the absence of the sacred, creating a desire for a more spiritually fulfilling life. The atmosphere of abandon and experimentation that permeated the late sixties was part of the problem, yes, but it was also part of a solution – many people felt that they were free to find the enlightenment and comfort once found in church elsewhere. They looked inward, they looked skyward, they looked to fiction or they looked east.

Such a one was David Bowie. In 1969, around the release of 'Space Oddity', Bowie's label distributed a press pack, which David had helped create himself. Among the documents was a timeline of his life, which ran thusly:

---

3. According to Derek Taylor, The Beatles' press officer at the time, a man called Caleb, who dressed all in white, was paid £50 a week to throw and read the I Ching at the start of each day and whenever tricky decisions had to be made.

4. This isn't a million miles away from JRR Tolkien's desire to write a new mythology for ancient Britain, despite being a strict Roman Catholic, hence *Lord of The Rings* and, especially, *The Silmarillion*.

Born: London 1947

15 - Didn't attend school much
    Played tenor sax with modern jazz group
    Buddhism

16 - Left school, went into ad agency and tripped on capitalism for six
    months as a commercial artist
    Re-read *On The Road*
    Formed progressive blues group

17 - More groups

18 - Frustrated with amps, went solo with an acoustic
    Back to Buddhism

19 - First LP

20 - Dropped out of music completely and devoted most of my time to
    the Tibet Society
    Helped get the Scottish monastery underway[5]

There is, of course, some Bowie myth-making in here. He highlights the stuff that makes him interesting, he embellishes quite a bit (a 'modern jazz group'? *The Kon-Rads?*) and he glosses over a lot. He never really 'dropped out' of music after the failures of *David Bowie* and 'Love You Till Tuesday'. There's a gap in his releases and conventional gigs, true, but David continued to be involved in music throughout 1968, writing and demoing songs while Pitt, having walked away from Deram and Decca, tried to find a new label. In May of that year, Bowie even recorded a session for John Peel's *Top Gear* programme, with Visconti onboard as musical director, and though he moved away from conventional rock gigs into a different performance medium he was, as we shall see, still performing music. It's true, however, that Bowie had a profound interest in Buddhism and spiritualism, which definitely spiked in 1967 and 1968, following the failure of his debut album.

The previous year, David had become acquainted with Jeff Dexter, the recovering mod, friend of Marc Bolan and regular DJ at Middle Earth, and the pair, along with other friends, took to having 'flying saucer meditation sessions' on Thursday nights at Dexter's Hampstead flat, where – he told Paul Trynka in *Starman* – 'we hoped that flying saucers would come and take us away'[6] while meditating and passing around a joint. The group were meditating based on teachings that David had picked up at a Buddhist Vihara near Hampstead[7].

---

5. Quoted in George Tremlett's 1974 book *The David Bowie Story*, from documents found in his own archive.

6. UFO-ology was intertwined in the dreamy new age spiritualism of the hippy era, hence the name of the Tottenham Court Road club night. If you weren't looking to the East, maybe you could look to the stars.

7. Several books and articles refer to this as 'Tibet House', however there wasn't a 'Tibet House' in London in the mid-sixties. The organisation/building known by that name today didn't open until 1994.

David's interest in Buddhism had started while he was still at school. He'd read *The Rampa Story*, a book written by a supposed monk called Lobsang Rampa, who despite being born in Devon and christened 'Cyril', claimed that his body was now possessed by the spirit of a Tibetan lama. It sparked an interest in Tibet, the country's then-recent occupation by China and the 100,000 Tibetans that the Dalai Lama had led into exile in India. In turn, that led to him reading more about Buddhism itself. The subject fascinated him, and he found that he could relate to its concepts of one-ness and emptiness. 'The idea of transience, and that there is nothing to hold on to pragmatically,' he told *The Telegraph* in 1996, 'that we do at some point or another have to let go of that which we consider most dear to us, because it's a very short life.' Once he was regularly travelling to London he began visiting the Vihara near Hampstead and the Buddhist Centre near Victoria several times a week. In 1966 he told *Melody Maker* that he wanted to visit Tibet for himself, searching for ancient secrets and the monks that could allegedly go long periods without food and live for centuries.

It was during his first visit to the Hampstead Vihara (into which he later claimed he had merely ducked inside in order to get out of the rain) that he met Lama Chime Rinpoche, a young monk that had fled the Tibetan occupation and one of only four lamas[8] then residing in the UK. According to Bowie the first thing that the lama said to him was, in broken English, 'You are looking for me'. He had meant '*Are you* looking for me?', or more generally 'Can I help you?', but David claimed that this simple statement, 'You are looking for me', was one he needed to hear at that moment in his life. Rinpoche became a mentor and also a friend – he was only six years older than David and the two built a relationship that would last for the rest of Bowie's life. David would later claim that he had helped establish the Samye Ling monastery in Scotland, a place of spiritual learning set up in an old hunting lodge under the auspices of two other exiled lamas, Chögyam Trungpa Rinpoche and Akong Rinpoche. Whether David did indeed 'help set up' the monastery is up for debate, but he claimed many times that he studied at the facility on multiple occasions in 1967 and 1968 and even came close to taking his vows. He was apparently talked out of it with less than a week to go by Chime Rinpoche himself – who felt he would make a poor monk and should focus on music, something that David had never been able to shake off. 'On the cushion it echoed through my meditation,' his future collaborator Mary Finnegan remembers him saying, in her book *Psychedelic*

---

8. A 'Lama' is a spiritual elder or teacher in Tibetan Buddhism, some of which, including Chime Rinpoche and the Dalai Lama, are believed to be 'Tulkas' – the hosts to specific reincarnated souls whose work they will continue. It's sometimes incorrectly used as a catch-all term for monks in general.

Suburbia, 'it was with me while out walking in the hills and, sooner rather than too late, I realised I was not being true to myself.'[9]

There has been some speculation that the whole 'nearly becoming a monk' aspect of the story was just typical Bowie fluff, adding some Eastern mystique (there's that orientalism again) to his persona, and possibly cashing in on The Beatles' recent dabbling in Indian mysticism. While that is possible – it would hardly be out of character – he was remarkably consistent in his story if so. He certainly attended the Samye Ling monastery at least once; Jeff Dexter remembers seeing his name in the visitors book there. Still, others felt that his spiritual commitment was never especially deep. Ken Pitt, who lived with Bowie in 1968, always thought his Buddhist credentials went no further than lighting some incense sticks every once in a while.

Marc Bolan also engaged in the spiritualism of the time, however his instincts took him down a different path. He was never a particularly religious person (his Jewishness was more about identity than actual practice), but still managed to build the sacred into his persona. With Marc, however, it was less about a concrete doctrine or creed, and more about the fantastical mumbo jumbo of the hippy era; absolutely embracing his new role as underground flower child. As with David and Buddhism, there's always been debate about how genuine Bolan's commitment to the hippy underground truly was; a suspicion that, having found himself in the right place at the right time, Marc rode the hippy horse for all it was worth, cynically adopting the look and trappings of the counterculture in order to build his audience. Tony Visconti says that the issue wasn't as black and white as it might seem. 'He certainly got it, he understood,' Visconti says. 'He was sensitive and poetic. All his songs were very, very sincere. The lyrics are just beautiful, there's a splash of Tolkien but there was a lot of pop philosophy too – he wasn't faking that.' He does admit, however, that Marc wasn't as committed to the cause as many of those around him: 'Marc wasn't really a hippy. When I was recording him he was still living with his parents, he never did hallucinogenic drugs. He certainly dressed the part [though]. It's a very grey area: a true hippy is probably someone who lives in a squat with twenty other people … who knows what defines a hippy?'

Others were less gracious and thoughtful in their responses. Joe Boyd, the founder of the UFO Club and sometime producer of Pink Floyd, recorded an early session with Tyrannosaurus Rex. He told Mark Paytress that he felt that 'Marc seemed like someone who had decided that being a hippie was the "in" thing, and had switched from taking Black Bombers[10] to smoking good Afghan

---

9. Chime Rinpoche was also introduced to Marc Bolan, who had at least one lengthy and private conversation with him, at which Marc acted uncharacteristically humbly, though he never became a devotee of Buddhism itself. Marc was happy to talk the talk of spirituality, but rarely had the patience to walk the walk.

10. A name for Duraphet, essentially speed pills beloved by mods.

hash. I felt there was no real conviction in his acousticness. It just … went along with the change of drug and the change of dress.' Simon Napier-Bell agrees, feeling that Marc's switch to flower-child was completely opportunistic – that the hippies were an audience prime for the plucking, and Marc shaped himself in their image in order to take advantage. It was just another route to the top. Not everyone is so cynical. Jeff Dexter, Marc's old friend and the DJ at Middle Earth, believes that the relationship between Marc and his audience was more symbiotic than parasitic, and that in that respect it truly represented the spirit of the time. 'Marc had been getting great encouragement from [Peel's] *Perfumed Garden*,' he told Lesley-Ann Jones. 'People were sending him the most tender letters, writing him really beautiful things. These were music fans taking note of someone doing something completely different. Marc responding to that was only logical, and genuinely heartfelt. They gave, he gave in return.'

He certainly looked the part. Marc had been immaculately dressing himself on the razor's edge of contemporary fashion since he was twelve, and there was nothing especially contrived about his embracing of the hippy look, except in the sense that *all* fashion is contrived. When he was a mod his immaculate dress sense had been an act of social rebellion, to be smarter, sharper, more unique than anyone else around him. The late sixties were simply the opposite extreme of the same perspective; instead of being the smartest, the sharpest, he was now the most ethereal, the most beautiful, the most waiflike. His tiny frame helped as it meant that he was able to wear girls' blouses, trousers and shoes, giving him an urchin-pixie quality that resonated perfectly with his songs. The hippies were the perfect audience to lean into – the weirder the imagery and stranger the sounds, the more they would lap it up, and Marc's unique voice and penchant for writing songs about Dwarven trumpet players, Parisian wizards and unicorns were a perfect match. The gentle, pastoral musical language he was using to interpret those lyrics felt very much of the hippy underground, with its fascination with earthiness, ecology and children's stories. Tyrannosaurus Rex were the musical equivalent of a someone dressed as an elf reading the poetry passages from Tolkien[11] in a macrobiotic restaurant. One of the first things he did when he and Tony Visconti began to work together was hand him a copy of *Lord of the Rings* saying it would help him 'understand me'.

Not that Marc wasn't prone to a little orientalism himself. The band's first album would begin with the striking of a gong and included songs called 'Afghan Woman' and 'Graceful Fat Sheba' before concluding with a piece called 'Frowning Atahuallpa (My Inca Love)', a song that includes a repeated chant of 'Hare, Hare Krishna, Hare Krishna, Krishna'. Their second album features a short ditty called 'Our Wonderful Brownskin Man'[12]. He might not have

---

11. Everyone skips these bits in *Lord of the Rings*. Go on, admit it.
12. A bit on the nose, you might think.

committed to a spiritual creed in the way that David or George Harrison did, but he knew to litter his lyrics and interviews with allusions to theology and mysticism. The very first issue of the underground magazine *Gandalf's Garden* carries an interview with Marc that is studded with classic examples of this.

> 'I never feel that it is just me doing it, it's more like my astral self. I do believe in the Guardian Angel scene. I don't think there's anything I do that isn't directed'

> 'God is the coolest thing of all. I think if I'm just a splinter out of his head, then he must be a bit like me ... not much though. I see him as a monster sun that opens in the middle and you could get sucked into it and out the other side.'

> 'You are born and born again until you reach the ultimate, until you reach another scene, get into another dimension. I have no doubt about reincarnation. It's just there, like I'm there. I can't conceive myself as any ultimate. I can't possibly see the end.'

This ethos was well represented on the first Tyrannosaurus Rex album, recorded with Tony Visconti across just two days in the spring of 1968 (with a further two days to produce mixes in mono and stereo). The LP was recorded and mixed using a state-of-the-art eight-track Advision mixing desk, which was both a blessing and a curse – the assigned engineer wasn't quite comfortable enough with the gear to get the best out of it. David Platz had okayed a budget of just £400 for the entire record, and Visconti and Bolan always felt that the songs were ultimately done a disservice by the rushed job ('We were victims of a low budget in those days, and we didn't know what we were doing', Visconti says. 'Mainly it was the tonality of the album, it was very thin and didn't represent the fullness of that amazing duo at the time.')

The recording was executed with what Visconti refers to as 'military precision', with each part carefully rehearsed and demoed at casa Visconti in Earl's Court. There might have been a shortage of time and money, but there was no shortage of material. Marc's song writing had exploded over the last year, and he had dozens of titles to choose from. A lot of really solid material he'd written before and during his stint with John's Children was put aside in favour of new compositions, meaning strong songs like 'Sara Crazy Child', 'Jasper C. Debussy', 'The Lilac Hand of Menthol Dan', 'The Perfumed Garden of Gulliver Smith' and others were abandoned completely. Only 'Hot Rod Mama' was carried over from his former band's set to a Tyrannosaurus Rex album. The new songs that Marc had been writing, which were crammed with cod-fantasy toybox mysticism, had an undeniably magical quality and they were musically rich and progressive. Bolan and Visconti had spent many hours nursing glasses of cheap wine while they dissected the work of The Beatles and Beach Boys, studying their immersive experimentation and atmosphere. Sonically there's little of either artist in the recordings the duo made, but there's something of their spirit, stripped down and rebuilt for a single acoustic guitar and a toy chest of percussion instruments. The songs are naive, absolutely, but they cast a spell.

The blend of Marc's rock 'n' roll instincts with the fey spirit of the times was probably the key to the record's creative success. His percussive guitar style and tendency to default to twelve bars and repeated phrases stopped songs like 'Strange Orchestra' and 'Scenescof' from drifting away on a cloud, while his creativity and craving for freaky oddness prevented 'Hot Rod Mama' and 'Mustang Ford' from being prosaic rockers, underpowered on acoustic guitar. The secret weapon was Steve Took, whose creative use of percussion instruments and instinct for exactly the right backing vocal added dimensionality and charm to Bolan's compositions. The album concluded with a reading of one of Marc's whimsical (and rather nonsensical) attempts at blending *The Lord of the Rings* with *The Wind In The Willows*, a charming if slight fairy story read with endearing earnestness by John Peel. It's one of the few moments on the record that goes fully and unashamedly into flower child hippy land, an indulgence the album, frankly, had earned.

Bolan titled the record, in the absolute spirit of the scene he inhabited, *My People Were Fair And Had Sky In Their Hair ... But Now They're Content To Wear Stars On Their Brows*[13], a nonsense phrase that nodded to Tolkien's Elvish law without actually quoting it directly. Many of Marc's friends and colleagues at the time would talk about his relentless ambition and drive – it's one of the aspects of his personality often used to discredit his claim to hippy ideals. If the album title does anything, though, it at least confirms Marc's willingness to double down on his underground credentials. The theme was underlined by the artwork, designed by none other than former Davy Jones sideman George Underwood. Having quit pop, The King Bees' best looking member had followed his passion and training into a career in illustration, and had come highly recommended by Bowie himself, who had by-now formed quite the clique with Bolan, Visconti and their girlfriends. Like the title, the artwork is heavily influenced by the imagery of Tolkien and William Blake and other lesser fantasy work and features a collage of demons, angels, mythical creatures, gods upon horseback, elves and other fantasy archetypes. Everything about the packaging of the record, which carried a dedication on the sleeve to 'Aslan and the Old Narnians', emphasised the other-ness of Tyrannosaurus Rex – they were nailing their weirdo credentials to the mast. Even in the age of *Sgt Pepper's Lonely Hearts Club Band* and *Ogden's Nut Gone Flake*, 'My People Were Fair And

---

13. A reminder here that David called his first album *David Bowie*. In some ways the London boys were very alike. In others, not so much.

Had Sky In Their Hair … But Now They're Content To Wear Stars On Their Brows' is not a snappy title for an intended chart topper. Choosing that name is the action of a man who either doesn't expect a hit and isn't bothering to seek one, or else whose confidence (or possibly delusion) is so bulletproof that they don't think a weird and wordy title will hold them back. Which one of these applies to Marc Bolan is left for the reader to decide for themselves.

As well as the twelve tracks that made up the album, the group's label, Regal Zonophone, also required a single, intended to be released ahead of the LP and not included on it (a relatively common practice in the era – artists often felt that including singles on an album meant that fans were unfairly required to purchase the same song twice[14]). Bolan, Took and Visconti chose one of Marc's newest songs, 'Debora', a catchy, rhythmic number with obvious crossover potential. The lyrics are essentially meaningless – the Debora of the title looks a bit like a zebra, dresses like a conjuror and, like a sunken ship off the Spanish Main, is full of mysterious promise. It's sing-song and nursery-rhyme-like, has a chugging rhythm and, of course, has a girls name as a title, in the tradition of Donovan's 'Jennifer Juniper', The Beatles' 'Michelle' or The Beach Boys' 'Barbara Ann'. It had a lot of potential. The single was released on 19 April 1968, almost a year to the day since David released 'The Laughing Gnome', and like that song, also a catchy number with high hopes riding on it, it got solid reviews across the board. There, however, the similarity stopped. Most reviews noted Marc's vocals, which were 'peculiar' (*Melody Maker*) and 'highly distinctive' (*Disc*) but more than that, critics picked up on the song's originality. *Record Mirror* called it 'ever so clever, ever so different', *NME* went with 'a fascinating debut … very clever and intricate', while the ever reliable Penny Valentine at *Disc & Music Echo* probably summed it up best when she described the song as 'pretty, in a strange way'. The release was buoyed by strong reviews, a small but loyal fanbase of hippies to spread word of mouth, a busy gigging schedule that included opening for Donovan at the Albert Hall and the group's first bona fide headline show at the Southbank Centre's Purcell Room as well as, of course, regular plays and plugs by John Peel. 'Debora' eventually went to number 34, and stayed in the charts for seven weeks, selling somewhere in the region of 30,000 copies – a minor but absolutely genuine hit. After six years of trying, one of the London boys was finally getting somewhere. Tyrannosaurus Rex had real momentum now. They'd graduated to headlining at Middle Earth and pulled decent crowds on the university circuit, even when John Peel *wasn't* there. In June 68 they played at a huge free show in Hyde Park arranged by

---

14. Compare this with the nineties trend for a single to come out on two CDs, a cassette and a 7", all with different b-sides to encourage fans to buy all four, with the song usually appearing on an album as well, to see how far the music industry changed.

Marc's new managers, Blackhill Enterprises, who also managed Pink Floyd,[15] with over 2,000 people in attendance. Shortly afterwards they headlined their biggest gig yet, at the 2,500 capacity Royal Festival Hall.

My People Were Fair And Had Sky In Their Hair ... finally made it into shops on 5 July, after a frustrating delay. Again, reviews were mostly strong. *International Times* got the album in a nutshell, noting that it was 'clothed in the deepest magic, with elves, fairies and pixies leaping about in gay abandon', though *Record Mirror* definitely takes the prize for the most succinct description of Tyrannosaurus Rex yet, describing the sound of the record as 'Jugband Psychedelia'. If Marc was faking his hippydom, then he certainly had the music press fooled. *Melody Maker* noted that 'the attraction of this simple duo lies in their simplicity, fun and beauty', while similarly *Disc & Music Echo*'s review pegged the appeal of the record as 'excellent, totally individual songs of love, beauty, fantasy and nature.' It wasn't just the music press who seemed to be buying (or empathising with, depending on your point of view) Marc's visions, hook, line and sinker – the album eventually peaked at number fifteen, outselling both Pink Floyd and The Jimi Hendrix Experience and hanging around the charts for nine weeks. Tony Visconti estimates that it sold somewhere in the region of 20,000 copies. After years of false starts and faltering sparks, Marc Bolan had released a genuine hit album. He was just getting started.

Regal Zonophone had sat on the debut Tyrannosaurus Rex album since April, by which point many of the songs on it were already a year or so old. Marc, as prolific at this point as he would ever be, wasn't about to abandon this particular seam of creativity and was churning out material at an unbelievable rate. Visconti had managed to sneak in some unofficial time at Trident Studios to track new songs while they waited for *My People Were Fair* to come out, booking the space behind his bosses' backs on the assumption that by the time the bill came, the first Tyrannosaurus Rex album would be a storming success, justifying his decision. [16] Before Marc's debut album had even been released, he had already recorded its follow up – *Prophets, Seers and Stars: The Angels of Ages*, ostensibly more of the same, though better recorded, leaning just as far into the mysticism, trippiness and (possibly faux) spirituality of the band's debut. The album's boldest move was to open with 'Deboraarobed', a re-recording of 'Debora' that, at the halfway point, flips and replays the first half again, this time backwards. It's a quirky trick, and one that few bands had the freaky chutzpah

---

15. Marc's new girlfriend, June – whom he had recently moved in with – an ex of Pink Floyd's Syd Barrett, had been working there when the pair met, but left after being given an ultimatum: dating a client (Marc) or keeping her job.

16. The sneaking wasn't very successful – his bosses soon cottoned on that he was recording unofficially on company time, and he's fairly sure that if it wasn't for the success of 'Debora' he'd have been sent packing back to Brooklyn.

to pull off. *Prophets, Seers and Stars* was released in November 1968, just five months after its predecessor. Again, it sold around 20,000 copies.

Tony Visconti's theory is that 20,000 was basically the UK's entire underground scene, all of whom dug Tyrannosaurus Rex. On the one hand, Marc had successfully captured and captivated his target market but on the other hand, things were going to need to change if he was to get beyond that audience. Flower child he may have been, but it would take more than patchouli oil and incense to mask Marc's ambition to be a star.

That summer, Tyrannosaurus Rex played a huge gig at the Royal Festival Hall, dubbed 'The Babylonian Mouthpiece Show', in which they slightly over extended themselves (a few sniffier reviews noted that there was not *quite* enough light and shade in the band's sound to justify the length of their set). Even so, it was a triumphant occasion – that an underground band with a weird, childlike 'Larry The Lamb' singer, using just acoustic guitar and bongos and singing about elves and unicorns, could play such a large and prestigious room tells us just how seriously London's arts scene was taking counterculture music, and how embedded into that movement Tyrannosaurus Rex were. Also on the bill that day were the folk guitarists Roy Harper and Stefan Grossman, the sitar player Vytas Serelis, and tucked away on the line up, thrilled at his friend's success, was David Bowie. He was miming.

Chapter Seventeen

Mime, All Mime

Through the tail end of 1967, right across 1968 and into 1969 it seemed like David dabbled in every kind of performance art *except* making pop records. It wasn't that his interest in the medium had faded, which was the explanation that he often gave later for the lack of progress he made at this point; he was still writing songs, still finding ways to perform them, still making demos, and still fascinated by the romance and culture of pop – it's just that no-one was especially interested in paying him to record any of it. Crisis talks were ongoing at Decca/Deram over David's future; the label wasn't threatening to *drop* David, but neither was anyone making any particular steps toward furthering his recording career. Having failed with the Visconti-produced 'Let Me Sleep Beside You', Ken Pitt had gone back to the label's selection committee suggesting they release the re-recorded version of 'When I Live My Dream'; the classiest ballad in David's repertoire, backed with a new Visconti produced number, 'Karma Man'; one a crowd pleaser you could take home to meet your mother, the other a niftily progressive pop tune that explored David's interest in Buddhism. The Decca committee again declined. A few months later Pitt offered another selection of new Bowie tunes recorded with Visconti, 'In The Heat of the Morning' and 'London, Bye Ta Ta', two propulsive, contemporary sounding and cinematic pop numbers, both displaying David's increasingly sophisticated songwriting, the latter of which being arguably the first of his recordings to sound more like the Bowie of the early seventies than that of the mid-sixties[1]. The Decca selection committee again declined both and by mutual agreement Pitt and Bowie walked away from the label. David's supporters at Deram were disappointed, but had been scuppered by their stuffier parent label at every turn; the relationship had clearly run its course. Flop, dropped (ish) and roll, yet again.

The Decca/Deram phase of Bowie's career had lasted two years, and was the most concerted and organised effort yet to boost him to the status of mainstream star. Decca had the means, the money and the contacts; David had the songs, the ambition, the imagination and the look – so why had it gone so badly wrong? Hugh Mendl, the label's A&R, put it down to happenstance, telling Paul Trynka that 'the fates were against us'. That's partly true: you can

---

1. So much so that Bowie and Visconti would record a new version in 1970, which sounds completely of a piece with the work he was doing at the time. It could even have slotted onto *Hunky Dory* the following year.

never underestimate the importance of 'right time, right place' in the pop world, of catching the wind just right, of circumstances coming together in perfect alignment. Who knows how many geniuses have remained in obscurity because the bus was late and they never got talking to that TV producer in the pub who would give them the break they needed? On the other hand, there's an argument that for an act that's genuinely special, well, another bus will be along in a minute. David, after all, *did* eventually become a huge star.[2] When Dick Rowe turned down The Beatles it wasn't the end of The Beatles. MGM told Walt Disney that cartoons about a mouse 'would never work'[3]. Twelve publishers rejected the same industry-changing manuscript for the first Harry Potter book. Hardly anyone makes it on the first try without some sort of Faustian pact.[4]

Bowie's music simply fell between the stalls. He had spent the first half of the decade surfing just behind the cultural wave, sometimes a follower of the cutting edge, sometimes a barometer of it, but never a leader. The stylistic shifts he'd made from 'Rubber Band' onward, culminating in the first *David Bowie* album, were a specific move away from what we'd now call the zeitgeist – an attempt to establish himself on his own terms, rather than as a poor man's version of The Who or The Pretty Things. There was the Anthony Newley influence, of course, but even that was a left-turn from the rock 'n' roll mainstream, a concerted and specific effort not to do what you'd expect a nineteen-year-old wannabe pop idol to do. Striking out in his own direction was an admirable and creative move. It's what we *want* our pop stars to do. Deram were happy to go on the journey, because everyone understood and trusted a specific vision – it's just that, unfortunately, however much you believe, however much you enthuse, there's only so far you can manipulate the excitement of others. David's Deram phase was the right idea at the wrong time, or possibly the wrong idea at the right time. It lit the touch paper, but the kindling never caught. Marc Bolan, meanwhile, had made the opposite choice – instead of leaning away from the public tastes, he'd found an existing scene to lean *into*. For all the gleeful creativity of *My People Were Fair ...*, for all of its big swings into weirdo-space, it was launching into a scene that already had Syd Barrett, The Incredible String Band, 'I Am The Walrus' and Donovan. 'Love You Till Tuesday' and 'Rubber Band' were, on the face of it, far more prosaic, safe, almost old-fashioned songs in comparison to 'Scenescoff' and 'Debora', which felt adventurous and mysterious but were released at a time when being the *right kind* of adventurous and mysterious was, ironically, a safer bet, at least in terms of finding a niche audience to build from. David had deliberately turned away from scenes and trends, while Marc had thrown himself headlong into one. Both tactics could

---

2. Spoiler alert.
3. Genuinely, because they thought a giant mouse on a cinema screen would scare housewives.
4. Often with Simon Cowell.

have failed or succeeded spectacularly, and it could easily have been the other way around.

For now, the major label dream was over. Pitt had been able to get tempting deals for Bowie in 1966 precisely *because* he was such an unknown quantity – a young man full of potential and a possible jackpot for the right lucky buyer. Now, though, he was damaged goods. He'd rolled the dice and lost. A half-century later we think of Bowie as an artist who constantly reinvented himself. Didn't like this Bowie? It's okay, there'll be a new one in a year or so. However, there was no reason why anyone in 1968 would be expecting that sort of creative evolution. Bowie was the 'Anthony Newley guy', the 'Laughing Gnome' guy. That version of Bowie had failed, and failed publicly. It would be a big ask for anyone else to take him on. Pitt, at David's request, tried to interest The Beatles' Apple records but found absolutely no interest there[5] or anywhere else, though he had at least been able to get Essex Music to agree to an extension to Bowie's publishing contract, squeezing another £1,500 of badly needed money out of David Platz and into David's pocket (he had earned just £322 in the whole of 1967). Pitt, thinking wistfully of the $10,000 that would have been arriving into the Bowie coffers had Ralph Horton not dropped the ball so badly, rolled up his sleeves and started thinking of ways that he could keep his boy in immaculate shirts and haircuts.[6] 'There were times,' he wrote rather mournfully in *The Pitt Report*, 'when I felt I was the only person in the world who believed in his talent'.

Given David's primary creative pursuits in 1968, it's unlikely that earning money was at the front of his thinking. In their final meeting with Decca, in which all agreed to terminate Bowie's recording contract, David told Hugh Mendl that he was planning to focus on a career as a dancer rather than as a musician. Mendl had felt that this unlikely move couldn't possibly be serious, and assumed that Pitt and Bowie had some grand plan to jump ship to another label with a guaranteed smash hit in mind. It proves that at least *someone* at Decca had faith in David's talent – perhaps more than he deserved at this point.

Despite Pitt's hopes, the 1967 *David Bowie* album had opened very few doors for his client. Indeed, it's tempting to think that Bowie's debut album might as well not exist for all the good it did his career in the long run – but this is not necessarily true. Pitt had purchased a stack of copies to send out to business contacts, TV and radio producers and other showbiz types;[7] this was one of the reasons he had wanted Bowie to record an album in the first place. 'We really planned the Deram album like a CV,' Pitt told Chris Welch in an interview for *Mojo* in 2003. 'We never thought it would sell or that anyone would buy

---

5. Presumably Caleb had cast that morning's I Ching and warned against David Bowie as an investment.

6. Things had gotten so bad at this point that David was working two part time jobs, one manning the photocopier at a Soho printing firm, and the other as a contract cleaner.

7. He also sent a copy to Bowie's parents, who apparently hadn't received one from David himself. There's gratitude for you.

it except ourselves.' One of those copies was sent to the dancer and acclaimed mime artist Lindsay Kemp, of whom Pitt's secretary was a fan. Kemp absolutely adored the record; he loved Anthony Newley, but was also switched on enough to hear other influences and ideas under David's facsimile – something that others had failed to do. For example, he heard the spirit of the dramatic Belgian crooner Jacques Brel, which is especially interesting when you consider that Bowie, who would become a huge fan of the singer, had yet to discover his music when he recorded his debut album; Kemp picked up the resonance between the two artists before David himself did. He also appreciated the echoes in the music of Victorian and early twentieth century music hall; the cockney singing style, the knack for storytelling and the sense of humour.

Kemp was working on the fringes of London's theatre and arts scene. He had trained with the Ballet Rambert school in London and with the great Austrian expressionist dancer Hilde Holger (who taught an almost meditative form of dancing in which body and mind were aligned as one) before going on to study with the legendary French mime Marcel Marceau. Kemp would spend his career blending theatre, dance, clowning, drag and mime to sometimes beautiful, sometimes comic, sometimes camp, sometimes erotic effect and would often be shunned by the dance world because of his mixing of such usually distinct disciplines. This creative blend would have been hugely attractive to Bowie, who had been flirting with combining pop and performance art since the days of the Lower Third, an itch he was briefly able to scratch with the Riot Squad. He knew that he could take it further. Kemp had been using 'When I Live My Dream', the grandest moment on the *David Bowie* record, in a show called *Clown*, running at the tiny Little Theatre Club, near Covent Garden, which featured Kemp as Pierrot, the tragi-comic 'sad clown' archetype which dates back to the seventeenth century. 'It was a *commedia dell'arte* musical, a sort of backstage circus with songs,' Kemp told Dylan Jones for his oral history of Bowie. 'The show was very much inspired by Picasso's early paintings of the blue and pink periods, of the hungry harlequins and Pierrot and their families and so on.' David was absolutely entranced by the show and keen to meet the principles afterwards. It was, as Kemp has put it in several interviews, 'love at first sight'.

Unfortunately, the old adage of 'if you can remember the sixties you weren't really there' does ring rather true in the case of Lindsay Kemp: he told his story many times across years of articles, biographies and documentaries, and the details varied significantly. We have to approach his account of their relationship with some caution – especially as there are few people left alive who can confirm the details (Kemp himself died in 2018). What we *can* say for sure is that within the next few days Bowie began attending Kemp's classes at the Dance Centre on Floral Street near Covent Garden, which he kept up for a while.[8] After one of the first classes he accompanied Kemp back to his flat and they became lovers.

---

8. It's often assumed that Bowie studied mime with Kemp, which is technically correct but doesn't tell the full story – Kemp's classes were in dance and movement, with mime as just one of the disciplines

Kemp's impact on David was fairly profound. Ken Pitt had introduced Bowie to a higher class, artsier scene and Ralph Horton had shown him London's more grown up gay life; Kemp, however, lived at an intersection of the arts, queerness and the counterculture, a scene closer to the one that had produced The Velvet Underground in New York; of drag queens, strippers, sex workers, fallen aristocrats, bohemians and the other fascinating exotica drifting around Soho's nightlife, living and working in – as Angela Bowie describes in her book *Backstage Passes* – a 'rad/lib/mystical/multisexual/commune.' For Bowie, who idolised Andy Warhol, was obsessed with the Velvets and had a swooning soft spot for the Weimar Berlin of Christopher Isherwood and *Cabaret*, it was another tribe to belong to, another facet of his personality to indulge; Kemp would later tell *The Guardian* that Bowie 'fell in love with the Bohemianism of my world', a view which Bowie himself very much backed up; 'His day-to-day life was the most theatrical thing I had ever seen, ever,' he told *Rolling Stone*. 'It was everything I thought bohemia probably was. I joined the circus'. Horton might have been the one who showed him the London gay scene, but it was only after meeting Kemp that he truly started to fold camp (with a hint of debauchery – not just the 'ooh ducky' caricature he'd occasionally played for laughs before this) into his persona, something that would serve him well in the coming years. Kemp considered there to be no difference between the tragi-comic, debauched Pierrot figure he presented on stage with its drama and indulgence, and his real bohemian life – David was learning that he could do the same. It was another building block in the facade he would create in the early seventies.

To all intents and purposes, Kemp was David's first 'boyfriend'. They didn't, as far we're aware, put a label on their relationship (although Kemp occasionally used the word 'boyfriend' when discussing David in interviews), but they did act as a couple; with Kemp inviting David very much into his life. Like many people who encountered Bowie over the years, Kemp was absolutely besotted from almost the very first moment he clapped eyes on him ('He became my muse', he told *Uncut* in 2017). David spent many nights at Lindsay's Soho flat being introduced to silent movies, music hall, the great French writer Jean Genet and new forms of theatre he had not yet come across; Japanese kabuki and mime, Ataud's 'theatre of cruelty' and Esslin's 'theatre of the absurd'. David, in turn, introduced Lindsay to the Tibetan Society and Buddhist Centre, hugely important in his life at that point, and even took him home to meet his parents, whom Kemp adored (though we have no record of what they made of him). When Kemp and company went on tour in 1968, he and Bowie shared a bed. Lindsay was clearly besotted, it oozes out of every interview that this warm, funny, engaging and extremely camp man ever did. The extent of David's own feelings are less clear – he never went into the details about his private

he incorporated.

relationship with Kemp, though he would talk about his respect for him as an artist, teacher and performer many times.

Lifestyle aside, it's almost impossible to understate the impact Kemp's lessons in movement and expression had on David's creativity as a performer. Kemp, like his own teacher, Hilde Holder, taught dance as a holistic artform, in which mind and body were linked. In 1976 his classes were attended by a young Kate Bush, very much a Bowie successor. She described his teaching style in an interview with *NME* in 1978: 'He taught me that you can express with your body ... he'd put you into emotional situations, some of them very heavy. Like he'd say, "right, you're all going to become sailors drowning and there are waves curling up around you." And everyone would just start screaming'. His classes with Bowie were very much along the same lines. Kemp's students were from all walks of life, actors and rock stars looking to improve their movement, professional dancers looking to widen their perspective and housewives and secretaries broadening their horizons. Kemp's focus was on expression through movement; to move and hold the body with physical, intellectual and emotional intent. He didn't so much teach routines and techniques as he taught *presence*. 'We spent a lot of time on breathing and improvising,' Kemp told *Uncut*. 'We'd improvise to everything from African drums to Carmen Miranda, Bach [and] Beethoven. He was really quite brilliant in improvising ... We did a lot of rolling around on the floor. Burning in the depths of Hell or drowning in the oceans to the swelling of Scriabin's music.' This wasn't about perfect dance forms, nor was it about showmanship. It was about inhabiting the body and imbuing it with the purpose and emotion of the piece being performed. 'I taught him to exteriorise,' Kemp would later tell Paul Stryka in *Starman*. 'To reveal his soul.' Alongside the courses in movement, David's experiences with Kemp and his theatre troupe were also great lessons in the power to be found in costume, lighting, staging and design – all of which would be hugely important in his future. Kemp was another great mentor, adding to the work already done by David's brother Terry, Owen Frampton and Ken Pitt; each contributing another layer of culture and subculture to the complex cocktail that Bowie was layering. Even Ken Pitt, who could be possessive of David when it came to other male influences in his life ('obsessively jealous' is how Bowie guitarist John Hutchinson puts it), describes Kemp as one of the 'great influences' on David's early career.

As with almost everyone important in David's life, Lindsay quickly became a collaborator. The two worked up a mixed media show together, part mime, part theatre, part songs, called *Pierrot In Turquoise*; 'Pierrot' for Kemp's favourite character, reprised again here, and 'Turquoise' for the colour's importance in Buddhism, where it symbolises eternity. David would play 'Cloud', the show's balladeer and one-man Greek chorus, performing songs that illustrated the silent themes evoked by Kemp's Pierrot and the Harlequin, who was played by the other member of the company, Jack Birkett, aka 'The Incredible Orlando'.

The trio, accompanied by set designer Natasha Korniloff, took their show on a small tour at the beginning of 1968, transferring to the Mercury Theatre in London for an eleven-night run in the spring,[9] before it was eventually worked into a one-off performance for Scottish television, renamed 'The Looking Glass Murders'. The show was relatively well received (the *Evening Standard*'s description of David as a 'fair swain with shining eyes' was a delightful contribution to his press clippings), and it was enough to confirm for Ken Pitt that David had a future in theatre ... and for David, that he had a future in mime.

Experimental theatre had a symbiotic relationship with the sixties underground, as the arts scene, buoyed by drugs and the sheer energy of London's swinging era increasingly blurred the lines between installation and theatrical event. It was where the capital's intellectual avant-garde and its free-thinking, acid frazzled lunatics[10] met in the middle. The first of London's 'Arts Labs', essentially a small theatre, gallery and cinema situated off Drury Lane, was founded in 1967 by Jim Haynes, one of those interconnected underground figures who played crucial roles in the capital's progressive culture. He was one of the co-founders of *International Times* and also, alongside Germaine Greer, the groundbreaking sex-positive newspaper *Suck*. He had also been partly responsible for transforming an old Camden rail shed into a multipurpose arts venue, the Roundhouse, which is still in use today. The Arts Lab was intended as an anything-goes performance and exhibition space, presenting out-there ideas not beholden to establishment values and concepts[11]. In the first of the regular newsletters about the space that Haynes would compose, he described an Arts Lab as a 'non-institution'. 'We all know what a hospital, theatre, police station and other institutions have in the way of boundaries, but a lab's boundaries should be limitless'. The basement contained a non-stop cinema with a floor covered in soft mats rather than seats, where those in the know could regularly be found snoozing through *Citizen Kane, Gilda* and arty pornography at 5 am, after having wandered dreamily out of Middle Earth up the road.[12] Lindsay Kemp himself worked up early ideas there, while John Lennon and Yoko Ono

---

9. Future shows were jeopardised after the second night of the tour, in Whitehaven near Carlisle, when Kemp discovered David in bed with Natasha. A distraught Lindsay Kemp inexpertly cut at his wrists and would have ridden his bike into the sea had he had one with him, while a heartbroken Korniloff threatened to overdose on sleeping pills. Both later dismissed these actually-quite-horrific events as dramatic grandstanding. David's two lovers spent the night sobbing on each other. He had to sleep in the hallway. The show went on. David had at least two other on/off casual girlfriends at this point, Dana Gillespie and Lesley Duncan, and it seems odd that Kemp might consider him monogamous – though he was far from the only one of Bowie's lovers to make that mistake.

10. Occasionally the same people.

11. Or capitalist ones, either. The Arts Lab was basically run at a loss, funded by donations from theatre greats.

12. There is some suggestion that the cinema at the Arts Lab was always full of people having sex, while others claim that it was full of people who had gone there in the *hope* of having sex only to

mounted their first joint exhibition in the space in 1968. One early play, *The Cage Show*, conceived by writer/poet/activist/face-around-the-underground Jeff Nuttall, involved the audience being padlocked into cages made from chicken wire and bed springs, and aggressively questioned about whether they were a person called 'Mrs Meadows'. Any unfortunate picked on by the cast had to prove they were *not* Mrs Meadows by any means necessary, while being pelted with offal and shot with water pistols[13]. The caged audience even had access to a telephone in case they needed to call a witness. Not *everything* was that terrifying – there were comedies, feminist monologues and angry political rhetoric; including a production of *Fuck Nam – A Morality Play*, written by The Fugs' Tuli Kupferberg, in which American GIs in Saigon were depicted as frustrated sexual inadequates. At one point an American officer and his wife eat their own child. The Lab, like much of London's avant-garde and underground theatre, was a mixed bag of the powerful and the baffling. On one night you could see the first ever self-written one-man show by Steven Berkoff, the next try to ignore someone getting a hand job on the next mat along while you attempted to stare fixedly at Andy Warhol's twin-screen art film *Chelsea Girls*.

Mime made up a surprisingly large portion of London's fringe theatre in 1967 and '68, often blended with contemporary dance and used to make profound political points. Like 'The Laughing Gnome', Bowie's mime career is something that is rarely taken seriously as the years go by, and is often used as a punchline[14], but it was something that David took *incredibly* seriously. Also like 'The Laughing Gnome', it was a career move that seems baffling now, but did genuinely make sense at the time. As well as working up *Pierrot in Turquoise* with Kemp, David performed at least once at the Arts Lab in an interpretive dance/ mime show called *Studies Toward An Experiment into the Structure of Dreams*, in which the Argentinian interpretative dancer Graziela Martinez performed improvised pieces to descriptions of dreams accompanied by Mark Boyle's 'Sensual Laboratory' lightshow, an incredible, immersive series of projections composed on the fly using oil and coloured inks, smoke, coated slides and pin scratches to create constantly swirling patterns that were different every night. Invariably the elected 'dreamer' who was supposed to supply material to work with failed to fall asleep, so Martinez and her fellow dancers improvised to the light show instead – an improvisation to an improvisation. There were over seventy performances of *Studies* ... though it's not known how many David was involved in.

---

find that the Lab's free love theatre floor was something of an urban legend. Perhaps both are true, depending on which night you went.

13. The water pistols were a daily presence, however much to Nuttall's annoyance, the actors refused to participate in offal throwing on most nights. He did get his way sometimes, however, and at least one or two audiences got the full works.

14. The deeply flawed 2021 Bowie biopic *Stardust* is a textbook offender.

By the summer of 1968, Bowie had devised his own solo mime performance which he had called 'Yet-San and the Eagle'[15], a twelve-minute interpretive mime in full whiteface, done to a sound collage incorporating his song 'Silly Boy Blue', which Bowie and Visconti had stitched together in an approximation of what they felt was 'Tibetan-style' sounds, tones and melodies.[16] The piece was intended to explore the Chinese occupation of Tibet, a subject very close to David's heart. He performed the piece – which those around at the time recall as being surprisingly good – at Marc Bolan's invitation at Tyrannosaurus Rex's huge show at the Royal Festival Hall, with a warm up performance at Middle Earth (which would be the first time that David met John Peel). Pitt proudly took out an advert in *Melody Maker* for 'David Bowie in mime ...' with a close up of Bowie in whiteface makeup and the two dates listed,[17] presumably baffling anyone who had bought the Deram album on the paper's recommendation the previous year, or who had heard Bowie on Radio One's *Top Gear*, neither of which suggested a move into wordless interpretative movement.

Mime, alas, was unlikely to put dinner on the table. [18] In retrospect we can see how the skills David learned at Lindsay Kemp's knee were absolutely crucial in building the performance persona that would give his career heft and permanence in the seventies. At the time, however, though a solid choice for underground art, it was not seen as the move of an artist headed for megastardom. It would be difficult for even David's greatest supporters to see any path leading from *Pierrot In Turquoise* and *Studies Toward An Experiment into the Structure of Dreams* to *Top of The Pops*, screaming fans and sell-out American tours. Ken Pitt believed in David completely, but he was also pragmatic. To Pitt, a manager of the old school, building a career was about solid work, and he was sure that following Tony Newley's lead as a quirky all-rounder, shining on the theatre stage or the silver screen, hosting television shows, writing for other artists and starring in musicals, was the most the sensible course for his client. Whether David still had these ambitions at this stage is hard to say – he never let go of his desire to act or to write a musical, certainly, however people who knew him at the time remember Bowie often complaining about Pitt's attempts to push him toward more mainstream ground. Meeting Kemp and the move into avant-garde theatre, with its connections to the underground, was something else entirely – that melding of art, the counterculture and debauchery suited David – but it was

---

15. Occasionally miswritten as 'Jetsun and the Eagle'.
16. Again, an example of hamfisted Western interpretations of Eastern culture for clout. (See chapter sixteen)
17. It also lists David's upcoming Radio One *Top Gear* session, although strangely doesn't specify that this is a live music performance, not part of his mime dates – giving the casual reader the intriguing idea that Bowie had found a way to perform mime on the radio.
18. It could, however, make you very good at pretending that you *did* have dinner on the table in case anyone was watching.

not a world which Ken Pitt, like Simon Napier-Bell, particularly understood or enjoyed.[19]

Though he had set major label ambitions aside for now, Pitt was still peddling David for all he was worth. During 1968 and '69 he had meetings, sent letters and arranged auditions for the likes of *Jackanory* (who weren't interested), at least one Broadway producer (David missed the meeting as he was with a girl), a film called *Alaine* (which appears to have gone unmade), the role of MC on a new pop show called *68 Style* (which didn't make it past the pilot stage) a part in the musical *Hair* (alas, rejected) and an advert for Lyons Maid ice lollies (this one actually happened). Also on the slate was David's new rock opera, *Ernie Johnson*, the plot of which was only revealed in 1996 after a demo tape came up for auction. *Record Collector* summarised the brief notes accompanying the tape:

'Ernie's staging a suicide party, at which Tiny Tim is one of the guests (cue a song); Ernie remembers his passing loves from the previous year; he has a racist conversation with a tramp; sings a song to himself in the mirror; rushes off to Carnaby Street to buy a tie for the big occasion of his suicide.'

Ken Pitt quotes a line of dialogue from the show in *The Pitt Report* ('Most exquisite party darlings. Everyone was there. They busted me for masquerading as a man. How dare they?') Sadly, it went the way of David's teleplay, *The Champion Flower Grower*, and *Kids On the Roof*, the musical he had planned with Tony Hatch – unproduced and unreleased to this day. Bowie did land one proper movie role that year, in John Dexter's hit *The Virgin Soldiers*. However, despite Pitt's hope of bagging a decent part for his client, he had to settle for a blink-and-you'd-miss-it walk-on having failed to impress in the audition. It was barely worth the short-back-and-sides he was given for the role.

Pitt had more success pimping David out as a songwriter. In March Billy Fury, one of British rock 'n' roll's first wave, covered 'Silly Boy Blue', though Parlophone frustratingly flipped the song from the A to the B-side at the last minute. One of Pitt's other acts, a throw-back beat group called The Beatstalkers, recorded several of David's songs, including 'Silver Treetop School For Boys', the delightful 'When I'm Five'[20] and a sprightly, Monkees-ish number called 'Everything Is You', featuring Bowie on guitar (the latter of which appears never to have been recorded by David himself). None were hits, but they gave Pitt confidence in David's commercial potential as a songwriter-for-hire. In

---

19. Neither objected to debauchery *per-se*; Napier-Bell is very open about the wild sex he had in the sixties, and though Pitt is far, far more reserved in his writing, others have hinted that he had some fairly specific predilections and kinks. It was the *hippyness* of it all that neither could understand, the dirty bare feet, the peace and love, the abstract psychedelics. The scenes which both men preferred may have been just as debauched as the 'free love' the hemp n' sandals set practiced; but they were far, far more *stylish*.

20. The combination of David's whimsical, cute lyrics and singer David Lennox's Glaswegian accent makes this arguably the first ever example of what would become known as Indiepop.

1967 Bowie gifted a cod-music hall piece called 'Over The Wall We Go', likely leftover from the Bowie/Hatch *Kids On The Roof* musical project, to one of Robert Stigwood's new artists, Oscar – aka Paul Nicholas, who would go on to success as an actor in The Who's *Tommy* and the sitcom *Just Good Friends*.[21] Alas, it was another (probably deserved) flop.

Most intriguing of all was an opportunity brought in by David Platz at Essex Music, who asked David to write English lyrics to a stirring French song, 'Comme d'habitude', originally by Claude François. Bowie contributed a completely original lyric which he retitled 'Only A Fool Learns To Love', and Pitt lobbied hard for the song to be Bowie's next single. The melody was beautiful; yearning and melancholic, swelling to a dramatic finale, with David's voice suiting it perfectly. It had astonishing hit potential. Unfortunately, the song's French publishers knew this too, and wanted a bigger name for the English version. David's lyrics were abandoned and 'Comme d'habitude' was eventually turned over to the Canadian singer/songwriter Paul Anka, who wrote his own version. The following year, David called Ken Pitt to tell him that 'Frank Sinatra recorded that French song!' By now, of course, it had been retitled 'My Way'.[22]

The final money-making venture dreamed up by Pitt in 1968 was a cabaret set. David had no band with which to tour the dance halls, and no chart hits that would get him into theatres, but Pitt thought – not unreasonably – that an artist as versatile as David Bowie should have no problems getting work on the cabaret club circuit; providing they could develop an act that worked. David was deeply resistant to this, but agreed after his father – whom he respected a great deal – impressed on him the importance of bringing in a wage. Pitt and Bowie put together a list of songs, with a handful of Bowie originals ('Love You Till Tuesday', 'When I'm Five', 'When I Live My Dream' and the aforementioned 'Only A Fool Learns To Love'/'Comme d'habitude') and some reliable covers, including a Beatles section complete with life-sized cardboard cut-outs of the cartoon Fab Four taken from *Yellow Submarine*.[23] The show also included a version of 'The Laughing Gnome' complete with a gnomish glove puppet, a Roger McGough poem and, at Bowie's insistence, a mime section. Pitt even provided David with a script, and the pair structured and choreographed the show right up to the placement of the microphone in the stand. The auditions came to nothing. In *The Pitt Report*, Pitt claims that one agent, Harry Dawson, told him that David was 'too good' before asking

21. Given that Fury was managed by Larry Parnes, Oscar by Stigwood and The Beatstalkers by Pitt himself, it's safe to say that the velvet mafia was still operating pretty well.
22. Years later Bowie would attempt to write something with a similar feel and spirit. The result, 'Life On Mars', probably means as much to Bowie fans as Sinatra's 'My Way' does to his.
23. At one point Bowie and Pitt were walking back to Pitt's flat carrying the life-sized Paul McCartney cut-out, only to be passed on the street by a smiling real-life Paul McCartney.

'but where can I book it?'[24]. Dawson himself remembered it rather differently when the writer Johnny Rogan questioned him for his 1988 book *Starmakers and Svengalis: The History of British Pop Management*. 'Let him have a good day job,' he remembers saying, 'he's never going to get anywhere'. The word 'cabaret' was never mentioned again.

The cabaret episode would be a millstone around Ken Pitt's neck for years, often cited as evidence that Bowie's manager simply didn't understand his style or potential. It's difficult to gauge the truth of this based on the level of enthusiasm for this venture in Pitt's own memoir, a fastidious work full of meticulously recorded dates and figures, useful but occasionally rather stuffy and dry. He talks about David's cabaret potential in the same tone he discusses discovering the white light and white heat of The Velvet Underground. Angie Bowie, in her memoir, mentions the words 'Ken Pitt' and 'cabaret' in the same breath several times, and never in an especially complimentary way. These two sources, supported by other interviews often quoting third hand, have between them given the impression that Pitt was a cabaret-type manager by nature, someone who would always be drawn to throwing his acts into the humiliation of the chicken-in-a-basket circuit. A letter he sent to David's father in July 1967 appears to support this.

> '… had David persisted with his work in the cabaret field he would have reached £100 a week … It was apparent to me that that was the one good and sure source of income and which would have kept him going until he got into other fields.'

Pitt denied several times that he wanted David to be a cabaret performer. 'Contrary to popular opinion,' he told Christopher Sandford for his 1998 book *Bowie: Loving The Alien*, 'I hated cabaret. In the course of four years, I mentioned it to David once. That was when he was broke and unable to feed himself.' Kevin Cann, the Bowie archivist and author of the comprehensive *Any Day Now: The London Years 1947-1974*, also interviewed Pitt. 'I never wanted David to go into cabaret at all' he said, 'it was simply a way of trying to help him make some quick money to appease his father'. The answer, in truth, is probably somewhere in the middle. Pitt was a professional agent and artist manager, and knew there was value in the cabaret circuit – it's entirely possible that his financial instincts would outweigh his tastes. What's more, David was giving him the raw material for just that sort of move. Many of the songs from Deram era would work perfectly in a lounge singer's act. Even the mime performance fitted into that context. That said, if we look at the circles David was now moving in – the Arts Lab, the Lindsay Kemp set, the acid rock

---

24. Which sounds like a kindly teacher telling a talentless but enthusiastic schoolboy footballer to hang back to give the other kids a chance.

of Syd Barrett and hippy gumbo of Marc Bolan and the absolute electricity of The Jimi Hendrix experience ... none of these associations feel of a piece with Pitt's cabaret dream. Still, the idea of being cajoled into the cheesy club circuit does seem to have stuck in David's craw – it's unlikely that Angie Bowie, Tony Visconti and John Hutchinson are all misremembering Bowie's complaints, or the impression he gave them that his former manager hadn't really understood him. Pitt would stay with Bowie for a couple of years yet, but it's arguable that from this point his days were numbered and the clock was counting down. Regrets? He had a few.

David, meanwhile, had more out-there (and less lucrative) ideas to pursue. His performance at the Tyrannosaurus Rex event at the Royal Festival earlier that year had been well received, aside from some heckling by a few token revolutionaries who felt that an attack on China's invasion of Tibet was somehow an attack on communism itself. *International Times'* review of the show, which was mildly critical of the headliners, was positively rapturous about David; noting that he 'received the longest and loudest applause of all the performers, and he deserved it. It was a pity that he didn't have a longer set.' He would reprise the piece the following year; opening for Tyrannosaurus Rex on their *For The Lion & The Unicorn In The Oak Forests Of Fern* tour. Quite what Marc's agenda was in looping in his old mate to perform a mime about Tibetan oppression ahead of his own performance is up for debate. Tony Visconti believes it was a specific attempt by Bolan to make sure he wasn't upstaged by his friend, while a more charitable interpretation might be that David was doing something genuinely interesting that would add some texture to the show, creating a richer experience than if they'd simply booked a couple of folk singers. Marc would have absolutely loved to be thought of as the type of artist who had mixed-media, exotic support acts at his happenings. It's a view that is borne out by Marc's other choice of support for the tour – sitar player Vytas Serelis. Of course, a slightly *less* charitable interpretation is that Marc knew full well that having an undercard consisting of unconventional Eastern music and mime would mean that his own set was going to feel breezier and more engaging to the audience. It's possible, of course, for all of these interpretations to be true at once. Whichever way you slice it, it's still a line-up that underlines the power of that 'Eastern promise'. It also illustrated a remarkable evolution for the London boys. Three years earlier, David and Marc had been a couple of mods setting the world to rights in Denmark Street cafes and comparing shirts; now one was commanding large audiences with his strangely compelling mewling and fantastical imagery, while the other was passionately defending an oppressed community through the medium of interpretive dance. You wonder what Les Conn would have made of it all.

Chapter Eighteen

'They're Selling Hippy Wigs
In Woolworths, Man'

L ondon's softer, flower-powered hippy dream lasted about a year – very
roughly from the Fourteen-Hour Technicolour Dream in April 1967 to
the violent protest and running battles between police and counterculture
demonstrators opposing the Vietnam War outside the US Embassy in Grosvenor
Square in March 1968, by which point things had begun to both evolve and
dissolve as the scene fragmented. The drugs were getting more serious and for
some they were becoming a way of life and an end in themselves – the values
were draining away.

Elsewhere there was politicisation and anger, now shorn of the peace and
tolerance that had marked the activism of the previous year. Faced with Enoch
Powell's famous (and famously revolting) racist call to arms 'rivers of blood'
speech, the wave of student protests in Paris, the movements for Black and
women's rights in the US and UK and the pointless brutality of the Vietnam
war, it was hard to espouse a life of gentle oneness with the universe and
harmony with the Earth. Finally, there was the usual case of subcultural
overspill. The small scene of hippies that comprised London's underground
had soaked to the point of saturation into mainstream consciousness, watering
down its power and creativity. This was no longer a subculture or a lifestyle
choice; it had become a hair style, a bunch of catchphrases, just another square
on the mood board. The 'weekend hippies', taking a break from their jobs at the
council, in the supermarket or doing outwork for catalogue companies to smoke
a little grass and let it all hang loose, far, far outnumbered the genuine radicals.
'There weren't really a lot of us' says underground mainstay Bob Rowberry in
Ian Marchant's book *A Hero For High Times*. 'There were a lot of people who
looked like the public perception hippies, dressing up like hippies, with their
long hair and smoking dope and taking acid, yeah, sure. And going to the festies
and whatever. But they weren't really there.'

Those who had hoped that a cultural, social and even political revolution
was coming now faced the miserable realisation that the self-sustaining and
unstoppable march of capitalism was having its usual wicked way with the
dream of peace and love. 'I really thought we were going to change the world,'
John Peel told Jonathon Green in *Days In The Life*. 'Quite clearly it came to
absolutely bugger all'. The atmosphere in the country was changing, the pound

was down, the tower blocks were up and there was a jump in crime and violence. It was reflected, as it always is, in pop music. In 1967, the Rolling Stones had sung 'She's A Rainbow' and all The Beatles had needed was love. In 1968, it was 'Street Fighting Man' and 'Revolution'.

Any pop stars surfing the waves of fashion were now finding themselves unsure what their next move should be. Underground music was entirely about authenticity, but popular success – provided you cared about it – was about knowing what would sell. Few acts get to have a foot in both camps for very long. Forging new creative directions can mean losing old fans, while staying put can stop you getting new ones. Attrification is the enemy of pop, but risk is the enemy of stability – it was a fine line to walk. Musical tastes were changing too: pastoral folk was being bleached out in favour of heavier blues rock like Fleetwood Mac, Free and Chicken Shack, very soon to be joined by Led Zeppelin. Jeff Beck and Eric Clapton were worshipped. All of this – the excessive drugs, the desperation to stay popular, the despair at the failure of the peace revolution, changing musical tastes – was causing a crisis of identity in the underground. The dream had splintered, and one of those fault lines ran straight through the middle of Tyrannosaurus Rex.

Though a cherished child of the underground[1] who genuinely bought into many of the ideals of the hippy era; Marc Bolan never quite managed to keep a lid on his ambition. He had wanted to be a star since he was a child. He was now monstrously successful by the standards of the hippy folk scene, but being a big fish in a small psychedelic pond was never really the goal. Marc had been telling people he was going to be 'bigger than Elvis' for years. Things were going well – the band now had a cult following and the press and radio (at least John Peel on *Top Gear* and, well, John Peel in *International Times*) were paying attention. It was, however, all balanced on the fracturing underground. It was difficult to see how a band with such a dream-like airiness to them could survive without that platform to stand upon. Tyrannosaurus Rex had teeth, but they were well hidden – to most they were a beautiful feather, floating on the breeze and easily crushed.

The band's second album, *Prophets, Seers & Stars: The Angels of the Ages* came out in November 1968. Visconti and Bolan, now feeling their oats, had given it a fuller, more detailed sound, though fundamentally it was a very similar record to its predecessor in terms of the structure of the songs. For all Marc's grandstanding in interviews about how much the duo's writing had moved on since they wrote their debut, the two albums are stylistically pretty interchangeable. If you'd never heard *My People Were Fair* you'd be impressed,

---

1. Marc's appeal was so caught up in the idea being an impish, childlike elemental that the nickname 'The Bolan Child' had caught on in fan circles, after it was discovered that words 'BOLAN CHILD' were written on the buzzer outside the front door to the flats where he lived. Since the flat's other occupant was called June Child, this was a little more mundane than those fans first supposed.

but the UK's underground was so small that, of course, pretty much everyone in that scene *had* heard it. *Prophets, Seers and Stars* was well reviewed but failed to make the charts at all, while a second single; another Bolan rocker called 'One Inch Rock', just about scraped into the top thirty. Visconti estimates that Tyrannosaurus Rex had sold around 40,000 copies of the two albums by the end of 1968, which was enough to keep his paymasters at Essex and Regal Zonophone happy, but the failure of the second album to chart still felt like a misstep for a band whose fan base should have been growing.

Marc and Steve were still astonishingly prolific however – and as their second album was released they were already settling down with Visconti to record their next, *Unicorn*, a far more versatile and grounded work than *Prophets* or *My People Were Fair*, and comfortably the best record the Bolan/Took version of Tyrannosaurus Rex would release. Recording would continue on and off into 1969, with Visconti expanding his bag of technical tricks and broadening the band's musical palette. *Unicorn* had far more creativity and versatility than either of its predecessors, nodding to the sound of Phil Spector and the Beach Boys' Brian Wilson, producers beloved of both Bolan and Visconti. While it was business as usual on 'Chariots of Silk' and 'Nijinsky Hind', other moments showed the duo stretching their sound. 'Cat Black (The Wizard's Hat)', a Bolan song dating back to before his time with John's Children, was augmented with a sprightly Tony Visconti piano part and Steve Took's full drum kit, while 'Iscariot' dissolved into a mournful harmonium. There's generally more space and atmosphere on the bluesier numbers, more variety in the percussion choices and more interesting twists in Took's always-inventive chromatic harmonies. Perhaps most significantly, Marc had reined in some of the florid poetry that marked his earlier work. The lyrics on *Unicorn* are, at least for the most part, both scannable and audible: not an accusation you could level at 'Dwarfish Trumpet Blues' or 'Salamander Palaganda'. Just as David's 'London, Bye Ta Ta' foreshadowed *Hunky Dory*, there are moments on *Unicorn* that point the way to *T.Rex*. Admittedly, John Peel is back narrating another one of Marc's 'woodland tales' but even this feels like an odder, more interesting story segment than the one that had appeared on *My People Were Fair*. It's a beautiful album, and one of the finest Bolan would ever write. *Unicorn* was preceded by a stand alone single, 'Pewter Suitor', another percussive Marc Bolan rocker, though far less obviously commercial than either 'Debora' or 'One Inch Rock', with an awkward rhythm and a twitching riff that verges on atonal in places. It suggests that Marc and his team were testing the waters to see what fans would respond to. They got their answer – the single, released at the start of 1969, didn't chart.[2]

---

2. Marc was actually against releasing 'Pewter Suitor' as a single, feeling it was more of an album track, but was talked into it by his label for reasons that were alas unrecorded. It's a curious decision, especially as the gorgeous and extremely commercial 'Cat Black (The Wizard's Hat)' was right there for the taking.

Fortunately, single sales didn't tell the whole story. When *Unicorn* was released in May 1969 it entered the charts at number twelve, though it fell out of the top twenty the following week and out of the charts altogether two weeks later. Its performance gives us a snapshot of the audience for Tyrannosaurus Rex in particular and underground bands in general as we move toward the end of the decade – they were loyal, they showed up, they bought albums in the first week or so or not at all, they didn't buy many singles and there weren't many of them. 'The underground was terribly small,' John Peel explained, speaking to Jonathan Green, citing the example of Berkeley psychedelic rockers Country Joe and the Fish. 'I said to the record company, "Why isn't this in the charts? Everybody I know has got a copy." What I didn't realise was that it was the other way around … the 300 that they'd sold were all to people that I knew.' Tony Visconti agrees: 'The first three albums were very limited in their audience – it was people that were John Peel fans. They wanted to go for the most underground thing going and they wanted to preciously hang on to that,' he says. 'We know what the amount of those people was – it was 20,000. We always hit the ceiling of 20,000 album sales'. To the pathologically ambitious Marc Bolan, however, that 20,000-strong audience wasn't a ceiling: it was a start.

Though some – both at the time and since – blamed him, Steve Took wasn't the reason that Tyrannosaurus Rex had yet to break out of their underground bubble. In fact, he was a large part of why they were doing as well as they were. It was Took that was adding the necessary dynamics that elevated songs beyond Bolan's fairly limited sonic palette. He was also crucial to the group's underground credentials: Bolan on his own was just an ambitious former mod with curly hair who looked great in Indian cotton smocks. Marc wasn't exactly a fake hippy, but neither was he a completely committed one, whereas Steve Took was the whole package, a true drop out. Marc talked the talk, while Steve walked the walk.[3] Bolan was hesitant to go deep into the counterculture but he still converted to vegetarianism when he met June and Visconti, could improvise vaguely authentic-sounding spiritual guff and genuinely did have a gentle soul and a positive outlook – he was a sweet person when he could get off the subject of his own genius (something Allan Warren, Simon Napier-Bell, Tony Visconti and his cousin Stephanie Keys all agree on). But he was also shallow. His politics and philosophy were fairly superficial, as were his ethics. He did a good impression of depth, but didn't have the intense commitment to art and ideas that David, for example, had – Marc had neither the discipline nor the inclination to practice movement and performance art or study Buddhism. He was always looking for shortcuts. The boy who had joined a band before he could even play a chord and cried because he hadn't been offered a record deal after one gig, hadn't changed all that much. As for the other main facets

---

3. Or at the very least 'sat the sit'.

of the underground – Marc rarely touched drugs[4] and was fairly unengaged politically.[5]

Steve was different. By 1969 he was deep in the Ladbroke Grove beatnik scene, hanging out with the anarchists and freaks for whom the underground had been an innately political and drug-fuelled experience. It suited him down to the ground. Took's unhappy upbringing meant that he was always going to respond to a close community that treated him like family, and that's what he found in the Ladbroke Grove set. Deviants singer and general anarchist-about-town Mick Farren, who in his book *Give The Anarchist A Cigarette,* described his clique as the 'Ladbroke Grove degenerate elite'[6] and, in a later piece for *Mojo,* 'the Bash Street Kids on drugs'. Also hanging around were Syd Barrett, recently ejected from Pink Floyd after his prolific acid habit had rendered him a liability, and the rowdier wing of the Pretty Things.

This was the darker end of the hippy dream, in which drug use became endemic, LSD blazed through bright minds until they burnt out and smack addiction was rife. Heroin use in the UK spiked into epidemic proportions for the first time toward the end of the hippy era. Prior to 1960 almost all recorded heroin addiction came from therapeutic use – mainly in people who had been prescribed it for pain relief. That changed during the sixties, with cheap heroin imported from North Africa, China and Afghanistan, partly thanks to the boom in immigration, partly brought directly into the scene via the 'hippie trail' – a fad that involved travelling overland from Turkey through the Middle East and on to India and Nepal, halting in Kabul or Goa. The blissful state induced by the drug appealed to the hippy mindset; it was the ultimate 'out of it' high, and its origin in the East tied into the oriental fetishisation that was bound up in counter cultural thinking. It was also, of course, lethally addictive. Further souring the mood was the introduction of organised crime into underground circles: Increased pressure from the government and changes in drug laws criminalised many of the substances beloved of the narcotically inclined. With no legal routes, the trade in hard drugs was turned over to an organised black market with its fair share of gangsters.

> 'The whole vibe had changed, the whole happy hippie pot-smoking thing had changed to smack, the whole Chinese heroin thing had completely changed the atmosphere. Because almost all the people that you knew previously, had partied with and clubbed with and this and that, they were all doing smack.'
>
> Underground scene stalwart Bob Rowberry, quoted in
> *A Hero For High Times* by Ian Marchant.

---

4. One of his few acid experiences was a result of being spiked; his subsequent trip was terrifying enough for him to never go near LSD again.
5. He was okay with the free love, though.
6. Another friend, Larry Wallis, interviewed by Fee Warner for her book *A Trip Through Ladbroke Grove,* described Farren and Took as 'the fucking heavyweights of the underground'.

Marc, his girlfriend June – who was increasingly taking on a behind the scenes role as an unofficial manager – and Visconti had no intention of letting Steve Took, a loose cannon who had already been busted and jailed once for possession of a small amount of pot, drag Tyrannosaurus Rex down into this murky world, just as things had started to look up. The grubby company that Steve was keeping worried Marc, who sensed momentum gathering behind his trip to the top and didn't want it spoiled. It came to a head during a show at London's Lyceum when Steve invited members of The Deviants and The Pretty Things onstage to plough messily through some Bo Diddley numbers. Bolan walked off.

Tyrannosaurus Rex were now being managed by the Bryan Morrison Agency, who helpfully also handled The Pretty Things, Syd Barrett and The Deviants. The organisation was so desperate to keep Steve Took away from bad influences and protect Marc, whom they considered their great hope, they went as far as to issue an edict banning all of their bands from playing on one another's records. Took, who was naturally collaborative, had already been jamming on current Pretty Things' drummer Twink's new project[7], and had played on tracks by Mick Farran and Syd Barrett as well as a Radio One session with David Bowie the previous year, handily sleeping on Tony Visconti's couch on a day when his services would come in useful. His management's ultimatum felt like a personal attack and sent him into a narcotic spiral that effectively spelled the end of the Bolan/Took version of Tyrannosaurus Rex. As Tony Visconti put it: 'Marc wanted to be a teen idol, he simply couldn't have a drug addict in his band'.[8]

There was, by now, a feeling in the Rex camp that *Unicorn* was a platform that could be built on, rather than a ceiling that stopped progress. Musically, Marc, still working with Took at this point, was expanding. Following the recording of *Unicorn* he had purchased a white Fender Stratocaster, and was becoming increasingly confident in wielding it. There was already electric guitar on much of the album (Marc had borrowed Visconti's), though it was used for texture rather than as a lead instrument; the duo now felt they could expand the notion of what Tyrannosaurus Rex was away from the fey folkies of 1967 and 1968. The result was 'King Of The Rumbling Spires', one of the great overlooked Marc Bolan singles. There were no traces of the dainty and mystical band of *My People Were Fair and Had Sky In Their Hair* here. 'King of The Rumbling Spires', featuring Took pounding his toy drum kit and Marc chugging on his Strat, is a *heavy* track; full sounding with fuzzed up guitars and Tony Visconti providing bass. A canny Chris Welch at *Melody Maker* dubbed the tune 'electrified teenybop', though the song itself has a heavier vibe than

---

7. Presumably they had run out of available drummers called 'Viv'.
8. Took was baffled by the idea that consorting with Notting Hill's most out-of-it rabble rousers could in any way harm the image of the band. 'I'd go, "What image?"' Took told *NME* many years later. 'I'm Steve Took, a well-known drug addict.'

this suggests. Welch predicted that it could finally give Bolan his big hit, while the *Daily Mirror* claimed the new commercial sound was going to 'ruin the underground image of Tyrannosaurus Rex'. They were both wrong. Though 'King of the Rumbling Spire' sold better than 'Pewter Suitor' at the start of the year, it still failed to make the top 40, stalling at 44.

Marc, much like he had been with 'The Wizard', was ahead of his time. Had 'King of the Rumbling Spires' come out in 1970, with heavier singles being more palatable, things might have been different. Had he released it in 1971 it would have been a guaranteed number one, entirely of a piece with the huge hits that he would enjoy at the time. This isn't the fey sound of Tyrannosaurus Rex, this is unmistakably a *T.Rex* single, though it would be a year before the band name was officially changed. Marc was now hurtling toward the future. He needed to hurry though if he wanted to get there ahead of the competition, because David Bowie had just written one of the best pop singles of all time...

1968 through 1970 was probably the point, outside of the mid-late Seventies, when David and Marc were at their closest; linked through both Tony Visconti and their shared history of being pinged from pillar to post by the Sixties pop-wannabe machine. For the first time in a couple of years they were moving in the same circles: David's work with Lindsay Kemp brought him into the underground scene of Middle Earth, the Roundhouse and freakout art happenings – in other words, the world in which Marc Bolan was currently among the top dogs. Bowie had started performing music regularly for the first time since parting ways with The Buzz in late 1966; his new act was a folk/dance/mime/poetry mixed-media group, initially called Turquoise, which also included his new girlfriend, Hermione Farthingale. Marc, June, David and Hermione would take drives out into the country, staying at Hermione's parents' posh pile in Sussex, sometimes accompanied by other friends in their circle. The mood in the little clique was briefly soured when Marc brought along Steve Took and another mutual friend, the photographer Ray Stevenson, turning the day into an 'impromptu' Tyrannosaurus Rex photoshoot. David, with some justification, felt that a pleasant weekend in the country with friends had been hijacked and his girlfriend's hospitality taken advantage of. Still, since it was exactly the sort of thing he himself would have done, the bitterness didn't last.

David and Hermione had met the previous year at Lindsay Kemp's dance classes, and were paired together during rehearsals for Kemp's BBC2 film *The Pistol Shot*, in which they both had small parts. Born Hermione Dennis (Farthingale was a stage name), David's new creative partner was a dancer, training in ballet and acting. She was a tall and elegant redhead with expressive eyes and beautiful manners – David was completely smitten, more or less on sight. The two became romantically involved very soon afterwards, though Bowie – ever one to compartmentalise the different aspects of his life – initially kept the relationship from both Lindsay Kemp and Ken Pitt, both of whom had a tendency to be a little possessive.[9] The Bowie/Farthingale partnership (which technically was a Jones/Dennis partnership) was instantly intense and creative. Hermione would later describe them as 'twin souls, very alike ... I was fascinated by this fey, elfin creature.'[10]. Within a few weeks David had moved out of Ken Pitt's flat into a top-floor bedsit in South Kensington, shared with Hermione; bringing him further away from Pitt's influence and closer to Tony Visconti (in Earls Court) and the Bolan-Child residence (in Notting Hill) – all three, Bolan, Visconti and Farthingale, were influences of which Ken Pitt, for one reason or another, never really approved. Though Pitt was still working hard for David, and David was still receptive to his ideas, the split in their perspectives was beginning to show. Mary Finnegan, whom Bowie lodged with in 1969, reported in her memoir that he complained about Pitt from the very first day she met him. 'He tells me he sees himself as a radical singer-songwriter', she wrote in *Psychedelic Suburbia*, 'but his manager, whose name I'm told is Ken Pitt, wants to turn him into a mainstream pop idol.'

The three piece band initially conceived as Turquoise was a bridge between Bowie's ambition as a singer/songwriter and his more recent interest in performance art, and it's interesting that its development coincided with Ken Pitt's doomed cabaret experiment. Turquoise's set comprised some acoustic Bowie originals – including sprightly new number, 'Ching-a-Ling'[11], 'When I'm Five' and the more folkish moments from the *David Bowie* LP like 'Sell Me a Coat', a cover of 'Strawberry Fields Forever', a dance piece performed by David and Hermione, a mime called 'the mask' performed by David alone[12] and a rendition of a Roger McGough poem, 'At lunchtime – A Story of Love'[13]. Considering that the cabaret set prepared by Pitt and Bowie also included Beatles songs, a mime and a Roger McGough poem, you'd be forgiven for

---

9. He maintained something of a triple-life at this point, hiding his time with Hermione by telling Pitt he was with Kemp, who he claimed was ill, and telling Kemp he was visiting his parents. He was only rumbled when Ken called Lindsay and inquired after his health. Neither were best pleased at finding out they had been played, particularly as Kemp was still smarting from the incident on tour and Pitt had just had to cover for David, who hadn't turned up for an important meeting with a Broadway producer during which, it turned out, he'd been with Hermione.

10. These lines are quoted in a feature based around a hastily conducted interview with the *Daily Mail* in 2016. The Mail tracked Hermione down in the wake of David's death and she bristles in the brief piece, saying 'I have spent all these years not speaking about me and him, so why should I start now? I want to remain true to what he always appreciated about me, which was that I never spoke about him and never kissed and told.' A class act. Nevertheless, the reporter – whose name, genuinely, is David Jones – managed to squeeze a few quotes out of her.

11. Hermione reckons this was an attempt to write a song that occupied the same sonic space as Tyrannosaurus Rex. Visconti was able to convince Platz to let him record it, though it remained unreleased for years. It's a perky, almost childish number that gets by on whimsy and charm. Despite the Visconti production, however, it really doesn't sound like Tyrannosaurus Rex.

12. This Marcel Marceau inspired routine was dubbed by Lindsay Kemp 'a load of old shit' during an interview for the documentary *David Bowie: Finding Fame*.

13. It's unlikely this latter was included in the trio's first performance, which was at the Roundhouse supporting The Scaffold, a band which actually included Roger McGough.

wondering why Bowie was so keen to avoid that route. It was a matter, of course, of context. In a cabaret, David would be performing to a club crowd on a night out in the West End. He'd be a turn. On the alternative circuit, playing venues like the Roundhouse and the Drury Lane Arts Lab, he'd be part of a scene, performing to a turned-on audience out to appreciate the art of like-minded scenesters. One was naff as anything, the other completely hip. Both involved David Bowie performing David Bowie songs. In some cases *the same* David Bowie songs.

The new act's first performance, on 14 September 1968, was at Camden's Roundhouse at a benefit show organised by Blackhill Enterprises, at the time also handling Tyrannosaurus Rex – It was Marc that had made the introduction. Present that night was Calvin Mark Lee, a beautiful, bisexual Asian American record exec with a PhD in Pharmaceutical Chemistry who customarily wore a trademark iridescent metallic disc adhered to his forehead, with whom David had already began a sexual relationship (presumably one that was unknown to Ken Pitt, Lindsay Kemp and Hermione Farthingale – David was not one to mix oil and water). With Calvin was his friend and occasional lover Angela Barnett, the future Angie Bowie, who recalled the gig in her memoir, *Backstage Passes*:

> 'David's act fit in perfectly at the Roundhouse. He was intense, intelligent, and "out there" in the right folky-trippy way. And although he was performing as part of a trio that night—Feathers, with John Hutchinson[14] and Hermione Farthingale—it was clearly his show. Charisma, you call it? Power, I call it.'

As Angela notes, David's time on the underground scene and his work on movement had magnified his stage presence to the point that even here, as part of a somewhat po-faced 'mixed media' trio, his rockstar potential absolutely shone through. This was no longer the try-hard wannabe R&B frontman of a million stolen beat groups, this was something new. David was stepping into his potential. His songwriting had evolved too. He was less content to croon, less wry, less knowing, more himself. There was still something of Anthony Newley in his voice – there always would be – but it had taken on a new complexity, partly as a result of his latest musical crush; Jacques Brel, whose 'Court of Amsterdam' was soon added to the set.

Bowie had been away from the pop scene for over a year – in theory the failure of his debut album should have killed his career stone dead; instead it had given him the room to expand creatively away from the self-conscious glare and external pressure of the mid-sixties pop market. *David Bowie* had begat a new David Bowie, more than the sum of his parts. It was a happier Bowie too

---

14. This is likely just Angela misremembering – John 'Hutch' Hutchinson, erstwhile of The Buzz, would replace Tony within the month, but did not perform at the Roundhouse show.

– John 'Hutch' Hutchinson, who replaced Tony Hill on acoustic guitar shortly after the first few Turquoise shows, at which point the trio renamed themselves Feathers, remembers a far more relaxed and comfortable in his own skin David than the one he had backed as a member of The Buzz – a change he partly put down to the sophisticated and easy-going Hermione. This was a contented and grown up David Bowie, or at least a *more* contented and grown up Bowie than the Soho mod so desperate to make it big back in 1966. Feathers played a handful of shows over the next few months; it was amongst the happiest times David had known, a time of musical chemistry, honeymoon-period love and a feeling of boundless creative potential.

Alas, it couldn't last. The couple were perpetually broke and as much fun as playing folk songs on the mattress-decked floor of the Arts Lab was, passing around the hat at the end of the gig, Hermione's heart was ultimately in her dance career – now stalling at the expense of David's enthusiasm for Feathers. In November 1968, around the time another Tyrannosaurus Rex album was reminding David how far he had fallen behind, Hermione passed the final round of auditions for a huge MGM movie musical, *Song of Norway*. It would mean a long shoot on location in New York, it would mean the end of Feathers, and it would inevitably mean the end of her relationship with David. Hermione would be leaving in early 1969. David was heartbroken. That agony did, however, hit the ignition switch on arguably the most important release of his career. Commencing countdown. Engines on.

Chapter Nineteen

Commencing Countdown

Ten.

Ken Pitt, still frankly baffled by the whole idea of Feathers, had been working on his latest brainwave intended to nudge David into the public consciousness: a sixty-minute television film initially to be called *The David Bowie Show*, but ultimately titled *Love You Till Tuesday*. He'd had the idea while filming a TV appearance with Bowie in Germany earlier in the year[1], and spent much of the latter half of 1968 putting the necessary funding and distribution in place. Some optimistic headlines indicated that the film would net Bowie somewhere in the region of £10,000, largely from German sources, however the proposed funding fell away and Pitt eventually paid for the whole thing himself. The film would involve promo clips for several Bowie solo songs, mostly taken from his Newley period, plus Feathers performing 'Ching-A-Ling'[2] and a new version of Bowie's 'Sell Me A Coat'. Hermione, who left for New York to film *Song of Norway* almost immediately after her parts were completed, appears along with Hutch in the promo for 'When I Live My Dream', the obvious sadness of her impending departure shining a new light on an already poignant piece as the pair held hands, danced slowly and gazed at each other wistfully. Also included was a mime piece, 'The Mask', which David had been performing at Feathers gigs[3], and finally a dramatic mini-sci fi piece, in which Bowie is blasted into space – with weightlessness achieved by a combination of a camera placed on its side, positioned so the floor isn't visible, and David's mime skills. The segment is, visually at least, probably the weakest and most dated in the whole of the film (only half of which was completed – it was abandoned with just thirty minutes shot and not released until the 1980s), featuring *Barbarella*-style space-babes and a cheap, tin foil costume and visor. The music that accompanied it, however, was something new for David – a

---

1. Germany and the Netherlands were amongst the few territories where David's Deram records had managed to achieve some modest success. Pitt had excellent connections in both countries, and as a result Bowie appeared on Dutch and German television several times in 67 and 68
2. The video, featuring the trio sitting cross-legged on cushions, makes the group seem more like Rod, Jane and Freddie, the in-house band on the 80s children's TV classic *Rainbow*. Hermione Farthingale reckons it's totally misrepresentative of what Feathers actually were.
3. This story, about a man who is killed by his own stage persona, foreshadows some of David's fears in the 70s, when he felt his Ziggy Stardust character was beginning to overwhelm him. 'The Mask' is also probably the origin of a persistent urban legend about Bowie telling a nervous child that he wears an invisible mask at all times to give him confidence.

melancholic duet between Bowie and Hutch that captured a unique feeling of alienation that felt very distant from the hippy-era's optimism and whimsy. In a nod to one of 1968's biggest movie releases, it was called 'Space Oddity'.

Nine.

According to Ken Pitt, 'Space Oddity' was the result of his request for a new piece for the *Love You Till Tuesday* film. 'I thought that the script badly needed a brand new song,' he wrote in *The Pitt Report*, 'a very special piece of material that would dramatically demonstrate David's remarkable inventiveness and would probably be the high spot of the production.' We don't have a date for this conversation, though it was certainly in the closing months of 1968. A year later, Bowie told the *NME* that he'd written 'Space Oddity' in November; while the earliest demos were recorded in December 1968 and January 1969 at David and Hermione's flat on Clareville Grove, South Kensington. It was the first song he played for Mary Finnegan, who became his new landlady – and, predictably, new lover – at her home in the London suburb of Beckenham a month or so later. For a while, David's opening gambit for meeting anyone seems to have been to play them 'Space Oddity'.[4]

The piece was originally composed on a Stylophone; a cheap 'pocket organ' played with a stylus, that generated a buzzing, space-age tone similar to the one that powers The Tornados/Joe Meek classic 'Telstar'. Though its size and ease-of-use made it seem like a toy (which, in fairness, it basically was) it was also a genuine, if limited, proto-synthesiser with a distinctive sound, readily available and cheap as chips at a time when actual synths, as used by The Beatles on *Abbey Road* that year, were monstrously expensive. The Stylophone was apparently a gift from Marc Bolan (something which both David and Marc remembered, though Tony Visconti maintains that it came from Ken Pitt), which makes sense given Tyrannosaurus Rex's association with toy instruments. Its sci-fi-style and other-worldly tone clearly sparked David's imagination.

Bowie added folky 12-string[5] chords to the notes he'd picked out on the little organ, which were then slightly jazzed up by Hutch, who also sang joint lead-vocals on early versions. With Hermione's departure, Bowie and Hutch had decided to continue as a folk duo (which they called, with some imagination, 'Bowie & Hutch'), and had divided the song's two characters ('Ground Control' and 'Major Tom') between them. When they performed live, Hutch would play David's 12-string, while David played the Stylophone. A few months later after Hutch returned to his wife and child and a more dependable income in Scarborough, dashing hopes that they could become 'The British Simon and

---

4. Frankly, if you'd written 'Space Oddity' you would do this too.
5. Though his guitar only had eleven strings due to one of the tuning pegs falling off – clearly David didn't have Marc Bolan's way with a pair of pliers.

Garfunkel', Bowie would perform 'Space Oddity' alone, while strumming along to a pre-recorded tape.

Despite what Hutch describes in his memoir (also imaginatively titled *Bowie & Hutch*) as the 'horrible buzzing sound' of the Stylophone, the two instruments pair beautifully, with the Stylophone's bass notes taking on the melancholy air of a cello played by a particularly musical, if rather depressed Cyberman, over which the ringing sound of a twelve-string guitar sounds bright and warm. Even the very early 'Space Oddity' demos, knocked out on a tape recorder in Clareville Grove, capture the unearthly and yet somehow achingly human atmosphere of the song.

Over this backdrop, Bowie wrote a paean to existential loneliness with his tale of a spaceman who drifts slowly into the cosmos until he becomes one with it – an absolutely direct lift from the finale of Kubrick's *2001: A Space Odyssey*, the title of which, of course, gives the song its punny name. The film had been a huge hit when it premiered in London the previous summer; an astonishing technical achievement that captured the era's fascination with space travel in state-of-the-art visual effects, coated in a uniquely Kubrickian sterility. Fifty years on, it's still a remarkable film. David saw it several times, while – or so he claims – high as a kite; the trippy visuals (particularly in the 'stargate' sequence) firing his already stimulated imagination[6]. Though this is a song with a fictional narrative and defined characters, it is clear that David had poured much of himself into it. 'Space Oddity' has an outer skin of science fiction, but the bones of a breakup song. His separation from Hermione would loom over all of the songs he wrote in the following months, most obviously 'Letters to Hermione', but it's 'Space Oddity' that best captures the peculiarly specific pain of a broken heart. It's a song about abandonment – Major Tom is, at the end of all things, absolutely alone.

---

6. The subject of David Bowie and drugs is an interesting one, which really belongs in a discussion of his seventies work. Many people who knew him in the sixties claim that he rarely went near drugs of any kind, simply holding and then passing on the endless spliffs circling every underground event worth its salt. It's another thing he had in common with Marc Bolan. In Marc's case he would tell people he was afraid of unleashing his inner demons, though in reality it's more likely he was worried about making a prat of himself. David, meanwhile, genuinely *was* scared that herbal or chemical enhancement would unlock some of the mental instability he saw in his mother's family, of which he was terrified. He would occasionally wax lyrical on-stage at the Arts Lab he founded in Beckenham in the Spring of 1969 about the dangers of drug use, and even hosted a lecture on the subject that was intended to bring older and younger people together to understand the issues. However, Mary Finnegan – with whom Bowie lived, worked and maintained a relationship with for several months, says that she and David would regularly get stoned. Bowie has also hinted that he tried heroin around this time, and there's some speculation that this dalliance is obliquely referenced in the lyrics to 'Space Oddity'. Hutch, who spent a lot of time with David around then, reckoned that this was nonsense. Bowie's tendency to ruthlessly compartmentalise his relationships makes it hard to say anything for sure.

Eight.

'Space Oddity' was a remarkable leap in Bowie's songwriting, and one that floored almost all of his friends. Ken Pitt was delighted, of course – though if Angie Bowie's recollections are to be believed, he didn't see a future in songs like this at all ('According to Ken, "Space Oddity" was a fluke, a novelty that meant nothing to David's future. There was no career to be had in rock' is how she remembers David's rants in her *Backstage Passes* memoir. Pitt himself often described the song more in terms of a launching pad). Bowie had excitedly played the demo to Marc Bolan, whose opinion he hugely respected and upon whom he often tested ideas; Marc's response was apparently one of pure brotherly joy ('Davie! It's gonna be a hit, Davie!') Mary Finnegan thought it was incredible, as did her two young children, who were thrilled by this strange, exciting man who had come to live with them. Finnegan recalls her son excitedly drawing pictures of spacemen and rockets, his own imagination fired. When it came time to shoot the 'Space Oddity' sequence for the *Love You Till Tuesday* film, Pitt remembered being taken aback by the cast and crew singing snatches of the song during their lunch break – something that hadn't happened with any of the other numbers – and realising that he may have something special on his hands.

Pitt didn't realise it at the time, of course, but 'Space Oddity' essentially rendered the *Love You Till Tuesday* film obsolete. The song was a stargate's journey beyond the Newley-style knees-ups and crooning of the title track or 'When I Live My Dream', both in terms of their composition and their themes. Those songs were, by now, nearly four years old. Even the newer numbers, 'Let Me Sleep Beside You' and 'When I'm Five', sounded like they came from a different era. The new addition leapfrogged those earlier influences of music hall, classic pop and balladeering – the area of David's repertoire with which Pitt was clearly most comfortable. Instead 'Space Oddity' had soaked in the Bee Gees, John Lennon, Simon & Garfunkel, Bob Dylan and even Tyrannosaurus Rex, and made no attempt to hide the fact: like many late sixties hits, at a time when styles and flourishes were freely traded and explicitly acknowledged, 'Space Oddity' carried its cool-but-relatively-conventional musical influences on its sleeve[7]. Its emotional and intellectual heart, however, was entirely David's own. Here he captured something innately of the age; a sense of the weirdness that was hanging in the air as the hippie dream slipped toward the unknown future of the 1970s. The decade that had changed everything had nearly run its course, and that brought with it an existential displacement which 'Space Oddity' captures masterfully. Bowie's earliest work, starting with 'Liza Jane', had sounded like every other pop act around at the time, more or less simultaneously, while his first album's desperation to be totally unlike any of

---

7. For The Doors to peck at.

the other mainstream pop released that year actually made it very apt for 1967[8]. 'Space Oddity' was pinned to 1969 in a completely different way. This was David Bowie's response to the death of a decade, a creative idea that only he, uniquely, could have generated. He'd been Pete Townshend, he'd been Howlin' Wolf, he'd been Anthony Newley, he'd been Lindsay Kemp. Now, finally, he was David Bowie. His space-age hymn to alienation and loneliness perfectly captured its author just as much as it did this last gasp of the sixties.

Seven.

Armed with incredible new material, Bowie was finally able to secure a new record deal – his first in two years. The groundwork had been done by Calvin Mark Lee, David's friend and occasional lover,[9] who worked at Mercury Records; an American label distributed through Philips in the UK. Lee was convinced that Mercury would be the label that finally took David Bowie into the mainstream[10]. He had Bowie & Hutch cut a set of acoustic tracks on a basic tape recorder, later released as *The Mercury Demos,* to send to his bosses overseas. The tape opened with 'Space Oddity', and included other folk-influenced new Bowie songs: 'Janine', 'Letter To Hermione', 'Conversation Piece' and 'An Occasional Dream'. With it, Lee was able to find allies at the label in the US, particularly Rob Oberman in the promotions department, a former music journalist who would become one of David's biggest (and only) stateside supporters in the coming years, and Simon Hayes, a Brit working high up in the firm's New York office.

Closer to home, Lee worked on his boss' girlfriend, Angela Barnett, first seducing her and then taking her to a Feathers show so that she could enthuse wildly about David to her partner, Mercury London boss, Lou Reizner. It worked … in a round-about kind of way. Reizner, who was never particularly fond of David's music, reluctantly succumbed to her enthusiasm and made the necessary calls. Angela, meanwhile, encountered Bowie again a few months later, once more in the company of Lee, fell hopelessly in love with him and scarcely left his side for the next four years – much to the surprise and annoyance of Mary Finnegan,[11] who was downgraded from lover back to landlady.

Lee's calculated campaign ultimately worked, despite the reservations of Ken Pitt who felt that Mercury wasn't a serious enough presence in the UK to be worth considering. Even Pitt had to be pragmatic: no other companies were

---

8. Unfortunately The Beatles, The Kinks and the rest had all had the same idea.
9. Like many of David's lovers during the sixties and seventies, Lee would later have a vague suspicion he was simply being indulged as a means to an end.
10. Presumably he hadn't spoken to the collection of broken-hearted A&R men David's career had left despairing in his wake at Vocalion, Parlophone, Pye and Deram.
11. Mary Finnegan's memoir, *Psychedelic Suburbia* is a cracking read for anyone interested in this specific period of Bowie's career. Finnegan is an experienced writer and journalist, which makes her memoir a cut above many of the others written by Bowie's bandmates and acquaintances.

knocking down his door to sign a consistently unsuccessful singer/songwriter who dabbled in mime and performance art. Pitt was able to negotiate a deal for both the single and, impressively, an album – which Angela Bowie takes some credit for, having apparently sweet-talked Mercury president Irving Green into going the whole hog and doing an LP. David signed his new record deal on 20 June 1969, the same day that recording began on 'Space Oddity'.[12]

Six.

Pitt's first choice to produce the new material had been George Martin, the genial studio genius responsible for the remarkable run of cutting edge Beatles recordings that began in 1962 with 'Love Me Do' and, as far anyone knew at that point, was still going strong. Martin, after ignoring Pitt for several weeks, sent a message via his secretary saying that he didn't care for the song ('GEORGE MARTIN IS FALLIBLE,' scrawled an exasperated Ken Pitt in his journal.[13]) The obvious next choice was Tony Visconti; the New Yorker knew Bowie's writing inside and out, and as David was still signed to Essex Music for his publishing, using Visconti would mean keeping things in the family. There was one issue, however: Tony Visconti *hated* 'Space Oddity'.

For what it's worth, Visconti has gone on record many, many times over the years to say that he was deeply wrong about Bowie's breakthrough single[14]. 'My mistake was seeing what was wrong externally with this song—the subtle rip-offs,' he wrote in *Bowie, Bolan and the Brooklyn Boy*. 'What I didn't realise at the time was that the music was just window dressing for a subtler subject— alienation—and the setting was outer space.' Visconti had quite rightly clocked the catalogue of contemporary influences that Bowie was channelling, notably John Lennon's post-*White Album* output and the Bee Gees' breakthrough American hit 'New York Mining Disaster 1941'. As a self-confessed 'principled young hippy', he also objected to what he felt was a cynical attempt to cash-in on the much-publicised US space-shot. He thought that 'Space Oddity' was essentially a novelty track exploiting the Apollo missions. It's something that Bowie always denied.

Space travel was certainly a fashionable topic at the time, with the whole world fascinated by the Apollo missions and the astonishing idea that a man would soon be landing on the moon. David, unconsciously or not, had tapped into that same mood; merging it with his stoned experiences watching *2001* the previous year. However, 'Space Oddity' was far more than a jaunty celebration

---

12. This was the second proper go at the song. Earlier in the year, Bowie and Hitch had recorded a more lightweight take, complete with an ocarina solo, for use in the film. It was clear to all involved that a punchier rendition was required for the single.

13. Whether Martin, at that moment making *Abbey Road*, his final album with The Beatles, ever even heard the song is up for debate.

14. 'I knew you'd come around!' was Bowie's response when Visconti apologised directly many years later, according to *Bowie, Bolan and the Brooklyn Boy*.

of NASA's finest. Bowie's intention, on a surface level, was to humanise the astronaut experience: 'The publicity image of a spaceman at work is of an automaton rather than a human being,' he told *International Times* in 1969, 'and my Major Tom is nothing if not a human being.' The song also served to puncture the hero-worship and pomposity that surrounded the Apollo missions: in Bowie's lyrics, the hero bathes in despair, while on Earth the media is scrambling to find out what brand of shirt he favours.

One potential worry here, as evidenced by 'principled hippy' Visconti, would be the reaction of the ultra-hip underground crowd; the Peel fans who flocked to throw flowers at Marc Bolan's tiny feet. The space race was hugely unpopular among radicals and revolutionaries, who regarded it as a waste of resources, and an example of geo-political machismo[15] and Cold War posturing. Fortunately, there was another element to 'Space Oddity''s thematic appeal: the hippies may have been against space travel as a form of resource-intensive proxy warfare, but they *loved* science fiction. The importance of sci-fi in the counterculture is often overshadowed by the back-to-nature drippiness of the Tolkien crowd, yet it's absolutely there if you look for it. The sixties saw the cementing of SF fandom in Britain and the growth of what was known as the 'New Wave of Science Fiction', moving on significantly from the boys-own adventure stories of the fifties and early sixties.

Short story magazines including *Science Fantasy* and *New Worlds* (the latter of which was edited by underground favourite Michael Moorcock) sold in their droves, with writers like Moorcock, J.G. Ballard and Brian Aldiss exploring hippy ideas of utopia and dystopia while crafting pointed anti-war parables and thinly concealed LSD-inspired landscapes. This chimes perfectly with the closing half hour of *2001: A Space Odyssey* itself (the film's co-writer, Arthur C. Clarke, was a giant presence in British SF fandom). 'Space Oddity' had built-in appeal for both the mainstream end of the pop market, with an audience desperate to know what the label inside Buzz Aldrin's collar said, and the radical underground, turned-on by its themes of alienation and anti-materialism. Both groups were convinced the song was aimed at them.[16]

While there are those that look back in bafflement at some of Bowie's sixties decisions – 'The Laughing Gnome', the miming – 'Space Oddity' sits in the opposite camp. It's commonly acknowledged as a masterpiece; David's first truly great moment and one of the best things he would ever write. To dismiss it as 'novelty' or a 'cash in' feels absurdly reductive and short-sighted. Again, as with 'The Laughing Gnome', that's judging the song by modern standards. At the

---

15. Have you seen the shape of the Saturn V rocket?
16. Terry Pratchett, who would one day become a colossus of British fantasy, was born a year after David, and in 1968 wrote a short story for *New Worlds*, 'Night Dweller' that echoed some of the themes of 'Space Oddity' – of floating into the unknown void; though in Pratchett's story something nasty is in that void with you. Despite Pratchett's later reputation, it is not a funny piece.

time it was still absolutely commonplace for short-lived acts capitalising on the memes of the day to be smash hits. Just a few months earlier The Bonzo Dog Band had a hit with the 'The Urban Spaceman', The Scaffold had managed a recent number one with a cod-musical hall shanty called 'Lily The Pink', Lulu had huge success with the fairly absurd 'Boom-Bang-A-Bang' and in August of that year the short-lived Zager & Evans had a one-hit-wonder number one with 'In the Year 2525 (Exordium & Terminus)', a song with a similarly creepy, alienated science fiction vibe to David's own. The year would close out with Rolf Harris claiming the Christmas number one with 'Two Little Boys', a frankly upsetting children's song about dying in war. 'Novelty' was hardly a dirty word in the music industry of the late sixties. Novelty sold.

In a sense, though, Visconti was actually right – from Mercury's perspective (and that of Ken Pitt) 'Space Oddity' *was* cashing in on the moon landings. They just didn't consider that necessarily to be a bad thing. A highly topical single that sounded like an obvious hit was part of David's appeal to Mercury, though their commitment to an album suggests that they saw more potential in David Bowie than a quick flash in the pan buck. Initially, however, the topicality actually worked against the song. Though many people saw no further than the space-age theme and catchy chorus, someone at Radio One was listening a little closer and BBC radio refused to playlist the song, deciding that a doomed-space-mission storyline might be in bad taste ahead of the extremely dangerous Apollo 11 launch.[17]

Five.

'Space Oddity', produced by Gus Dudgeon (who had none of Tony Visconti's hippy principles), featuring bass from a young session pro called Herbie Flowers and mellotron[18] by a youthful polymath called Rick Wakeman[19] was released to moderate fanfare on 11 July in both the UK and US, the week before the Apollo 11 mission got underway. London crowds had already been introduced to the song the previous week at the Rolling Stones' famous free concert in Hyde Park, where it was played several times over the PA to the 200,000-strong

17. The Apollo 11 mission was so precarious that US president Richard Nixon had two speeches ready on his desk – one to announce to the American public that all had gone well, and another to deliver in the event of their deaths, stranded just as Major Tom was.

18. The mellotron is an analogue precursor to the sampler, with samples recorded to actual tape and attached to each key. It enjoyed some popularity in the late sixties after The Beatles used it on 'Strawberry Fields Forever'. Dudgeon brought in Wakeman on Visconti's recommendation, as he'd used him on the Junior's Eyes album earlier in the year and said he was familiar with the instrument. Later, of course, Dudgeon would realise that whatever went on under the hood, a mellotron had a standard keyboard and any pianist could probably have managed the job eventually.

19. Both Flowers (who Dudgeon booked because he had a 'fucking cool name') and Wakeman would bridge the London boy divide in the seventies. Flowers played bass on Bowie's *Diamond Dogs* tour and later joined Bolan in T.Rex, while Wakeman played piano on both David's 'Life On Mars' and Marc's 'Get It On'.

crowd. It was also broadcast between acts at a pop proms event at the Albert Hall featuring Fleetwood Mac and Led Zeppelin.

The reviews were amongst Bowie's best ever. Most enthusiastic of all was *Disc & Music Echo*'s David Bowie correspondent Penny Valentine, who claims that she made a bet with her colleagues that the song would be a huge hit. Valentine was overjoyed to find that David had dropped his 'nasty knack for sounding like Tony Newley', saying that she 'listened spellbound throughout, panting to know the outcome of poor Major Tom and his trip into the outer hemisphere … the sound is amazing.' The shrewd critic also took careful note of the influence of The Moody Blues, Simon and Garfunkel, The Beatles and, very specifically, the Bee Gees' 'New York Mining Disaster'. Chris Welsh at *Melody Maker*, another Bowie (and Bolan) champion, predicted the song could be a 'huge hit and escalate Bowie to the top', though he too notes the similarity to the Bee Gees, while *Record Mirror*'s review was tiny but positive ('An off beat, pertinent, topical production, full of gimmicky sounds but also full of an authoritative vocal performance from David. Commended. Four stars,' ran its write up, in full.)

Despite the BBC issuing a blanket just-in-case ban on space-based records that week, many in the Bowie camp were anticipating a hit, and in the case of Bowie and Pitt, absolutely desperate for one. After so many years and so many failures, Ken Pitt even resorted – apparently for the only time in his career – to trying to buy the single into the charts. Bowie had been approached by a shadowy figure called 'Tony Martin' who allegedly worked in advertising at *NME*. Martin, who apparently kept his sunglasses on at all times, reckoned that for a mere £300 he could guarantee a top ten placement in both the *NME* and *Record Retailer* charts. Determined to get his boy a hit 'by means fair or foul' (*The Pitt Report* again), Pitt stumped up the first half of the cash the next day.[20]

On 24 July, as the world watched, NASA astronauts Neil Armstrong and Buzz Aldrin became the first humans in history to set foot on the surface of the moon. At Mary Finnegan's house in Beckenham, David's home since the spring, housemates and friends, including Angela and the photographer Ray Stevenson, crowded around Mary's black and white set to watch the BBC's coverage of one of humanity's most astonishing achievements. There was screaming and crying, with Mary and Angela, David's most recent lovers, clinging to each other as they watched the impossible scenes – it wasn't *just* that man had landed on the moon, it was that the BBC, surprising everyone, had chosen to soundtrack the moment with David Bowie's 'Space Oddity'. Somewhere across London, at the home of an as-yet unidentified girl, David himself was watching too,

---

20. In the *Pitt Report*, Ken made no attempt to excuse his actions, quoting Oscar Wilde by saying that instead 'I explain them', before launching into the history, mechanics and innate unfairness of the British record industry, going on for a page and a half. Twenty years later it was clearly still niggling at him.

gobsmacked, and thanking his lucky stars that the music department at BBC Television paid a lot less attention to lyrics than the one at BBC Radio. Amazing reviews? A dodgy chart buy-in? A showcase soundtracking a pivotal point in human history, watched by most of the country? 'Space Oddity' couldn't fail to be a hit.

Four.

'Space Oddity' became the tenth consecutive David Bowie single to flop. At least at first. In truth, the BBC's ban on space songs had killed its chances of being an immediate post-moon-shot hit stone dead. Most people wouldn't have heard 'Space Oddity' until the BBC One moon coverage, and pop fans were more likely to be watching the popular satirist David Frost hosting a 'Gala Moon Party' on ITV, featuring performances by Cilla Black, Lulu, Mary Hopkin and Cliff Richard. Despite the mass exposure, few BBC viewers actually went out to find a copy. Bowie was still a no-name, and Philips, Mercury's UK distributors, didn't exactly hammer the publicity. There were decent reviews in *Disc & Music Echo* and *Melody Maker*, sure, but *Record Mirror*'s entire coverage had been a single sentence at the bottom of page nine and *New Musical Express* had ignored it altogether. David's promotional appearances were next to none – he did no television and his only gigs were at the Arts Lab that David and Mary Finnegan had set up in Beckenham, which were extremely popular for an event held in the backroom of a pub, but hardly the launchpad for a hit single. Under those circumstances Major Tom was never going to get off the ground, let alone achieve orbit.

By August, David and Pitt seem to have almost written it off as a loss, and aside from Pitt writing a few strongly-worded letters to Philips and Mercury, very little more happened at their end. In truth, David had rather lost interest in being a pop star – he told Finnegan that he considered himself a 'radical folk singer' – so the failure of his song would have smarted substantially less than it had with 'Love You Till Tuesday' or 'You've Got A Habit of Leaving Me'. Besides which, work was already well underway on David's first album for Mercury. Recording had commenced on the same day as the Apollo 11 mission had lifted off, 16 July, and Bowie and Visconti – back in the producer's chair, having deemed the rest of the album in line with his values[21] – were already deep into the process. Wary of the hodgepodge of styles and ideas that had compromised Bowie's first album, Visconti and his boss at Essex, David Platz, were determined to give this second bite at the cherry a distinct identity, leaning into a very late-sixties, transatlantic folk-rock sound. At its prettiest there was a debt to Simon & Garfunkel ('Janine', 'Letter To Hermione'), while

---

21. After hearing the results he had achieved on 'Space Oddity', Visconti fully expected Gus Dudgeon to be given the rest of the album to do as well. He was genuinely touched when Bowie told him he had no intention of working with anyone else.

the influence of Bob Dylan was obvious at the rowdier end, particularly on 'Unwashed and Slightly Dazed', which skirted so close to Dylan territory as to be practically a facsimile. Elsewhere the omnipotence of The Beatles was clear, notably on 'Cygnet Committee' and in the outro of 'Memory of a Free Festival'; a shameless attempt to create a 'Hey Jude' singalong moment. There's a fair smattering of Tyrannosaurus Rex here too, which given David's admiration for Marc's work and the presence of Tony Visconti was probably inevitable. Anthony Newley was nowhere in sight.

The album, which was to be released in November, was titled *David Bowie*, presumably under the assumption that no-one buying this folk-rock-longhair workout was likely to remember another record with the same name which came and went with little fanfare two years earlier (subsequent reissues would rechristen the album *Space Oddity* to avoid confusion).[22] It's appropriate for David's first two albums to share the same name, and to be self-titled – they both represent different facets of the artist he was. *David Bowie* (1967) was all over-thought artifice and polish, telling stories and making smart, wry asides, while *David Bowie* (1969) was sincere, turned on and emotional, scrappier and more honest. Neither is wholly satisfying, and David wouldn't really crack his artistic voice until he learned to combine the two, something hinted at here with 'Space Oddity', but not really anywhere else. This is far from the only time in Bowie's career that he would channel deeply personal pain into his lyrics, but it *is* the only time he would do something as completely frank as writing a song about a girl called Hermione who broke his heart and calling it 'Letter To Hermione'. He would learn to build far more layers into his writing. Recording continued on-and-off into the autumn, ahead of a tour in which David was booked to open for Humble Pie, a new band featuring two old friends: Steve Marriott of the Small Faces (and very nearly of the Lower Third) and Peter Frampton, the son of David and George's old art teacher.

Calvin Mark Lee had, by this time, left Mercury Records (a fact he hid from Ken Pitt), but continued to work on Bowie's album in an unofficial capacity, booking studio time and charging it to the label without their approval, and acting, alongside Angela – much to Pitt's growing annoyance in both cases – as if he was David's manager. Pitt was beginning to sense that his influence on David was slipping away as his young charge leaned increasingly on Angela Barnett, Calvin Mark Lee and Tony Visconti, with priorities and ideals now quite removed from the professional showbiz world that Ken Pitt understood. 'David became unmanageable,' he sighed, speaking to Johnny Rogan for his

---

22. Those who enjoy playing 'compare and contrast' with the London boys can read what they will into Marc Bolan calling his first two albums *My People Were Fair and Had Sky In Their Hair But Now They're Content To Wear Start On Their Brows* and *Prophets, Seers & Sages: The Angels of The Ages*, while David Bowie called his *David Bowie* and *David Bowie*.

1988 book *Starmakers and Svengalis*; one of the most candid and waspish interviews he ever gave. 'I was manager in name only'.

Three.

The dichotomy between Ken Pitt's businesslike approach and the sort of artist that David felt he was becoming – the one that wrote 'Space Oddity', a song about alienation and abandonment, not the one that wrote 'Space Oddity', a song about space travel during a space craze – was never more apparent than in the months after the initial release of the single. While David recorded a folk rock album (complete with a ten-minute epic that railed against hippy complacency) and invited gurus, protest singers, poets and performance artists to the Beckenham Arts Lab, Pitt had arranged two appearances at schmaltzy European song festivals, one in Malta and another in Italy. These were rather old-fashioned, small-scale versions of the Eurovision Song Contest, a format popular on the continent right into the nineties (there are still some going today). During the former David would sing his grandest ballad, 'When I Live My Dream' – of all his songs, probably the least representative of where he was as an artist at that point – and a Maltese song for which he would write English lyrics.

Though these cheesy-sounding festivals seem to highlight Bowie's manager's distance from his latest incarnation, it's important to note that Ken Pitt thought that the Maltese and Italian events were nothing more than an excuse for a nice holiday on expenses, and that the two men (joined in Italy by Angela, who dropped jaws in a sheer dress with nothing beneath[23]) enjoyed themselves immensely. There's no indication that Pitt planned to push David onto the circuit of song festivals and competitions that littered the continent. Still the fact that Pitt moved in these circles at all emphasised the gulf between them. In her memoir – a lively, bitchy document that should probably be taken with a pinch of salt – Angela remembers David calling her from Malta in a foul mood, complaining about the people, the atmosphere and the suit that Pitt was forcing him to wear. Pitt's account, however, describes a jolly holiday that neither man took seriously. Even so, the cognitive dissonance generated by competing in events like this – David took second place at the Maltese festival, and was given an award for 'Best Produced Song' in Italy – must have spun the head of an artist that had written a song like 'Space Oddity' and ran an underground folk club.

This was a time of change and questioning for David, as he started to find the kind of artist he was, the kind of career he wanted and the kind of people he wanted to share that life with; a balance of creative and ideological sixties instincts, and good old-fashioned pop star ambition. In a real sense, it marked a

---

23. 'A great collective gasp went up … I don't think those people had ever seen high-class hippies before' wrote Angela in *Backstage Passes*.

cut off point between David's future career and his past one. When he'd walked away from his previous record deal he had been trying to be one type of artist; in signing his next one, in writing 'Space Oddity' and recording the 1969 *David Bowie* album, he knew he had become another. That this pivot point happened at the very change of the decade, with a string of sixties failures behind him and a blast of wild seventies success ahead, is beautifully appropriate.

This change of epoch was underlined with a personal tragedy. David returned to London on 3 August, just in time to play his regular role as MC and star-turn at the Beckenham Arts Lab and it was there that Mary Finnegan informed him that his father was unwell. John Jones, who had suffered ill health since he was a young man, had contracted pneumonia and was gravely ill, his thin frame weakened by years of stomach ulcers. David rushed to his bedside, showing him the trophy he had won in Italy and receiving a weak but undeniable smile from his proud father in return. Two days later, while working on the new album at Trident studios, David received word that John Jones had died.

Bowie's relationship with his parents had always been complicated. The previous year David and Hermione, as Feathers, had been interviewed by *The Times* for a sort of state-of-the-nation piece on youth culture, entitled 'The Restless Generation', which also included interviews with Mick Jagger and Mary Hopkin.[24] In the interview, David talked at length about the generation gap between himself and his parents. 'My father tried so hard', he told journalist Sheila More, 'but his upbringing was so different that we can't communicate. He and all his friends were in the army during the war and he takes naturally to iron discipline … to get emotional about something, well that's only fit for the servants' quarters'.[25] It was more complex than David makes out. John had fought in the war, of course, and not just as a conscript; he'd been a territorial in the 1930s and enlisted fully as soon as war broke out, serving with dedication in the Royal Fusiliers. Prior to that, though, John had been a bit of a scoundrel; a wannabe-impresario, a creative entrepreneur, a music fan, an alcoholic and a womaniser. Despite David's harsh words in *The Times* about how little they had in common, the apple hadn't really fallen that far from the tree. John had always nurtured and encouraged David's creative side, taking him to shows as a child, buying him his first guitar and first saxophone, and lending him money to support himself while trying to 'make it'. Ken Pitt's files were full of polite letters between the two men, with Pitt reassuring John about his son's future and finances, and John clearly feeling that David was in capable and grown-up hands.[26] It often feels as if the two were discussing an errant child. There was

---

24. Remarkably, neither Mary nor Mick took the main spotlight – the piece was led by a classy picture of Feathers themselves.
25. 'That must have gone down well at Plaistow Grove', observes Hutch in *Bowie & Hutch*.
26. When John helped David move his things into Pitt's Manchester Street flat, he apparently remarked approvingly that the decor was 'very masculine'.

clearly a lot of mutual respect – when Pitt published his 1983 memoir, *Bowie: The Pitt Report*, it carried the dedication 'In memory of Heywood Stanton Jones (1912–1969).' David, for his part, was fond of his father – certainly fonder than he was of his mother – and repairing their relationship had been on his mind at the time of John's death. In a 1993 BBC TV interview with Hanif Kureishi, the Bromley-based author of *The Buddha of Suburbia*, a TV adaption of which Bowie was soundtracking, David said that his father's death had occurred 'at a point when I was just beginning to grow up a little bit and appreciate that I would have to stretch out my hand for us ever to get to know each other ... I felt so ... Damn! Wrong time! Not now, not now!'

The death of a parent is a titanic moment for most people – the removal of one of life's constants, a presence literally since birth, can be seismic. However, it's not necessarily true to say that John Jones' passing was the creative and career watershed for Bowie that some have made it out to be. The journey to becoming the decadent, smart colossus of seventies rock was already well underway. Perhaps the removal of his father's judging eye allowed David to lean more into his flamboyant side, but then perhaps not – after all his mother was still alive throughout the periods that marked his most shocking behaviour. It did, more likely, mean that David no longer had anyone to feel beholden to. He had tried to appease and placate John throughout his career, most recently during his doomed dalliance with cabaret, and now there was no-one left for whom David would make such compromises. John's death also severed another of the ropes tying Bowie to Ken Pitt – it's possible Bowie would have hesitated to distance himself from his mentor, a career decision that his more old-fashioned father would have been opposed to, had John lived. All of this, obviously, contains an element of speculation. What is undeniably true is that the passing of Heywood 'John' Jones added another layer of separation between David and his past.

Two.

A month on from the release of 'Space Oddity', all was quiet on the Bowie front. The single had come and gone and scarcely made a ripple. There had been some talk at Philips of withdrawing the record but Ken Pitt had begged them to keep it in the machinery of the label for a little longer. The single finally crept into the official *Record Retailer* chart on 6 September at number 48, before dropping out again. There are certainly versions of this story where 'Space Oddity' peaked at 48 and that was that. Fortunately, in *this* reality Philips had just employed Olav Wyper as General Manager. This young exec had come from CBS, where he had overseen the release of the label's catalogue in the UK. He'd already been instrumental in the success of Georgie Fame, Fleetwood Mac and Marmalade and had jumped to Philips hoping to nurture similarly hopeful new talent.[27] One of the artists he'd been looking forward to working with was David Bowie. Not many people had bought 'Space Oddity' at this point, but one of the few that had was Olav Wyper, who loved the record and was fully expecting it to already be a hit when he started his new gig – he was therefore genuinely shocked to discover that it had disappeared. With no major releases on the label's slate in the first few weeks of his tenure, he decided to concentrate the company's resources on a loose thread with potential. This is why, for a couple of weeks in September 1969, the entire might of the Philips organisation was focused on selling David Bowie's 'Space Oddity'. Wyper's PR team worked every angle in order to get David into the papers, resulting in his first major music press features, while his sales team were turning up in regional record shops with the sole purpose of getting copies of 'Space Oddity' onto the shelves and his promotions team took out quarter-page adverts in *Melody Maker* and *NME* declaring 'Didn't you know it! David Bowie's SPACE ODDITY has cracked the chart barrier – is heading topwards'. It was an optimistic claim[28], but it turned out to be absolutely true. The following Sunday, 28 September, the single re-entered the chart at number 25, and would climb every week until November. 'Space Oddity' would remain in the top 40 until 13 December.

On 2 October David finally had the validating experience craved by most would-be sixties music stars (and seventies, eighties, nineties and early-2000s ones), when he appeared on BBC One's flagship music show *Top of the Pops*.

By 1969, with other mainstream pop shows like *Ready, Steady, Go!* long off the air, *TOTP* was appointment-to-view television, watched by every school kid in the country, alongside their curious mum and tutting dad. It was genuinely career-making, and a solid appearance on the show could be the trigger for a hit single ... Bowie and his team were determined that the appearance went as well as possible. For almost all of the iconic show's 42-year run, the majority of performances were done in the presence of a studio audience, often on a central stage, surrounded by a crowd of awkwardly dancing teenagers.[29] As visually interesting as this could be, it also created at least three or four awkward moments in every episode where slightly gormless youths would stare into the camera, wave, stumble or simply turn out to be visibly terrible dancers. Ken Pitt was adamant that David wasn't going to be upstaged by a pillock in a tank top. Pitt was able to talk producers into shooting David's section on a separate stage in order to preserve the atmosphere of the song, and rather than have cutaways to a studio audience, David's performance was mixed with evocative shots of

27. He would go on to found the label's Vertigo imprint, home to some of the biggest rock acts of the seventies, and was responsible for coming up with its iconic 'swirl' logo.
28. 'Space Oddity' had only 'cracked' the chart barrier at number 48 when this advert ran in the 13 September issue of both papers. Had any reader thought to cross reference the advert's claim with the actual chart printed toward the front of the issue, they might have found the ad a little suss.
29. I hate to go all 'kids today' here, but honestly ... kid's today cannot know the impossible, glamorous dream of somehow getting a ticket to be in the *TOTP* studio audience.

the Apollo 11 mission. Gus Dudgeon, as the song's producer, felt it was his duty to come along to ensure the BBC's in-house orchestra didn't mangle the backing track[30] while Calvin Mark Lee provided David with a beautiful silver jacket and belt. Also in attendance (at least according to *Disc & Music Echo*) was Peggy Jones, David's recently widowed mother, who was brought along in order 'to cheer her up'. The episode aired on 9 October; the following day Pitt wrote to Bowie, who was playing a show in Birmingham, to tell him that the 'reaction to *Top of the Pops* is E-N-O-R-M-O-U-S'. He wasn't wrong.

One.

The following week, 'Space Oddity' jumped to number eight in the charts and when the *Top of the Pops* performance was repeated on 16 October, the single was pushed further to number six. By now the publicity machine was hurtling along. Penny Valentine had interviewed David on the set of the show, and 11 October's edition of *Disc & Music Echo* became the first music paper to feature David Bowie as the main cover star. Valentine's piece is undeniably gushing – presumably winning her bet had put her in a good mood – 'His charm,' she says, 'is so overpowering that it has given him more freedom to achieve his ideals than you would have thought possible.' She ends her piece by predicting that '"Space Oddity" is the first tenuous link in a long chain that will make David Bowie one of the biggest assets, and one of the most important people British music has produced in a long, long time.' Those words were echoed later that day when David was interviewed for Belgian radio station BRT. The host, Ward Bogaert signed off his piece by saying: 'We saw him as the symbol of the youth and England and the World of tomorrow.' That week's edition of *Melody Maker*, also published on 11 October, carried a feature by David's other press champion, Chris Welch. In the piece Welch is a shade less excitable than Valentine, downgrading *Disc's* description of David as 'one of the most important people British music has produced in a long, long time' to a more cautious prediction that 'David's current success could mean the start of a whole new career for an extremely talented and likeable person'. David himself does a fairly good job of playing down his own skills; 'I really don't consider myself a performer,' said the man who had spent the last year taking mime classes and headlining his own folk club. 'I really wouldn't like to make singing a full-time occupation'.

Like it or not, however, singing and performing *had* suddenly become a full time occupation for David, at least for now. As 'Space Oddity' continued its rocketing ascent up the chart, he was out on tour for the first time since

---

30. Musician's Union rules had scuppered artists miming to their hits at this point, and acts would either perform fully live, pre-record a new backing track to sing over – providing all the musicians used were present on stage – or use the BBC's in-house orchestra and band. These rules would last right into the seventies.

1966. Dubbed 'Changes '69', the shows were headlined by Humble Pie, with support from Welsh blues act Love Sculpture and short-lived psyche rockers Samson.[31] Andrew Loog Oldham, the former Rolling Stones manager who was now handling Humble Pie, had originally booked Bowie to do a mime performance, presumably because he was interested in the same mystic variety bill vibe that Marc had wanted on the *Lion and the Unicorn* tour. Conveniently, a problem with the backing track before the first show meant that David had to accompany himself, so of course a mime performance was out of the question. More conveniently, Bowie just happened to have his guitar with him. Much to Oldham's annoyance, David played a conventional acoustic set at every show, including a rendition of 'Space Oddity'. According to a review in *NME*, it received 'the biggest applause of the night'.

A week of great press and shows was capped with a session on BBC Radio One for Dave Lee Travis. David, backed by Junior's Eyes – the band used by Visconti for much of the new album – performed an incredible folk-rock re-interpretation of 'Let Me Sleep Beside You', his abandoned 1967 single, here completely rehabilitated.[32] It's a riveting performance, capped off by DLT playing out interview segments and the single version of 'Space Oddity'. The press, the adverts, the radio and the tour all did their work, just as Olav Wyper had hoped. On the official chart for 26 October 1969 'Space Oddity' entered the top five. A genuine, iron-clad and unarguable hit single.

Lift off.

---

31. Not to be confused with the late-seventies New Wave of British Heavy Metal band of the same name. See also the mid-sixties British psychedelic band Nirvana, once recorded by Tony Visconti, not to be confused with the other Nirvana who covered Bowie's 'The Man Who Sold The World', a song originally produced by ... Tony Visconti. It's a small world, when you get down to it, and it apparently contains a finite amount of nouns.
32. You can find this version of 'Let Me Sleep Beside You' on *Bowie at the Beeb* and it is absolutely worth your time. It should be considered the definitive take on the song.

Chapter Twenty

The Prettiest Stars

Marc was delighted for David when 'Space Oddity' was a hit – he had, after all, predicted that it would be. Though Bowie was the older of the two, the more well read and the more worldly, their power balance still very much tilted toward Marc whom, according to Ken Pitt, David absolutely idolised. Bowie had the bigger hit now, but Bolan was still the underground darling with the solid fan base and records that were commonly thought of as substantive work, while there were many ready to chalk David up as a one-hit-wonder. In late 1969, while speaking to *NME*'s Gordon Coxhill, Bowie described Bolan as 'a great influence on me, not so much with his music, but with his attitude to the pop scene. He shuts himself off from the destructive elements and prefers to get on with his work. That's how I intend to be.'

When discussing Bowie and Bolan the word 'rivals' is used as often as the word 'friends'[1], but really the rivalry would come later. The playing field had been level when they'd first met, and any traces of bitterness in their friendship were rooted in sniping from the lowest rung at those doing better than them. Since then, it was Bolan's career that had taken off, and David had only now begun to catch up. Later, both would have a brief spell of bitterness at the other's expense (Bowie's seems to have evaporated around the mid seventies, by which time his dominance was firmly established), with Marc being the more scathing of the two, especially as he watched his friend gaining ground on him with his Ziggy Stardust project. Marc, as Tony Visconti puts it, 'was in competition with everyone'. In 1969 both he and David had naturally sorted themselves into first and second place, at least for now, and felt no bitterness about those roles. It meant that Marc got to feel magnanimous and impressive, gracing Bowie with his benediction and attention. Bowie, meanwhile, had something to aim for. Tony Visconti, however, thinks there was more going on under the surface. 'It was Marc who was covertly in awe of Bowie,' he told Mark Paytress. 'He secretly admired him.'

While Major Tom shot beyond the outer hemisphere and into the stars,[2] Marc had been rather busy. 'King of the Rumbling Spires', a fine song in its own right, had been released just a week after 'Space Oddity' but had been sucked into the same black hole in which Bowie's single was temporarily

---

1. A special award goes to *The Guardian*'s Alexis Petridis, who in a 2020 retrospective went with 'frenemies'.
2. Or at least number five in the charts.

trapped. Tyrannosaurus Rex's latest, alas, would never achieve the necessary escape velocity. While David headed for the toppermost of the poppermost, Bolan found himself dealing with issues closer to home than outer space. He and Took had already begun work on a follow-up to *Unicorn*, planned as a more electrified, less pastoral album that was focused around Marc's growing obsession with playing lead guitar and riffs. Took, however, would never complete the sessions. By this point the two halves of Tyrannosaurus Rex were in different worlds. Took, damaged and vulnerable, was falling far deeper into substance abuse, while Marc was starting to let the hippy mask slip, revealing his uncompromising ambition. In an already toxic situation, Steve Took made the ultimate faux pas.

> 'The thing that totally wrote Steve off was when he said "I'd like to do some of my own songs now." He was the George Harrison of Tyrannosaurus Rex, whereas the Beatles didn't fire George Harrison, Marc did fire Steve. That was the last straw, that with his drug abuse and wanting to be a fifty-fifty creator was too much. Marc couldn't take it'.
>
> Tony Visconti

You can sympathise with poor Steve. The group, after all, was called 'Tyrannosaurus Rex', not 'The Marc Bolan Band', and he wasn't a hired hand or a side man, but rather Bolan's foil. In the press, the band were always discussed in terms of being 'Marc and Steve', a duo and while it was common knowledge that Bolan was the driving force, it was also obvious to anyone paying attention that Took was an important creative element, quite apart from his hippy authenticity. And he was a songwriter – he had been for years. He played guitar and piano and he wrote songs; you can't blame someone like that for getting tired of sitting to the side, tapping the bongos and singing the 'la la las', however much they'd enjoyed their 'two idyllic summers of second division rock stardom, parading the King's Road in aviator shades and a pink velvet cape' (as Mick Farren once wrote in *Mojo*).

'When we started off, Marc would look after the melody part of a song and I'd be responsible for the percussion and the arrangement,' Took explained to the *NME* in 1972. 'And it worked very well. Then I started writing things of my own and instead of being on the fantasy part of the trip they were about what happens to the kids on the street around here. But the record company started objecting to words like "breast" or "drugs" and it frustrated me greatly.' Tony Visconti – who was genuinely very fond of the younger man – remembers Took's work having a bigger problem than edgy themes, however: 'He slept over my place on occasion,' he told Bolan biographer Mark Paytress, 'and we'd do some of his songs ... but they were awful.'

Aside from the songs and the bad company, it seems clear that by this point Steve Took was a mess. Still just nineteen, he was a starving monkey with the keys to the banana plantation – few young men of that age have the self control to stay on the straight and narrow, particularly not when they were – in the words of Tony Visconti – 'a fairly damaged person'. Took was under pressure from many sides at once; recording and performing with an increasingly judgey bandmate who considered himself in charge, while balancing a growing interest in revolutionary politics and environmental activism at odds with the peaceable image imposed on him; dealing with having his songs roundly rejected along with the inbuilt implication that he was supposed to shut up and do as he was told. Faced with so much, Took simply fell apart. 'I was [supposed to be] a flower child, and there's things that a flower child can't do,' he explained to *Melody Maker* in 1972. 'Being a natural born rebel I wanted to do all the things I was not meant to do. That caused a lot of raps with the management, and a lot of raps with Marc. I couldn't get together looking at all those kids, and if I went into a heavy rap Marc would get freaked out.'

It was eventually, inevitably, decided that Steve Took would leave Tyrannosaurus Rex following the duo's upcoming US tour. In later interviews, Took would always refer to himself as having 'quit' the band, while June Child and Tony Visconti have both used the word 'sacked'. We can at least say that his association with Marc Bolan ended through mutual agreement – Marc, interviewed in 1971, even used the phrase 'we decided to break up', though who mutually agreed to what is unclear. 'We're just not playing together any more,' Marc told Chris Welch of *Melody Maker* in October 1969, before lying through his teeth. 'There's no bad vibes between us whatsoever, we just both want to do different things.' Two days after the decision to part ways was made, Tyrannosaurus Rex left for their first American tour, and Steve Took's last round of dates. Took, having partied into the early hours, nearly missed the flight. He was so out of it that friends had to break into his flat, slap him awake and put him into a taxi. When the tour was done, Steve – who had met a girl and got stranded at her place – missed his flight home. Marc and June boarded their plane and left him there, taking the future of Tyrannosaurus Rex with them.

Quite what that future might have looked like had it included Steve Peregrin Took is unclear. Aside from Tony Visconti himself, Took was by far the most musically collaborative partner that Marc Bolan would ever work with, and his continual influence could have curbed a lot of Bolan's future misdirections, especially the musical stagnation that cost him his place at the top in the mid-seventies. The prospect of an all-electric Tyrannosaurus Rex that included Steve Took is one of the great missed opportunities in British rock. Took would also have made a hell of a pop star. On the other hand, perhaps the manoeuvres and pivots of the next year or so, positioning Marc as a heart-throb rock 'n' roller, needed to be undertaken alone to be effective. We will, alas, never know. As it was, Tyrannosaurus Rex mark-one bowed out in the United States, where the duo undertook an eventfully chaotic US tour, occasionally very well received, occasionally met with indifference or bafflement. The shows, at least, sound anything but boring, evidenced by a review of the band's appearance at the Cafe Au Go Go in New York City's Greenwich Village:

'The final number was wild, from its opening jungle-like screeching by Took, through Bolan's singing ... through Took's playing of the gong he knocked over and struck with a thrown chair. He then pounded a tomtom with maracas, shattering one ... Tyrannosaurus Rex is quite an act.'[3]

Fred Kirby, *Billboard*

Alas, this freak-out, underground-friendly incarnation of Tyrannosaurus was abandoned at the airport with Steve Took's unused plane ticket. Never again would Marc Bolan's music and career feel quite this creative or unpredictable. And perhaps that was for the best. What Marc wanted more than anything, what he had wanted since he was a little boy, was to be a superstar, an icon, an idol. It's arguable that he could have got there with Took in tow, but it's equally arguable that someone with Steve's principles, outlook and creative instincts (not to mention his pride and his addictions) would ultimately hold the band back from those lofty, populist heights. He didn't need a partner any more, he needed a yes-man. He needed an enabler for his vision, not someone who might feel they could question it, and certainly not someone who could jeopardise it. It's a callous mode of thinking, it's not very hippy, but it was commercially sound. Steve Took had played his part in bringing Marc's music to the world's attention. It was time for someone else to take up the supporting role.[4]

As the end of the decade approached, both Marc and David were trying their best to establish the foundations of their careers and personas. Marc was easing himself out from under the expectations and cliches of the sixties counterculture dream, though it would take another year for him to really free himself of it and find his next audience. David, meanwhile, still had a stake in the alternative world, though he considered himself separate from the well-

---

3. This show was woefully under attended, probably as it took place simultaneously with the Woodstock festival happening up-state.
4. The story of Steve Took's career post-Tyrannosaurus Rex is a frustrating and sad one. Later, when asked where Steve was now, Marc replied cruelly 'in some gutter somewhere', and while that's not quite true, it's also not quite wrong either. Steve never hit a complete rock bottom, and his savings from the band and very occasional Tyrannosaurus Rex royalties were able to keep him clothed, fed and housed, but his addiction issues never fully went away and his career never recovered. He, Farren and Twink formed The Pink Fairies, but the only gig they played made the infamous full-band Tyrannosaurus Rex show at the Electric Garden sound like a masterclass in professionalism. When the Pink Fairies finally got themselves together to play again, it was without Took. Several other musical projects came and went: Shagrat, Steve Took's Horns, numerous shambolic solo performances, guest slots with Mick Farren, Hawkwind, Syd Barret and Twink, but ultimately he was never able to get out from under the shadow of his addictions. This sweet, talented and troubled man died in 1979, choking to death on a cocktail cherry after a heroin binge funded by his latest Tyrannosaurus Rex royalty cheque, aged just 31.

meaning flower power era of the mid-late sixties. On the one hand he was withering about the hippies ('Middle-class kids rebelling against their parents. They aren't underprivileged when they can afford to buy kaftans,' he sniped in *Disc & Music Echo*), saying that the underground had been dying for two years anyway. On the other hand, his interviews at the time are largely concerned with the Arts Lab he was running with Mary Finnegan in Beckenham, which he told *Melody Maker* he considered his 'chief occupation'.

Bowie and Finnegan had begun their Arts Lab – initially just called the Beckenham Folk Club until they decided to expand its remit – at the start of the year in the backroom of the Three Tuns pub, the landlord being happy to take the night's bar takings as payment. Following the success of the original Drury Lane Arts Lab the concept had taken off, and copy-cat venues and nights had mushroomed across the UK, operating in the same spirit of experimentalism and creative freedom as the original. A combination of a very late-sixties willingness to engage with the arts (so long as they were framed as *alternative* arts) and David's own magnetism as a compere and performer meant that the Beckenham lab's popularity built quickly, and a true local arts community grew around it – at one point, David said, they were even considering taking over a whole street and creating a commune. Finnegan produced a weekly newsletter, *Growth*, also the name she gave to their organisation, which was distributed at the club. David would play lengthy sets and book friends and artists he admired – Lindsay Kemp, Marc Bolan, Chime Rimpoche, The Strawbs, Keith Christmas and Ralph McTell all appeared to sing, perform or lecture. Bowie, Finnegan and their co-organisers encouraged poetry, dance, mime, speeches, light shows and local musicians ('I never knew there were so many sitar players in Beckenham,' Bowie told *Melody Maker*.) The Beckenham Arts Lab reached its community peak when Bowie, Angie, Finnegan and their friends put on the Beckenham Free Festival at a local park bandstand in August 1969, just a week after the death of David's father.[5] The event was a huge success, with over a thousand people turning up (some estimates have said 3,000) to enjoy local artists, stalls, a reggae version of 'Space Oddity'[6] and Angie's money-spinning burger stand constructed out of a wheelbarrow. Despite not charging for entry, the event generated a badly needed £200 for the Arts Lab – not pocket change in 1969. According to Finnegan's book, David, grief stricken and in a foul mood, sniped viciously at

---

5. And a week after the song festivals in Malta and Italy, which much to Mary Finnegan's utter annoyance had taken David, who was in charge of the music, away from his responsibilities at the eleventh hour.
6. David was backed by Tony Visconti and an unknown drummer at this event. Visconti records it as being John Cambridge from Junior's Eyes behind the kit, but Cambridge confirms in his book *Bowie & Cambo* that the band were touring in Germany at the time. Sadly, no-one filmed or recorded audio at the event, so this unique version of 'Space Oddity' went undocumented.

Mary and Angie as they glowed with pride – 'You make me sick, you're just a bunch of bread heads, you don't care about anything except money'.[7]

He might have been down on the notion of the hippy underground as it was commonly understood, but in the Arts Lab and the free festival he was absolutely living its values, and in a way that he felt was more valid than the middle class pretentiousness of the city crowd ('There's a lot of talent in the green belt and a lot of tripe on Drury Lane,' said David Bowie, one of the stars of *Studies Toward An Experiment into the Structure of Dreams* at the original Arts Lab, Drury Lane, in *Melody Maker*). A theme of many of his interviews at the time stressed the importance of the Arts Lab and of an enriching and valuable body of cultural experiences over the idea of hit singles – which, of course, is easy to say when you've just had a hit single.

While the back end of 1969 and first half of 1970 saw Marc Bolan concentrate upon his ambitions and sharpen his idea of what sort of artist he was, Bowie seemed to descend further into an identity crisis. He saw himself as a radical, the maverick owner-operator of a community performance art project who had just made a deeply personal folk rock album; a troubadour and an artist. He was also very aware that he had just had what amounted to a novelty hit single, and the contrarian in him was reacting against anyone judging him for that. In November, ahead of the release of his second album, he spoke to *NME*'s Gordon Coxhill and came out swinging against the snobs who might look down on him for daring to have a hit. 'A lot is said and written about music snobbery with the fans, but I think the groups are just as bad,' he sniffs. 'For some reason even the words 'entertainer' and 'cabaret' make them shudder.' This is quite a breathtaking display of hypocrisy from a man who, not two years ago, had auditioned for cabaret clubs under extreme duress, and whose manager knew he loathed every second of it. And yet David doubled down in the interview, saying that he was 'determined to be an entertainer – clubs, cabarets, concerts, the lot.' David's friends at the time remember him loathing the idea of being considered an all-round entertainer, a Tommy Steele or a Cliff Richard, and yet here he was declaring he was just that, and happy with it. Those that point a finger at Ken Pitt's lack of credible ambitions for David should note that Bowie himself didn't seem to know what or who he was.

His final interview of the 1960s was with *Music Now!* magazine, and moved David even further away from the purist, the idealist, the art-for-art's-sake free spirit his interviews of just months earlier seemed to hint at. 'I want to be known,' he told journalist Kate Simpson. 'I want my songs to be known. Otherwise I wouldn't go on writing, because I don't write for myself – there are lots of things I could do besides writing songs. I enjoy it, and [I enjoy] making money out of

---

7. The day, of course, was commemorated on David's album as 'Memory of a Free Festival', though the carefree and joyful nature of the music belies the fact that Bowie was heartbroken and miserable at the time.

it at the same time.' It sounds, oddly enough, like something Marc Bolan would say. Elsewhere in the interview he rails against the clueless do-gooders of the underground. 'They're so apathetic,' he says. 'So lethargic; the laziest people I've met in my life. They don't know what to do with themselves, looking all the time for people to show them the way. They wear anything they're told, and listen to any music they're told to. People are like that.' Here, he was discussing the song 'Cygnet Committee', the epic and angry centrepiece of the new album, a song inspired by the community that ran the Beckenham Arts Lab that he had spent so many of 1969's interviews espousing. David Bowie was finishing the sixties pulled in two directions – community-minded folkie, or entertaining pop singer? Post-hippy cynic or artsy idealist? Idol or ideals?

One thing he absolutely showed is that he was a brazen liar – he told *NME*'s Coxhill that he had spent the money from 'Space Oddity' on a big car and 'bought a nice little house.' The car part was true – he'd treated himself to a roomy, secondhand Rover 100 – but the 'nice little house' he had 'bought' was a flat he was renting; comprising a couple of bedrooms, a kitchenette and a living room, which he and Angie shared with Tony Visconti, his girlfriend, Sheila, and a friend called Roger Fry,[8] who would drive David to shows and on tour. The space was carved out of Haddon Hall, a large house on Beckenham's Southend Road which had been partitioned into flats. Though the portion they rented was fairly small, it did include the house's impressive entrance and staircase – meaning that visitors were treated to the impression of a grand Victorian mansion; the kind usually referred to as a 'pile', albeit one where the stairwell led to doors that had been sealed up; the rooms behind them being used as flats accessible through other exterior entrances. The landlord also let Bowie and Visconti build a practice space in the cellar, while Angie created an interior design scheme that leaned into the building's faded opulence. A visiting journalist from *Jeremy*, the discreet gay lifestyle magazine to which Pitt had pitched a feature in the hope of capturing the pink pound, described the space:

> 'Ramshackle yet strangely beautiful in its decay. Sweeping staircase. Huge stained glass windows. Moulded ceilings. Carved and tiled fireplaces. Liberty print blocks. Art Deco lamps. William Morris screens. There is an almost childlike excitement about the way he pounces on each new treasure, it's infectious.'

Haddon Hall would become HQ for Bowie and his growing entourage of friends and musicians as his career began to galvanise.

If Bowie was struggling to work out what kind of artist he was and what kind of audience he had, the reception that awaited the release of *David Bowie*

---

8. Known as 'Roger the Lodger'. Obviously.

(1969) didn't help matters.[9] 'Space Oddity' had been a huge success, but its parent album far from replicated this. The two sides of the sleeve seem to further highlight the weird duality of David's ambitions and frame of mind – the front cover featured David himself, or at least his head, crowned with a halo of hair, looking directly – and seriously – at the camera, with none of the softness or playfulness of his previous album cover. The picture is superimposed over a blue and green polka-dotted background; a little psychedelic, a little space age, and somehow quite uninviting. Ken Pitt, who had nothing to do with the packaging, absolutely hated it. The back cover, meanwhile, had been painted by George Underwood in the same style in which he'd rendered the first Tyrannosaurus Rex sleeve – the two images would sit beautifully together framed side-by-side[10]. The rear cover incorporates whimsy, anger, surrealism and science fiction – with a bonus sketch of Hermione Farthingale peering through the clouds in the top left. Neither is a completely representative piece of art for the songs, though the reverse does a far better job at inviting the viewer to listen, suggesting more of the depth they might find.

Neither piece of artwork seemed able to convince the public to part with their money. 'Space Oddity' had sold almost 140,000 copies by the end of the year; the album on which it could be found would sell less than 5,000 during its first six months on sale. It didn't help that neither Philips nor Mercury seemed to especially believe in the work. Olav Wyper, the great champion of 'Space Oddity' at Philips, had been unimpressed by the album and hesitant to push it in the same way he had the single, while Calvin Mark Lee, who had brought David into Mercury in the first place, had moved on from the label and was gradually being frozen out of the Bowie operation altogether after bungling the press invites for David's big showcase at the Royal Festival Hall's Purcell Rooms.[11] Ken Pitt, loyal as ever but increasingly defanged, continued to lose influence to Angela, Tony Visconti and Marc Bolan, none of whom owned record stores, booking agencies or promotions companies. The album had precious few people in its corner.

As the Haddon Hall family hunkered down for their first Christmas – minus Angie, who was spending the holidays with her family in Cyprus – a question mark hung overhead. If David Bowie was a radical folk singer with an album of

---

9. 'What was your first album called?' John Peel asked during a live session the next year. 'Also *David Bowie*? Okay. I suppose David's third album is going to be called *David Bowie* too. His fourth one will be called *Elvis Presley*".

10. Actually, this is a brilliant idea, and I'm going to do it later.

11. 'An Evening With David Bowie' had been booked at the venue by Ken Pitt an entire year in advance in the desperate hope that Bowie would have made an album at that point and have something to promote. Calvin, meanwhile, had approached the same venue about booking David, prompting its office to contact Pitt to work out what on earth was happening. A livid Ken Pitt turned the whole arrangement over to Calvin Mark Lee to handle. The result was a well-received press showcase with barely any press in attendance. Angie Bowie is convinced that Pitt made a point of not working his own contacts to make his young rival look bad.

meaningful work, then why wasn't he having the critical success he deserved? If he was a populist entertainer with a huge hit single to his name and a knack for giving the audience what they wanted, then why hadn't that audience showed up to buy the album? As 1970 dawned, the crucial question was 'who is David Bowie?'

A far easier question to answer was 'who is Marc Bolan?' The man dubbed by *Melody Maker* as 'The bopping elf' knew exactly which direction he was travelling in, what fine lines between credible and populist he needed to tread and the kind of person he needed to help him achieve it. Steve Took was now out of the picture, and while Marc was perhaps not quite self-aware enough to know what big shoes his replacement had to fill[12], he thought he knew exactly what he was looking for. Someone who looked great, who sounded, ya know, *fine*, and was easy to work with. June Child, Marc's girlfriend, was convinced that if they got in someone who more or less looked the part, no-one was going to be able to tell the difference anyway.

In early October an advert appeared in *Melody Maker*:

> *TYRANNOSAURUS REX*
> *WANTED: to work with T. Rex a gentle young guy who can play*
> *percussion i.e Bongos and Drum Kit, some Bass Guitar and Vocal Harmony.*
> *Photos please.*
> *BOX 8679, % Melody Maker, 161-166 Fleet Street, London, E.C.4*

Marc was inundated with over three hundred applications. As it turns out, he didn't actually need to look at any of them. Steve's replacement had already been found. He was an acquaintance of Jeff Dexter and another former mod of 1947 vintage from the suburbs: Michael Norman 'Mickey' Finn. There's two stories as to how the pair met. The official line is that Finn, who was a painter and decorator at the time, was painting a wall at Seed, a macrobiotic vegetarian restaurant in the West End beloved of hippies[13], when he was approached by a short figure in women's shoes and a velvet cloak, who turned out to be Marc Bolan, digging his look. The other, more likely explanation is that Jeff Dexter introduced Marc and Mickey because he knew they'd work well together. Finn wasn't a musician, he couldn't really sing and he hardly had any experience, however he had three important things going for him. Firstly he was *beautiful*, quite as beautiful as Marc in fact. He had impeccable style, incredible cheekbones and a louche attitude. He looked cool whatever he was doing, and when you pointed a camera at him he practically glowed. Secondly

---

12. Presumably pointy ones, with bells on.
13. The two brothers that owned Seed would go on to invent the veggie burger before moving into chocolate under the name Green & Blacks, now a leading global brand in the field of overpriced confectionery. The company is now owned by the multinational conglomerate formerly known as Kraft, which just goes to show that nothing is sacred.

he was sweet – placid and pliable, happy to do as he was told and enjoy the ride. It was exactly what Marc wanted in a sidekick. Finally, he was five-foot-eight, only slightly taller than Marc himself, which was useful in photos, and once Marc started performing guitar standing up rather than cross legged, would be vital in not highlighting how tiny and elfin the Bopping Elf actually was once the boppin' started. The lack of musicianship wasn't deemed a problem. Steve Took had been a master percussionist, dextrous and inventive, and he had given Bolan's songs complexity and depth, at this stage, however, with the kind of music Marc wanted to make, such dexterity wasn't actually that necessary. In fact, not having someone over-complicating Marc's boogies might be an advantage. Ultimately, it was decided that playing the bongos (which, unlike his predecessor, is all Mickey really did) wasn't actually all that hard, so long as you can keep time – which thankfully, Mickey Finn could. Just about.

Bolan and Finn commenced work on the new Tyrannosaurus Rex album *A Beard of Stars* at Halloween, with Visconti once more overseeing proceedings. Finn's first gig as a member of Tyrannosaurus Rex happened a week later at Leeds University, where they stood in for Pink Floyd who had pulled out at the last minute. The album was completed by the end of the year. The majority of the record had been tracked after Marc returned from the US, however a couple of songs had already been recorded with Steve Took, meaning Visconti had to artfully erase the former percussionist's contributions. His back-up vocals were re-done by Marc, and his percussion replaced with a simpler part by Mickey.[14] Finn's musical contribution to the album was fairly basic – his congas do the absolute minimum required of them and nothing more – but his contribution to mood and morale was much higher. 'The album was made in a really good atmosphere, helped no end by Finn's positive spirit, which led to the sessions being very creative and experimental,' explains Visconti.

That experimentation was almost entirely based in the electric guitar, of which Marc was now a complete devotee. Throughout his career he had been watching and learning – he'd played gigs with Jimi Hendrix – arguably the greatest of all time – and been mesmerising by his emotional, fluid solos and creative playing, he'd been on tour with The Who and watched Pete Townshend windmill and thrash, channelling his energy and his anger through his instrument until he couldn't resist smashing it across the stage. More recently he and June had been hanging out with June's friend Alice Ormsby-Gore, the posh socialite who was dating Eric Clapton. Sitting in the guitarist's country manor, Marc had watched,

---

14. A fairly dirty trick was pulled on Took at this point. As he had left the band apparently voluntarily (the reality of which is still unclear) he was told by Marc's managers that he was in breach of contract for not finishing the album and invoiced for £3,000. It kept him from trying to get money out of the band, or interfering with the record. Took never forgave Bolan for allowing it to happen.

mesmerised, as Clapton jammed blues licks. Later he would tell Tony Visconti that 'I sat at the feet of the master and I watched his hands the whole time'[15].

Though *A Beard of Stars* doesn't quite have the charm or atmosphere of either *Unicorn* nor Bolan's next album, *T.Rex*, it works as a solid stepping stone between the two. Marc continues the journey he had begun on *Unicorn*, his lyrics becoming increasingly stripped down – still beguiling and unusual, but also digestible. They worked as surreal slogans pasted together. The previous year, Marc had published a poetry collection, *The Warlock of Love*, and between the two most recent Tyrannosaurus Rex albums and the book you can trace a development in Bolan's words. He's moving further away from the head-in-the-clouds drifting of mid-sixties hippiedom. His imagery is still fantastical, still defaulting to whimsy, but there's far more economy of language, tighter rhyming and better scansion.

The new-found economy in Bolan's words is more than balanced by the budding self-indulgence in his guitar playing. Marc with a Fender Stratocaster was a child with a new toy, and he drenched *A Beard of Stars* in licks, noodles, riffs and scales – all hidden artfully and deployed carefully by Visconti, who was developing quite the bag of production tricks. The percussive rhythms were still predominantly acoustic, but the embellishments gave them new dimensions, used particularly well on 'Woodland Bop' – an obvious single that was weirdly overlooked – on which an acoustic jangle panned to the left speaker is joined on the chorus on the other speaker by a swooping, down-stepping riff. It comes to a head on the album's centrepiece, 'Elemental Child', an entirely electric piece built around a rockabilly hook that eventually resolves into a chugging riff and a lead guitar workout, more a string of funky rock 'n' roll licks than a shredding solo. Technically proficient it is not, but gutsy and heartfelt it certainly is.

A Beard of Stars, would be released the following March – meaning that 1970, like 1968, would see two Marc Bolan albums (the second, *T.Rex* would be released at Christmas), a speed boost in his prolificity that would carry him into the mid seventies. *A Beard of Stars* is probably the least self-contained and satisfying of Bolan's early records, capturing him in a transitory phase both musically and in terms of approach and identity. Finn's contributions are so minimal and Bolan's so maximalist that it may as well be a Marc Bolan solo album, and indeed this was the point in his career where Bolan's ego was starting to override some of his other instincts.

Marc had always been a little self-obsessed – he was well known for talking about himself constantly – but for most of his career thus far it had been tempered with an endearing earnestness. His ambition came off as cheeky, even charming. In private, that charm seemed to be withdrawing, revealing more entitlement and ruthlessness. Whether it was the fading of the hippy fairydust,

---

15. The exact same reaction that David had to seeing Howlin' Wolf back in 1964.

or whether the replacing of Took (a creative partner) with Finn (an affable yes man) had emboldened him, Bolan was becoming harder to work with for those tasked with capturing his ideas. Visconti became an adept Bolan-wrangler, learning when to stroke his ego to get the best results and when to tiptoe around his moods. The presence of anyone else in the studio was always met with an oversensitivity on Marc's part, due to his not wanting to appear embarrassed or undermined. This wasn't restricted to visitors either, it extended to recording engineers and even Mickey Finn. Visconti had to find tactful ways of telling Marc that his guitar was out of tune – an issue with his playing since the days of John's Children – and carefully manoeuvre his less palatable ideas into the scrap pile and come up with better ones, while getting him to think they were his own suggestions all along.[16] This new (or at least newly uncovered) attitude was a double edged sword. On the one hand, it made working with this more volatile Marc occasionally wearying (thankfully tempered for Visconti by Mickey Finn's good nature), on the other he was becoming increasingly driven, energetic and focused in the studio, something which impressed his producer as they forged forward. The cover of the album, though displaying the words 'Tyrannosaurus Rex', featured a picture of Bolan alone, looking arguably at his prettiest and most Byronesque. The previous three album covers had featured both members. A solo portrait of Mickey Finn and the album's title were to be found on the reverse, but it's not the back cover that looks out at you from the record store racks. There was now no denying whose band Tyrannosaurus Rex was.

The album was preceded by a single – for once taken from the record itself – 'By The Light of A Magical Moon', a perfect snapshot of its parent album. The track finds proper Bolanic charm in its textbook percussive-acoustic-over-bongos frame, augmented by little bluesy licks and descending swoops. It was another strong Tyrannosaurus Rex single, and one that – especially after the success of *Unicorn* – might have had some prospects for success. Marc would certainly be eyeing the gigantic sales of 'Space Oddity' and wondering if he could pull the same trick; whether his decision to theme the song around the moon was intentional or not we can only speculate. The last ever single to be released under the name 'Tyrannosaurus Rex', alas, was another dead-on-arrival sinker, finding no favour with radio and thus no traction with the public. Bolan was deflated, though he could take some comfort from the performance of *A Beard of Stars* a few months later. The album stalled in the charts at number 21, a full nine places below *Unicorn*'s peak at 12, but it also continued to sell whereas *Unicorn* had dropped straight out. It was a sign that, though the singles market had not yet been cracked, his audience was definitely growing beyond the crumbling counterculture. It became the best selling Tyrannosaurus Rex

---

16. This is at least as valuable a skill in a record producer as understanding how to mic up a drum kit, or work out a harmony part. Visconti says he handled Bolan in the same careful way he would handle a school bully.

album yet. What would have pleased him even more, had he known, was that it would be five years before one of his singles missed out on the top forty again. Marc Bolan was just eleven months away from beginning a chart run that would place him in the top five *ten times in a row*.

Just days before 'By The Light of the Magical Moon' was released, Marc found himself playing lead guitar in very different circumstances. A lot of thought had been given to David's follow up to 'Space Oddity', and originally Philips had talked about releasing 'Janine', a pretty but relatively slight cut from the album, while Mercury in the US wanted a new version of 'Memory of a Free Festival'. David, however had suggested another stab at recording 'London Bye Ta-Ta', one of the numbers Decca had rejected two years earlier, and also had a new song in mind, a swooning, romantic throwback called 'The Prettiest Star', a song he'd played down to the line to Angie in Cyprus over Christmas before asking her to marry him. Studio time was booked for 8 January, David's twenty-third birthday. Visconti, who had been impressed with Marc's recent guitar playing on *A Beard of Stars* invited Bolan along to put a part down on 'The Prettiest Star'.[17]

The session was an uncomfortable one, and the first real indication that Bowie and Bolan could be less than thrilled with each other's success. Visconti had assumed everything was going well – Marc was delighted to be considered as a guitarist as it was further validation of his skill as a lead player and though the part he eventually composed wasn't exactly innovative – he essentially just copies Bowie's vocal line – there's real charm and heart to his playing. Marc was hardly a virtuoso, but he was the right musician for the right moment and his guitar absolutely sings. David was delighted with his friend's work on the song – when it was re-recorded three years later for *Aladdin Sane*, he had guitarist Mick Ronson replicate Bolan's part practically note for note.[18] Unfortunately, there was more going on than a solid guitar lick. The recording was suffused with a weird atmosphere from the moment Marc, accompanied by June, entered the studio. 'I remember a very strange attitude in the studio,' Bowie said many years later. 'We were never in the same room at the same time. You could have cut the atmosphere with a knife.'[19]

17. It's possible he also played on 'London Bye Ta-Ta', as both were recorded on the same day, though nobody involved can remember if Marc worked on the track or not. The lack of a distinct lead guitar in the song makes it difficult to judge.

18. Debates over which is the better cut have raged across fan circles for decades. Nicholas Pegg, for example, the author of *The Complete David Bowie* is absolutely in the Ronno camp. For me though, there's a sweetness to Bolan's playing and a care-free vibe to Visconti's production on the 1970 version that has the edge. Visconti's super melodic bassline is also a highpoint.

19. This is quoted by Mark Paytress and Nicholas Pegg in their respective Bolan/Bowie books, but I have been unable to find the original source. It's also curious that David should recall that they weren't 'in the same room at the same time' – that was certainly true in 1972, but definitely untrue in early 1970 when they were still part of the same circle.

What exactly was the problem? Bowie says in the same interview that he can't remember what the argument was about. It could certainly be jealousy on Marc's part – he was happy for David when 'Space Oddity' was first a success, but 140,000 sales, the cover of *Disc* and photoshoots for *Jackie* and *Mirabelle* were more than he could have expected. Bowie had also scooped some end-of-year awards, including 'Brightest Hope For 1970' from *Disc* – a position that Marc felt very much belonged to him. On the other hand, it's clear that 'Space Oddity' was a one off, at least for now. The album had sold appallingly in comparison with the single, and Marc must have known that. Considering how well his own albums had done – each outselling Bowie's four times over – he presumably still felt he had the upper hand. What's more Tony Visconti remembers Marc simply being happy to be involved. He told David Buckley in 1999 that 'for the first time, Marc wasn't feeling any rivalry; he was simply grateful to be acknowledged as a good guitar player. He was actually feeling genuine camaraderie towards David for the first time'. It's important to remember that both Bowie and Visconti were speaking decades after the fact here, and neither is notorious for having perfect recall (for example when Visconti was interviewed by Paul Trynka for his 2011 book *Starman*, he changes his story, saying that 'Marc comes in and the atmosphere just chills up … it was daggers.') Whether the disagreement was something trivial and recent, or whether it was a more deep seated bitterness, no-one now can remember. Just a month earlier Bowie had told an American magazine that Marc was his only friend in the music industry, and two months later Marc was clear about his admiration for David's work in an interview in *Zigzag*. 'I really dig David,' he says. 'I like his songs and we have a very good head thing.'[20]

Everyone agrees on one thing: it was Marc's girlfriend June that seemed to be in a spiky mood that day. She had watched the recording from the control room alongside Ken Pitt, who had popped in unexpectedly and who she turned to and accused of being 'David's mister ten percent'.[21] Pitt had the idea that she and Marc were opposed to the conventional bread-head corporate world of rock management, feeling that music industry businessmen were out for themselves and not their artists. June had been involved in the industry for several years at this point, and had been round the block working with Pink Floyd's managers (she'd also dated Syd Barrett and Eric Clapton) and the experience had obviously jaded her. Though Marc did have managers and agents in this period, they never seemed to last very long. In truth it was June, formidable and fierce, that was managing Marc's career. After the session came to an end and she and Marc prepared to make an exit, she rounded on Bowie: 'This song is crap. The

---

20. Bolan, camp as ever, is quick to add to that ' … but we don't make love. To make love wouldn't be repulsive to me. It would just be a bit of a bore with bums, and it'd hurt.'
21. Pitt's reply, as he tells it to George Tremlett, was 'I don't work that cheaply'.

best thing about it is Marc's guitar,' before turning on her heel and leaving the room. It soured the atmosphere between the two London boys for a while.

Marc and June would marry a few weeks later, with David and Angie following them down the aisle in March – yet another example of the two men's lives mirroring each other. The two women would be absolutely instrumental in their husband's successes in the coming years: styling them, negotiating for them, helping mastermind and actualise their ideas. Both Marc and David could be passive (and passive-aggressive) people, often in need of a nudge. Angie and June were smart, stylish and supportive women ready to provide that nudge, and the occasional shove. Had neither London boy met their particular London girl, things may have turned out differently.

'The Prettiest Star' was released in March to reviews that other artists might kill for, but sold in amounts that verged on the humiliating. The 'Space Oddity' sales of 140,000 were reduced to just 800 for its follow up, numbers as low as David was getting in 1967. Combined with the low sales of the album, it indicated a downward trend in Bowie's career that, potentially and for all anyone knew, suggested the seventies were likely to go the way of the previous decade. David was disappointed, naturally, but not devastated. He was young, talented, confident and newly married. What's more, he'd just started a rock band with an incredible guitarist from Hull by the name of Mick Ronson who played exquisite, spidery lines, and his new songs – robust, heavy, fascinating – were amongst the best he had ever written. There was plenty of time for things to look up.

Meanwhile, with *A Beard of Stars* maintaining steady sales, Marc and Mickey were starting to notice a shift in the audience at their shows. The hippies were still turning up, but they were being elbowed out the way by a younger teenage crowd. All of a sudden there were a *lot* of girls. A few months later, a band called Mungo Jerry had a novelty hit with a catchy shuffle called 'In The Summertime' on which singer Ray Dorset sang in the same warbling, Larry-the-Lamb voice that Marc Bolan had always been told was too weird for hit records. Marc felt ripped-off, true, but also vindicated. There was a space at the top for him, just as he'd always known. The same week that 'In The Summertime' went to number one, Marc, Mickey Finn and Tony Visconti were in Trident studios working on a new album; not the fifth album by Tyrannosaurus Rex, but the first by 'T.Rex'. That week they recorded a brand new Bolan composition, a sharp, elegant, minimal boogie a world away from the dense poetry and busy arrangements of *My People Were Fair And Had Sky In Their Hair* ... It was called 'Ride A White Swan'. The 1970s were just getting started.

The End. *The Beginning.*

Selected Bibliography

Books about David Bowie and related

Bowie, Angela & Carr, Patrick – *Backstage Passes: Life On The Wild Side With David Bowie* (Berkley, 1993/Lume, 2020)

Broakes, Victoria & Marsh, Geoffrey – *David Bowie Is* (V&A, 2013)

Buckley, David – *Strange Fascination* (Random House, 1999)

Cambridge, John – *Bowie, Cambo & All The Hype* (John Cambridge, 2021)

Cann, Kevin – *Any Day Now: David Bowie The London Years* (1947-1974) (Adelita, 2010)

Doggett, Peter – *The Man Who Sold The World: David Bowie and the 1970s* (Vintage, 2012)

Edwards, Henry & Zanetta, Tony – *Stardust: The David Bowie Story* (McGraw-Hill, 1986)

Finnegan, Mary – *PSYCHEDELIC SUBURBIA, David Bowie and the Beckenham Arts Lab* (Jorvik, 2016)

Gillman, Peter & Gillman, Leni – *Alias David Bowie* (New English Library, 1987)

Goddard, Simon – *Bowie Odyssey: 70* (Omnibus Press, 2020)

Hagler, Tony – *We Could Be: Bowie And His Heroes* (Cassell, 2021)

Hutchinson, John – *Bowie & Hutch* (Lodge Books, 2014)

Jones, Dylan – *David Bowie: A Life* (Penguin, 2017)

Jones, Lesley-Ann – *Hero: David Bowie* (Hodder & Staunton, 2016)

Lancaster, Phil – *At The Birth Of Bowie: Life With The Man Who Became A Legend* (John Blake, 2019)

Leigh, Wendy – *Bowie: The Biography* (Gallery Books, 2014)

Lemieux, Patrick – *The David Bowie Chronology, The Recording & Release History Volume 1 1947-1974* (Across The Board Books, 2018)

Morely, Paul – *The Age of Bowie: How David Bowie Made A World Of Difference* (Simon & Schuster, 2016)

Paytress, Mark & Pafford, Steve – *Bowie Style* (Omnibus Press, 2000)

Pegg, Nicholas – *The Complete David Bowie* (Titan Books, 2016)

Pitt, Kenneth – *David Bowie: The Pitt Report* (Lume Books, 1983)

Tremlett, George – *The David Bowie Story* (Futura, 1976)

Trynka, Paul – *Starman* (Sphere, 2011)

Books about Marc Bolan and related

Bolan, Marc – *Pictures of Purple People* (Wintergarden, 2019)

Brammell, John – *Marc Bolan – Beautiful Dreamer* (Music Press, 2012)

Danielz – *T.Rextasy: The Spirit of Marc Bolan* (Wymer, 2012)

Dicks, Ted and Platz, Paul – *Marc Bolan A Tribute* (Essex Music, 1978)

Jones, Lesley-Ann – *Ride A White Swan: The Lives and Death of Marc Bolan* (Hodder & Staunton, 2012)

McLenehan, Clifford – *Marc Bolan 1947-1977: A Chronology (Revised and Update)* (Helter Skelter Books, 2019)

Peytress, Mark – *Marc Bolan: The Rise and Fall of a 20th Century Superstar* (Omnibus Press, 2009)

Rolan, Paul – Metal Guru – *The Life & Music of Marc Bolan* (Extradition, 2017)
Thompson, Dave – *John's Children: A Midsummer Night's Scene* (Dave Thompson, 2012)
Warner, Fee – *A Trip Through Ladbroke Grove: The Life and Times of Underground 'Hero' Steve Peregrin Took* (Independent Publishing Network, 2021)
Warner, Fee – *'London Boy' The Guide To The Bolan Sites* (TAG, date unlisted)
Welch, Chris & Napier Bell, Simon – *Marc Bolan: Born To Boogie* (Plexus, 2008)
Willans, John & Thomas, Caron – *Marc Bolan: Wilderness of the Mind* (Xanadu, 1992)

Contemporary memoirs

Altham, Keith – *The PR Strikes Back* (Blake Publishing, 2001)
Bailey, David – *Goodbye Baby & Amen: A Saraband for the Sixties* (Coward McCann, 1969)
Bowie, Angela – *Lipstick Legends* (Mary A Jones, 2019)
Boyd, Joe – *White Bicycle: Making Music In The 1960s* (Serpent's Tail, 2006)
Evans, Bob – *DRUMSHTICK: The Second Part of The Riot Squad* (Bob Evans Flag, 2015)
Faith, Adam – *Poor Me* (Foresquare, 1961)
Farren, Mick – *Give The Anarchist a Cigarette* (Pimlico, 2001)
Gillespie, Dana – *Weren't Born A Man* (Hawksmoor, 2021)
Hall, Eric – *Monster! True Tales from a Showbiz Life* (Boxtree, 1998)
Mason, Nick – *Inside Out: A Personal History of Pink Floyd* (Weidenfeld & Nicolson, 2004)
Napier-Bell, Simon – *You Don't Have To Say Your Love Me* (Ebury, 2005)
Ravenscroft, Alexandra, Ravenscroft, Florence, Peel, John – *John Peel Margrave of the Marshes* (Corgi, 2006)
Shapiro, Helen – *Walking Back to Happiness* (HarperCollins, 1993)
Visconti, Tony – *The Autobiography: Bowie, Bolan and the Brooklyn Boy* (HarperCollins, 2007)
Wyman, Bill – *Stone Alone* (Da Capo Press, 1990)

General Music Reference

Bullock, Darryl W – *David Bowie Made Me Gay: 100 Years of LGBT Music* (Duckworth Overlook, 2017)
Bullock, Darryl W – *The Velvet Mafia: The Gay Men Who Ran The Swinging Sixties* (Omnibus Press, 2020)
Chapman, Rob – *Syd Barrett: A Very Irregular Head* (Faber & Faber, 2011)
Cohn, Nik – *Awopbopaloobop Alopbamboom: Pop from the Beginning,* (Weidenfeld & Nicolson, 1969)
Gamer, Ken – *The Peel Sessions: A story of teenage dreams and one man's love of new music* (BBC Books, 2007)
Gill, John – *Queer Noises* (Cassell, 1995)
Hoskins, Barry – *Glam! Bowie, Bolan and the Glitter Rock Revolution* (Faber & Faber, 1998)
Long, Pat – *The History of the NME* (Portico, 2012)
MacDonald, Ian – *Revolution in the Head: The Beatles' Records and the Sixties* (Pimlico, 1988)
Miles, K G & Lees, Jackie – *Bob Dylan In London, Troubadour Tales* (McNidder & Grace, 2021)
Napier-Bell, Simon – *Black Vinyl, White Powder* (Ebury, 2002)
Norma, Philip – *Shout!: The True Story of the Beatles* (Pan, 1981)
O'Neil, Andrew – *A History of Heavy Metal* (Headline, 2018)
Reynolds, Simon – *Shock & Awe, Glam Rock and Its Legacy* (Faber & Faber, 2016)
Rogan, Johnny – *Starmarkers & Svengalis* (Queen Anne Press, 1988)
Stanley, Bob – *Yeah Yeah Yeah: The Story of Modern Pop* (Faber & Faber, 2013)
Wale, Michael – *Vox Pop* (Harrap, 1972)

Post-War History/General History reference

Garfield, Simon – *Our Hidden Lives: The Remarkable Diaries of Postwar Britain* (Ebury, 2005)

Hennessy, Peter – *Having it So Good: Britain in the Fifties* (Penguin, 2007)

Ings, Andrew – *Rockin' At the 2 I's Coffee Bar* (Pavilion View, 2010)

Jenkins, Simon – *A Short History of London* (Viking, 2019)

Kynaston, David – *Austerity Britain, 1945-1951* (Bloomsbury, 2008)

Kynaston, David – *Family Britain, 1951-1957* (Bloomsbury, 2010)

Kynaston, David – *Modernity Britain, 1957-1962* (Bloomsbury, 2013)

Russell, Michael – *East End at War And Peace* (Matador, 2015)

Sandbrooke, Dominic – *Never Had It Go Good: A History of Britain From Suez to the Beatles* (Abacus, 2005)

Sandbrooke, Dominic – *White Heat: A History of Britain in the Swinging Sixties* (Abacus, 2006)

Various – *Memories of Bromley* (True North Books, 2000)

1960s, Subcultures and the CounterCulture Reference

Cruickshank, Dan – *Soho: A Street Guide To Soho's History, Architecture and People* (Weidenfeld & Nicolson, 2019)

Curtis, David – *London's Arts Labs and the 60s Avant-Garde* (John Libbey Publishing, 2020)

Green, Jonathan – *Day's In The Life: Voices From The English Underground, 1961-71* (Pimlico, 1988)

Hewitt, Paolo – *The Sharper Word: A Mod Anthology* (Helter Skelter, 1999)

Johnson, David – *Gear Guide, 1967: Hip-pocket Guide to Britain's Swinging Carnaby Street Fashion Scene* (Old House Books, 2013)

Miles, Barry – *London Calling: A Countercultural History of London since 1945* (Atlantic, 2010)

Said, Edward William – *Orientalism* (Pantheon Books, 1978)

Newspapers, Magazines and Periodicals

Bromley & Kentish Times
Daily Express
Daily Mail
Disc & Music Echo
Fabulous
Gandalf's Garden
History of Rock
International Times
Interview
Jackie
Jeremy
Mannheimer Morgen
Melody Maker
Mirror
Mojo
Music Now!
New Musical Express / NME
New York
New York Times

Q
QX
Record Mirror
Rolling Stone
Telegraph
Time
Town
Uncut

Web resources
BBC.co.uk
BowieBible.com
Bowiesongs.wordpress.com
DavidBowie.com
DavidBowieWonderland.com
LondonShoes.blog
MainMan Podcast
Mainmanlabel.com
Marc-Bolan.net
NME.com
OfficialCharts.com
The A-Z of David Bowie podcast
TillDawn.Net
Trynka.net
udiscovermusic.com/in-depth-features/decca-records-label-history/

Documentaries, Films and Television
A Technicolour Dream (dir. Stephen Gammond, 2008)
Dandy In The Underworld (dir. John Piper, 1997)
David Bowie – Finding Fame (dir. Francis Whately, 2019)
David Bowie – Five Years (dir. Francis Whately, 2010)
David Bowie – The Last Five Years (dir. Francis Whately, 2017)
David Bowie: The Calm Before The Storm (Sexy Intellectual, 2012)
Expresso Bongo, (dir. Val Guest, 1959)
Marc Bolan: Cosmic Dancer (dir. Jeremy Marre, 2017)
Marc Bolan: Ride On (dir. Mike Parkinson, 2005)
Marc Bolan: The Final Word (dir. Mark Tinkler, 2007)
Marc [episode 6] (dir. Nicholas Ferguson, 1977)
Rolling Stone: Life and Death of Brian Jones (dir. Danny Garcia, 2019)
The Beatles: Get Back (dir. Peter Jackson, 2021)
The Rolling Stones: The Quiet One (dir. Oliver Murray, 2019)
The Strange World of Gurney Slade, (dir. Alan Tarrant, 1960)
Urban Myths [series 2, episode 5] – 'David Bowie & Marc Bolan' (dir. Jim O'Hanlon, Sky Comedy, 2018)
World In Action – '1964 pt. 2: The Flip Side' (exec producer Alex Valentine, 1964)
World In Action – '1967: Mick Jagger' (exec producer Alex Valentine, 1967)